PRODUCTION FOR

GRAPHIC DESIGNERS

ALAN PIPES

THIRD EDITION

 Laurence King Publishing

Published 1992, 1997, 2001 by Laurence King Publishing
an imprint of Calmann & King Ltd
71 Great Russell Street
London WC1B 3BP
Tel: + 44 020 7430 8850
Fax: + 44 020 7430 8880
email: enquiries@calmann-king.co.uk
www.laurence-king.com

A catalogue record for this books is available from the
British Library.

ISBN: 1 85669 268 X

Editor: Kara Hattersley-Smith
Designer: Cara Gallardo, Area
Cover designer: Frost Design
Printed in Hong Kong, The Hanway Press Ltd

About the typefaces used in this book

Main text: 10.25/12.5pt Scala Sans

Scala Sans was designed by Dutch designer Martin Majoor. The seriffed
Scala was originally designed in 1988 for the Vredenburg Music Centre
in Utrecht. In 1991, FSI FontShop International published FF Scala as
the first serious text face in the then-new FontFont Library. In 1993
FF Scala was augmented with a sans-serif version, FF Scala Sans.

The sans and the serif versions complement each other, following
the same principle of form. The second largest newspaper in Holland
(Algemeen Dagblad) uses both FF Scala and FF Scala Sans for text
and headlines.

Martin Majoor was born in Baarn, Netherlands in 1960 and has
been designing type since the mid-1980s. After a student placement at
URW in Hamburg, he started in 1986 as a typographic designer in the
Research & Development department at Océ-Netherlands. There he
carried out research into screen typography and worked on the production of digital typefaces for laser printers.

In 1994, Majoor started working on the design of the Dutch
telephone directory, for Dutch phone company PTT Telekom for which
he created a new typeface Telefont in two weights: Telefont List and
Telefont Text. As a reaction to this formal work, Majoor designed FF
Scala Jewels in 1997; a quartet of classic decorative typefaces based on
the capitals of FF Scala Bold.

Caption text: 8/9.8pt Scala Sans

Manifesto in Design Trailblazers text:
8/11.25pt Neue Helvetica Light Condensed

Helvetica was originally designed by Max Miedinger in 1951–53 as Neue
Hass Grotesk, renamed Helvetica in 1957 (see p. 51). In 1983, Linotype
staff redrew the entire Helvetica family to correct differences in alignment and make all the weights and widths work together as one family.
This new drawing is called Neue Helvetica (German for New Helvetica).

Other production notes

Screen ruling: 175 lines per inch
Text paper: 113 gsm Japanese matt art
Cover: 350 gsm one-sided board with oriented polypropylene lamination
Binding: sewn in 16-page sections, cover four scored with 6mm hinges
on either side of spine

CONTENTS

▶

▶

■ PREFACE

When the first edition of this book was published, way back in 1992, computers were rarely seen in graphic design studios — there were some expensive turnkey systems around, mainly used for producing national newspapers — but the predominant means of layout was the mechanical. Now computers are not only ubiquitous in every area of the design-to-production cycle, but it is hard to imagine how books and magazines were ever produced without them. The drawing board has been confined to a quiet corner of the studio, and that once so expensive PMT camera to the scrapyard. A graphic designer without a computer and email account is an endangered species.

In prepress too, that once analog world of lenses, photographic emulsions, and baths of chemicals has gone digital. Direct computer-to-plate, and even plateless print are becoming more familiar. Xerography and the newer digital print technologies are being used to produce customised short-run jobs on demand. And all the paraphernalia of prepress, currently the province of the repro service bureau, is being brought inhouse.

In the past few years a completely new medium (to designers at least) has shot to prominence — the internet. There was no mention of the internet in the first edition of this book. In the second edition it was deemed important enough to deserve its own chapter. Through the internet, designers are able to break the bounds of traditional print and incorporate dynamic online resources that could only have been dreamt about when the first edition was put to bed. Despite the rise of the internet, print is still a large part of our lives. According to Printing Industries of America, Inc, printing is still one of the largest manufacturing industries in the USA —

employing over a million people in almost 50,000 establishments, and selling over \$155.7 billion of products in 1999. The industry is dominated by small- and medium-sized businesses, most employing fewer than twenty employees — along with their computers.

This completely revised third edition addresses the exciting changes that have taken place since the first two editions of *Production for Graphic Designers* were published. There is now an even greater need to master the fast-moving world of computing. Pre-digital methods of production are still important to know, but have been repositioned into a more appropriate historical and pedagogical context. A development in the second edition was to include, in-between chapters, inspirational profiles of important practicing designers along with portfolios of their work. This coverage has been expanded in the third edition.

I should like to thank the friends and colleagues who helped in the production of the first edition, particularly my editor Ursula Sadie at Calmann & King, picture researcher Elizabeth Loving, designer Richard Foenander, Chris Myers at Bookworm Typesetting, and Rosemary Bradley, who commissioned me to write it. Grateful thanks are also offered (almost alphabetically) to Aldus UK (now Adobe) for a copy of FreeHand (now back with Macromedia) with which to produce the line drawings; Joty Barker of Face to Face; the staff of Brighton Polytechnic (now the University of Brighton) Library at St Peter's House; Jane Brotchie for access to her HP DeskWriter; Roger Burg of Monotype Typography; John Christopher of Strong Silent Type; Eleanor Curtis, formerly at the Royal College of Art, London; Bob and Sue Harrington of RH Design; Nikki Morton and Ruth Jindal for their help in locating and retrieving books; Stan Noble of Towers Noble Design; William Owen; Kanwal Sharma of Lewis Sharma Design; Martin Shovel for the use of his StyleWriter; and Elvis the goldfish RIP for his or her calming influence.

For the second edition I should like to thank my editor Damian Thompson at Calmann & King and designer Cara Gallardo at Area for making my text and picture ideas a joy to read. Cara also art directed the cover and chapter opening spreads, and I should also like to acknowledge and thank: photographer Toby McFarlan Pond; London Graphic Centre for the use of the keyboard introducing Chapter 2; Peripheral Vision, London, for the circuit board (Chapter 5) and cable (Chapter 7); The Pale Green Press, London, for the printing inks introducing Chapter 6. I would also like to mention Philip and Dave Clark of Brighton Print Centre for tirelessly explaining to me the finer points of practical printing; and finally to Lesley Ripley Greenfield, Editorial Director, College & Fine Art at Calmann & King for commissioning me to write this update.

For the third edition I should like to thank my editor Kara Hattersley-Smith at Calmann & King, whose encouragement and support contributed far more to this new edition than can be guessed from this small credit, Cara Gallardo at Area for once again designing my words and pictures into a pleasing and accessible whole, Michelle Clair at Tenazas Design, Kelli Daley at David Carson Design, Tim Kong at Tomato, Kevin Smith at Research Studios, Jane Spencer for lending me her precious books, and my colleagues at the Brighton Illustrators Group for providing images.

Alan Pipes, Spring 2001

ONE

INTRODUCTION

INTRODUCTION

Words and pictures. Paper and ink. And now zeroes and ones — binary digits. These are the raw materials of the graphic designer. They are about to meet, go on a journey, and undergo several transformations, before ending up in a printed and finished or electronic publication that you designed. Something that will communicate ideas and images to large numbers of people.

But how do words and pictures get on to the printed page or website? Printing has always been a mysterious craft. And until recently, graphic designers were excluded from its secrets. Now the print production process is well within the designer's realm. And designers are ever being asked to expand their expertise into newer media. The purpose of this book is to demystify and help you understand some of those arcane and cutting-edge processes.

There is a long-standing misconception that to learn the craft part of any profession can be a chore. The temptation is to jump right in there and get on with the creative stuff. Print production, in particular, with its many different stages and processes, can seem dull, the very sound of words like "mechanical" at once conjuring up visions of production lines of automatons cutting and pasting like galley slaves. On the other hand there are some designers, and many typographers, who are so in love with the process that they forget the purpose of the job they are doing. What use is a beautiful piece of design or typography, without meaning or content? The graphic designer's role, first and foremost, is that of communicator. But if you can communicate cost-effectively with wit, economy, and elegance, then you are a very good graphic designer indeed.

In graphic design, free expression cannot exist in isolation from the process. Walter Gropius, the modernist architect and founder of the Bauhaus — a German art school that has become the model for mo of our present schools of art, communications, and design — suggested in his manifesto of 1919 that a cannot be taught, but that craft can. "A foundation in handicraft is essential for every artist," he said. "It is the that the primary source of creativity lies."

Graphic designers are both artists and craftspeople. This book does not major on how to be an artist, b it will tell you much that you need to know about the craft of printing. And when you have learnt all about pri production, the creativity will be able to come shining through. A sound understanding of all stages of the pri production process will at the very least prevent your designs from failing for technical reasons.

The chapters are arranged to follow the tracks of both the design process and the print process — from th choosing of type and the preparation of illustrations and photographs, through their arrangement on the pag or website, to the printing and finishing of the publication. The design process may follow a linear path, b many of the design decisions up front are affected by processes downstream. Every stage of the print produ tion process will exert some influence on your design.

The choice of paper and print technology, for example, will affect the kind of typefaces you can use and th way in which halftones are treated. In turn, the size of print run determines the print technology. You may b asked to design a range of product labels, for example — some to be printed on art-paper stock using high quality litho presses, while others will be printed directly on to plastic yogurt pots using flexography or screen printing. You may even be expected to "repurpose" the designs for multimedia or the internet. Your design will have to work well across a range of substrates and media.

■ SOME HISTORY

When you open the parcel from the printer, and you look at the finished copy of your design, it is as well to pause and appreciate that this printed product is a tribute to every advance in printing technology since the first wooden block was inked and pressed against a sheet of paper.

The history of printing began in the East: in China, Korea, and Japan. Paper was invented in China — its invention was officially announced to the Emperor by Ts'ai Lun in AD 105 — and printing using wooden blocks had become a flourishing fine art by the tenth century. The oldest known printed book, the *Diamond Sutra*, is dated at AD 868, though books were almost certainly being printed a century before. Words and pictures were carved together on to the same wooden blocks, and a fresh set of blocks had to be cut for each new book. Printing presses with type cast from individual pieces of clay that could be used time and time again were in use in China by AD 1041, and Korean printers were casting metal type before AD 1400. But because the languages of the East use symbols for whole words — some tens of thousands of them — rather than putting together words from relatively few characters in an alphabet, the development of so-called "movable" type was not so significant there as it later was in Europe.

Textiles have been printed in Europe since at least the sixth century, and playing cards were certainly being printed, using wooden blocks similar to those

" It is now forty years (1785) since I worked. like you, at this press, a journeyman printer."

Franklin

BENJAMIN FRANKLIN.

THE PRINTING-OFFICE OF MESSRS. COX BROTHERS, GREAT QUEEN-STREET, LINCOLN'S-INN-FIELDS.

THE HOUSE IN WHICH FRANKLIN RESIDED WHEN AGENT FOR PENNSYLVANIA; NO. 7, CRAVEN-STREET, STRAND.

1.1 Benjamin Franklin (1706–90) is perhaps America's most famous printer. This wood engraving shows him at the London print shop of Cox & Sons in 1785; note the wooden screw press.

of the Chinese printers, by the 14th century. But it is Johannes Gutenberg (1398–1468) who is credited with the invention of printing in the West, some time before 1440, and who printed the first book in Europe in 1445.

Gutenberg was a goldsmith by trade, living in Mainz, in what is now Germany. All the technology necessary for the invention of printing was in place at the time — it was just waiting for the right mind to put all the pieces together. He knew how to cast objects in metal, there were presses already available (for wine-making), he had ink and paper. And he saw a market opportunity for mass-produced books, to stock the libraries of all the universities being founded at that time.

Before that, in the Middle Ages, all books were created by hand. Scribes and artists worked together to create one-off books, often copying from existing texts. They were beautiful objects, mostly "illuminated" with ornamental letters, paintings, decorative borders, and gold blocking. There was even a form of mass-production in operation. In scriptoria, a chief scribe would dictate aloud the text to be copied by a team of under-scribes. Nevertheless, it was a slow process, and books could be possessed only by the very rich.

Gutenberg's invention was the process of letterpress: the concept of casting individual letters that could be assembled into words, printed, then cleaned and put away, and used over again. First he cut a steel punch for each character and punctuation mark. This punch was then struck into a softer metal to

form the matrix in which the type was cast. Finally lead, with the addition of some antimony for hardness and tin for toughness, was poured into the mold and the type cast. The most original part of Gutenberg's process was a mold of adjustable width, used to hold the different sizes of matrix. (See Chapter 2, p. 34, for a fuller description of the process of hot-metal typesetting.)

Gutenberg's original idea was to imitate in type the handwritten books of the scribes (but without the graphic embellishments). To do that he had to create a set of over 300 characters, including all the variations of letterforms and joined letters that a scribe might use. In comparison, a modern printer's alphabet might contain only 50 or so characters.

1.2 Title page from *The Whole Booke of Psalmes* (1640), the first book to be published in North America, by Stephen Daye of Cambridge, Massachusetts.

The invention of printing spread across Europe. The first book in English was printed by William Caxton, who learnt his craft in Cologne, Germany, and set up a press in London in 1476, using Flemish equipment. Printing was brought to America by Joseph Glover, who imported a press and three printers from Cambridge, England, to Cambridge, Massachusetts. Sadly, Glover died on the voyage, but the press was installed by Stephen Daye and his two sons in 1638, and operated under the auspices of Harvard College (Fig. **1.2**).

Progress in the technology of printing was slow until the Industrial Revolution. Wooden wine-type presses with huge screws (Fig. **1.1**, p. 13) were gradually replaced by iron presses operated by a simpler lever mechanism. The first was developed by Earl Stanhope in 1804, and this was followed by the more ornate Columbian and Albion presses. By 1812, there were presses in operation powered by steam, and huge rotary machines followed soon after.

Printing became a more industrialized process with the invention of automatic typesetting machines, first from Linotype in 1886, and from Monotype in 1887. Until the beginning of the 20th century, however, it was very difficult to combine type and pictures on the same printed page.

1.3 Until the end of the 18th century, the only way to print type and illustrations combined on the same page was by using woodcuts. These have period charm but lacked the capacity for fine detail, as is obvious from this depiction of the 1456 visit of Halley's Comet, from Conrad Lycosthenes' *Prodigiorum ac ostentorum chronicon*, 1557.

Printing pictures

Letterpress is a relief method of printing, in which a raised surface is inked and pressed against the paper. However, throughout the early history of printing almost every method of reproducing images used the **intaglio** process. The only exception was the woodcut — a relief process that predates printing — which could be used for decorative initials and simple illustrative work (Fig. **1.3**). Woodcuts are made with a knife on the long grain of the wood. The result is a rather rough image, but one that can be printed with the type.

For fine illustrative work, the only alternative was the intaglio process. Intaglio is the opposite to relief. Here it is the incised lines that print. A plate is inked, wiped almost clean, and the ink that remains in the grooves is drawn out, under pressure, to form the image on the dampened paper. Both engraving and etching are intaglio methods of printing (Fig. **1.4**).

So, before the Industrial Revolution, letterpress was used for printing text, in large print runs. Intaglio was used for refined work, where the print run was relatively small and the expense not so crucial. Artists had been making engravings on copper plates since the Renaissance. By the 18th century, the process was used commercially for printing invitation cards, banknotes, and stamps. The engravers used a sharp instrument called a burin to incise lines on to copper plates. And because any lettering had to be drawn by hand, it was often very elaborate. Hence

1.4 Because etching is an intaglio process, illustrations had to be printed separately from the text and were "tipped in" when the book was bound. This baker's shop, 1635, comes from a series of 22 etchings on the arts and crafts by Jan Joris van der Vliet.

the term "copperplate" is now used for a particular kind of formal handwriting. In the late 19th century, methods were developed for engraving on steel plates (Fig. **1.5**), which are more durable than copper.

A later development was etching, in which marks are made with a needle or any other sharp instrument to scratch off an acid-resistant coating on the surface of a copper plate. This is then placed in a bath of acid, and the drawing is etched chemically into the surface of the plate. The image on an etched plate was usually tidied up and detail added by hand, by engraving directly into the plate with a burin.

Another intaglio process was mezzotint, in which a burnisher is used to smooth the rough texture on the surface of the plate, created previously by the action of an abrasive "rocker" (the smooth areas would be white on the finished printed material). Aquatint is a type of etching that builds up tones using resin and stopping-out varnish. **Resist** is applied to the plate to prevent the non-printing areas from etching. Both these latter processes were used mainly to reproduce watercolor paintings. All of these methods are still used today by artists to produce limited edition prints, but are no longer used by commercial printers.

From Gutenberg's time until the Industrial Revolution, it was common for images in books to be printed separately from the text using an intaglio process. They were tipped-in (inserted among the text pages) during the binding process.

Things improved, however, when Thomas Bewick (1753–1828) developed the art of wood engraving (Fig. **1.6**). At last publishers had at their disposal the means to print fine line work and areas of rich black, in among the text.

1.6 An Arabian horse from Thomas Bewick's *General History of Quadrupeds*, 1790. Bewick had the bright idea of cutting boxwood on the end grain, and thus invented wood engraving. Despite its name, this is a relief method, which is capable of a dazzling tonal range and delicacy of line.

4   HISTORY OF QUADRUPEDS.

THE ARABIAN HORSE.

THERE is scarcely an Arabian, how poor soever in other respects, but is possessed of his Horse, which he considers as an invaluable treasure. Having no other dwelling but a tent, the Arabian and his Horse live upon the most equal terms: His wife and family, his mare and her foal, generally lie indiscriminately together; whilst the little children frequently climb without fear upon the body of the inoffensive animal, which permits them to play with and caress it without injury. The Arabs never beat their Horses; they speak to, and seem to hold friendly intercourse with them; they never whip them; and seldom, but in cases of necessity, make use of the spur. Their agility in leaping is wonderful; and if the rider happen to fall, they are so tractable as to stand still in the midst of the most rapid career.—The Arabian Horses, in general less than the Race-Horses of this country, are easy and graceful in their motions, and rather inclined to leanness.—It is worthy of remark, that, instead of

1.7 The tradition of Bewick is carried on today by contemporary wood engravers such as Nick Day, who are more likely to be seen cutting vinyl floor tiles than boxwood.

Wood engraving is a relief process, despite the similarity of its name to copper engraving, which is an intaglio process. Wood engravings are made with tools similar to those of the engravers, most commonly on the end grain of boxwood (Fig. **1.7**). Scratchboard, or scraperboard, is a contemporary method of illustration that simulates the appearance of a wood engraving.

By the middle of the 19th century, wood engraving had become an industry, and engravers such as Joseph Swain and the Dalziel brothers were as famous as the illustrators whose work they interpreted. Magazines such as the *Illustrated London News* used a system of separating large blocks into more manageable pieces, sending them out to a team of engravers, then reassembling them — an overseer had the job of disguising the joins. Journalistic accuracy came second to visual impact, with the same blocks used over and over, whenever there was a public hanging or a shipwreck.

1.8 The process of lithography revolutionized print production, but it was a long time coming. Early lithographic illustrations, like engravings, had to be printed separately from the text, but were used extensively for color work. This express train was first published in 1870 by Currier & Ives in New York as a color lithograph. Note that here it has to be reproduced as a halftone from a photograph of the original.

Enter lithography and photography

In fact, there was a process that could quite easily combine type and pictures on the same page, and it had been around since the end of the 18th century.

It was lithography (Fig. **1.8**), invented in Prague by Alois Senefelder around 1796–9. Neither a relief nor an intaglio process, it is better described as a planographic process. It is based on the principle that oil and water do not mix (much more in Chapter 5), and in effect everything happens on a flat surface.

Ironically, it was the versatility of the process that prevented it from being taken up more universally. Almost any greasy mark made on the lithographic stone, or, from the end of the 19th century, on a prepared metal plate, will print. Illustrators could at last work directly and spontaneously. By the end of the 19th century, greetings cards, postcards, decorative "scraps," maps, sheet music, and posters were all being mass-produced by lithography.

Offset lithography — in which the image is transferred from the stone or plate to a rubber roller, and then to the **substrate** — entered the scene surreptitiously. The process was first used in about 1875 for printing ornamental decorations on to tinplate, for applications in packaging.

Type produced by letterpress could be transferred on to the stone using special transfer paper, but this was not a totally satisfactory process. One more ingredient was necessary before lithography could take over from letterpress as the most versatile of all the printing processes: the invention of photography in the late 1830s.

Photography — analog or digital — is the basis for every print production process in use today. The first application of photography to the reproduction of illustrations was quite modest, however. It was used to sensitize the surface of the boxwood used for wood engravings. These still had to be cut by hand, but the illustrator's original drawing could be preserved and, furthermore, the method could be used to reproduce photographs.

Early photographers were eager to reproduce their work in large

1.9 It was the experimental photographers of the late 19th century who pushed forward the technology of print production, inventing better methods of reproducing continuous-tone artwork and the technique of producing color separations. This picture of Joseph Bazalgette, the architect of London's sewerage system, was first reproduced by Woodburytype — a form of collotype patented by Walter Bentley Woodbury in 1866 — a process said to produce hard and brilliant prints.

quantities. They were an extremely experimental group of individuals, and many of the pioneering developments in print production were made by them. **Collotype** (Fig. **1.9**) was the first method used for reproducing photographs, and this slow and expensive process was soon followed by photogravure.

Collotype — the name comes from the Greek word for glue — uses a plate coated with photographically sensitive gelatin which hardens in proportion to the amount of light falling on to it. A negative is exposed in contact with the plate, which is then moistened and absorbs more water where there was less light. Impressions are taken using greasy ink, as in lithography. Collotype gives an almost facsimile reproduction of pencil, pastel, and crayon. To date it is the only commercial process that can print continuous-tone originals without having them first converted, by screening, into a pattern of dots.

Photogravure, first developed in 1852, is an intaglio process characterized by rich tones and the absence of regularly patterned dots. However, the process does involve a form of screening to create the "grains" on the plate or cylinder. On

etching, the grains are eaten away in proportion to the tone values on the original — the blacks become the deepest and the whites the shallowest. On printing, the darker areas are created by a greater amount of ink being deposited on the paper, and the grains are obliterated by the spread of the ink. The process relies on quick-drying spirit-based inks, and for this reason many of the early reproductions appeared in sepia or green. Photogravure is used widely to this day, and is discussed more fully as a printing process in Chapter 5.

The breakthrough that allowed images to be printed by letterpress was the development of the process block. The line block, for black and white work, was invented in Vienna by Paul Pretsch in 1853 and used a process resembling collotype — the softer portions of sensitized gelatin on the surface of the plate swell into relief. An electrotype cast is made, and the resulting plate is mounted on to a wooden block (hence the

name — the block brings it up to the height of the type). This can then be assembled with the type. By the mid-1880s, zinc plates were being etched photographically from original artwork, and the profession of process engraving, or blockmaking, was born.

The early process blocks could handle only relatively simple areas of black and white, and the style of illustrators such as Aubrey Beardsley and William Heath Robinson owes much to the constraints of the process (Fig. **1.10**). For the first time, an illustrator was free to draw at larger sizes than the work would be appearing in print.

Tints could be added by the blockmaker (see Fig. 3.2, p. 82), where indicated by the illustrator. Ben Day tints, the first commercially available tints, were introduced in 1901. These were sheets of celluloid stretched in wooden frames. Each sheet was embossed with a pattern and was transferred to the block,

1.10 The line art of such artists as Aubrey Beardsley and William Heath Robinson was as much influenced by the invention of the process block as by the importation of Japanese art at the end of the 19th century. At last an artist's spontaneity could be reproduced directly from artwork — as can be seen in this illustration by Robinson from Hans Andersen's *Fairy Tales* (1913).

1.11 Old meets new. This 16th-century woodcut of printers at work is given a contemporary treatment courtesy of Photoshop, the image manipulation program from Adobe.

turous designer even further. What you saw on the mechanical was what you got in the printed product.

It was a natural next step to want to design on the computer screen, once WYSIWYG (What You See Is What You Get) displays became available in the early 1980s. Both text and graphics could be treated equally in the eyes of the computer, and could be subjected to an almost infinite variety of manipulation (Fig. **1.11**).

The introduction of PageMaker for the Apple Macintosh in 1984, along with the PostScript page-description language and the LaserWriter, are just some of the many recent milestones in the history of print production for graphic designers.

Now the internet, once the domain of computer scientists, has further liberated graphic designers, setting them free to expand their horizons beyond the world of printed ink on paper and into digital screen-based multimedia.

As with the invention of lithography, it is often difficult to foresee the effect of an isolated discovery on the overall history of printing. Lithography had to wait for the development of photography before it could become a commercial proposition. In the same way xerography, invented in 1938 by Chester Carlson, has leapt forward with laser and computer technology. Who could have predicted the growth of the internet in the past few years? In just half a decade, it has become as commonplace as the telephone and television, complementing print-based media with a degree of inter-activity and immediacy undreamt of by Gutenberg.

before etching, using a roller inked with lithographic ink. Areas not requiring a tint were first painted out with gum to repel the ink.

The reproduction of continuous tone by means other than collotype had to await the invention of the halftone screen. The photographer Fox Talbot first suggested in 1852 that tones could be reproduced by means of "photographic screens or veils." But it was Frederick Ives of Philadelphia who patented a method of converting a photograph into dots. This was refined in 1882 by George Meisenbach, who used a single-lined screen that was turned 90 degrees during exposure. Ives, in collaboration with Louis and Max Levy, replied in 1890 with the first cross-lined screen. Now illustrations and photographs could be freely combined with type on the same page, and printed together at the same time.

The invention of the halftone screen also paved the way for full-color printing, using three and later four "process" colors to reproduce all the colors of the rainbow (see p. 91).

The first rotary offset lithography machine for printing on paper was

introduced in 1906 by Ira W. Rubel, but it was not until the 1950s that it began to take over from letterpress.

Photocomposition systems could set type, not in pieces of lead, but on rolls of photographic bromide paper or transparent film. These could be cut and pasted into designs that could then be transferred directly to a lithographic plate and printed. This technological breakthrough, and the explosion of print that followed, gave a huge boost to the young profession of graphic design. Over the years, the printing industry had become fragmented — there were separate typesetters, process engravers, and printers — and someone had to step in to plan and coordinate printing projects. That job fell to the graphic designer.

There was greater creative freedom too. No longer were graphic designers constrained to what could be done with metal type and process blocks. Type on paper could be positioned anywhere, alongside any images that could be recorded by the camera.

It was the age of camera-ready artwork — the mechanical. And the introduction of display faces in the form of dry-transfer rub-down lettering such as Letraset liberated the adven-

Milestones in the history of production technology for graphic designers

3500 BC Sumerians use cuneiform alphabet on clay tablets

2400 BC Earliest surviving papyrus scroll with writing

AD 105 Paper invented in China by Ts'ai Lun

868 *Diamond Sutra*, first printed book, in China

1041 First presses with clay movable type in China

1150 First paper mill opened in Europe, in Xativa, Spain

1400 Koreans printing with metal movable type

1445 Johannes Gutenberg printed first book in Europe

1446 Earliest known copper engraving: The Scourging of Christ, by a German artist

1477 William Caxton issued first printed book in England

1638 First American press established by Stephen Daye at Harvard College

1690 First American paper-mill established in Germantown, Pennsylvania, by William Rittenhouse

1790 Thomas Bewick perfected process of wood engraving

1796–9 Lithography invented by Alois Senefelder

1798 Papermaking machine invented by Nicolas-Louis Robert

1804 Iron press devised by Earl Stanhope

1810 First Fourdrinier papermaking machines in operation

1812 The *Times* (of London) printed on steam press

1822 J. N. Niepce first to fix images in a camera obscura on metal and glass plates

1829 Amos H. Hubbard's mill at Norwich, Connecticut, first American paper-mill to install a Fourdrinier machine

1837 Invention of Daguerre photographic process

1839 Negative/positive photography invented by Fox Talbot

1841 First paperbacks produced by Tauchnitz Verlag, Germany

1852 Photogravure invented by Fox Talbot

1853 Line block invented by Paul Pretsch

1860 Photographically sensitized boxwood process developed by Thomas Bolton

1860 Principle of color separation by filters demonstrated by Clerk Maxwell

1861 First color photograph by Clerk Maxwell

1872 Process line block invented by Alfred Dawson

c. 1875 Offset litho used for printing on tin

1881 Halftone process invented by Frederick Ives

1884 Punch-cutting machine invented by Linn Boyd Benton

1886 Linotype machine invented by Ottmar Mergenthaler

1886 First Linotype installed at New York Herald Tribune

1887 Monotype machine invented by Tolbert Lanston

1890 Four-color separation process invented

1890 Aniline coal-tar process (later called flexography) demonstrated at Bibby, Baron & Sons in Liverpool, England, but later abandoned

1901 Ben Day mechanical tints introduced

1906 First rotary offset litho machine invented by Ira W. Rubel

1920s Aniline process developed for printing on non-absorbent stock such as cellophane

1938 Xerography invented by Chester Carlson

1948 Color scanner invented by Kodak

1952 Name "flexography" coined for aniline coal-tar process

1955 Linofilm photocomposing system introduced

1959 First Linofilm installation at National Geographic

1960 Laser invented at Hughes Laboratory

1967 Computerized Linofilm typesetter introduced

1968 Crosfield Magnascan four-color scanner introduced

1968 Ted Nelson coins the terms "hypertext" and "hypermedia"

1969 ARPAnet, the precursor to the internet, established

1971 Email invented by Ray Tomlinson of BBN

1971 Project Gutenberg began at the Illinois Benedictine College aimed at collecting as many texts as possible in electronic format

1976 Inkjet printing announced by IBM

1981 IBM PC announced

1982 Lisa, the precursor to the Macintosh, introduced by Apple

1982 Adobe Systems founded

1984 Apple Macintosh and Linotronic 300 laser imagesetter launched

1984 CD-rom invented: Parke Lightbown builds a computer application that runs from a computer-based version of the compact disc

1985 Adobe PostScript used to set type on LaserWriter and Linotronic imagesetter at different resolutions

1985 Aldus PageMaker launched, and term "desktop publishing" coined by Aldus founder Paul Brainerd

1987 Mac II and QuarkXPress launched

1987 Adobe Illustrator launched

1990 Windows 3 released by Microsoft

1990 Adobe Photoshop launched

1991 TrueType format and System 7 introduced by Apple

1992 Tim Berners-Lee of CERN develops software for the World Wide Web (WWW)

1993 NCSA releases Mosaic, the first WWW browser

1993 Adobe Acrobat launched

1993 First digital presses, the Indigo E-Print 1000, and Xeikon's DCP-1 launched

1993 Intel introduces the 80 MHz Pentium chip

1993 Motorola ships the first 80 MHz Power PC 601 chip

1994 First PowerPC Macs launched

1994 Aldus and Adobe merge

1994 Netscape Navigator launched by Mosaic Communications

1995 Windows 95 released

1996 Internet Explorer released by Microsoft

1997 Apple launches Mac OS 8

1998 Intel releases the 350 MHz and 400 MHz Pentium II processors

1998 Steve Jobs introduces the Apple iMac

1998 Microsoft releases Windows 98

1999 Intel announces Pentium III processor

1999 Apple Computer releases the 400 MHz Power Mac G4 computer and 22-inch LCD flat-panel Cinema Display

1999 Adobe InDesign and PressReady launched

2000 Adobe InProduction launched

2001 Apple OS X launched

■ GETTING STARTED: STUDIO EQUIPMENT

Some graphic designers claim to get by with just a pad of layout paper, a pencil, and a book of type specimens. The typographer Erik Spiekermann (see p. 76) used to boast (before he bought his first Apple Macintosh) that he could communicate clearly with his type-setter by means of a written set of instructions. This was a type specification that could be dictated down the telephone, if need be — with no graphic layout necessary. Well, you may argue that typographers have it a lot easier than graphic designers. They don't have to deal with pictures, or color.

So maybe in the past the more unprofessional graphic designers just sent rough layouts covered in keylines and instructions to the printer and hoped for the best. These days, it is more likely that you will present your computer-generated layouts to an image-setting bureau or repro house on a CD-rom, or down the telephone wire via ISDN. And you will already have a very good idea of how the printed result is going to look.

What do you need to get started? A sturdy tabletop or, better, a drawing board with an adjustable angled surface and built-in parallel motion (a straight edge that moves up and down, always perfectly horizontally) is very useful. The drawing board has become synonymous with the cyclical nature of the design process. How many times have you heard the phrase "back to the drawing board" when pernickety clients changed their minds about what

they really wanted? Even in design studios with computers, drawing boards are still seen — they are good places at which to plan and think, to scale and crop illustrations, and are ideal for spreading around the design elements during the sketch stage of design.

A surgical scalpel and a heavier-duty craft knife (such as an X-acto) are useful for cutting paper and board and making up dummy publications. Use a cutting mat with a "self-healing" surface for trimming artwork, and clean off any stickiness regularly with lighter fuel. For sticking and mounting you will need rubber cement or aerosol adhesive, such as Scotch Spray Mount, for wrinkle-free mounting. For safety's sake, adequate ventilation is essential while using spray glue. Buy a brand that uses a CFC-free propellant, to protect the environment. Many graphic designers used to use hot-wax coaters for sticking paper to board; they also kept the studio warm in the winter! Low-tack masking tape and matte frosted "magic" tape are useful for mending, and for attaching tissue or acetate overlays to delicate artwork.

Other accessories include plenty of non-reproducing light-blue pencils, including some greasy pencils (Chinagraphs) for writing on glossy surfaces, and maybe an electric pencil sharpener. A large soft brush is indispensable for removing debris from the work in progress, and a supply of talcum powder will come in handy for degreasing and "lubricating" surfaces. However, keep it away from finished work! A bulk stock of paper towels is useful to mop up spillages. It is always good policy to keep things clean and tidy.

Paint called "process white" is used by designers for correcting mistakes and adding highlights to drawings. It is still considered good advice to buy the finest-quality sable brushes (sizes 00, 1 and 3 would be a good selection). Look after them — they should be washed and rinsed straight after use (they must never be left point down in a jar of water) and stored with the points upward. There are some very good synthetic substitutes available.

A loupe, linen tester, or eyeglass (Fig. 1.12) is a mounted magnifying glass that will prove its worth over

■ **1.12** A loupe, or linen tester, is a magnifying glass which is useful for examining transparencies and proofs, often in conjunction with a lightbox.

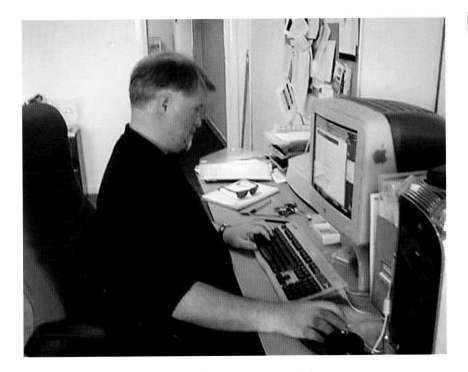

and over. It can be used to check the dots in a halftone, examine a color transparency for suitability and any defects, and to scrutinize proofs for printing problems.

A lightbox that fits on the table-top, and comprises a translucent surface illuminated from below by fluorescent lights conforming to the **standard lighting conditions** used by printers, is invaluable for properly examining the color temperature of transparencies. It is also a great aid to experimentation. You can try out different designs on a lightbox, tracing over those parts of an original design you wish to retain. A lightbox can also be used to check the registration of color separations. If you are to be checking and correcting color proofs, set up a corner of the studio according to **standard viewing conditions**, with the light source surrounded by neutral gray.

A proportional scale, or just a plain old calculator, will help you work out percentage reductions and enlargements. And there are all kinds of other measurement devices. A stainless-steel pica rule will become a lifelong companion, and there are plastic rules available for measuring the depth of type in

different sizes, useful for casting off (calculating the length of a text) and copy fitting (making sure your type-setting will fit the space you have left for it in the layout). A transparent grid will assist you in checking that design elements are square, and well aligned, although computer layouts will always be perfectly square! A photocopier capable of enlarging and reducing is a very useful addition to any studio, as is a fax machine and computer connected to the internet to keep in visual touch with the client and printer.

The computer and its peripherals (Fig. **1.13**) are now almost indispensable. And here's a word of warning, right at the start of the book. A computer can be a tireless and uncomplaining assistant, but you cannot talk to it in such subjective terms as "increase the spacing here" or "less orange there" as you would with a typesetter or the scanner operator at your repro house. Compositors and scanner operators have had years of experience in delivering the results they think you want. They can almost read your mind. They have a common understanding of what is acceptable, and what is good. The computer, on the

other hand, can do either nothing or anything — depending on what instructions you give!

The computer might never question your unusual requests and never charge you for changes of mind. But it will expect you to do all the thinking, and be able to tell it exactly, to the thousandth of an inch, centimeter, or percentage point, where things should be moved. Not only does that make more work for you, but you have to know in minute detail exactly what you want — and you will have to take responsibility for the outcome.

Typesetters were in fact among the first users of computers — they could recognize a good thing when they saw it. Your computer is not going to replace printers, and they will probably always be one step ahead of you. So think of your system as complementing their computers, acting as a front end to their systems.

Use your computer responsibly, to improve the quality of design communication between your studio — the ideas house — and the printers — the production house. Their centuries of hard-won expertise are there to be used. And they will appreciate the knowledge you have of their processes, gained from reading this book.

SAUL BASS

LIFE STORY ■ From the 1960s onward, Saul Bass and his Sunset Boulevard-based design company Saul Bass Associates (later Bass/Yager & Associates; now Citigate Bass Yager) fashioned the corporate face of America, with logos for AT&T, Quaker Oats, Rockwell, and Warner Communications. But he was much more than a graphic designer for print, and is perhaps better known for his film work, notably the much imitated "paper cut" title sequence for *Anatomy of a Murder* in 1959 and for collaborating with Alfred Hitchcock on the shower scene in *Psycho* in 1960. He worked as "visual consultant" on many of Hitchcock's 40-plus films, including many Hollywood classics. His more recent film credits for Martin Scorsese, which he designed with his wife and collaborator Elaine Makatura, include *Cape Fear, Goodfellas,* and his last film *Casino*.

> "His titles are not simply unimaginative identification tags ... When his work comes up on the screen, the movie itself truly begins."

Bass was born in 1920, grew up in the Bronx, and studied at the Art Students' League in Manhattan from 1936 to 1939, then under modernist Gyorgy Kepes at Brooklyn College from 1944 to 1945. In 1948 he headed west to Los Angeles to work in advertising for motion pictures, and set up on his own in 1955. His poster for Otto Preminger's *The Man with the Golden Arm* broke new ground in 1955 with its use of bold graphic elements — before Bass, movie posters were mainly a formulaic blend of star billing, big headlines, and photo-realistic imagery. Bass's publicity design was so dramatic that Preminger asked him to create the film's opening title sequence, which marked the beginning of a long partnership.

Bass was multi-talented, and maintained that designers should never confine themselves to a single discipline — as well as designing for print and film, he was an accomplished maker of short films (notably the Oscar-winning *Why Man Creates*), photographer, writer, and actor. He died aged 75 in 1996, but his strong, iconic, and instantly memorable approach to graphic design remains an inspiration to a new wave of web designers.

◀ ▶ Bass simplified AT&T's Bell trademark in 1969, and after the break-up of AT&T into "Baby Bells," he designed a much-imitated logo for AT&T. The Bell trademark is still used by BellSouth.

MANIFESTO ■ **Symbolize and Summarize**
"Bass's graphic work looked like what Matisse might have done if he'd grown up in the Bronx and had listened to jazz," says film critic Jim Supanick. Martin Scorsese once said: "His titles are not simply unimaginative identification tags, rather they are integral to the film as a whole. When his work comes up on the screen, the movie itself truly begins." A number of critics maintained his titles were in some cases better than the films that followed.

In a 1969 interview for *Communication Arts* by Richard S. Coyne, Bass said: "Years ago, if you created a modern design, it was news. You would be singled out for awards and acclaim for doing what seems now to be a janitorial job ... removing ugliness and clutter ... simplifying and utilizing new visual thinking.

"Magazines were full of great photography at a time when the equivalent was not happening in film. That's what distinguished my initial work in films. I was bringing to bear the visual standards that I had developed in the graphic field. That was very startling, and that's what made the work that I did then look so wild.

"Now everybody can make beautiful shots of sunsets, long-lens foreground-to-background change-focus shots ... the nose-to-nose close-ups, fast cutting, zoomy overlaid double-image opticals ... and suddenly it's just a tool. It's understood. It's available to everyone. You can still do it poorly, but chances are, if you're reasonably proficient at what you do, you will do it well. So now the real question is: what are you trying to say?

"This process also occurred in design. Initially, the fight was to de-uglify the print environment ... to make it more beautiful, more exciting, more visually appetizing. With that done, the issue of the day was: what does it mean? We were into content. This kicked off another swing of reaction. Ugly was beautiful — because it helped to eliminate the so-called obscuring elements. It began to undress the communication so that its essential body showed."

The AT&T corporate identity
One of Bass's most significant corporate-identity jobs was begun in 1968 for AT&T (then known as American Telephone and Telegraph). AT&T then comprised 28 companies, 22 of which were regional telephone companies operating with a considerable amount of autonomy. The project was assigned by the parent company, AT&T. If and when they approved the designers' concept, it was still subject to the acceptance of the Bell System.

▶ Film director Otto Preminger liked Bass's 1955 poster for *The Man with the Golden Arm* that he asked him to design the film's opening titles — the start of a long and creative partnership.

▼ Neil Gower's 1994 series of posters for the British Heart Foundation were (with Bass's permission) heavily influenced by Bass's cut-up technique, in particular his design for *Anatomy of a Murder*

The drab look of the previous identity was designed during the depression of the 1930s. In those days the idea of a job, any kind of job, was terribly important. Institutions like the telephone company held out a solid promise of future job security. People regarded such organizations as dependable — not subject to the wild economic waves then stirring much of the business community. But with AT&T's move into the new technologies of communications and computers, it was time for a change.

The bell symbol, a trademark since 1889, was simplified, and the type within the bell deleted. New fonts were explored, but abandoned in favor of the simplicity and legibility of a modified Helvetica Medium. The corporate identity also specified stripes, borrowed from the world of racing and athletics, which said: "competitive, alert, dedicated." (Stripes were also used on the AT&T globe logo designed by Bass in 1982, when the US Department of Justice decreed that AT&T divest itself of the 22 Bell operating telephone companies.)

Bass used a large sound stage in Tucson for the big presentation, which comprised eight slide and three film projectors. After the films, the screen lifted up to reveal a live set with vehicles, a simulated office, and personnel modeling proposed uniforms.

Bass's implementation manuals read more like courses in design than like the usual list of orders and prohibitions one expects. "We're still engaged in winning people over," Bass said three years after implementation had begun. "Winning them over not by charm, not by jokes, and not by fear. It's a very conscious process of patiently and logically winning them over to the program, and being so careful in our own thinking that, when we are questioned, there can be a complete openness on the reasons for what we are doing."

The full interview is available on www.commarts.com/creative/bass/index.html

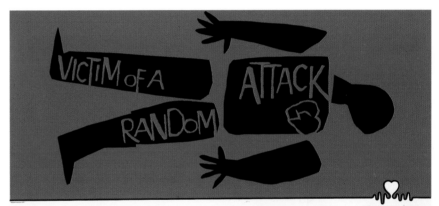

HALF OF ALL DEATHS ARE FROM HEART AND CIRCULATORY DISEASE. HELP US FIGHT BRITAIN'S No 1 KILLER.

British Heart Foundation
The heart research charity

WORKSTATION

- Website: www.saulbass.co.uk
  (Flash-based fan site created by Brendan Dawes and Victor Helwani, includes many interviews, images, and filmography)
- Philip B. Meggs (ed.), *6 Chapters in Design: Saul Bass, Ivan Chermayeff, Milton Glaser, Paul Rand, Ikko Tanaka, Henryk Tomaszewski*, Chronicle Books, San Francisco, 1997
- Gerry Rosentswieg and Saul Bass *The New American Logo*, Madison Square, New York 1998
- Saul Bass on the web:
  Interview by Richard S. Coyne, *Communication Arts*
  www.commarts.com/creative/bass/index.html

TWO TEXT & TYPE

TEXT & TYPE

The ability to use type effectively is an essential skill for successful graphic design. Just a few basic principles open the way to an infinite variety of design possibilities for all kinds of printed products. Graphic designers must make type work hard, in harmony with other graphic elements, such as illustration, photography, and color. They are dealing with practical situations, in the real world of tight deadlines, specific briefs, and competitive pitches.

Since the introduction of digital design systems, the graphic designer has been confronted with a bewildering choice of typefaces, as well as the means to manipulate them. It has never been more important for graphic designers to become familiar with the craft and knowledge of the printers and typographers who have gone before.

People like Gutenberg designed their own type, cut the steel to make it, cast it into lead, composed it into pages, printed their own books, and bound them. They concocted their own ink, and probably made their own paper as well.

Computers give graphic designers the opportunity to take back the responsibility for almost as much of the production process as they are willing, or capable enough, to handle. But to go forward, one must first know what is possible.

This chapter aims to give the graphic designer an insight into type and how it is used. It will explain the vocabulary of print and typography, both ancient and modern. For in print production we commonly use both terminology handed down through generations of printers and typesetters, and jargon introduced from computing and digital prepress.

The chapter is divided into three sections. In the first we talk about type itself — letters and words, the basic building blocks with which graphic designers work. We see how type originated from the handwriting of medieval scribes, detail the work of pioneering printers, and learn the all-important methods of measuring type.

Then we turn to the relationship between text and house style, investigate how different typefaces are recognized, and discover how to choose the best typeface for the job.

Finally we learn how type is created. Here we discuss the systems of typesetting — from hot metal, through photosetting, to the computer systems that make the craft of typography accessible to anyone possessing a power socket.

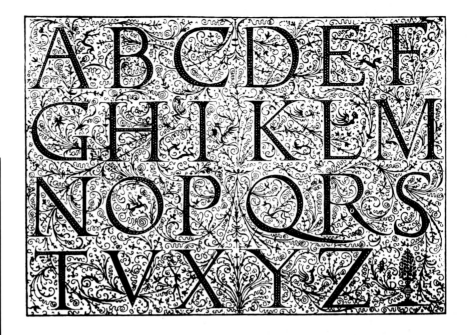

2.1 A decorative alphabet drawn as a sampler by Daniel Hopfer of Nuremburg, Germany, dated 1549. The letterforms are based on the lettering on Trajan's Column in Rome. Note the absence of J, U, and W.

What equipment do you need to get started?

- ✔ a sturdy tabletop or drawing board
- ✔ type specimens
- ✔ a pad of layout or tracing paper
- ✔ a supply of fibertip pens (ballpoints may damage artwork) and soft black pencils
- ✔ a pencil sharpener
- ✔ a non-reproducing light-blue pencil
- ✔ a stainless-steel pica rule or plastic typescale
- ✔ a set of standard proof-readers' marks
- ✔ a calculator

and optionally:

- ✔ computer: an Apple Macintosh, an IBM PC, or PC compatible such as a Compaq
- ✔ software for word processing and page layout
- ✔ a desktop printer
- ✔ a photocopier capable of enlarging and reducing
- ✔ a fax machine to keep in visual touch with the client and printer
- ✔ access to the internet

■ TYPE

The essence of writing and lettering, according to typographer Fernand Baudin, is to make language visible and retrievable. Spoken words pass away; written words are here to stay.

Type is the basic building block of print production. The design of type is a very subtle craft, dealing with the sometimes microscopic details that distinguish one typeface from another. It is also a thankless and humbling profession. "The best typography never gets noticed," American typographer Herb Lubalin has been quoted as saying. (Typographer means here a person who designs type and designs with type. The term **compositor** is used for someone who sets type.)

Or, as another famous American typographer Beatrice Warde has pointed out, perhaps more eloquently: "Good typography is like a crystal wine glass, thin as a bubble and just as transparent, its purpose to reveal rather than hide the beautiful thing it is meant to contain. Good graphic design and typography should help people communicate with all the clarity an idea deserves."

When we are taught to write the alphabet at school, it probably never occurs to us that there are thousands of ways that 26 simple letters can be constructed. It is only through looking at printed matter in later life that we begin to realize that a letter g, for example, comes in two main varieties: g and g.

And while an alphabet with 26 letters and eight punctuation marks will be adequate for a message on a noticeboard, a set of over a hundred different characters and marks may still fall short of some tasks facing the graphic designer.

Some history

Our Western alphabet was invented by the Phoenicians around 1100 BC somewhere on the eastern shores of the Mediterranean Sea. Capital letters derive from Roman incised lettering, with its distinctive serifs (the little marks made by the chisel to neaten the ends of letters), slanted stress, and variations in stroke thickness. The chiseled capital letters carved on Trajan's Column in Rome (Figs **2.1** and **2.3**, p. 30) in around AD 114 are still regarded as the "perfect" **roman** letters. Lower-case lettering comes from a more rounded form of handwriting, known as the uncial, developed for everyday use in the fourth century.

◄ **2.2** In medieval times all books were created individually, copied out slowly but lovingly by scribes. Only the very rich could afford books.

In the Middle Ages, scribes or scriveners created all books by hand, usually copying from existing books (Fig. **2.2**). They were beautiful objects, often "illuminated" with ornamental letters, paintings, and gold blocking (Fig. **2.4**).

The clear and manageable script established by the educational reforms of Emperor Charlemagne (742–814) in the latter part of the

ABCDEFGHIJ KLMNOPQR STUVWXYZ& 1234567890$

◄ **2.3** (left & opposite page) The lettering on Trajan's Column is the prototype for most present-day roman typefaces, including Adobe's display typeface (left) designed in 1989 by Carol Twombly and called, appropriately enough, Trajan. Note how our serifs derive from the chiseled finishing-off marks made by the Roman stonecutter.

◄ ▲ **2.4** Some medieval books were illustrated or "illuminated" with watercolors and gold embellishments. The names of the artists and scribes are long forgotten, and those with recognizable styles are now known only by the names of their patrons — the Master of Mary of Burgundy, for example. To squeeze as many words as possible on to a page, most scribes used the up-and-down form of writing called textura lettering, as on this French depiction of the Montpellier riots of 1379 (left). Other manuscripts, like the 14th-century Lancelot Grail (above), used a freer, open, rounded form of script more akin to uncial, or roman lower-case, writing.

▼ **2.5** Archaic English characters, including the thorn — an obsolete character that sounds like "th" but looks like a "y" (bottom row, fifth from left).

8th century and early 9th — known as Carolingian minuscule — was rediscovered and refined in the Italian Renaissance by the humanists, and is the basis of the present-day roman alphabet.

In medieval Europe, there were two kinds of script: "book" hands, used in literary and liturgical manuscripts; and the more functional "charter" or "court" hands, used for business documents. In northern Europe, a narrower and heavier style of writing emerged. The use of a broad pen produced angular strokes, and the resemblance of a page written in this way to a woven pattern (*textus*) led to the name "text," "textura," or "black letter." Paper, parchment (the prepared skins of sheep or goats), and vellum (from calves, lambs, or kids) were expensive, and the scribes were encouraged to fit as many letters to a line as possible. The result is a closely packed page, with much more black than white. The humanists called this style "gothic" because of its resemblance to the pointed style of architecture in fashion at the time.

While scriveners could take their time to produce beautiful manuscripts for libraries, the clerk or secretary of a law court was more interested in speed writing and evolved a more cursive style known as "secretary," also commonly used in correspondence. By the 1450s, a more upright seriffed minuscule called "littera antiqua" was all the rage — a cursive and slightly inclined version called "italic," first used in the papal Chancery, developed from this. It did not catch on in England, however, until around 1550.

It was first used alongside secretary, particularly for quoted matter and marginal asides, but came to dominate and by 1620 had become known as the "mixed" or "round" hand.

The first italic face was cut in Venice by Aldus Manutius in about 1500. It was not until two centuries later that it became partnered with roman, or plain text, and an essential part of the type family.

▲ **2.6** Type foundry Crazy Diamond Design produce historically accurate typefaces with extensive character sets.

2.7 Johannes Gutenberg is credited with the invention of movable type in the western world. No portraits of him survive from the period; this artist's impression in woodcut, made much later from the carvings on Gutenberg's tomb, shows him reading proofs while his assistant works the printing press.

2.8 To imitate the lettering of the scribes, Gutenberg's font had to contain a set of over 300 characters, whereas a modern printer's alphabet might contain only 50 or so.

Other scripts included "chancery" hand, used for royal letters and patents in the Royal Chancery at Westminster, and the hand used by lawyers at the courts of the Common Pleas and King's Bench. These were banned by an act of parliament in 1733 and replaced by the round hand.

Many characters in common use in medieval England have long since disappeared. These include the thorn, which looked like a "y" and sounded like "th" (Fig. 2.5). It lingers on in examples such as Ye Olde Shoppe, which means The Old Shop.

Historical typefaces containing extended sets of characters are available from type foundries such as Crazy Diamond Design (Fig. 2.6) and Scriptorium.

The first movable type in the western world, invented by Johannes Gutenberg (Fig. 2.7), closely imitated the writing of the scribes. He created a set of over 300 characters, to accommodate all the variations of letterforms and **ligatures** (joined letters, such as fi and fl) that a scribe might need to use (Fig. 2.8).

2.9 The design for a hot-metal letter-form had to go through many stages on its way to the printed page, and at each successive stage the image had to be reversed (laterally inverted).

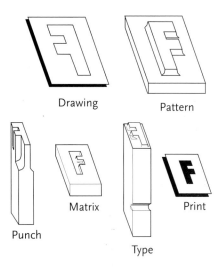

Drawing

Pattern

Matrix

Print

Punch

Type

2.10 The title page of a Shakespeare edition of 1623. By the time his plays were being published, the more readable roman humanist style of type — still in common use today — had replaced the denser textura faces of the scribes.

Gutenberg's masterpiece, known as the 42-line Bible, was an impressive achievement by any standards. Each two-volume work (48 copies survive from an estimated print run of 200) comprises 1286 pages, and was probably Gutenberg's financial undoing.

But his major legacy was the process of **hot-metal setting**. A steel punch for each character and punctuation mark is struck into a softer metal **matrix**, into which the lead type is cast.

Lead was used because it melts easily, flows evenly into the matrix, and expands slightly to make an exact replica of the punch. It hardens sufficiently to print repeatedly with acceptable levels of wear. Type for letterpress was always designed "the wrong way round" in mirror image, the production sequence being: drawing (wrong), pattern (right), punch (wrong), matrix (right), type (wrong), print (right) (Fig. **2.9**).

The fact that, in letterpress, characters have initially to be carved from steel has had a strong influence on type design ever since. It was only with the introduction of photosetting, in the 1950s, that some of the constraints were lifted.

As the skills of printing spread across Europe, craftsmen adapted their type to match the kind of lettering their customers preferred. William Caxton, the first printer in England, learnt his craft in Cologne, Germany, and bought Flemish equipment, so his books adopted the textura type.

Caxton's first book was printed in 1477. By 1509, English printers were already using roman type, mainly because of French influence. Shakespeare's plays were first printed in roman type (Fig. **2.10**), and the heavy textura type, or black letter is now rarely seen — outside of German-speaking countries — except on newspaper mastheads, banknotes, college certificates and diplomas, on signs advertising "Ye Olde Worlde Tea Shoppe" and for the logos of heavy-rock bands.

MR. WILLIAM
SHAKESPEARES
COMEDIES,
HISTORIES, &
TRAGEDIES.

Publihed according to the True Originall Copies.

LONDON
Printed by Iſaac Iaggard, and Ed. Blount. 1623.

2.11 A complete font. This font — ITC Clearface — is based on a face originally designed for American Type Founders by Morris Fuller Benton in 1907, and was redesigned in 1979 by Victor Caruso.

The language of type

A **font** is a complete set *in one size* of all the letters of the alphabet, complete with associated ligatures (joined letters), numerals, punctuation marks, and any other signs and symbols (Fig. **2.11**). The word font, or fount as it is sometimes spelt in Europe, derives from "found" as in type foundry, and reminds us of the days when molten metal type was cast in molds.

Typeface, often shortened to **face**, is the name given to the *design* of the alphabet and its associated marks and symbols. Every typeface has a name. This can be the name of its designer, for example Garamond, Bodoni, or Baskerville. It can take the name of the publication it was originally designed for, for example Times New Roman or Century. Or it may just have a fanciful name intended to convey the "feel" of the face, for example Optima, Perpetua, and Futura.

The letters of the alphabet, the numerals, and all the associated marks and symbols are collectively known as the **alphanumeric character set**. Individually, they are known as **sorts**. The expression "out of sorts," meaning unwell or depressed, comes from the typesetters finding that they have run out of a particular sort when composing a job.

The two words "font" and "typeface" are often used interchangeably. This has come about because in hot metal there will be a different font for each size of type. In photosetting, as we shall see later, it is common for one design to be enlarged or reduced to make all the sizes. This confusion is compounded in a digital page-layout system or word processor, in which a computer menu item labeled "font" will display to the user a list of available typefaces.

ABCDEFGHIJKLMNOPQRSTUVWXYZ
abcdefghijklmnopqrstuvwxyzfifl.,"-:;
()ÆæŒœ?&–$£1234567890

ABCDEFGHIJKLMNOPQRSTUVWXYZ
abcdefghijklmnopqrstuvwxyzfifl.,"-:;
()ÆæŒœ?&–$£1234567890

ABCDEFGHIJKLMNOPQRSTUVWXYZ
abcdefghijklmnopqrstuvwxyzfifl.,"-:;
()ÆæŒœ?&–$£1234567890

A complete set of sorts will also include some or all of the following:

- alternative letters, for the ends of lines, for example, and ornamented or "swash" capitals (but avoiding setting whole lines of swash letters!)

- diphthongs, such as æ and œ
- ligatures, such as fi and fl (in books of poetry, you may even see a ligature between c and t)
- accented letters or "floating" accents for setting foreign languages, such as à (grave), é (acute), ô (circumflex), ü (diaresis), ç (cedilla), ñ (tilde)
- numerals or figures, which can be lining or non-lining (sometimes called "old-style" numbers). Some fonts have both (Fig. **2.12**)

2.12 Lining and non-lining ("old-style") numbers. The old-style ones have more charm, but lining numerals are easier to incorporate into tabular matter.

1234567890   1234567890

- punctuation marks, such as , (comma) and ; (semi-colon)
- reference marks, such as * (asterisk) and ¶ (paragraph)
- fractions and mathematical signs, also known as **pi characters**, such as + (plus) and = (equals)
- and other signs and **dingbats**, such as & (ampersand, see left), F, and © (copyright)

A font of roman type will comprise three alphabets:
- capitals, also called majuscules or upper case, so named because of the position of the letters in the compositor's typecase (abbreviated to caps or u.c.)
- small letters, also known as minuscules or lower case (abbreviated to l.c.)
- and perhaps small capitals, which are the height of a lower case letter

ABCDEFGHIJKLMNOPQRSTUVWXYZ
abcdefghijklmnopqrstuvwxyz
ABCDEFGHIJKLMNOPQRSTUVWXYZ

Helvetica Roman
Helvetica Italic
Helvetica Bold
Helvetica Bold Italic

Helvetica Heavy
Helvetica Heavy Italic
Helvetica Black
Helvetica Black Italic

2.13 A type family contains all the fonts associated with a particular design.

Italic and bold fonts contain just two alphabets: capitals and lower case.

A **family** is a set of fonts related to the basic roman typeface which may include italic and bold plus a whole spectrum of different "weights" (Fig. **2.13**). These range from ultra light to ultra bold. It will also include different widths, ranging from ultra condensed to ultra expanded.

Univers, for example, was designed by Adrian Frutiger in 1957 to have 21 fonts, in five weights and four widths (Fig. **2.14**). In the original numbering system for Univers, the tens figure indicates the weight, the units figure the width. Odd numbers are roman, even numbers italic.

A **series** is a complete range of sizes in the same typeface.

How type is measured

The way type is measured dates back to the days of hot metal. Type sizes used to have quaint names such as nonpareil, long primer, minikin, minion, and brevier. Only "pica" remains in common usage.

In 1737, the Frenchman Pierre Fournier *le jeune* invented the **point** system of measurement, by dividing the French inch into 12 "lines" which were further subdivided into six points. Some half century later, around 1785, another Parisian, François-Ambroise Didot, settled on a standard — the **didot point** — that is used in continental Europe to this day.

In the United States, the point was standardized by the American Type Founders' Association in 1886 to be 0·013837 inch (or 0·03515 mm). Recently, the point has been further rationalized to make it exactly $^1/72$ inch (0·01389 in or 0·3528 mm). This may seem like splitting hairs, but it means in practice that the pica rules and typescales (Fig. **2.15**) designed for traditional typesetting will give inaccurate readings when used with digital layout.

There are 72 points to the inch. A **pica** is 12 points, and so measures $^1/6$ inch. (The didot equivalent to the pica is the cicero.) Although with computerized systems type can be of any height, its size is still generally measured in points, abbreviated to pt.

The use of points to specify size refers back to metal letterpress type. When a font is described as 6 pt or 18 pt, what is really being measured is the height of the body of lead that the letter sits upon (Fig. **2.16**). This is the total height from the lowest extremity of a **descender** (the long vertical stroke of a p or q) to the top of the tallest **ascender** (the long vertical stroke of a k or d), with a little extra space top and bottom. Thus in Linotype Times, for example, the distance from the top of a 10 pt letter k to the bottom of a

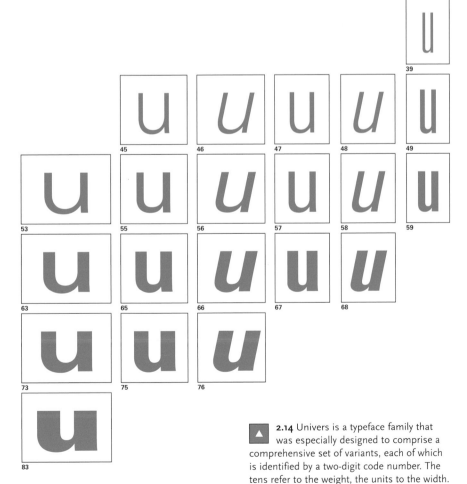

2.14 Univers is a typeface family that was especially designed to comprise a comprehensive set of variants, each of which is identified by a two-digit code number. The tens refer to the weight, the units to the width. Odd numbers are roman; even numbers italic.

Points	Picas	Inches	Millimeters
10	1		
20	2		
30	3		10
40	4		
50	5		
60	6	1	20
70	7		
80	8		30
90	9		
100	10		
110	11		40
120	12		
130	13	2	50
140	14		
150	15		
160	16		60
170	17		
180	18		70
190	19	3	
200	20		
210	21		80
220	22		
230	23		90
240	24		
250	25	4	
260	26		100
270	27		
280	28		110
290	29		
300	30		
310	31	5	120
320	32		
330	33		130
340	34		
350	35		
360	36	6	140
370			
380			150
390			
400			
410			
420			
430			

▲ **2.15** (left and right) Type is still mainly measured in points and picas. There are 12 points to the pica, and 72 points to the inch. Here the two most commonplace fonts — Times New Roman and Helvetica — are shown in various point sizes.

HxHx 36pt
HxHx 30pt
HxHx 24pt
HxHx 20pt
HxHx 18pt
HxHx 16pt
HxHx 14pt
HxHx 12pt
HxHx 11pt
HxHx 10pt
HxHx 9pt
HxHx 8pt
HxHx 7pt
HxHx 6pt

HxHx 42pt
HxHx 48pt
HxHx 54pt
HxHx 60pt
HxHx 66pt
HxHx 72pt

Shoulder
Face
Body or point size
Beard or bevel
Shank
Nick, for compositor to find front of type
Foot
Width, or set

◄ **2.16** The point size of a font refers back to metal type — to the top-to-bottom size of the body that the letter sits upon, not the distance from the uppermost part of a letter to the lowermost.

2.17 A more logical method for measuring the size of type is to measure from the top of a letter k to the bottom of a letter p: the so-called k–p distance.

2.18 Different typefaces have different proportions of ascender/descender in relation to the bowl, say, of a letter b. So two faces of the same point size may appear to be different sizes in print. The x-height — the height of a typical lower-case letter — is a good guide to the apparent size, and thus legibility, of a particular typeface.

letter p (the **k–p distance**, Fig. **2.17**) is not 10 pt but only 7·973 pt. The k–p distance of a named face can vary depending on its source, so the only sure way to identify type size is to compare your sample with suppliers' example settings.

A more exact way of defining point size is to say that it is the distance from **baseline** to baseline when type is set solid (without leading — see p. 41).

Some typefaces have longer ascenders and descenders than others, so it is quite possible for two typefaces to be exactly the same point size but to appear smaller or larger. A more visually accurate method for describing size is to use the **x-height** (Fig. **2.18**). The letter x is used because all its terminals touch a line of measurement.

Type below 14 pt is called **body type**, text, or book type. Type above 14 pt is called **display type**. Some display types are so decorative as to be unsuitable for text setting and are available in capitals only.

Width and spacing

The width of a letter is called the **set**. Every character sits on a body (real in hot metal, imaginary in computer systems) that is a number of "set points" wide, each set point being the same as the point which defines the height of the type. Typefaces with a narrow set, such as Bembo, will fit more words per page than wider typefaces, such as Baskerville.

On a regular typewriter, each letter, whether it is a thin i or a fat W, occupies the same width. The carriage moves forward the same distance each time a key is struck. The design of a typewriter font accommodates that shortcoming to

some extent. Look at the length of the serifs on a typewritten i, for example, or on a t (Fig. **2.19**).

Some letters are naturally wider than others, so, in typesetting, the "body" (the letter itself plus some space either side) is divided into vertical slices or **units**. In hot metal, an 18-unit system is employed. Thus the letter i occupies 5 units, while an M occupies the maximum of 18. Numerals are normally all 9 units wide, for ease of setting tables.

A regular typewriter uses a 1 unit, or monospaced, system. An example of a monospaced computer font is Courier. A "proportionally spaced" typewriter, such as the IBM Selectric, uses a 9-unit system. In comparison, photosetting systems use as

2.19 In a typewriter face such as Courier, all the letters are of equal width — note how the i is elongated to match the m. In more sophisticated typefaces, the width of letters varies, from the slimline l to the more expansive w. Thus different letters are allocated different numbers of units according to their set, or width.

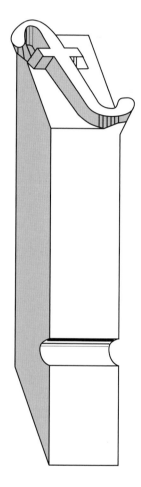

many as 96 units, the subtleties being apparent only in the very largest sizes of type.

In graphic design, the space around type is often as important as the letterform itself. When characters are allocated units, they are also given units either side to prevent consecutive sorts from touching. These are called **side bearings**, and the information about horizontal spacing built into a typeface by its designer is known as its **font metrics**.

Ems and ens

The width of a line of setting, or the column width of a publication, is called the **measure**, and is sometimes measured in picas. Other dimensions, particularly relating to page size and the positions of blocks of type, are generally measured in inches or millimeters. (In the United Kingdom, measure is also more usually in millimeters.)

Another convenient method of measurement is the **em**. This is the width of a capital M (or, strictly speaking, the width of a square space called an em **quad**). Half an em is an **en**, which is the width of a capital N. A complete font also provides the graphic designer with two types of dash, an en rule and an em rule — this book uses spaced em rules.

The em is not an absolute measurement like the pica. Its size will vary depending on the set of the typeface and its point size. A one em indent in 10 pt type is 10 points; a one em indent in 18 pt type is 18 points. But it is often convenient to ask the typesetter for a paragraph indent of say an em, so that it will

always be in proportion with the rest of the setting. A column width should never be specified in ems, however, for it will be different for each different font used. A 12 pt em is called a **pica em** — not to be confused with a regular pica!

Kerning and tracking

By overriding the unit allocation for pairs of certain letters, such as L and T, it is possible to bring them closer together and improve their visual appearance. This is called **kerning** (Fig. **2.21**).

In hot metal, kerning was only possible by physically cutting away, or mortising, the metal body of the type. Kerning characters are made with portions of the face overhanging the body (Fig. **2.20**). With computer systems, there are no restrictions on the extent of kerning possible. Most systems have routines already pre-programmed to adjust the spacing between kerning pairs automatically.

Yo! World.
Yo! World.

2.21 To improve the visual spacing between certain pairs of letters, especially those with overhanging parts, they are kerned according to rules laid down by the type designer. It is also possible to fine-tune the kerning later, by eye, depending on the context and on the size of the type.

Adjusting the spacing between *all* the letters is called **tracking** (Fig. **2.22**). Tracking should not be confused with kerning, which only takes place between pairs of letters.

Tracking was never really feasible with hot-metal setting, except in special places such as the title pages of books. On the rare occasions when it was done, different materials were used to make spaces between letters: brass for 1 pt, copper for $^1/_2$ pt, stainless steel for $^1/_4$ pt, and paper for the finest letterspacing of all.

In computer systems, it is common practice to use negative tracking to tighten up the spacing of text, particularly with sans-serif faces.

Leading

Spacing between lines of type is called **leading**, pronounced "ledding", and named after the strips of lead that were placed between lines of type in hot-metal setting (Fig. **2.23**). **Set solid** means without leading, for example, written 10/10 pt and spoken ten on ten point. To write 10/11 pt means to ask for 10 pt type with a 1 pt space (leading) between the lines, although in hot metal it actually meant to cast 10 pt type on to an 11 pt body.

Jo was very busy in the garret, for the October days began to grow chilly, and the afternoons were short. For two or three hours the sun lay warmly in the high window, showing Jo seated on the old sofa, writing busily, with her papers spread out upon a trunk before her, while Scrabble, the pet rat, promenaded the beams overhead, accompanied by his oldest son, a fine young fellow, who was evidently very proud of his whiskers. Quite absorbed in her work, Jo scribbled away till the last page was filled, when she signed her name with a flourish, and threw down her pen, exclaiming:

"There, I've done my best! If this won't suit I shall have to wait till I can do better."

▲ SCALA SANS 12/13PT NORMAL TRACKING

Jo was very busy in the garret, for the October days began to grow chilly, and the afternoons were short. For two or three hours the sun lay warmly in the high window, showing Jo seated on the old sofa, writing busily, with her papers spread out upon a trunk before her, while Scrabble, the pet rat, promenaded the beams overhead, accompanied by his oldest son, a fine young fellow, who was evidently very proud of his whiskers. Quite absorbed in her work, Jo scribbled away till the last page was filled, when she signed her name with a flourish, and threw down her pen, exclaiming:

"There, I've done my best! If this won't suit I shall have to wait till I can do better."

▲ SCALA SANS 12/13PT NEGATIVE TRACKING

Jo was very busy in the garret, for the October days began to grow chilly, and the afternoons were short. For two or three hours the sun lay warmly in the high window, showing Jo seated on the old sofa, writing busily, with her papers spread out upon a trunk before her, while Scrabble, the pet rat, promenaded the beams overhead, accompanied by his oldest son, a fine young fellow, who was evidently very proud of his whiskers. Quite absorbed in her work, Jo scribbled away till the last page was filled, when she signed her name with a flourish, and threw down her pen, exclaiming:

"There, I've done my best! If this won't suit I shall have to wait till I can do better."

▲ SCALA SANS 12/13PT POSITIVE TRACKING

2.23 The space between lines of type is called leading after the strips of lead that were used in letterpress. Thus 12/12 pt is said to be set solid. The 12/13 pt has 1 pt leading. Type can also be set with negative leading, producing lines with ascenders and descenders touching.

To aid legibility (see p. 60) it is now common to use 1 pt or 1¹/2 pt leading in text setting. Computer systems often add 1¹/2 pt leading by default. Always take into account the x-height of a typeface when deciding on a leading value. A good rule of thumb is: the larger the x-height, the more the leading; the smaller the x-height, the less the leading.

With computer systems, it is now allowable to specify all measurements in either inches or millimeters, or even mixtures of the two. However, against all odds, the point and pica persist!

Jo was very busy in the garret, for the October days began to grow chilly, and the afternoons were short. For two or three hours the sun lay warmly in the high window, showing Jo seated on the old sofa, writing busily, with her papers spread out upon a trunk before her, while Scrabble, the pet rat, promenaded the beams overhead, accompanied by his oldest son, a fine young fellow, who was evidently very proud of his whiskers. Quite absorbed in her work, Jo scribbled away till the last page was filled, when she signed her name with a flourish, and threw down her pen, exclaiming:

"There, I've done my best! If this won't suit I shall have to wait till I can do better."

▲ SCALA SANS 55 12/11PT

Jo was very busy in the garret, for the October days began to grow chilly, and the afternoons were short. For two or three hours the sun lay warmly in the high window, showing Jo seated on the old sofa, writing busily, with her papers spread out upon a trunk before her, while Scrabble, the pet rat, promenaded the beams overhead, accompanied by his oldest son, a fine young fellow, who was evidently very proud of his whiskers. Quite absorbed in her work, Jo scribbled away till the last page was filled, when she signed her name with a flourish, and threw down her pen, exclaiming:

"There, I've done my best! If this won't suit I shall have to wait till I can do better."

▲ SCALA SANS 12/12PT

Jo was very busy in the garret, for the October days began to grow chilly, and the afternoons were short. For two or three hours the sun lay warmly in the high window, showing Jo seated on the old sofa, writing busily, with her papers spread out upon a trunk before her, while Scrabble, the pet rat, promenaded the beams overhead, accompanied by his oldest son, a fine young fellow, who was evidently very proud of his whiskers. Quite absorbed in her work, Jo scribbled away till the last page was filled, when she signed her name with a flourish, and threw down her pen, exclaiming:

"There, I've done my best! If this won't suit I shall have to wait till I can do better."

▲ SCALA SANS 12/13PT

Jo was very busy in the garret, for the October days began to grow chilly, and the afternoons were short. For two or three hours the sun lay warmly in the high window, showing Jo seated on the old sofa, writing busily, with her papers spread out upon a trunk before her, while Scrabble, the pet rat, promenaded the beams overhead, accompanied by his oldest son, a fine young fellow, who was evidently very proud of his whiskers. Quite absorbed in her work, Jo scribbled away till the last page was filled, when she signed her name with a flourish, and threw down her pen, exclaiming:

"There, I've done my best! If this won't suit I shall have to wait till I can do better."

▲ SCALA SANS 12/14PT

TABS AND PARAGRAPHS

Try to use the tab and paragraph commands in your word processor to format text, rather than taps on the spacebar. Type will line up better and won't cause problems later if it has to be reflowed. Better still, learn how to use the style-sheet commands included in most word processors — it will save you time in the long run, and ensure consistency within the document. Output your text in RTF (Rich Text Format) — not everyone has Microsoft Word!

Most word processors and page-layout programs let you specify left, right, and first-line indents for paragraphs (a paragraph to a computer is all the text until you reach a carriage return, and includes headlines). So try to kick the typist's habit of hitting the tab key when you begin a new para — give the paragraph a first-line indent.

And if you're setting text that's ranged left and want to move a sticking-out word over to the next line, use a forced break or soft return (shift-return) rather than a return or lots of spaces.

2.24 Type is commonly set ranged left (ragged right). It can instead be ranged right, centered, or asymmetrical. If type is to be set justified — neatly aligned on both left and right sides — variable spaces must be introduced between words to make each line the same length. Failing this, some words must be broken, or hyphenated.

Justification and hyphenation

A regular typewriter produces rows of type that line up on the left-hand side but give a ragged appearance on the right. In typesetting, this is called ragged right, **ranged left**, or flush left. Type can also be set ragged left, **ranged right**, centered, or asymmetrical (Fig. **2.24**).

In books and magazines, it is usual to see columns of type with neat edges on both sides. This is called **justified** setting, and it is achieved by introducing variable amounts of space between the words. More often than not, especially with the narrow columns used in newspapers and magazines, it is not possible to justify a line merely by increasing the space, and so words must be divided, or **hyphenated**.

Compositors have been taught to break words according to certain rules, as found in handbooks such as *Hart's Rules for Compositors and Readers*. A word is usually hyphenated between syllables, pairs of consonants, or pairs of vowels. The part of the word left at the end of a line should also suggest the part commencing the next line. Thus starva-tion is to be preferred to star-vation. Other rules instruct to hyphenate before -ing, except in a one-syllable word such as ring, and unless preceded by d, t, or h.

Rules for hyphenation can be programmed into computer systems, along with tables of exceptions, to avoid **bad breaks**. However, it is still common to see howlers. Some careless word breaks can create unwanted meanings: the-rapist is a memorable example.

It is also generally considered good design to avoid too many

For two or three hours the sun lay warmly in the high window, showing Jo seated on the old sofa, writing busily, with her papers spread out upon a trunk before her, while Scrabble, the pet rat, promenaded the beams overhead, accompanied by his oldest son, a fine young fellow, who was evidently very proud of his whiskers.

▲ RANGED LEFT

For two or three hours the sun lay warmly in the high window, showing Jo seated on the old sofa, writing busily, with her papers spread out upon a trunk before her, while Scrabble, the pet rat, promenaded the beams overhead, accompanied by his oldest son, a fine young fellow, who was evidently very proud of his whiskers.

▲ RANGED RIGHT

For two or three hours the sun lay warmly in the high window, showing Jo seated on the old sofa, writing busily, with her papers spread out upon a trunk before her, while Scrabble, the pet rat, promenaded the beams overhead, accompanied by his oldest son, a fine young fellow, who was evidently very proud of his whiskers.

▲ CENTERED

For two or three hours the sun lay warmly in the high window, showing Jo seated on the old sofa, writing busily, with her papers spread out upon a trunk before her, while Scrabble, the pet rat, promenaded the beams overhead, accompanied by his oldest son, a fine young fellow, who was evidently very proud of his whiskers.

▲ ASYMMETRICAL

For two or three hours the sun lay warmly in the high window, showing Jo seated on the old sofa, writing busily, with her papers spread out upon a trunk before her, while Scrabble, the pet rat, promenaded the beams overhead, accompanied by his oldest son, a fine young fellow, who was evidently very proud of his whiskers.

▲ JUSTIFIED

2.25 One of the general rules of good layout is to avoid creating "orphans" — one or a few words alone on a line at the end of a paragraph — or worse still, a "widow" a single word floating at the top of a new page or column.

An occasional Newsletter for graphic designers, printers, and typographers that is published once a millennium, if ever at all.

¶ Type *Tymes*

Alphabet soup

Writing text that is meant to represent body type in layouts and type specimen books is probably the most difficult task a writer can ever be asked to undertake. Ideally, the text should contain examples of all the letters and sorts – in Roman, *italic* and **bold** – and include a range of words of average length so that it looks right. Above all, it shouldn't draw attention to itself. The text is not meant to be read, merely looked at – but invariably someone somewhere will grab a magnifying glass, read it and then criticize any attempted jokes therein.

Some designers take the easy route and use real or bogus Latin text, most often a famous piece of text that begins: "Lorem ipsum dolor sit amet, consectetur adipscing elit, diam nonnumy eiusmod tempor incidunt ut labore et dolo..." These are, according to the FAQ (frequently asked questions) of the newsgroup **comp.fonts**, the slightly jumbled remnants of a passage from Cicero's *de Finibus Bonorum et Malorum*, written in 45 BC, a treatise on the theory of ethics, which begins: "Neque porro quisquam est qui dolorem ipsum quia dolor sit amet, consectetur, adipsici velit..." (There is no one who loves pain itself, who seeks after it and wants to have it, simply because it is pain.)

This text has been the industry's standard dummy text ever since some printer in the 1500s took a galley of type and scrambled it to make a type specimen book; it has survived letter-by-letter essentially unchanged except for an occasional "ing" or "y" thrown in. The nonsense Latin was as incomprehensible as Greek: so the phrase "it's all Greek to me" and the term "greeking" have common semantic roots!

But this does contain some strange, to English eyes, letter combinations. Few, if any, English words contain the sequence "eiu," for example. When short pieces of text are called for, try to make a sentence containing all the letters of the alphabet with as few duplications as possible. These are called *pangrams*.

Whatever else you do, try always to avoid widows.

The classic pangram used by typographers is: "The quick brown fox jumps over a lazy dog". Good score: all 24 letters of the alphabet in a 33-word sentence that makes sense. "Pack my box with five dozen liquor jugs" is better, with one letter less. Another common albeit longer one is: "How razorback-jumping frogs can level six piqued gymnasts!"

This one is not so good: "In the vocation of typesetting, dexterity can be gained by means of quiet, judicious and zealous work." It is more appropriate to the printing trade, but comprises 83 letters! And what about this: "Wherever civilization extends, the services of expert and judicious typographers and printers must always be quickly called upon". Is that grammatically correct? I don't think so. Or this: "The bank recognizes this claim as quite valid and just, so we expect full payment". Hmm.

Probably the shortest French pangram, at 29 letters, is: "Whisky vert: jugez cinq fox d'aplomb." Some pangrams of exactly 26 letters do exist, but rely heavily on the kind of obscure words that Scrabble players collect plus the odd Welsh and Hebrew word, such as cwm (a Welsh valley) and qoph (the nineteenth letter of the Hebrew alphabet) and, of course, proper nouns (which could in fact be made up from the left-over letters): "Vext cwm fly zing jabs Kurd qoph" is a good example. And try not to leave any orphans!

Page 1

2.26 A drop cap is an embellishment found at the beginning of a chapter in a book or in the opening paragraph of a magazine article, in which the first letter is enlarged and set into the body of the text. Its historical precedent can be found in illuminated medieval manuscripts like the ornamented title page of 1496 from the Cistercian monastery at Zinna reproduced above.

For two or three hours the sun lay warmly in the high window, showing Jo seated on the old sofa, writing busily, with her papers spread out upon a trunk before her, while Scrabble, the pet rat, promenaded the beams overhead, accompanied by his oldest son, a fine young fellow, who was evidently very proud of his whiskers.

For two or three hours the sun lay warmly in the high window, showing Jo seated on the old sofa, writing busily, with her papers spread out upon a trunk before her, while Scrabble, the pet rat, promenaded the beams overhead, accompanied by his oldest son, a fine young fellow, who was evidently very proud of his whiskers.

consecutive hyphens. Three lines ending with hyphens or other punctuation marks is the maximum that can be tolerated. The designer should also be on the look-out for **rivers** of space running vertically in the middle of chunks of type. And for **widows** and **orphans** (Fig. **2.25**).

A widow is a single word on the last line of a paragraph carried over to the top of a column, and is best avoided by asking the copywriter or author to lose a word from earlier on in the paragraph. Orphans are single words, or small groups of words, left at the ends of paragraphs. There will be more discussion on the principles of layout in Chapter 4 (p. 110).

A revival from medieval manuscripts is the **drop cap** (Fig. **2.26**), mainly because it is easy to do on a computer system. A drop cap is an initial letter signaling the beginning of the text. It is usually enlarged to a size equivalent to three or more lines of type, with the type adjacent to the drop cap indented to make room. Drop caps work best when the first sentence begins with a single letter, such as A or I. Failing that, avoid short words, especially ones with only two letters. And take care with those words that form different words when the initial letter is removed, such as T-he, E-very, and S-elf. Another common error is to forget to remove the first letter of the body text that follows.

2.27 An author's manuscript must be marked up by a copy editor before it goes to the printer for typesetting. This process brings the raw text into house style, corrects any errors, and can involve some degree of rewriting. Either the editor or the designer will also need to instruct the compositor as to which typefaces, sizes, and measures to use when converting the text into type.

■ TEXT

Text is the "meaning" part of type: just plain words plus the spaces between them, devoid of any information about the typefaces, sizes, measures, or weights being used. In print production, raw text is called **copy**.

One of the designer's tasks has traditionally been **copy preparation** — adding the instructions that define how the text is going to look, either by keying them directly into the computer or by **marking up** the manuscript for the typesetter (Fig. **2.27**).

For type to remain consistent within a long document, or from issue to issue of a magazine, the graphic designer will write down and send to the compositor a **style sheet** or **type specification** (Fig. **2.28**). This will define the size, typeface, and measure of the body text, captions, headlines, and so on. In this book, for example, the text is set in 10^1/4 / 12^1/2 pt Scala Sans Regular, headings in various sizes of Scala Sans Bold, and chapter titles in 60 pt Scala Sans Bold.

The type spec may also lay down a **grid** (see pp. 112–3) which restricts type to certain areas of the page.

Collectively, a text document is called a **manuscript**, abbreviated to Ms or ms. A single sheet is called a **folio**. (A folio is also the term given by publishers to the page numbers in books.) Each folio should be numbered and identified with a tag or catchline, usually the name of the author or job, in case the Ms is dropped or otherwise gets out of sequence. It is also customary for short pieces of setting to indicate

2.28 The style sheet for this book.

Correcting text proofs

~~**Proofing and proof correction**~~

Once type has been set, it must be checked to make sure that it has been keyed correctly. The old proofreaders on newspapers were adept at reading type back to front, but for mere mortals, a proof must be taken. The first proof is called the galley proof. Several pulls are made so that the various professionals involved in the production can each read the proof. The printer's reader is the first, and ~~he or the~~ marks the printer's mistakes to be corrected, usually in green ink.

(Run on) One proof is designated the **master proof**, and others *(of the galley)* go to the author or copywriter and to the copy editor, who decides which corrections should be incorporated on to the master proof. So-called **author's corrections** are *bold* marked in blue and have to be paid for, while any other printer's errors are marked in red. *n.p.* Typing errors such *bold* as transposed letters are called **literals**, and probably constitute the bulk of the corrections. Note that it is possible in hot metal and photosetting to introduce new, more serious errors into a text when attempting to correct a relatively trivial one! So that there can be no chance of misunderstanding between the copy editor and the compositor, corrections are marked neatly both in the setting and with an accompanying marginal symbol, according to an internationally agreed convention

2.28 (Fig. **2.?**). *If something is wrongly corrected and needs to be reinstated, it should be marked with dotted underlining and the word stet written in the margin.*

Although there are no physical galleys in photosetting, the

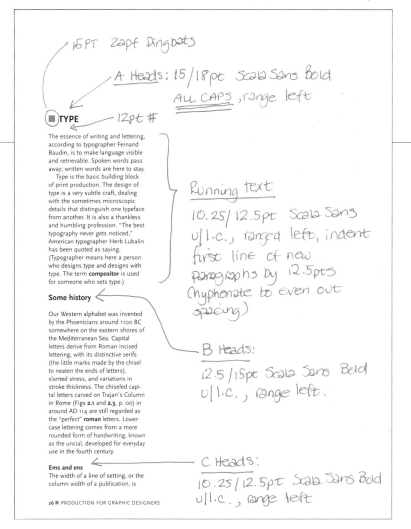

15PT Zapf Dingbats

A Heads: 15/18pt Scala Sans Bold ALL CAPS, range left

12pt #

■ TYPE

The essence of writing and lettering, according to typographer Fernand Baudin, is to make language visible and retrievable. Spoken words pass away; written words are here to stay.

Type is the basic building block of print production. The design of type is a very subtle craft, dealing with the sometimes microscopic details that distinguish one typeface from another. It is also a thankless and humbling profession. "The best typography never gets noticed," American typographer Herb Lubalin has been quoted as saying. (Typographer means here a person who designs type and designs with type. The term **compositor** is used for someone who sets type.)

Running text
10.25/12.5pt Scala Sans u/l.c., ranged left, indent first line of new paragraphs by 12.5pts (hyphenate to even out spacing)

Some history

Our Western alphabet was invented by the Phoenicians around 1100 BC somewhere on the eastern shores of the Mediterranean Sea. Capital letters derive from Roman incised lettering, with its distinctive serifs (the little marks made by the chisel to neaten the ends of letters), slanted stress, and variations in stroke thickness. The chiseled capital letters carved on Trajan's Column in Rome (Figs **2.1** and **2.3**, p. 00) in around AD 114 are still regarded as the "perfect" **roman** letters. Lowercase lettering comes from a more rounded form of handwriting, known as the uncial, developed for everyday use in the fourth century.

B Heads:
12.5/15pt Scala Sans Bold u/l.c., range left.

Ems and ens

The width of a line of setting, or the column width of a publication, is

C Heads:
10.25/12.5pt Scala Sans Bold u/l.c., range left

BOOKWORM TYPESETTING
4 Harthill Street, Manchester
T: 0161-832 3034

Calmann & King
Production for Graphic Design
24.2.97 [Own Disc & Pi]
David Newton [254G]

W9808FIG.FOL

Correcting text profs

Once typ has been set, it must be checked to make sure that it has been keyed correctly. The old proof-readers on newspapers were adept at reading type back to font, but for mere mortals, a proof mûst be taken. The first proof is called the galley proof. Several pulls are made so that the various proffessionals involved in the production can each read the proof. Several pulls are taken so that the various proffessionals involved in the production can each read the proof The printers reader is the first, and marks the printer's mistakes to be corrected, usually in green ink.

One of the galley proofs is designated the **master proof**, and others go t the author or copywriter and to the copy editor, who decides which corrections should be incorporated on to the master proof. So-called **author's corrections are marked in blue and have to be paid for, while any other printer's errors are marked in red.**

Typing errors such as trasnposed letters are called *literals*, and probably constitute the bulk of the corrections. Note that it is possible in hot metal and photosetting to introduce new, more serious errors into a text when attempting to correct a relatively trivial one! so that there can be no chance of misunderstanding between the copyeditor and the composer, corrections are marked nearly both in the setting and with an accompanying marginal symbol, according to an internationally agreed convention (*Fig.* 2.27. If something is wrongly corrected and needs to be reinstated, it should be marked with dotted underlining and the word stet written in the margin. Although there are no physical galleys in photosetting, the same procedure applies. The designer and/our copy editor usually will receive a set of photocopies of the bromide print, which is treated in exactly the same way as the hotmetal galley proof. Once corrected, another proof may be sent, but it is more likely that the next chance to check that the corrections have been made will be on the page proof, a proof of the mechanical complete with runinning headlines, captions, and line illustrations in palace.

With apologies to Bookworm Typesetting, who set the galley proofs very cleanly.

2.29 Once the marked-up copy returns from the typesetter in the form of galley proofs, it must be read, checked, and marked for correction using standard proof correction signs, as shown overleaf. Here we show the original marked-up copy (Fig. **2.27**), the typesetting after being marked for correction (right), and, after another journey to the typesetter's, the resulting "clean" setting (below), incorporated into the layout.

marks the printer's mistakes to be corrected, usually in green ink. One of the galley proofs is designated the **master proof**, and others go to the author or copywriter and to the copy editor, who decides which corrections should be incorporated on to the master proof (Fig. **2.29**). So-called **author's corrections** are marked in blue and have to be paid for, while any other printer's errors are marked in red.

Typing errors such as transposed letters are called literals, and probably constitute the bulk of the corrections. Note that it is possible to introduce new, more serious errors into a text when attempting to correct a relatively trivial one! So that there can be no chance of misunderstanding between the copy editor and the compositor, corrections are marked neatly both in the setting and with an accompanying marginal symbol, according to an internationally agreed convention (Fig. **2.30**, p. 47). The marginal symbol is most important because compositors run their eyes down the edges of proofs to locate corrections. If something is wrongly corrected and needs to be reinstated, it should be marked with dotted underlining and the word **stet** written in the margin.

Although there are no physical galleys in photosetting, the same procedure applies. The designer and/or copy editor will usually receive a set of photocopies of the bromide print, which is treated in exactly the same way as the hot-metal galley proof. Once corrected, another proof may be sent, but it is more likely that the next chance to check that the corrections have

on each folio whether *more follows* or that the copy *ends*.

Copy should always be clean and legible, typed or printed out on one side of the paper in double spacing with wide margins, leaving enough room for the copy editor's corrections. Some publishers used to provide authors with **templates**, sheets printed with feint blue guidelines, for the purpose. Any matter not to be printed, such as instructions to the typesetter, should be encircled.

Correcting text proofs

Once type has been set, it must be checked to make sure that it has been keyed correctly. The old proof-readers on newspapers were adept at reading type back to front, but for mere mortals, a proof must be taken. The first proof is called the galley proof. Several copies are made so that the various professionals involved in the production can each read the proof. The printer's reader is the first, and

2.30 To ensure that designers, proof-readers, editors, and typesetters can communicate with each other effectively, an internationally agreed standard for proof-correction symbols has been developed.

STANDARD PROOF CORRECTION SIGNS

EXPLANATION	MARGINAL MARK	TEXT MARK
Delete letter(s) or word(s)	⌒	I've doner my best
Close up; delete space	⌒	I've done my best
Delete, and close up word	⌒	I've done may best
Let it stand as it is	stet	I've done my best
Insert space	#	I've donemy best
Equalize spacing	eq #	I've done my best
Insert hair space	hL #	1398–1468
Letterspace	LS	I'VE DONE MY BEST
Begin new paragraph	¶	I've done my best! [If
Don't begin new paragraph; run on	no ¶	I've done my best! If this won't suit
Move type one em	⊐	] I've done my best
Move type two ems	⊐⊐	] I've done my best
Move right	]	I've done my best]
Move left	[	[I've done my best
Center	][	] I've done my best [
Move up	⌐ ⌐	I've done my best
Move down	⌐ ⌐	I've done my best
Flush left; range left	fL	[I've done my best
Flush right; range right	fr	I've done my best
Straighten type; align horizontally	=	I've done my best
Align vertically	‖	‖ I've ‖ done
Transpose; swap the order	tr	I've done my bset
Set in *italic* type	ital	I've done my best
Set in roman type	rom	*I've done my best*
Set in bold type	bf	I've done my best
Set in lower case	Lc	I've done MY best
Set in UPPER CASE (capitals)	cap	i've done my best
Set in SMALL CAPITALS	sc	I've done my best
Remove blemish	X	I've done my best
Make superscript figure	∨⁰	1024 is 210
Make subscript figure	∧₂	101012
Insert comma	∧	There I've done my best
Insert apostrophe or single quotation mark	∨	Ive done my best
Insert period	⊙	I've done my best∧
Insert question mark	?	Have I done my best∧
Insert colon	:/	She exclaimed "I've done
Insert hyphen	/=/	Black and-white print
Insert en dash	⊢N⊣	1398–1468
Insert em dash	⊢M⊣	I've done my best∧
Insert parentheses.	(/)	∧ I've done my best∧
Insert brackets	[/]	∧ I've done my best∧

been made will be on the **page proof**, a proof of the page layout complete with running headlines, captions, and illustrations in place.

With a digital design system, it is tempting to go straight to page layout once the text has been input. It is much safer to print out the text and to read it as if it were a galley proof. In this way there is **hardcopy** — a record of the corrections made. This also goes for website design — print out your pages and proofread them away from the computer. Better still, get a colleague to read the proof — mistakes are often invisible to those who make them. Proofreading is vital now that designers are expected to set text as they are laying out designs.

Keeping track of changes to a manuscript as it travels from computer to computer is quite diffi-cult as word processors and layout programs always present you with a "clean" copy of the text. It is very difficult to see where any changes have been made. Programs such as Microsoft Word and Adobe InCopy, which works with layout program InDesign (see p. 118) can, however, track editorial changes, including insertions, deletions, and moved text. You can display or hide each kind of revision, or display change bars in the margin of a document. To track revisions, you can label changes by user, time, and date, and navigate between them. Revisions are stored with the document until they are accepted or rejected.

And beware of computer spell checkers — they can give a false sense of security. For example, if a word is wrong but spelt "correctly," i.e. you typed "cat" but meant "cut,"

it won't be picked up by a spell checker. Irritatingly, spell checkers also stop at every proper noun and most numbers!

Casting off and copy fitting

Casting off is estimating the number of words in a manuscript. **Copy fitting** is assessing how much space text will take up in a printed document. Both are tedious and produce only approximate results, but are important in ensuring that you do not end up with pages of **overmatter**. Nowadays, authors rely

on the word-processing program to keep track of the word count. Traditionally, one would encourage the author to type the same number of lines per page, and across a measure containing a round number of characters that is straightforward to calculate.

A regular typewriter does not have proportional spacing, so each letter takes up the same amount of space. One would rule a pencil line down the right-hand edge of the typing, placed so that the visual area of the type to the right of the line equals the area of white space to the

Characters per line

Font size	Pica Measure												
	18	19	20	21	22	23	24	25	26	27	28	29	30
8 pt.	59	62	65	68	72	75	78	81	85	88	91	94	98
9 pt.	52	55	58	60	63	66	69	72	75	78	81	83	86
10 pt.	46	48	51	53	56	58	61	64	66	69	71	74	76
11 pt.	42	44	47	49	51	54	56	58	61	63	65	68	70
12 pt.	38	40	43	45	47	49	51	53	55	57	60	62	64

2.31 Copy-fitting tables help estimate the space needed by copy in a particular typeface and point size. The above old-style table is for Century. In the two-part table below, each typeface is given a value. A number from the first table is used to read off characters per pica from the second.

left. This establishes the average number of characters per line. A less accurate method is to count the number of characters per line for the first, say, ten lines and find the average. Then count the number of lines, marking, say, every hundredth line in pencil. It is assumed that, in English, an average word is five letters plus one space long, so the number of characters divided by six gives the number of words.

Most word processors use proportional spacing, which makes character counting more difficult. However, most now have built-in word counters. These are often approximate, depending on what the program decides constitutes a word. Different programs can give different word counts for the same piece of text.

The amount of space required when the text is set into type will vary depending both on the type size and the typeface. For hot metal and photosetting, the type foundries would supply copy-fitting tables (Fig. **2.31**), which gave you the information that, for example, 11 pt Bembo averages 66 characters (11 words) in a line 24 picas long. It was thus possible to find out how many pages the copy would fill once set in type.

For smaller jobs, a plastic type gauge was used to measure the number of lines that a particular size of type would occupy. If you calculated that five lines of text would give you seven lines of type, for example, it was possible to count them off using the gauge. Many type gauges also had scales with which to count typewritten characters. On typewriters, the number of characters per inch is

called the **pitch**: the normal 10 pitch is called pica (no relation to the typographic pica!), and the smaller 12 pitch is called elite. Always overestimate the number of words, to be on the safe side. It is easier to deal with white space than to find room for unexpected text.

With computer setting, there is a lot of variation in set width between the same named typeface from different suppliers. The only way to be safe is to base your calculations on a piece of sample setting from your chosen font and use *exactly* the same font for the eventual setting. This is particularly important when using a bureau which may claim to hold the same font: when the proof arrives you may find the words are not where you wanted them.

It is all too easy to make copy fit an awkward space by altering the tracking, the size of type, or the leading by just the tiniest amount, with a resulting inconsistency of "color" within the document. This is a temptation that should be resisted.

House style

There are few absolutes in life, and in some cases a usage is neither right nor wrong. But **house style** is a way of standardizing spelling and codifying the way, say, that ships' names, like the USS *Enterprise*, are always italicized. There will normally also be guidelines to avoid sexist and racist usages creeping into print.

House style will regulate how the date should be written, and will also

Alphabet lengths for different sizes
Laufweitenkennzahl für verschiedene Schriftgrößen
Longueur d'alphabet pour différents corps

alphabet length ref. no. at 10 pt / Laufweitenkennzahl in 10 pt / de longueur d'alphabet en 10 pt

pt	6	7	8	9	10	11	12	14	16	18	20	24	30	36	42	48
mm	2,25	2,63	3,00	3,38	3,75	4,13	4,50	5,25	6,00	6,75	7,50	9,00	11,25	13,50	15,75	18,00
85	51	59	68	76	85	93	102	119	136	153	170	204	255	306	357	408
87	52	60	69	78	87	95	104	121	139	156	174	208	261	313	365	417
88	52	61	70	79	88	96	105	123	140	158	176	211	264	316	369	422
90	54	63	72	81	90	99	108	126	144	162	180	216	270	324	378	432
92	55	64	73	82	92	101	110	128	147	165	184	220	276	331	386	441
93	55	65	74	83	93	102	111	130	148	167	186	223	279	334	390	446
95	57	66	76	85	95	104	114	133	152	171	190	228	285	342	399	456
97	58	67	77	87	97	106	116	135	155	174	194	232	291	349	407	465
98	58	68	78	88	98	107	117	137	156	176	196	235	294	352	411	470
100	60	70	80	90	100	110	120	140	160	180	200	240	300	360	420	480

Characters per line (Pica)
Zeichen pro Zeile (Pica)
Caractères par ligne (Pica)

determined alphabet length ref. no. / ermittelte Laufweitenkennzahl / de longueur d'alphabet déterminés

Pica	1.00	10	12	14	16	18	20	22	24	26	28	30	32	36	40	45
50	6.74	67	81	94	108	121	135	148	162	175	189	202	216	243	270	303
52	6.48	65	78	91	104	117	130	143	156	168	181	194	207	233	259	292
54	6.24	62	75	87	100	112	125	137	150	162	175	187	200	225	250	281
56	6.02	60	72	84	96	108	120	132	144	156	168	181	193	217	241	271
58	5.81	58	70	81	93	105	116	128	139	151	163	174	186	209	232	261
60	5.62	56	67	79	90	101	112	124	135	146	157	168	180	202	225	253
62	5.43	54	65	76	87	98	109	120	130	141	152	163	174	196	217	245
64	5.27	53	63	74	84	95	105	116	126	137	147	158	168	190	211	237
66	5.11	51	61	71	82	92	102	112	123	133	143	153	163	184	204	230
68	4.96	50	59	69	79	89	99	109	119	129	139	149	159	178	198	223
70	4.81	48	58	67	77	87	96	106	116	125	135	144	154	173	193	217
72	4.69	47	56	66	75	85	94	103								

489, 494, 504, 513, 518, 528, 537, 542, 552, 561, 566, 576, 585, 590, 600, 609, 614, 624, 633, 638

RECOGNIZING TYPEFACES
To recognize a typeface you're not familiar with, look at the capital Q, the lowercase g and the ampersand (&) first for the earmarks (distinguishing features) of the face. Collect as many type sample books as you can — catalogs are often given away by type foundries — and, if you have time, try asking your supplier: some type vendors offer a type-recognition service.

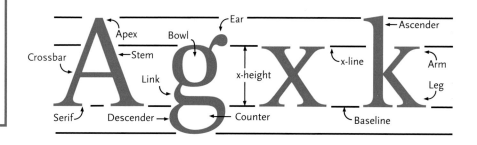

include instructions as to whether acronyms should be given periods or not (dots per inch as d.p.i. or dpi, or even dots/in), set all caps or all lower case (both WYSIWYG and wysiwyg, for example, could be used to mean "what you see is what you get").

The keyword is consistency — within a publication, and within an organization.

Choosing and recognizing typefaces

To be able to choose the right typeface for the job, one must first know something about how typefaces are constructed and classified (Fig. **2.32**).

Each face has its own personality (Fig. **2.33**), and typefaces are described by typographers in the same hallowed tones used by connoisseurs to talk about wine. Garamond is said to be "quiet"; Bodoni "sparkles".

Each has its place in the graphic designer's toolkit: for a bank's annual report, for example, you may wish to use a well-established "classic" face like Garamond to convey tradition and solidity; a music magazine aimed at young people will look better with a fashionable type. Some typefaces are chosen for practical reasons. Newspapers tend to use faces with large x-heights and open counters, because the ink spread on low-grade paper would fill in less robust faces.

2.33 Some typefaces are so familiar as to be virtually invisible — Times and Helvetica are the main culprits — while others, such as Futura and Gill, come regularly in and out of fashion every few years.

Vertical stress
(Times)

Inclined stress
(Goudy Old Style)

2.32 Each letter has its own anatomical details, and knowing the names for the component parts of a letterform is a great aid to identifying and specifying a particular typeface.

Establishment
Times New Roman

Professional
Rotis serif 55

Fun and Friendly
Dolores Bold

Bland but safe
Helvetica

Traditional
Baskerville

Powerful
Franklin Gothic Heavy

Fashionable
Meta

Elegant
Garamond Italic

Serif or sans serif?

The most obvious distinguishing feature of a typeface is whether it has a serif or not (Fig. **2.34**). **Serifs** are marks or flourishes around the extremities of letters, on the baseline and at the top, usually at right angles to the direction of the stroke. They help to make type more readable (see p. 60), and take several different forms: bracketed, with a smooth curved "fillet" between the serif and stem; slab, with sharper corners and almost the same thickness as the stem; hairline; or wedge. The best known serif typeface is Times.

A typeface without serifs is called **sans serif**, or just sans. The old name was grot, from grotesque, and in America they are also known as Gothic faces. The first sans typeface for text was cast in 1835 and called Seven Lines Grotesque, though sans faces have long been used for display setting and for signwriting. They did not become popular until the beginning of this century, first with Edward Johnston's 1916 typeface — still in use — for London Transport. Later came Univers, and Max Miedinger's Helvetica, perhaps one of the most popular typefaces currently in use. Contemporary classics include Meta and Verdana.

 2.34 All typefaces can be classified according to whether they do or do not have serifs. Some serifs have brackets — smooth "fillets" between the horizontal and upright — and some do not. The size of the serif can range from slab to hairline.

Sans serif (without serifs)   Square or slab serifs   Bracketed serifs

Thin or hairline serifs   Round serifs

Novelty serifs   Cupped serifs

GgyQap&4
Helvetica

GgyQap&4
Univers

GgyQap&4
Futura

GgyQap&4
Gill

GgyQap&4
Clearface

GgyQap&4
Times

GgyQap&4
Baskerville

GgyQap&4
Garamond

2.35 Earmarks are the distinguishing features of a typeface design. Easily identifiable letters include the capital Q and the lower case g, and don't forget the ampersand.

■ Helvetica

In the years following the Second World War, Swiss-style typography was the in thing. Switzerland's neutrality had allowed a continuity of development from the grid-bound modernist graphic design of the 1930s, with its integrated text and image, use of photomontage, and above all its reductive unadorned type, serving only the functional needs of communication. According to Joseph Müller-Brockman (1914–96), unornamented sans-serif typefaces expressed the age and were suitable for any job — and the typeface of choice was Berthold's Akzidenz Grotesk, aka Standard. It was favored over geometric fonts like Futura, because it could provide a closer fit of letters. It had, however, been around since 1896 and so the race was on to find a more up-to-date successor.

Max Miedinger (1910–80) was born in Zürich and trained as a typesetter, but worked most of his life as a customer service and sales representative for the Haas Type Foundry in Münchenstein, near Basle. At the age of 46, he became a freelance graphic designer in Zürich. Then in 1956, Edouard Hoffmann of Haas asked Max to redesign Akzidenz Grotesk with a higher x-height and give them something to sell. The result was Neue Haas Grotesk (1951–53), renamed Helvetica (the Latin word for Switzerland) in 1957 when it was licensed to German type foundry Stempel. The commercial package was launched in 1961. Linotype took complete control of Haas in 1989 and produced a full family of variants.

Linotype's limited licensing forced a large number of unauthorized copies of Helvetica, including Helios, Geneva, Megaron, Triumvirate, and Swiss 721. Forty years after its introduction, Linotype listed 115 fonts for the family, with Helvetica Rounded being probably the least known. Max Miedinger died in 1980. Other typefaces designed by him include: Pro Arte (1954) and Horizontal (1964).

Despite the challenge of the more radical and modern Univers, designed by Adrian Frutiger in 1954 in both a photosetting and metal version and in 21 logical variants, Helvetica — a simple response to market demand — became, along with Times New Roman, one of the most popular typefaces of the 20th century.

Successors to Helvetica include Ariel, designed in 1989–90 for Microsoft by Robin Nicholas and Patricia Saunders of Monotype, and, of course, "the Helvetica of the 90s," Erik Spiekermann's Meta.

Helvetica:
ABCDEFGHIJKLMNOPQRSTUVWXYZ
abcdefghijklmnopqrstuvwxyz
Akzidenz Grotesk:
ABCDEFGHIJKLMNOPQRSTUVWXYZ
abcdefghijklmnopqrstuvwxyz

Find out more
Website: Nicholas Fabian, *Helvetica, Serendipity, and Max Miedinger,*
webcom.net/~nfhome/miedinge.htm

Earmarks

Each typeface has its own distinctive characteristics, called **earmarks** (Fig. **2.35**), named after the distinctive "ear" on the lower case g. These enable us to identify one design from another. To distinguish Helvetica from Univers, for example, look for the vertical downstroke in the capital G, the curly tail of the lower case y, and the angled tail through the bowl of the Q.

Soon you will be spotting the more subtle differences. For other typefaces, a good strategy is to start with the Q (a letter so infrequently used that typographers often have fun with it, making it their trade-mark), then the ampersand, then the J, G, and W. Try the lower case g, then a, j, and y. For numbers, look first at 3, then 7, 5, and 2. Real italics, not the sloped oblique versions of roman type found in DTP systems, are usually distinctive and easy to identify.

Other features that help distinguish different typefaces are the overall proportions (the relation of x-height to ascenders and descenders, for example), the stress (is it oblique or vertical?), the contrast between thick and thin strokes, the formation of the serifs. Are the characters wide and loose fitting, or compact and tight? Some are easy: script and "black-letter" faces, for example, stand out from all the others. To the untrained eye, others look virtually indistinguishable.

Type has long been classified into groups, such as "old face," "transitional," and "modern." These sometimes vague classifications have been codified, first by French typographer Maximilien Vox, and later by national and international standards, into nine groups (Fig. **2.36 a–g**). The categories may not seem at first sight to be of great use to the graphic designer when choosing type, but they are a considerable aid to communicating with the typesetter and printer.

ZUZANA LICKO

LIFE STORY ■ Zuzana Licko was born in 1961 in Bratislava, Czechoslovakia, and emigrated to the USA at the age of seven. She graduated with a degree in graphic communications from the University of California at Berkeley in 1984.

It was also in 1984 that Licko, together with her Dutch-born husband Rudy Vanderlans, started *Emigre* magazine, a journal for experimental graphic design. The magazine garnered much critical acclaim when it began to incorporate Licko's digital typeface designs — Emperor, Emigre, and Oakland — which were created on the Macintosh computer. The 128k Macintosh was launched just as the second edition of *Emigre* was in production. The exposure and success of these typefaces in the magazine led Licko and Vanderlans to set up Emigre Inc. to manufacture and distribute the fonts to a wider audience.

When Licko designed her first fonts for the Mac (the Emperor, Emigre, Oakland, and Universal families) in 1984, bitmap fonts were the only kinds available. Her intention was to create a series of legible fonts for the 72 dpi computer screen and dot-matrix printer. After laser printers and outline fonts were introduced, she imagined that these bitmaps would be relegated to the status of novelty fonts, but with the current interest in multimedia CDs and the World Wide Web, they have been re-evaluated.

As a graphic design team, Emigre has worked for clients ranging from large multinationals such as Apple Computer to independent art organizations such as San Francisco's Artspace. Their work has been published in *Blueprint*, *Baseline*, *Axis*, *I.D.*, *Eye*, *Communication Arts*, *Print*, and numerous design magazines and books throughout the USA, UK, Holland, Germany, and Japan. Their writing has been published in the *AIGA Journal*, *I.D.*, *U&lc*, and *How*. Selections of their work are included in the permanent collections of the San Francisco Museum of Modern Art, the Design Museum in London, The National Design Museum in New York, the Italian traveling exhibit "Pacific Wave," and in the Walker Art Center design retrospective "Graphic design in America."

Emigre was the 1994 recipient of the prestigious Chrysler Award for Innovation in Design and, also in 1994, New York publisher Van Nostrand Reinhold published a ten-year retrospective book entitled *Emigre: Graphic Design into the Digital Realm*.

> ### "Integrating design and production, the computer has reintroduced craft as the source of inspiration"

Licko's interest in creating more traditional typefaces for text was a result of *Emigre* magazine's publication of in-depth articles, which required fonts appropriate for lengthy text setting. Her revival of the Baskerville typeface, named Mrs Eaves, after Sarah Eaves — the woman who became John Baskerville's wife — presented her with the opportunity to design some fanciful ligatures which helped create visual interest and are reminiscent of customized lettering.

As well as designing fonts, Licko also makes and sells stoneware pots with the same restraint and simplicity of design as her typefaces, and she has even designed sleep wear (pajamas).

MANIFESTO ■ **Puzzles**

What is a typeface? A typeface is the ornamental manifestation of the alphabet.

If the alphabet conveys words, a typeface conveys their tone, style, and attitude.

"Ever since I was first introduced to graphic design, I heard everybody say how bad digital type looked and how it was impossible to make it look any better. This really intrigued me. Whenever anyone makes a statement like that, I have difficulty agreeing. I was reading books on the history of graphic design and in the final chapter they would always mention something about digital type and show typefaces like OCR A and B. Some of them were interesting but never really any good for setting text.

"So I saw that here was something unexplored and interesting and I wanted to try my own hand at it. But every time I asked for advice, people kept telling me it was really a lost cause, that it couldn't be done. So I thought that anything I would do would be better than what was out there.

"I enjoy things that are like puzzles; anything that is tremendously restrictive, where there are very few choices but you have to make it work. If I get too many choices, I become overwhelmed. I just don't have the time and patience to look at every possible scenario. This is the problem I have with graphic design. I never got the feeling that I found the final solution to a problem. Although I now design more traditional and less modular typefaces, I still get most of my creative energy out of solving these problems. When nobody is able to make something work, I get inspired to find out what I might do with it.

"Integrating design and production, the computer has reintroduced craft as the source of inspiration. Because the computer is an unfamiliar medium, designers must reconsider many basic rules previously taken for granted. This has brought excitement and creativity to aspects of design that have been forgotten since the days of letterpress. With computers many alternatives can be quickly and economically reviewed. Today's designers must learn to discriminate intelligently among all of the choices, a task requiring a thorough understanding of fundamentals."

WORKSTATION

- Website: www.emigre.com
- Rudy Vanderlans and Zuzana Licko, *Emigre* (the book): *Graphic Design into the Digital Realm*, Van Nostrand Reinhold, 1994
- *Emigre* (the magazine): published quarterly by Emigre Inc., 4475 D Street, Sacramento, CA 95819, USA

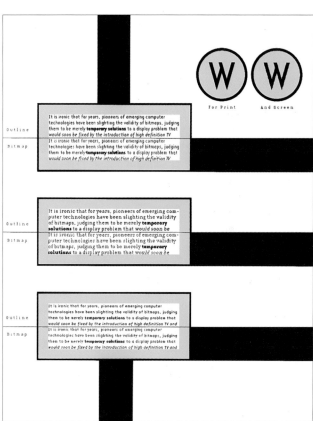

▲ **Base-9 and Base-12** These fonts were designed by Zuzana Licko in 1995. The basic concept for the Base-12 family started with the 24- and 36-point screen fonts that Licko designed for use on the Emigre website. The result was one serif and one sans serif family based on 12-point screen fonts called Base-12, and one family based on 9-point screen fonts named Base-9 — a total of 24 individual faces.

PostScript fonts come in two parts (see p. 72): the screen font or bitmap and the device-independent outline font or printer font. Usually, the printer-font characters dictate the look of the screen-font characters, but Licko tackled the problem from the opposite direction, designing the screen fonts first to set the exact character widths within which the outline characters were adjusted to fit.

When using Base-9 and Base-12 in situations where character display and spacing on the screen are of primary importance, such as in multimedia, they should be used at multiples of their "base." For example, Base-12 is best used at 12 point, 24 point and above. Base-9 is best used at 9 point, 18 point and above. Carefully hand-edited screen fonts are provided at these sizes for the best possible screen display. But although Base-9 and Base-12 were designed for a specific function, the goal was also to create a comprehensive family of typefaces suitable for traditional print.

Solex
Solex Regular

Solex
Solex Medium

Solex
Solex Italic

Solex
Solex Medium Italic

Solex
Solex Bold

Solex
Solex Black

Solex
Solex Bold Italic

Solex
Solex Black Italic

▲ **Solex** was Licko's first release in nearly two years. Inspiration came from two principal sources: Alternate Gothic and Bauer Topic (designed by Paul Renner, who also designed Futura). Solex revisits postmodern themes seen in Erik Spiekermann's Meta Sans and its cousin, Officina Sans.

Group 1: Humanist

These faces are characterized by an inclined bar on the lower case e, which points to their calligraphic origins. They are light in weight, with bracketed serifs, and an oblique stress. Also known as Venetian. An example is Centaur.

Humanist: Centaur.
Mind your Ps & Qs
ABCDEFGHIJKLMNOPQRSTUVWXYZ
abcdefghijklmnopqrstuvwxyz
1234567890
(.,.;*?$["&"]'%'!)

It was after sun-up now, but we went right on and didn't tie up. The king and the duke turned out by and by looking pretty rusty; but after they'd jumped overboard and took a swim it chippered them up a good deal. After breakfast the king he took a seat on the corner of the raft, and pulled off his boots and rolled up his britches, and let his legs dangle in the water, so as to be comfortable, and lit his pipe, and went to getting his "Romeo and Juliet" by heart.

Group 2: Garalde

The faces in this group still have an oblique stress, but are less script-like, with a horizontal bar on the e. The name Garalde is a contraction of *Gara*mond and *Ald*us, though where the e comes from is a mystery. Other examples include Bembo, Plantin, and Caslon (Fig. **2.37**). Collectively, Humanist and Garalde are called "old face" or "old style." Old style, however, does not mean old-fashioned: Galliard is a face designed with the aid of a computer by Matthew Carter in 1978–81.

Garalde: Caslon.
Mind your Ps & Qs
ABCDEFGHIJKLMNOPQRSTUVWXYZ
abcdefghijklmnopqrstuvwxyz
1234567890
(.,.;*?$["&"]'%'!)

It was after sun-up now, but we went right on and didn't tie up. The king and the duke turned out by and by looking pretty rusty; but after they'd jumped overboard and took a swim it chippered them up a good deal. After breakfast the king he took a seat on the corner of the raft, and pulled off his boots and rolled up his britches, and let his legs dangle in the water, so as to be comfortable, and lit his pipe, and went to getting his "Romeo and Juliet" by heart.

The US Declaration of Independence, 1776, set in Caslon.

2.36c

Group 3: Transitional

Here the axis of the curves has become vertical, with bracketed oblique serifs. The construction of each letter is based on a mathematical formula, and the major example is Baskerville, which is wide for its x-height.

Q

Transitional: Baskerville.
Mind your Ps & Qs
ABCDEFGHIJKLMNOPQRSTUVWXYZ
abcdefghijklmnopqrstuvwxyz
1234567890
(.,:;*?$["&"]'%'!)

It was after sun-up now, but we went right on and didn't tie up. The king and the duke turned out by and by looking pretty rusty; but after they'd jumped overboard and took a swim it chippered them up a good deal. After breakfast the king he took a seat on the corner of the raft, and pulled off his boots and rolled up his britches, and let his legs dangle in the water, so as to be comfortable, and lit his pipe, and went to getting his "Romeo and Juliet" by heart.

2.36d

Group 4: Didone

There is an abrupt contrast between the thick and the thin strokes; the axis of the curves is completely vertical; and serifs are horizontal, unbracketed, and hairline. This grouping is also called "modern." The name is a contraction of Didot and Bodoni, and other examples include Caledonia.

P

Didone: Bodoni.
Mind your Ps & Qs
ABCDEFGHIJKLMNOPQRSTUVWXYZ
abcdefghijklmnopqrstuvwxyz
1234567890
(.,:;*?$["&"]'%'!)

It was after sun-up now, but we went right on and didn't tie up. The king and the duke turned out by and by looking pretty rusty; but after they'd jumped overboard and took a swim it chippered them up a good deal. After breakfast the king he took a seat on the corner of the raft, and pulled off his boots and rolled up his britches, and let his legs dangle in the water, so as to be comfortable, and lit his pipe, and went to getting his "Romeo and Juliet" by heart.

Mechanistic: Rockwell.
Mind your Ps & Qs
ABCDEFGHIJKLMNOPQRSTUVWXYZ
abcdefghijklmnopqrstuvwxyz
1234567890
(.,:;*?$["“&”]‘%’!)

It was after sun-up now, but we went right on and didn't tie up. The king and the duke turned out by and by looking pretty rusty; but after they'd jumped overboard and took a swim it chippered them up a good deal. After breakfast the king he took a seat on the corner of the raft, and pulled off his boots and rolled up his britches, and let his legs dangle in the water, so as to be comfortable, and lit his pipe, and went to getting his "Romeo and Juliet" by heart.

 2.36e

Group 5: Mechanistic
Also known as slab-serif or Egyptian, these faces have heavy square-ended serifs, with or without brackets. Examples include Clarendon, Melior, and Rockwell.

P

Neo-grot sans serif: Helvetica.
Mind your Ps & Qs
ABCDEFGHIJKLMNOPQRSTUVWXYZ
abcdefghijklmnopqrstuvwxyz
1234567890
(.,:;*?$["“&”]‘%’!)

It was after sun-up now, but we went right on and didn't tie up. The king and the duke turned out by and by looking pretty rusty; but after they'd jumped overboard and took a swim it chippered them up a good deal. After breakfast the king he took a seat on the corner of the raft, and pulled off his boots and rolled up his britches, and let his legs dangle in the water, so as to be comfortable, and lit his pipe, and went to getting his "Romeo and Juliet" by heart.

 2.36f

Group 6: Lineal
Better known as sans serif, these faces are further subdivided into:
- Grotesque, the original 19th-century faces with a "closed" appearance, e.g. Grot and Headline;
- Neo-grot, which are rounded and open with a monoline weight, e.g. Helvetica and Univers;

Group 6 Lineal continued
- Geometric, based on the geometric shapes promoted by the Bauhaus, such as circles and straight lines, e.g. Futura;
- Humanist sans serif, based on more classical proportions, e.g. Gill Sans and Optima.

Geometric sans serif: Futura.
Mind your Ps & Qs
ABCDEFGHIJKLMNOPQRSTUVWXYZ
abcdefghijklmnopqrstuvwxyz
1234567890
(.,:;*?$["&"]'%'!)

It was after sun-up now, but we went right on and didn't tie up. The king and the duke turned out by and by looking pretty rusty; but after they'd jumped overboard and took a swim it chippered them up a good deal. After breakfast the king he took a seat on the corner of the raft, and pulled off his boots and rolled up his britches, and let his legs dangle in the water, so as to be comfortable, and lit his pipe, and went to getting his "Romeo and Juliet" by heart.

Group 7: Glyphic
These faces look chiseled rather than written, with blunt elephant's-foot serifs. The example shown here is Albertus.

ABCDEFGHIJKLMNOPQ
RSTUVWXYZ
abcdefghijklmnopqrstuvwxyz
1234567890

Group 8: Script
Script faces imitate cursive or "copperplate" writing. They can be formal, e.g. the Berthold Script shown here, or informal, e.g. Flash. They are not normally used as text faces, but are reserved for jobs such as wedding invitations or menus.

ABCDEFGHIJKLMNO
PQRSTUVWXYZ
abcdefghijklmnopqrstuvwxyz
1234567890

Group 9: Graphic
This group includes faces that look as if they have been drawn, rather than written. Examples are Dom Casual (shown here) and Klang.

ABCDEFGHIJKLMNO
PQRSTUVWXYZ
1234567890

ABCDEFGHIJKLMNOPQRSTUVWXYZ
abcdefghijklmnopqrstuvwxyz

ABCDEFGHIJKLMNOPQRSTU
VWXYZ
abcdefghijklmnopqrstuvwxyz

ABCDEFGHIJKLMNOPQRSTUVWXYZ
abcdefghijklmnopqrstuvwxyz

ABCDEFGHIJKLMNOPQRSTUVWXYZ
abcdefghijklmnopqrstuvwxyz

ABCDEFGHIJKLMNOPQRSTUVWXYZ
abcdefghijklmnopqrstuvwxyz

ABCDEFGHIJKLMNOPQRSTUVWXYZ
abcdefghijklmnopqrstuvwxyz

2.38 Many classic letterpress typefaces have been redesigned over the years, first for phototypesetting and lately for digital systems. Note how recent versions often have greater x-heights, thicker serifs, and a more condensed appearance. This is to accommodate changing needs in both technology and fashion. Shown contrasted here are Monotype's Century Old Style and ITC's Century Book, and both Monotype and ITC versions of Garamond and Garamond Italic. (ITC faces are printed in blue.)

To this classification scheme ought to be added a group to include the digital faces created on computer systems (see pp. 67–74) mainly for the style magazines of the 1980s, e.g. Modula and Emigre, and the so-called "intelligent" faces such as Beowulf.

Despite the best efforts of the classifiers, there still remain some typefaces that defy categorization, and which can only be described as being "hybrids." These include the best-known typeface of all — Times New Roman — which has to be described as a Garalde/ Didone hybrid. There are two other points to make about typefaces: first, not all versions of a named typeface are the same (Fig. **2.38**). There are many versions and interpretations of Univers and Times for example, and if you are not precise in specifying a particular vendor's Univers, you may be in for a surprise, especially when an accurate cast-off has been attempted.

Second, for copyright reasons, the same design of typeface may have a different name (often thinly disguised to give a clue to its origin) when obtained from a source other than its originator. For example, Bitstream's version of Plantin is called Aldine 721, Linotype's Futura Book is called Spartan Book and Compugraphic's Helvetica is renamed Helios.

Legibility and readability

One of the most important concerns of the graphic designer is to ensure that any type used is legible and readable. The intention, after all, is to communicate the author's or copywriter's ideas to the reader as efficiently as possible. If the type makes an aesthetically pleasing "picture" on the page as well, then that's a bonus.

For legibility, context is everything (Fig. 2.39). Novels, cookery books, and telephone directories are all read in different ways. The designer has to know the conditions in which the type will be read, who will be reading it, and why.

Faces with quirky letters, like the Q in ITC Bookman and the *g* in Galliard Italic, can begin to annoy when set in continuous text. And a display face for advertising or a logo has a completely different purpose to that of a face for a children's book. A logo, for example, may initially be harder to read, but in the long term is more memorable and recognizable. The instant legibility of type on freeway signs is a matter of life and death.

Legibility, however, is a cultural matter. Unless they are German-speaking, many people find "black-face" lettering difficult to understand. Graffiti on subway trains are unreadable by most people over 15. Designers such as David Carson (see p. 00) are often attacked by purist typographers for alleged illegibility, but in cases like *Ray Gun*, where the style is often more important than the content, a more adventurous approach to type is often expected.

There has been much research on the legibility of sans versus serifed

faces. The outcome seems to be that, with some exceptions, faces with serifs are easier to read continuously over long periods than those without. Serifs serve several purposes. They help letters to keep their distance. They link letters to make words, for we read by recognizing the shapes of words. They also help to differentiate letterforms, particularly the top halves, which are apparently more critical for rapid recognition. Faces with a large x-height, favored by newspapers, do not guarantee legibility, for the relatively short ascenders and descenders may have a negative effect on the overall shape of a word.

Sans serif faces, especially geometric ones like Futura, have a

(purposely) high degree of similarity between sorts. Try to distinguish for example 1, I, and l out of context! For some faces there are versions specially designed for continuous setting. Futura Book, for example, is just such a version of Futura. But the matter is highly subjective. Some assert that sans serif faces set in blocks of text look monotonous and hence intrinsically less attractive.

Italic is said to be less legible than roman, so much so that the typographer Sir Francis Meynell recommended that poetry be set in italic because it ought to be read slowly!

For print to be legible, words should be set close to each other, and certainly closer than the space ebp

← ascender
← x-height →
baseline →
point size
descender →

ebp

← x-height →
point size

Above: Letters with a small x-height. On the facing page letters with a large x-height. The size is identical in both cases. The difference is in the contrast between the normal letters and the ascenders & descenders. All ascenders line at the top. All descenders line at the bottom. But the normal letters are much deeper on the facing page. And the descenders & ascenders are shorter accordingly. Traditionally the smaller x-height is for book-typography. The Italian Renaissance marked a return to the Carolingian alphabet & the progressive elimination of Gothic letter-

forms. The black letter, however, was never totally eliminated. In Germany, in Switzerland it is ever present. Nor is it absent in Britain & the U.S. It would be a real loss for typography & calligraphy if it were to disappear altogether. A larger x-height has been popularised by newspapers. The poor quality of newsprint & the speed of the printing process combine to fill in the bowls of a b d e g o p q. Technology may change. Not so the letterforms, the text columns. For more than a century the newspaper has met the expectations of millions. It is therefore easier to carry on than to try to change their visual habits.

between lines of type. If the gap between words is too great, the eye will skip to the next line rather than the next word. So all continuous text matter is made easier to read by increasing the leading. Of course, there are some exceptions to this rule — for television graphics and on traffic signs, for example.

Legibility also has a part to play in deciding the width of columns. If the line is longer than about 12 words (or seven words in newspaper setting), the eye will have difficulty in returning to find the next line.

Black on white setting, too, is considered to be more readable than **reversed out** white on black (abbreviated WOB), where hairline serifs, for example, can be lost and horizontal spacing can look too cramped. Text all set in capitals, as in telexes, can be very tiring on the eye. On the internet, text that is set all in capitals means you're shouting!

Legibility is a major issue when designing typefaces for the computer screen. Verdana, designed by Matthew Carter, and named after the verdant Seattle area, has a large x-height, yet not so big that it's hard to distinguish lower case from upper case. It is extended and has extra space between characters so they don't touch, particularly with letter combinations such as "fi," "fl," and "ff," that would be ligatures in print. The bolds are very bold, so you can always tell the difference between bold and roman, yet the bold characters will not fill in, even at small sizes (you can still read it at 4 pt, at least in Windows).

Special care has been taken with letters like 1, I, l, i, and J , adding serifs to the capital I and J, so that they are easily recognized. The lower-case "i" is slightly shorter than the lowercase I, which also makes them more distinct. Curves are kept to a minimum and lower-case characters are a pixel taller than their upper-case counterparts at key screen sizes.

Legibility can be achieved by observing common-sense rules like these. Readability is something else. It entices readers to continue reading what you have designed, and that takes care, skill, and talent!

2.40 Text does not necessarily have to be typeset. Typographers like Fernand Baudin are very fond of their own handwriting, as demonstrated in these pages from his manual *How Typography Works (and Why it is Important)*.

■ TYPESETTING SYSTEMS

There are many ways of producing type. Most graphic designers will eventually be using offset lithography for print, and this process demands input in the form of film — a photographic image of the page to be printed. This was once made from a **mechanical** (see Chapter 4) but now most likely comes direct from a computer system. The typesetting used as raw material in compiling a mechanical may in turn have come from metal type, in the form of a reproduction proof, or it may have been a bromide print from a phototypesetting machine, a laser print, or even a piece of hand lettering.

Other print technologies, such as flexography and silkscreen, rely on similar processes — some

JUST LEFTHAND: ABCDEFGHIJKLM
NOPQRSTUVWXYZABCDEFGH
IJKLMNOPQRSTUVWXYZ12345
67890!@#£$.%^&*()_+<>?

Eric Righthand: ABCDEFGHIJKLMNO
PQRSTUVWXYZabcdefghijklm
nopqrstuvwxyz1234567890
!@#£$%^&*()_+<>?

newspapers once even printed on letterpress machines from photo-typeset mechanicals. Each method of typesetting has its role and its place, though some methods (e.g. so-called "strike-on" from the IBM Selectric typewriter) have become obsolete, and are discussed here only for the sake of completeness.

Hand lettering and calligraphy

It is an amusing exercise to try to work out the very least expensive way to produce a book, magazine, or any other publication. If you have all the time in the world, the cheapest production method of all must be to handwrite every single copy. Fernand Baudin's book *How Typography Works (and Why it is Important)* has been produced almost entirely by reproducing the author's best handwriting (Fig. **2.40**). Since the development of photolithography and, more recently, the introduction of fast, high-quality photocopying machines and inexpensive desktop scanners, the idea of handwriting a whole book is not as crazy as it may first appear. Many books have been produced this way, and curiously it is often typographers who tend to favor this quirky approach.

Calligraphy is handwriting's beautiful cousin (Fig. **2.41**), and is often used on the title pages of books. A grounding in calligraphy is essential for a proper understanding of good typography and graphic design, and its practice is to be encouraged. The famous German designer Jan Tschichold wrote in 1949, "All my knowledge of letter spacing, word spacing, and leading is due to my calligraphy, and it is for this reason that I regret very much that calligraphy is so little studied in our time."

Handwriting and calligraphy have long been copied in type. Script and brush faces are "cleaned-up" versions of hand lettering. And with computers it is possible to invent your personal font based on your own hand (Fig. **2.42**).

2.43 Rub-down lettering, from suppliers such as Letraset, revolutionized graphic design in the 1970s. It had to be applied carefully to prevent break-up.

"Strike-on" or "cold-metal" setting

Cutting and pasting of existing type, as in the punk blackmail-style designs of album covers by Jamie Reed in the late 1970s, is a form of **cold-metal setting**. Another form is the rub-down dry-transfer lettering used for display type from suppliers such as Letraset. The vinyl letters were transferred one by one on to paper or board, and then pressure applied through the backing sheet to "fix" the lettering in place. This is called **burnishing** (Fig. **2.43**).

With **strike-on setting**, the marks made at the time of setting are those that will go under the camera or scanner for printing by the offset litho process. There is no intermediate processing required.

Type *can* be set using a regular typewriter (for menus, for example). Typeset-quality typewriters designed for the purpose were introduced during the 1960s. The IBM Selectric had fonts of 88 characters arranged around a "golfball" print head. It used a nine-unit system of proportional spacing, and had "real" fonts such as Univers and Times. For justified setting, each line had to be typed twice, as the first attempt was used to calculate the amount of space needed between words.

The VariTyper had an open carriage, to tackle greater widths of setting than the IBM, and could handle two fonts at a time, each of 99 characters. These machines represented a breakthrough at the time, and replaced hot metal for many low cost jobs, but by today's standards the setting looks crude and poorly spaced.

2.44 Inserting sorts from the lower typecase into the composing stick, where type is set, line by line, before being transferred to the chase.

Hot metal: hand and machine setting

The method of setting type from hot lead remained virtually unchanged from the time of Gutenberg until the invention of the punch-cutting machine by the American Linn Boyd Benton in 1884. This paved the way for the Linotype machine in 1886 and the Monotype machine a year later.

But whereas machine setting has been superseded by phototypesetting, handsetting is still used whenever beautiful typography is demanded for some high-quality publications and limited-edition poetry books.

For handsetting, the compositor takes individual metal sorts and spaces from a typecase and places them one by one into a **composing stick** (Fig. **2.44**) that has been adjusted to the correct measure. Capital letters are taken from the upper case, and small letters from the lower case. The sizes of the compartments in the typecase reflect the popularity of certain sorts. You will need more "e"s, for example, than "z"s in an average job. Less frequently used fonts are kept in drawers under the typecase.

When the composing stick is full, the setting is transferred to a **galley** on the **imposing table**, and the compositor returns to the typecase to set the next couple of lines. When the galley is full, a **proof** is taken on a hand-operated **proofing press**, and any mistakes are picked up and corrected by the proofreader, the designer, or copy editor.

A galley proof is a long, thin strip of paper, and gives the designer an

2.45 When the type, leading, and any process blocks are all flat and in place, the chase is packed with metal or wooden "furniture" and locked up. It is now called a forme and is ready to be inked and printed.

▶ **2.46** The Linotype machine automated hot-metal setting. As the compositor keyed in the text, matrixes would fall into place and the type was set line by line from molten lead.

opportunity to see the setting before it is divided up into pages. This proof, when corrected, may be good enough to be used as a **reproduction proof**, or **repro**, if the setting is going to be cut up using a scalpel and incorporated into a mechanical.

If the setting is going to be printed — and hot-metal setting is the only kind of setting discussed here that *can* be printed directly — then the type is taken from the galley and placed into a page-sized contraption called a **chase**, and "locked up" (Fig. **2.43**, p. 65). The spaces and leading used to fill up the rest of the chase, often of wood, are collectively known as furniture. The locked-up chase is called a **forme**.

For small runs, the printing is made direct from the type in the chase. But for large jobs, and for newspapers and magazines, for example, where the type must be wrapped around a cylinder, a one-piece duplicate of the type, called a **stereotype** or **stereo** (Fig. **2.47**), has

to be made from a *papier-mâché* mold called a **mat** or **flong**.

Once the stereo has been made, or the pages printed, the type is then cleaned and returned (the word used in the trade is "distributed") to the typecases. Extra care has to be taken to get this right, compositors being told to "mind their 'p's and 'q's."

The **Linotype** machine (Fig. **2.46**) was invented by Ottmar Mergenthaler of Baltimore in 1886 to automate the casting of type. Whole lines of type (hence the name, from "line o' type") called **slugs** are set in one operation. A compositor keys in the text, and, as it is typed, molds of the letters to be cast fall into place. Wedge-shaped spacers are inserted between words, and when a line is complete, the compositor pulls a lever and these push the words apart to fill out the justified measure. Lead pours into the assembly, and out comes a slug of type. After the setting has been used, the slugs are melted down for re-use.

The **Monotype** machine, developed by Tolbert Lanston of Washington DC in 1887, sets type in individual sorts and, unlike the

◀ **2.47** Metal type cannot be used directly on a rotary letterpress machine. It must first be made into a curved plate known as a stereotype, which is then wrapped around the press cylinder ready for printing.

Linotype, uses a two-stage process. The compositor sits at the keyboard and inputs the text, which is coded on to a perforated roll of paper. When the end of a line approaches, a bell rings and it is left to the compositor's skill to calculate the spaces needed between words to justify the line. This information is keyed in at the end of each line. When the job is complete, the roll of paper is inserted into a typecasting machine *back to front*, so that the spacing information precedes the text it adjusts, and the type is cast individually.

The advantage of the Monotype machine over the Linotype one was that corrections could be made using precast sorts. This was especially useful for book production. With the Linotype method, the whole line had to be reset and replaced. As a consequence, Linotype machines were mostly used for newspaper and magazine work where speed is of the essence, and where the effect of spilling the type, a catastrophe known as "printer's pie," was minimized.

Phototypesetting

The popularity of offset litho as a printing process led to the development of new ways of setting type. With letterpress, it is not easy to mix text with illustrations and photographs, and the opportunities for creative design are limited.

Phototypesetting, or **photosetting**, was first demonstrated to the American Newspaper Publishers' Association in 1949 by Rene Higgonet and Louis Marius Moyroud, but did not become popular until the 1960s. Like a Monotype system, it comprised two separate parts. The compositor sat at a keyboard and generated paper or magnetic tape. This was then transferred to the **imagesetter**, where the bromide or film was exposed. In the earliest systems, light was projected through a matrix of tiny photographic negative images of the font's sorts on to photosensitive bromide paper or film. Later, the fonts were stored digitally, and reconstructed using CRTs (cathode ray tubes); then lasers were used (Figs **2.48** and **2.49**).

Photosetting provided the designer with many advantages over hot metal. Letters could be set closer together. They could be set touching, or even overlapping.

It was also possible, by means of mirrors and prisms, to distort type. Oblique (slanted) letters could be created from roman type, and headlines could be condensed or expanded to fit a given width.

Type produced by photosetting was sharper than the equivalent hot-metal setting. Hot metal was always proofed to paper, and no matter how carefully the ink was applied, it was squeezed between the face of the type and the paper and there was some spread. A typeface such as Bodoni, with its extremely fine serifs, was designed to be pressed into paper — photoset versions of Bodoni had to be redesigned with thicker serifs.

With photosetting, type could be set ahead of a type specification — the text was keyed in and the size, face, and measure were added later. The same text could be used over and over, in different forms. Any metal type to be reused had to be stored as "standing matter." This was costly and took up lots of space. With photosetting, type for dictionaries and telephone directories, for example, could be stored on tape, and updated later.

Computer systems

A photosetting machine may have looked like a regular computer, but setting was all it could do. A computer system, on the other hand, makes use of a standard off-the-shelf PC or Mac to produce information that is then input to the imagesetter that generates the bromide paper, film or plate. It does much more besides.

More choice of typefaces

Perhaps the most apparent effect of computers on graphic designers is that they have a much greater range of typefaces to choose from. With early photosetting, and even more so with strike-on technology, the user was offered any typeface ... so

2.50 Photosetting and digital software can concoct a kind of italic by slanting the roman font. This is better termed an oblique variant, as a true italic has different designs from the roman for most letters, with more cursive serifs.

Roman & afg
Oblique & afg
Italic & afg

long as it was Times, Univers, or Helvetica. There are currently many thousands of different typefaces available that can be used with computer systems. So-called "expert sets" add ligatures, small caps, swash caps, non-aligning numerals, fractions, and superior/ inferior figures to the basic fonts.

To produce a typeface in hot metal was an enormous and costly undertaking, requiring a huge investment in both time and money. Most of the great typographers of the past are known for just one or maybe two typefaces. The same was true for photosetting. Particular typefaces were tied to particular machines. Thus if you had a Linotype machine, you could use only faces from the Linotype library. Similarly, if you had a Berthold machine, you could use only type from Berthold.

If a typographer went to Berthold with a new idea for a typeface, its production would be extremely expensive and its distribution limited

to the number of Berthold machines in operation worldwide.

But with a computer system it is possible to design a brand new face, copy it on to a CD-rom or upload it to the internet and distribute it for use by thousands of other designers within days.

Quality and flexibility of digital type
The pace of progress in computing means that the few advantages of other technologies quickly disappeared. Computers have been universally adopted by both the printing and the design industries. Yet hot metal has always held two advantages over photosetting, that of visual and tactile quality.

In hot metal, each size of a typeface has been designed individually. Thus, for the sake of legibility, the small sizes have a relatively larger x-height and a wider set width. Bigger sizes have daintier serifs and more subtle distinctions between the parts of the letterform, created by enlarging or reducing one of these **font masters**.

In computer systems, all sizes are created by **scaling** (enlarging or reducing) one font master, usually 12 pt, designed as the best compromise. There have been some concessions to creating different designs for different sizes. Times Ten Roman, for example, is a version of Times New Roman that works better at small sizes. But the problem of legibility at smaller sizes has usually been solved by tracking.

Photosetting machines could be used to expand and condense type, but this always distorted the overall proportions of the letterform. A Futura E, for example, when condensed, will have a vertical stroke thinner than the horizontals.

By sloping roman letterforms, a photosetting system could create an oblique — but not an italic — version of the typeface. A true italic font has entirely different designs for many of its letters. Look at the *a*, *f*, and *g* of an italic face (Fig. **2.50**).

Any computer system can perform these kinds of distortions. They can embolden letters, too, and produce combinations of italic, bold, outline, and shadow (Fig. **2.51**). But the results bear little aesthetic relationship to the original "plain" letterforms. The design intention of the typographer will have been lost.

2.51 Computer software can also take a roman font and "style" it in various ways. Most programs can create bold, outline, shadowed, and reversed-out variants. More specialized software, such as FreeHand and Illustrator, can be used, for example, to set type along a curve, and to apply "stroke and fill" to a letterform.

2.52 New custom fonts can be designed letter by letter using programs such as Fontographer. These programs can also import existing typefaces, which can then be adapted to your own taste.

2.53 An envelope feature in programs such as FreeHand and Illustrator can be used to distort letters and words mathematically. Previously, the lettering would have to have been drawn laboriously by hand or distorted photographically.

Multiple Masters from Adobe is a technology that incorporates non-linear scaling into typefaces. It uses mathematical formulas to retain relationships between the stroke weights of individual letterforms, and inter-character spacing, or tracking, is adjusted appropriately. It is possible to encode a font master with information that describes the shapes of small, medium, and large versions of the typeface, and the computer will interpolate all the gradations in between. There is also an application in Acrobat PDF (Portable Document Format) documents, where Adobe Sans MM and Adobe Serif MM can simulate fonts used by a designer that readers do not have installed on their computers. They will automatically generate an accurate weight/width shape variation for any specified size.

With computer setting, the graphic designer has never been restricted to the small and standard list of point sizes available from the hot-metal type foundries. In page-layout systems such as Adobe InDesign and QuarkXPress, for example, type can be set at any size in any increment, leading can be defined in increments or percentages, and letters can be kerned interactively.

Type manipulation and custom font design

Page-layout systems, such as Adobe InDesign and QuarkXPress, are able to adjust the size of type to fit a certain space, condensing or expanding it to the limits of legibility.

Drawing programs (more of which in Chapter 3, p. 100), such as Macromedia's FreeHand and Adobe Illustrator, allow text to be set, for example, around an ellipse or along a freeform curve — and create even more extreme distortions (Fig. **2.53**). The designer is able to create graphic "envelopes" into which the text is squeezed and contorted to fit.

With programs such as Fontographer (Fig. **2.52**), you can tweak existing faces to your own preferences or create entirely new faces from scratch. It is this power that horrifies traditional typographers. Here, a knowledge of typography, however rudimentary, is essential to prevent the novice from falling into the pitfalls learnt the hard way throughout the history of type.

Many digital fonts are revivals of traditional fonts, adapted to the limitations of the technology. There are also several fonts designed specifically for the process, and for

McVAY S.T,
  18 Swan Copse,Mansfield Rd 25...708 0761
  T, 9 Hollington Cres 33 ....784 7037
McVEAGH J.G.R, 211 Castle La,Solihull .. 743 3266
  W, 69 Damson La,Solihull 705 7866
McVEICH S, 171 Jayshaw Av 43 ......357 5933
McVEIGH A, 63 New Coventry Rd 26 ..742 8955
  D.F, 5 Bernard Pl,Brookfield Rd 18 ...554 2068
  G, Warwick Rd,Solihull 705 6922
  J, 16 Harvington Rd,Oldbury 422 4789
  J.D, 17 Winton Gro,Sutton Coldfield ...351 4406
  J.M, 99 Miranda Clo 45 ....453 9681
  J.P, 49 Round Moor Wlk 35 ....747 8542
  M.F.P, 27 Prospect La,Solihull 744 5227
  R.M, 8 Chiseldon Croft 14 .....474 5165
McVEIGHTY D, 82 Audley Rd 33 ....786 2946
  D, 39 Este Rd 26 ....783 0454
  D, 67 Hilleys Croft 37 ....770 1737
  R, 62 Clarence Rd 13 ....444 4088
McVEITH T, 37 Frankley La 31 .....478 0534
MACVENAN M, 15 Overbrunton Clo 31 ...477 2547
McVERRY B.P, 4 Chalybeate Clo 45 ....453 8277
  D, 24 Goodrest Croft 14 ......430 4084
  D.J, 17 Duncalfe Dv,Sutton Coldfield ...308 5672
McVEY C.F, 19 Brownley Rd,Shirley 745 1015
  J, 31 Beeches Wy 31 ....477 8434
  J, 158 Jayshaw Av 43 ....357 4988
McVICAR A.J, 158 Swan Gdns 23 ...373 0289
  E.W, 38 Moorfield Dv,Sutton Coldfield ...373 8366
McVICKER N.M, 78 Northdown Rd,Solihull ..705 8822
  R.P, 43 Heybarnes Rd 10 .....773 7558
MACVIE F.E,
  Fiddlers Gn,Blackford Hl...Henley-in-A 2819
  Mrs M.H, 72 Marsh Hl 23 .....373 2702
McVITTY P.J, 312 Sarehole Rd 28 ....777 5775
McWALTER I.M,
  30 Upper St. Mary's Rd,Smethwick..429 1297
  J.W, 66 Hawkstone Rd 29 .....475 6246
  S.G, 207 Court Oak Rd 17 .....427 9694
McWALTERS S.B,
  11 Chadwick Rd,Sutton Coldfield..378 3693
McWATTS A.C,
  6 Bannersgate Rd,Sutton Coldfield..355 1647
McWEE R.M, 29 Stanmore Gro,Halesowen .. 422 7767
McWEENEY L, 114 Junction Rd 21 ....523 3828
McWHINNEY S.J, 6 Longmore Rd,Streetly ...353 7526
McWHINNIE J.R.K,
  282 Eachelhurst Rd,Sutton Coldfoield..351 2022
  J.R.K,
  282 Eachelhurst Rd,Sutton Coldfield..351 3382
  W.R, 22 Widney Manor Rd,Solihull ...705 8842
McWHIRTER D,
  9 Spring Ho,Cooks Ct,Chester Rd 36..770 0970
  D.C, 30 Greenfield Rd 17 ......427 9679
  D.L, 24 Fugelmere Clo 17 ......429 4883
  J, 28 St. Michaels Rd,Sutton Coldfield ...354 6521
  John D, 23 Maxholm Rd,Streetly ...353 2850
  P.J.K, 92 Devon Rd,Smethwick 429 1213
  R, 17 Aldbourne Wy 30 ......459 4503
  R.M, 127 Manor La,Halesowen 550 1718
  W.H.P, 188 Northfield Rd 17 ....427 1736
McWILLIAM A.R, 30 Waldrons Moor 14 ...444 2414
  I, 38 Corbridge Rd,Sutton Coldfield ...354 2558
  I.R, 50 Meriden Rd ....Hampton-in-A 2015
  J.W, 55 Colesbourne Rd,Solihull 742 3228
  R, 108 West Av 20 ....554 4261
  R.C, 20 Galton Tower,Civic Clo 1 ...236 4901
McWILLIAMS A.G,
  32 Sandhills Cres,Solihull..704 9547
  B, 126 Kingswood Rd 31 .....477 6225
  B.V, 4 Dornton Rd 30 ....444 3788
  C, 203 Albert Rd 6 ....328 4676
  C.P, 20 Hatherton Gro 29 ....427 6854
  E, 20 Somerset Rd 23 ....384 4951
  G, 306 Prince of Wales La 14 ..430 3917
  J.B, 18 Milner Rd 29 ....472 7085
  J.D, 3 Newells Rd 26 ....742 1801
  K, 103 Ashbrook Rd 30 .....472 5807
  N, 98 Manor Ho La 26 ......743 2498
  P.W, 56 Hodge Hill Rd 34 ....783 7477
  R, 28 ...
  R, 5 ...
  R, 14 ...
  S, 48 ...
  W.K, ...
MACWI...
MACZK...
MADAH...
  J.S, ...
  T, 84 ...
MADAN...
  V.P, ...
MADDA...
  A.D, ...
  B.M, ...
  D.G, ...
  G.W, ...
  H, 41 ...
  J, 21 ...
  J.L, ...
  M, 1 Chantry Dv,Halesowen 422 4339
  R.G, 714 Hagley Rd Wst,Oldbury 422 7826
  Sidney C, 4 Griffins Brook Clo 30 ...459 3814
  T.A, 212 Highters Hth La 14 ....430 2472
MADDEN A, 54 Strathdene Rd 29 ...472 1469
  A, 2 Wilford Gro,Sutton Coldfield ...351 3998
  A, 256 Witton Ldg Rd 23 .....350 6119
  A.C, 41 Galton Tower,Civic Clo 1 ...233 2935
  B, 113 Heather Rd 10 ....771 2140
  C, 4 Sycamore Terr,Vicarage Rd 14 ...444 0919
  C, 257 West Boulevard 32 ....427 6313
  C.A, 548 Bromford La 8 .....786 2021
  C.W, 6 St Johns Rd,Oldbury 544 7941
  D, 23 Court Oak Gro 17 ......427 9851
  D, 12 Elmwood Rd,Sutton Coldfield ...353 3807
  D, 40 Middle Dv 45 ....445 2002
  D, 73 St. Agathas Rd 8 ......327 2379
  D, 4 Sunnydale Wlk,W Bromwich ...525 1518
  D.M.J, 40 Sheldonfields Rd 26 ....743 4350
  D.S, 134 Kingsdown Av 42 ....357 6662
  E, 23 Eileen Rd 11 ....449 0807
  E, 105 Manor Ho La 26 ......742 6515
  E, 1/4 Ward End Pk Rd 8 .....327 6308
  F, 34 Cecil Rd 24 ....373 4542
  F, 19 Greswolde Ho,Cole Hall La 34 ...784 9304

MADDEN H.A, 85 Naseby Rd 8 ....327 5567
  I, 11 Boldmere Clo,Sutton Coldfield ...350 6027
  I.M, 74 Worlds End Rd 20 .....554 7649
  J, 44 Amberley Gro 6 ....356 8558
  J, 266 Galton Rd,Smethwick 429 6179
  J, 140 Knowle Rd 11 ....777 8672
  J, 3 Minster Dv 10 ....773 3675
  J, 37 Roughley Dv,Four Oaks 308 4882
  James, 347 St. Benedicts Rd 10 ...772 0748
  J, 68 Tomey Rd 11 ....772 0813
  J, 137 Wellsgreen Rd,Solihull 743 2015
  J, 5 Welwyndale Rd,Sutton Coldfield ...373 6663
  J, 61 Windmill La,Smethwick 565 3634
  J, 21 Windsor St Nth 7 ......359 0115
  J.A, 91 Pinewood Dv 32 .....422 0066
  J.E, 64 Pitts Fm Rd 24 .....350 5780
  J.T, 100 Alston Rd,Solihull 704 1390
  K.W, 37 Varlins Wy 38 .....458 6997
  L, 26 Chartley Rd 23 ....328 3751
  L, 7 Clodeshall Rd 8 ....328 3186
  L, 51 Ercall Clo 23 ....356 0845
  L, 331 Yardley Wood Rd 13 ....449 8241
  M, 12 Cecil Rd 24 ....373 8447
  M, 323 Guardian Ct,
    Francey Beeches Rd 31..477 5078
  Michael, 101 Livingstone Rd 20 ...356 0701
  M, 55 Norfolk Rd 23 ....373 0753
  Michael, 232 Somerville Rd 10 ...773 9922
  M, 7 Yew Tree La 26 ....706 6797
  Michael A, 51 Courtenay Rd 44 ...360 4605
  M.A, 75 Harrow Rd 29 ......472 1056
  M.J, 48 Brookvale Rd,Solihull 706 3076
  M.J, 29 Link Rd 16 ....454 7864
  M, 50 Moorend La 24 ....384 4518
  N, 88 Pritchett Tower,Arthur St 10 ...773 8947
  P, 21 Ebley Rd 20 ....523 9924
  P, 7 Rawlins Croft 35 ......749 3961
  P.B, 101 Clodeshall Rd 8 ....328 7530
  P.J, 48 Broadway Ave,Halesowen ...550 7879
  P.J, 135 Oxhill Rd 21 ......523 9704
  R.F, 55 Hill La,Sutton Coldfield ...308 4990
  R.J, 3 Whitwell Clo,Solihull 744 7724
  R.N, 303 Dovedale Rd 23 .....382 7236
  S, 27 Gladstone Rd 26 ......706 5469
  S.D, 14 St. Michaels Rd,Sutton Coldfield ...355 5701
  S.J, 376 Queslett Rd 43 .....360 1421
  T, 228 Millhouse Rd 25 ......784 0182
  T, 30 Station Rd 21 ....554 2344
  Timothy, 16 Westbury Rd,Wednesbury ...526 3558
  T.A, 22 Avenue Rd 14 ......444 1597
  T.H, 53 Allcroft Rd 11 ......778 1379
  T.J, 68 Hazelbeach Rd 8 .....326 0974
  T.S, 8 Daniels Rd 9 ....773 1741
  W, 7 Hilldrop Gro 11 ....426 3667
  W.A.L, 340 Hagley Rd Wst,Oldbury ...422 8554
MADDERS G.R, 37 Quarry La,Halesowen ...550 5409
  G.T, 23 Rowton Dv,Streetly 353 6668
  J.L, 9 Stourton Clo,Sutton Clodfield ...329 3193
  Max A, 6 Selly Clo 29 ......472 1670
MADDIX C, 8/8 Broadmeadow Clo 30...459 4724
  D, 33 Calder Tower,Birchfield Rd 20 ...356 5853
  Martin, 15 Heanor Croft 6 ....328 3670
  J, 2/24 Taylor Rd 13 ....444 0057
  J.M, 1 Chartwell Ct,Beardmore Rd,
    Sutton Coldfield..373 1815
  J.M, 40 Dower Rd,Sutton Coldfield ...308 1476
  E.L, 16 Harbury Rd 12 ....440 2185
  F.M, 512 Kingsbury Rd 24 ....350 2007
  G, 31 Daimler Clo 36 ....747 0199
  I.F, 824 Pershore Rd 29 .....472 2636
  J, 1 Denise Dv 17 ....427 2395
  J, 28 Tinmeadow Cres 45 ....453 5355
  J.C, 1 Overbury Clo,Halesowen ...550 4642
  M, 8 Raven Hays Rd 31 .....477 2201
  N, 29 Marsham Rd 14 ......430 5180
  P, 38 Daisy Fm Rd 14 ......474 5939
  P, 46 Middle Pk Rd 29 ......476 9146
  P, 1 Pagnell Gro 13 ....443 3851
  R.A, 178 Franklin Rd 30 .....458 7198
  R.C, 119 Bell Holloway 31 ....477 3973
  R.S, 178 Gregory Av 29 ......477 3372
  S, 34 Hodgetts Clo,Smethwick 429 2362
  S, 25 Pettit Clo 14 ....430 5011
  S.C, 48 Rowheath Rd 30 .....459 0944
  V, 8 Cherry Tree Ct,Woodfall Av 30 ...451 3284
  W, 73 Longmore Rd 31 ......354 5745
  W.L, 129 Kineton Gn Rd,Solihull ...708 2684
MADDON J, 229 Manningford Rd 14 ...430 6295
MADDOX A, 192 Farnborough Rd 35 ...747 8584
  A, 12 The Hurstway 23 ......382 5280
  A.A, 84 Hales Rd,Wednesbury 556 1092

MADDOX B.T, 235 Hay Green Rd 30 ...475 6050
  C.D, 347 The Ridgeway 23 ....331 4687
  C.R, 37 Coniston Av,Solihull 743 6397
  C.R, 26 Libbard Ho,Stonebow Ave,Solihull ...705 8876
  D, 1 Alcombe Gro 33 ....784 9496
  D, 20 Ashton Rd 25 ....784 5873
  D, 73 Newlands Rd 30 ......451 2736
  D.C, 38 Duncumb Rd,Sutton Coldfield ...378 3508
  D.M, 71 Babbington Rd 21 ....523 0145
  E, 139 Garretts Green La 26 ...742 5777
  E, 149 Nuthurst Rd 31 ......476 6364
  E, 2 Arbor Ct,Penns La,Sutton Coldfield ...351 5636
  E.S, 89 Monmouth Rd 32 ....475 1892
  F.C, 49 Milstead Rd 26 .....784 6434
  G, 54 Harleston Rd 44 ......360 2212
  G, 57 Surrey Cres,W Bromwich 502 1184
  G, 26 Elm Croft,Windmill La,Smethwick ...565 1169
  H, 15 Bucknall Cres 32 .....550 5836
  H, 5 Middleton Rd,Shirley 744 4732
  I, 41 Ansell Rd 24 ....373 1003
  J, 8 May La 47 ....Wythall 824209
  J.R, 142 Birdbrook Rd 44 .....360 1132
  John W, 18 Elmfield Rd 36 ....747 5667
  K, 2 Ingram Gro 27 ....778 2433
  K.A, 28 Ebrington Rd,Sutton Coldfield ...355 3522
  K.J, 2 Linford Gro 25 ......783 5073
  L, 801c Warwick Rd 11 .....706 1305
  L.L, 9 Ferndale Rd,Streetly 353 7885
  M.E, 83 Stanton Rd 43 .....358 7530
  M.I, 510 Chester Rd 36 .....770 5083
  M.K, 42 Teesdale Av 34 .....730 2350
  M.P, 48 Amberley Gro 6 .....356 7517
  N, 3 Western Rd,Sutton Coldfield ...354 9278
  P.W, 31 Marlborough Rd 36 ....747 2149
  R, 78 Grestone Av 20 ....554 0267
  R, 197 Newton Rd 43 ....357 1863
  Roy A, 182 Northfield Rd 17 ....427 3322
  R.L, 33 Wharf Rd 30 ....459 2660
  S, 2 Greenway Clo 43 ......360 5791
  S, 50 Vimy Rd 13 ....444 1945
  S.L, 12 Boldmere Clo,Sutton Coldfield ...373 3765
  W, 3 Westholme Croft 30 ....478 8782
MADDRELL Simon, 48 Ellesmere Rd 8...326 8979
MADDY K.P, 3 Meerhill Av,Solihull 745 5813
MADELEY A, 128 Dudley Rd Est,Oldbury ...552 4887
  A, 7 Walton Ct,High Farm Rd,Halesowen ...503 0184
  A.C, 98 Triumph Wlk 36 .....749 2685
  A.E, 56 Farnhurst Rd 36 .....328 3619
  B, 7 Dauntsey Covert 14 .....458 6910
  B.W, 27 Leaford Rd 33 ......784 0412
  C.E, 17 Marldon Rd 14 ......444 7677
  D, 89 Braemar Rd,Solihull 706 0366
  D, 30 Macmillan Rd,Rowley Regis ...559 2793
  D.H, 252 Coleshill Rd 36 .....747 4575
  E, 5 Pryor Rd,Oldbury 544 4518
  E.A, 17 Mynors Cres 47 .....Wythall 826651
  E.G, 27 Queens Ct,Alderham Clo,Solihull ...705 6750
  E.S, 117 The Ridgeway 23 ....356 7835
  I, 449 Lugtrout La,Solihull 704 9849
  Theo M, 38 Redthorn Gro 33 ....783 7684
  W.E, 126 Spouthouse La 43 ....357 6503
MADELIN A.E,
  305 Beaconview Rd,W Bromwich..588 2099
  D, 152 Powis Av,Tipton 557 7026
  H, 55 Glebefields Rd,Tipton 557 9450
  K, 415 Sycamore Rd,Tipton 520 4748
  M, 20 Kipling Clo,Tipton 557 5572
MADEN M.A, 44 Steel Rd 31 .....476 6493
MADER R, 107 Birmingham Rd 48 ...445 2366
MADEW E.A, 39 Witton Ldg Rd 23 ...350 0522
  J.T, 226 Rectory Rd,Sutton Coldfield ...378 3495
MADGE A,
  60 Bampfylde Pl,Thornbridge Av 42..358 2139
  C, 19 Andrew Rd,W Bromwich 588 6693
  C.J, 5 Rectory Pk Av,Sutton Coldfield ...378 0353
  G, 1 Ravenhill Clo 34 ....748 7534
  G.H, 78 Hathersage Rd 42 ....360 2845
  H, 118 Fernley Rd 14 ......355 4840
  H.E, 36 Homecroft Rd 25 .....783 4867
  H.S, 11 Parkhall Croft 34 .....747 0129
  J, 27 Walsham Croft 34 .....748 5736
  J.E, 86 Preston Rd 26 ......708 0883
  J.M, 42 Cambridge Dv 37 ....770 4121

MADGE M.J, 1 Station Approach,Vesey Ldge,
    Sutton Coldfield..353 6347
  W.H, 68 Drayton Rd 14 ......443 2047
MADGWICK D.J,
  239 Ulverley Green Rd,Solihull..706 1349
  G, 3 Beresford Cres,W Bromwich 353 3637
  H.A, 78 Coopers La,Smethwick 558 8623
MADHAL C.S, 11 Raglan Rd,Smethwick ...565 1487
MADHAS N, 34 Chantry Rd 21 .....554 7075
MADHOO G, 10 High Trees 20 .....523 8532
MADIGAN A, 693 Hagley Rd Wst 32 ...421 3971
  E.G, 183 Bucklands End La 34 ...747 8988
  E.J, 206 Gravelly La 23 ......350 7814
  J.J, 48 Cranmore Rd,Shirley 745 4407
  J.J, 48 Shakespeare Rd,Shirley ...745 1712
  M, 711 Kingstanding Rd 44 ....355 5221
  M.J, 4 R.A.F Houses,Chester Rd 35 ...748 6327
  S, 175 Balden Rd 32 ....429 3689
  W, 18 Blakeland Rd 44 ......356 9967
MADILL W, 64 College Rd,Sutton Coldfield ...354 8566
MADIN J, 34d Wentworthrd 17 ....427 7430
  M.L.K, 182 Lightwoods Hl,Smethwick ...429 2530
  W.H, 131 Park Hl Rd 17 .....427 1634
MADISON J.O, 132 Raglan Rd,Smethwick ...558 4789
  N.A, 34 Teesdale Av 34 ......748 1201
MADKINS A.H,
  76 Somerville Rd,Sutton Coldfield..355 3613
  A.J, 39 South Gro 23 ....350 8551
  P.E, 20 Hinton Av 48 ....445 2966
  T.W, 433 Birmingham Rd,Walsall ...358 1512
  W.E, 110 Meadthorpe Rd 44 ....360 3535
MADLAM K, 73 Caldwell Gro,Solihull ...711 1215
MADLEY Gwyn, 48 Neville Rd,Shirley ...744 4881
MADOURIE C, 31 Glendower Rd 42 ...356 1081
MADRELL K.W, 95 Silhill Hall Rd,Solihull ...705 2477
MAECHER Pictureproducts
    Ltd..Snodland 243450
MAEER C.W, 5 Lingard Ho,Fox Hollies Rd,
    Sutton Coldfield..351 7629
  F.W.C, 70 Clay Pit La,W Bromwich ...553 2571
  G, 3 Park La 21 ....525 3628
  J.E, 12 New St,W Bromwich 556 0285
  K.M.F, 81 Riland Rd,Sutton Coldfield ...378 5549
  M.A, 42 New St,W Bromwich 502 1718
MAEERS G.A, 119 Kingsbury Rd 24 ...373 3909
MAER G.J, 14 Spiral Ct,Monkskirby Rd,
    Sutton Coldfield..378 1979
MAESE R, 34 Southcote Gro 38 ....459 8562
MAETINEAU B.E,
  Good Rest Camp Site,Good Rest La 38..459 1481
MAFFIN R.W, 64 Woodgate Gdns 32 ...422 1769
MAFLAHI M, 11 Birkdale Gro 29 .....471 4011
  M.S, 22 Aubrey Rd 10 ......773 8415
MAGAHRAN E, 46 Doveridge Rd 28 ...744 5756
MAGAR K.S, 2 Greenside Rd 24 .....373 3709
MAGDZIARZ A, 14 Hamstead Rd 19 ...554 1014
MAGEE A, 20 Holte Rd 6 ......327 0796
  ...7957
  ...9226
  ...8046
  ...2119
  ...0339
  ...8640
  ...1630
  ...1666
  ...5134
  ...0260
  ...1923
  ...5979
  ...9070
  ...7482
  ...8897
  ...6654
  R, 20 The Scotchings 36 ......747 9215
  R.H, 153 Castle La,Solihull 743 9893
  T, 11 Pavillion Av,Smethwick 429 5635
GEEAN J.J, 9 Leatherhead Clo 6 ...359 8471
GEED R, 27 Whetstone Clo 15 ....454 3927
GEN J.W, 80 Coronation Rd 43 ....358 6283
GENIS I, 52 Oxford St 30 ......459 8501
GGS B.E, 389 Warwick Rd,Solihull ...704 3235
  .D, 20 Greenwood Clo 14 ....443 4936
  .I, 10 Harleston Rd 44 ......350 5654
  , 32 Pitleasow Clo 30 ......451 2997
  .O, 3 Garnett Av 43 ....360 3103
  .D, 7 Meerhill Av,Shirley 745 9427
  .R, 21 Whitley Ct Rd 32 .....422 0127
  V.J.T, 17 Nevison Gn 43 .....325 0098
  V.S, 24 Cherrywood Ct,Solihull ...743 5528
GILL B, 11 Inkberrow Rd,Halesowen ...550 4366
  .R, 24 Morven Rd,Sutton Coldfield ...354 2746
  red, 172 West Hth Rd 31 .....475 4518
  , 201 Wyndhurst Rd 33 ......783 2748
  , 114 Clent View Rd 32 ......422 1576
  .G, 2 Bishbury Clo 15 ......455 0101
GINLEY T.H, 57 St. Peters Rd 20 ...523 3415
GINNIS A.F, 10 Chapel St,Halesowen ...501 3269
  A.R, 22 Cross St,Halesowen 550 4024
  J.E, 14 Grosvenor Rd,Solihull 704 2707
  L.A, 43 Barcheston Rd ....Knowle 6840
  T.W, 676 Chester Rd 36 .....770 7022
MAGNAY Dr A.R, 18 Crosbie Rd 17 ...427 3433
MAGNER P.F, 74 Fredas Gro 17 ....427 9846
  R.D, 10 Lottie Rd 29 ....472 7916
MAGNESS C.R,
  50 Slater Rd,Bentley Hth....Knowle 3189
MAGONS F, 61 Burney La 8 ......783 6389
MAGOR D.C,
  6 Linden Ct,Hampton La,Solihull..704 9722
  M, 7 The Avenue,Rowley Regis 559 1674
MAGOWAN S.C, 21 Tansy Badgers Bank Rd,
    Sutton Coldfield..308 3265
MAGRATH G.F, 90 Wentworth Rd 17 ...426 2485
MAGRAW W.L,
  42a Maney Hl Rd,Sutton Coldfield..354 5063
MAGRI S, 69 Tedstone Rd 32 .....427 5127
MAGRIS G.L,
  5 Far Highfield,Solihull..378 2470
MAGSON A.G, 109 Stoney La 25 ....783 0170
  A.M, 243 The Avenue 27 .....707 3712
  D, 250 Scott Rd,Olton 706 9854

the changing needs of the graphic designer. Erik Spiekermann's Meta (Fig. **2.55**) has been described as an ecological face, designed to look attractive even in small sizes on problematic papers such as coarse, thin, and recycled stocks. Designers Banks and Miles developed an economical typeface for British Telecom's telephone directories and managed to achieve savings in paper of over 10 percent (Fig. **2.54**).

Some typographers are using the power of the computer to incorporate "intelligence" (or rather, chaos) into their typefaces. Beowulf from Dutch designers Erik van Blokland and Just van Rossum, for example, is a "random" font in which the letterforms mutate subtly each time a character is produced (Fig. **2.56**). Three versions of Beowulf have differing levels of randomness built in, and they imitate the effects of wear and tear on metal and wooden type.

In a way, faces like Beowulf are a modern counterpart to Gutenberg's efforts to emulate the scribes' humanized typography. A similar point could be made about computer simulations of hand lettering in comics.

Meta Normal:
ABCDEFGHIJKLMNOPQRSTUVWXYZ
abcdefghijklmnopqrstuvwxyz
1234567890!@#£$%^&*()_+‹›?

META CAPS:
ABCDEFGHIJKLMNOPQRSTUVWXYZ
ABCDEFGHIJKLMNOPQRSTUVWXYZ
1234567890!@#£$%^&*()_+Ø≠?

Meta Bold:
ABCDEFGHIJKLMNOPQRSTUVWXYZ
abcdefghijklmnopqrstuvwxyz
1234567890!@#£$%^&*()_+¨Æ?

R21: ABCDEFGHIJKLMNOP QRSTUVWXYZabcdefghijk lmnopqrstuvwxyz1234567 890!@#£$%^&*()_+‹›?

R22: ABCDEFGHIJKLMNOP QRSTUVWXYZabcdefghijk lmnopqrstuvwxyz1234567 890!@#£$%^&*()_+‹›?

R23: ABCDEFGHIJKLMNOP QRSTUVWXYZabcdefghijk lmnopqrstuvwxyz1234567 890!@#£$%^&*()_+‹›?

2.55 Erik Spiekermann's ecological face Meta was designed as a reaction to the overuse of Helvetica, which he describes as "the Federal font" because of its widespread use by German business and government.

2.56 Building randomness into a font's characteristics creates subtly mutating type. Beowulf from Dutch designers Erik van Blokland and Just van Rossum was the first "anarchistic" font.

2.54 The condensed typeface designed by Colin Banks of London-based designers Banks and Miles also addresses green issues. It allows four columns per page of the telephone directory, and this, along with the decision not to repeat surnames, has resulted in huge savings in both paper and ink. As only one size (5.75 pt) was required, Banks was able to design the bitmaps pixel by pixel. Note the **traps** in some letters to prevent ink spread from filling in the junctions.

ABC ABC ABC

PostScript and TrueType

Almost every machine or device in print production encountered today — from computer screens and scanners to high-resolution imagesetters — works on the **raster** principle. A raster (from the Latin for "rake") is the line that makes up the picture on a television screen. On digital devices like a computer screen, each line is divided into a series of dots called **pixels**, and the **resolution** of the screen is described in terms of the number of pixels horizontally by the number of lines vertically. Thus the screen of a computer monitor may have a resolution of 640 x 480 or 1024 x 768.

Another way of measuring resolution is by the number of dots per inch, or **dpi**. Thus, measured in this way, a Mac's screen has a resolution of 72 dpi; a PC monitor is 96 dpi.

2.57 PostScript is an outline description format, developed by Adobe and adopted worldwide as a de facto standard. Letterforms are described in terms of outlines using the math of Bézier cubic spline curves. These outlines are then converted to bitmaps appropriate to the resolution of the output device.

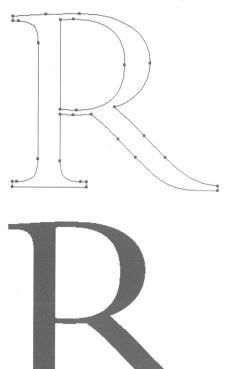

The higher the resolution, the better the quality. A laser printer typically has a resolution of 600 dpi. A production-quality imagesetter will have a resolution of 2550 dpi or higher.

The same type has to look good (or at least be recognizable) on all kinds of different devices with all kinds of resolutions. A designer may work initially on the computer screen, proof the results on a laser printer, and then send off a CD containing all the type information to a bureau for high-quality bromide prints or film, or to the printers for direct digital printing.

Type descriptions have to be stored in a device-independent format, and converted to a form readable by the particular device as and when necessary. **PostScript**, developed by Adobe, is such a format (Fig. **2.57**).

PostScript describes the outline of the letterform in terms of vectors (lines and curves) rather than dots, and this outline is converted by software into a pattern of dots specific to each output device. PostScript is, strictly speaking, a page-description language (more in Chapter 4; see p. 118) that describes not only letterforms, but also drawings created on the computer, and the layouts of type and drawings on pages.

As PostScript is a proprietary piece of software, anyone wanting to make PostScript-compatible typefaces or printing devices has to pay Adobe a license fee. To try to break Adobe's monopoly, Microsoft, the developers of Windows for the PC, and Apple developed a rival format called **TrueType** (Fig. **2.58**).

2.58 TrueType is a rival format to PostScript, developed jointly by Apple and Microsoft. It is similar in principle to PostScript, but its mathematical basis is different — it uses quadratic curves. It is linked to Apple's operating system, but also runs under Windows on an IBM PC. These samples were produced using TypeMan from Type Solutions, Inc.

The two systems will work together in the same document, but PostScript fonts will not print well on the cheaper inkjet printers that TrueType fonts will. ATM (Adobe Type Manager) is a program that improves the appearance of scaled-up fonts on the computer screen and on low-resolution printers.

Adobe's licensed fonts are called Type 1 PostScript fonts. Other PostScript fonts are called Type 3. There is no Type 2! Type 1 fonts have **hinting** (Fig. **2.60**), which subtly changes the shape of a character so that it better fills the pixel grid of the target device. It is not the same as non-linear scaling.

Before PostScript and TrueType, fonts were stored as arrays of dots called **bitmaps** (Fig. **2.59**). These can, when printed, be every bit as good as the equivalent PostScript version, but you needed a separate bitmap for every font and every resolution of the target device. With PostScript you need just two: a screen font to give an idea of the look of the typeface on the relatively low resolution of the computer screen; and a printer font, to cover all the different kinds of output device. TrueType uses just one: the printer font is used to generate the screen font.

2.59 A bitmap is a pattern of dots that approximates the outlines of a letterform. On a low-resolution device, such as a computer screen or dot-matrix printer, a bitmap looks crude and jagged. But on a high-resolution device, such as an imagesetter, the dots would be too small to see.

72 dpi 144 dpi 300 dpi

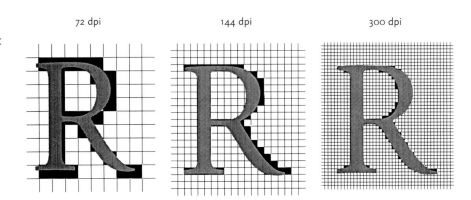

2.60 Hinting is the name given to the process of slightly adjusting the pixels in a scaled bitmap to give a consistent weight and to make the letterform more legible at smaller sizes.

Inconsistent weights Consistent weights

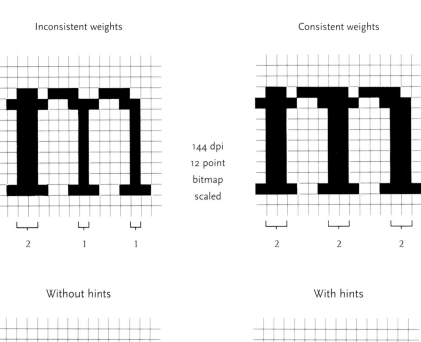

144 dpi
12 point
bitmap
scaled

2   1   1   2   2   2

Without hints With hints

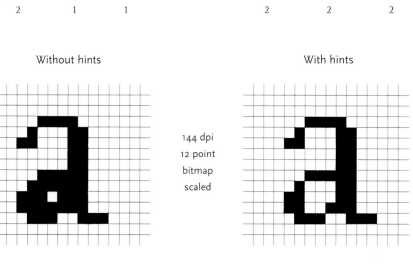

144 dpi
12 point
bitmap
scaled

■ SUMMARY

What, then, are the pros and cons of the various typesetting technologies?

Hot metal or letterpress

■ **Advantages** Quality: each font designed specifically for its particular size; printed result gives an impressed look and feel which conveys care and expense. Uses original type designs. Can be quick to set up for small jobs such as business cards. Nowadays reserved mainly for short-run prestigious invitations, overprinting diplomas, and for private press editions of poetry books.

■ **Disadvantages** Handsetting is labor-intensive, and thus costly. Must hold a large inventory of metal type, which takes up space. Can run out of sorts in the middle of a job. Machine setting is noisy and highly skilled. Metal type is inflexible, does not enlarge well, and cannot be set close. Limited availability.

Cold metal or strike-on

■ **Advantages** Quick and direct setting by relatively unskilled operators. Inexpensive.

■ **Disadvantages** Poor selection of typefaces, crude intercharacter spacing. Justified setting difficult. Low quality.

Photosetting

■ **Advantages** Fast and relatively inexpensive. Wide range of typefaces. Letters can be set closer than in hot metal. Set by skilled compositors, ensuring a good-quality result.

Disadvantages All sizes produced by one font master. More "sterile" look than hot metal. Mechanicals usually needed to produce pages.

Computer setting

■ **Advantages** Wide range of typefaces available. Type can be adjusted and manipulated in different ways. Type can be imported directly to page make-up systems, so no intermediate mechanical stage required. Possibility of "do-it-yourself" setting, so no typesetting costs.

Disadvantages Designs of traditional typefaces vary between suppliers. Unless set by skilled compositor, possibility of errors going unchecked. Choice of sizes, leading, tracking can result in unimaginative use of defaults. New skills to be learnt.

ERIK SPIEKERMANN

LIFE STORY ■ Erik Spiekermann was born in 1947, in Stadthagen, Germany. He funded his own studies, in art history at the Free University in Berlin, by setting metal type and operating a printing press in the basement of his home.

He spent seven years working freelance in London in the 1970s, principally for Wolff Olins and Pentagram. He also lectured at the London College of Printing, consolidating his involvement with all aspects of typography, including type design. Spiekermann calls himself a typographic designer: "A typographic designer starts from the word up; a graphic designer starts from the picture down." His trademark signature is a "tectonic" narrow rectangle or bar bleeding off the confines of the page, usually in just one of two colors: black or red, with type dropped out in white.

Never long away from Berlin, Spiekermann also developed a successful relationship with Berthold AG, which led in the late 1970s to commissions to redraw and digitize some of their classic typefaces. He returned to work in Berlin, founding the first incarnation of MetaDesign with Dieter Heil (based in London) and Florian Fischer in 1979. In 1984, the company was bought by Sedley Place Design, while Spiekermann worked nearby as MetaDesign Mk 2. The first Mac computer (in Germany) arrived in 1985.

> "A typographic designer starts from the word up; a graphic designer starts from the picture down."

MetaDesign Mk 3 was set up on 1 January 1990 with Uli Mayer and Hans Christian Krüger. MetaDesign is the largest design studio in Germany, with major design contracts for Adobe, Apple, AT&T, Audi, BVG (Berliner Verkehrsbetriebe, the Berlin transportation authority), the city of Berlin itself, the German Green Party, Hewlett-Packard, IBM, Nike, Springer Verlag, Texas Instruments, and Volkswagen.

In 1992 Spiekermann co-founded MetaDesign West in San Francisco, with Terry Irwin and Bill Hill, ostensibly because he needed "a work excuse to spend more time in California." In 1995, to close his typographic circle, Spiekermann formed a partnership with Tim Fendley and Robin Richmond in London, completing what has become an international network.

As a type designer, Spiekermann is best known, so far, for ITC Officina, FF Info and FF Meta (see p. 71), which is now approaching a Helvetica-like ubiquity. Meta began life as a corporate typeface for the German post office to try to end the "chaos" created through the use in the organization of dozens of versions of Helvetica, but ended with the client's decision to stick with Helvetica because to change would "cause unrest." He recently designed a "phonetic" typeface for "Glasgow 1999: UK City of Architecture and Design," with echoes of Charles Rennie Mackintosh and lots and lots of ligatures.

In 1992, Spiekermann was commissioned to design a set of stamps commemorating the Olympic Games for DTT, the Dutch Post Office — the first "foreigner" to get such a brief. In 1996, he was honored as one of the "I.D.

MANIFESTO ■ You Cannot *Not* Communicate

Spiekermann's philosophy is: think before you act, do a little more than is required, and keep it simple. "Each single solution has to function in every small detail," says Spiekermann, "while at the same time being seen as part of a larger total. Nothing is irrelevant: a picture chosen arbitrarily, sloppy printing, inappropriate choice of paper or messy typography can destroy even the most profound design concept. The aim is always to achieve a distinct, coherent visual style, which can be identified and attributed even without showing the logo."

Spiekermann's specialty is creating order from chaos: information design. This is achieved through care in type selection, sometimes type creation, and especially through typographic clarity.

"We're constantly bombarded by messages," says Spiekermann, "all trying to make us look, to make us listen, to make us react. Some of these messages, however, are more important than others. How you interpret some information could even be a matter of life or death. The difference between being a survivor and a casualty may be as simple as finding the 'Way Out' sign.

"When the design of information is left to chance, the result is information anxiety. And when things become too complex, when an environment defies common sense, when technical requirements are allowed to prevail over human considerations, then someone has to intervene.

"Many designers regard the design of information as something that is somehow beneath them; they'd rather be left alone to design posters, logos and glossy brochures, which probably pay better anyway.

"But more and more businesses are now discovering the advantages of clear communications. Good information design must communicate by convincing us, not just browbeating us. And information designers need to know, as clever advertising people have long known, that nothing convinces people more than being entertained. Show me a form that's fun to fill out, a sign that makes me smile, or a set of instructions I'll want to take to bed to read, and maybe all this information won't seem so painful after all."

After the fall of the Berlin Wall, public transport in the unified city needed new passenger information. Signs, schedules, maps, bus stops, stations, and printed matter had to be redesigned for people in the East and West; after thirty years apart they had nothing much in common any more. By late 1990, MetaDesign had developed an information system that worked well enough for other transport corporations in the Berlin region to adopt it for their own systems. The design work was awarded the German Design Prize in 1991, which encouraged the team to continue towards a complete corporate design program — from letterheads to the styling of new tramcars and even complete subway stations. Spiekermann's familiar bleeding rectangle was forbidden by the client.

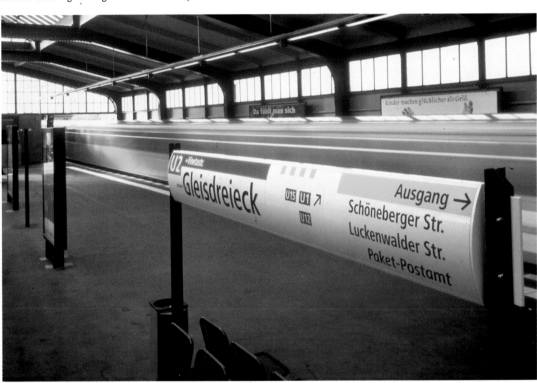

Today the Berlin transport system sports friendly colors, with clear up-to-date messages showing a new attitude and regard for the customers. The strategy has also led to changes within the company: for example, by standardizing seat covers and other fittings across a wide range of vehicles and developing a modular signage system it has been shown that good design can also save money!

In March 1994, *Fortune* magazine recognized the BVG corporate design program with the prestigious Beacon award.

WORKSTATION
• Website: www.metadesign.com
• Erik Spiekermann, *Rhyme and Reason: A Typographic Novel*, H. Berthold AG, Berlin 1987
• Erik Spiekermann and E. M. Ginger, *Stop Stealing Sheep and Find Out How Type Works*, Adobe Press, CA 1993
• Fay Sweet, MetaDesign: *Design From the Word Up*, Thames and Hudson 1999
• *Emigre*, 11, 1989 Ambition/Fear issue
• Mike Daines, "Erik Spiekermann: Serious But Not Solemn," *Baseline*, 19, 1995, pp. 22–7
• William Owen, "Meta's Tectonic Man," *Eye*, 18, 1995, pp. 34–45
• *I.D.* magazine Jan/Feb 1996, p. 78

Forty," *I.D.* magazine's fourth annual selection of leading design innovators.

No conference about type and typography is complete without an appearance by Erik Spiekermann. If not in person, then on tape or by satellite link. The newcomer in the audience is struck first by his bilingual articulation and then by his humor, at once acerbic and self-deprecating. His ability to communicate ("not called speaker-man for nothing") has speeded his international recognition.

Erik Spiekermann is Professor for Communication Design at Bremen University, Vice-President of the German Design Council, and President of the International Institute for Information Design.

THREE | ILLUSTRATION

ILLUSTRATION

"A picture is worth more than a thousand words," says the ancient Chinese proverb. Well, that may be a gross undervaluation in our image-rich and visually literate society. And while beautifully set typography can have "shape," "form," and "color," there is nothing to compare with the real thing.

Words and pictures are the raw materials of the graphic designer. We have looked at the production of words, and now it is the turn of images in all their diversity.

Until the middle of the nineteenth century, there were very few ways that images could be combined with type. Today, any image is immediately accessible to the resourceful graphic designer. How individual designers choose to communicate the message of their particular publication is no longer limited by printing technology. But an understanding of the process is essential if designers are to realize their dreams.

We explore the differences between line and tone, find out the finer points of flat color and the four- and six-color processes, learn the secrets of successful screening, and discover how the digital scanner "sees" the copy we put before it. We look at practical methods of sizing and cropping images, and investigate the best ways of preparing artwork and photographs for the service bureau, repro house, or printer.

We look at the psychology and symbolism of color and how to take into account the needs of disabled people. Finally, we investigate the important issue of copyright and develop some winning ways to get the best from our professional colleagues, the illustrators and photographers.

3.1 Line art includes much more than just black lines on paper, as can be seen in this Victorian engraving of Prince Albert by D. J. Pound, from an original photograph by Mayall. Look closely at the full picture and at the detail opposite and you will not be able to see anything that cannot be reproduced directly.

■ LINE AND TONE

Line, to the printer, is any copy that will print in a single color requiring no other intermediate treatment. When the printer mixes ink, the machinery is not capable of diluting it to produce grays, or tints of a color. Black cannot become gray; dark green cannot become pale green. The ink is either there on the paper or it's not. Line means solid areas, dots, or lines of a single color, with no gradation of tone.

There are ways of fooling the eye into perceiving tints and tones. Illustrators use techniques such as stippling or cross-hatching to simulate tones. Victorian engravings can look almost photographic, but look closely and you will see only lines and dots of one color (Fig. **3.1**).

The line process is both the cheapest and the most satisfactory for printing on inferior papers. As mentioned in Chapter 1, the line block for letterpress was invented by Paul Pretsch in 1853, and, by the

3.2 "Overcoming the difficulties of serenading in New York City," a cartoon with a mechanical tint, from William Heath Robinson's 1934 collection *Absurdities*.

3.3 Before computers, graphic-design studios used a combination of process camera, like this WLTC 184, and PMT machine to produce enlarged or reduced copies of line art good enough to use on the mechanical.

mid 1880s, zinc plates mounted on wooden blocks were being used to reproduce black-and-white illustrations in newspapers and books.

For the first time, an illustrator was able to work at larger sizes than the image would appear in print; any imperfections of the line would thus be proportionally reduced. It became common, therefore, to work "half-up" — at 45 x 30 to become 30 x 20 — or "twice-up," at 60 x 40 to become 30 x 20. Too great a reduction, however, can lose much of the original quality and spontaneity of the work, and over-reduced lines may break up or disappear under the pressure of printing.

From 1901 onward, the blockmaker could add Ben Day **mechanical tints** to a line drawing as indicated (usually with a blue wash on the original) by the illustrator (Fig. **3.2**). Later, self-adhesive film such as Letratone, printed with various tints and patterns, could be added to line work to achieve the same effect.

For offset litho, line illustrations were reproduced photographically on high-contrast **bromide** paper, usually reduced down in size from the original. This print was then pasted on to a board along with the typesetting. Bromide prints were also produced as **PMTs** (photomechanical transfers), or **diffusion transfers**, by a proprietary method developed by Kodak (Fig. **3.3**). It was a much drier process than the original method, in which the bromide paper was processed in trays of photographic chemicals in a darkroom.

To produce a PMT, original artwork was exposed on special negative paper through a process camera. This negative was then fed into a processor which activated the in-built developer and then laminated it to a receiving sheet of paper or film. After a short delay, the two sheets were peeled apart and the line image was revealed. It was also possible to obtain reversed-out (white on black) images using appropriate paper.

If more than one copy was required, or there was a need for the image to be retouched, a negative film was first made from the original. (It is easier, for example, to clean marks on the white areas of an image by opaquing out the black areas on a negative.) This was then used to produce contact prints on bromide paper, by means of the conventional and messy method of processing.

For low-cost work, it is also possible (and much cheaper) to reduce artwork on a laser photocopier using smooth, good-quality paper.

3.4 Tone art, such as this print of Bill Gates, has to be converted into a pattern of dots before it can be printed, by a process called screening.

3.5 A conventional halftone contains dots of different sizes, but in a regular array conforming to the screen being used. Light areas are represented by small black dots. At 50 percent, you will see a checkerboard of black-and-white squares, while the darker tones appear as white dots on black. It is rare to find either pure white (no dots at all) or pure black (a solid area of black) on a halftone.

Screens and halftones

A **halftone** is any photograph or piece of artwork that contains tonal values other than just plain black and white (Fig. **3.4**). Before an original containing continuous or intermediate tones can be printed, it must first be converted to "line" — into a form in which there can be either ink on the paper or not. The most common method is to use a halftone **screen** which converts the continuous tone original into a pattern of single-colored dots (Fig. **3.5**).

Screening is done digitally these days, but used to be achieved by placing a glass or plastic screen between the lens of the process camera and the bromide paper or film being exposed. As mentioned in Chapter 1, the method devised by George Meisenbach in 1882 used a single-lined screen that was turned 90 degrees during exposure. The first cross-lined screen was introduced in 1890 by Frederick Ives, in collaboration with Louis and Max Levy.

Halftone screens came in two varieties: glass screens and the cheaper plastic contact screens. Glass screens had a finely ruled grid pattern and were situated between the lens and the film. Contact screens contained a pattern of vignetted holes and were placed in direct proximity with the film. The term halftone is perhaps a misnomer: they are thus named because it was thought that half of the tone is eliminated during the process. Half the image maybe — but *all* of the tone. Just black and white remain.

3.6 Imagesetters can make various shapes of dot electronically. Elliptical dots score over conventional ones, as they are less prone to dot gain — the abrupt darkening of areas where the dots are beginning to join up.

3.7 When two screens are superimposed and are not quite in alignment, there is a good chance that moiré patterns will result. This happens most commonly when a previously screened halftone, cut from a magazine, for example, is put through another screening process.

3.8 Detail of Rajarani Temple at Bhuvanesvar, India, at screen rulings of 65 (coarse), 120 (general purpose), and 175 (the ruling used throughout this book).

The optics of how this happens is not really important to know. Suffice to say that different tones are converted into dots varying in size, shape, and number, which when viewed from a distance seem to melt back into continuous tone.

The traditional crossed-line screen of 1890 gives a round dot, which becomes a square in the midtones — a checkerboard pattern at 50 percent density. More recently, various shapes of dot have been tried. An improvement on the conventional screen is one with elliptical holes which produce kite-shaped dots that join first in one direction, then the other, giving a much smoother gradation in the middle tones.

On modern electronic image-setters, the dots are "written" on to the bromide paper or film directly by a laser beam — no screen is involved. These machines are capable of producing any shape of dot you like: square, round, or elliptical (Fig. **3.6**). The operator at the repro house will choose the best type of dot for the printing process and paper stock being used, and the tonal quality of the original.

Halftone screens are measured in lines per inch (lines per cm in continental Europe), usually abbreviated to **lines** or lpi (Fig. **3.8**). The higher the number of lines, the finer the dot pattern, and the better the quality of the reproduction. But there is a trade-off. Newspapers, for example, use cheap, rough paper and thin ink that is prone to spread. Too fine a screen, and the dots in the darker areas of the image will merge and **fill in**. Thus, for newsprint, a coarse dot pattern of 55 or 65 lines for letterpress and 100 or 120 lines for offset is standard. Magazines are printed on smoother papers, and so a finer screen of, say, 150 lines can be used. The very finest screens are reserved for glossy art papers (see Chapter 6, pp. 163–73, for an in-depth discussion about paper).

The lines of the screen are usually aligned at 45 degrees to the horizontal, as this seems to produce the pattern that is easiest on the eye. There are dangers, however, when screening photographs containing regular patterns — on a person's clothing, for example. The screen dots and the pattern in the picture can interfere with each other to produce **moiré** (wavy or basket-weave) patterns (Fig. **3.7**). This can be avoided or lessened by adjusting the angle of the screen. The moiré effect is put to good use in devices that can tell you what screen is being used in a printed publication.

There are also special-effect screens available that convert continuous tone into straight lines of varying weight, wavy lines, concentric circles, and textures that simulate canvas, linen, and random grain (Fig. **3.9**).

Conventional screening is now referred to as **AM** (amplitude-modulated) screening: the dots are arranged in regular columns and rows, but vary in size. In **FM** (frequency-modulated) screening, all the dots are same size, but they are randomly scattered (Fig. **3.11**). This eliminates the possibility of moiré patterns, and produces much smoother vignettes. And because the final image is built from single pixels, rather than composite halftone dots, the imagesetter can be run at lower resolutions. However, subsequent platemaking is so sensitive it must be carried out in almost "clean-room" conditions. Note the absence of the familiar rosettes you see when you magnify areas of constant color in four-color work. FM screening is also sometimes called **stochastic** screening, from the Greek for "random."

Halftones are generally squared up, i.e. rectangular in shape. Sometimes you might want to specify a thin black border or keyline around them to define the edge. There are other effects that can be

used by the discerning graphic designer (Fig. **3.10**). These include **cut-outs**, in which extraneous matter is opaqued out (once by hand, now using an image-manipulation program such as Photoshop); **drop-outs**, in which the dots in the very whitest areas are eliminated to accentuate the highlights; and **vignettes**, usually oval, in which the image fades gradually to nothing at the edges.

In work destined for offset lithography, halftones were once made into negative film and "stripped in" later, occupying the clear holes on the negative page left by black squares placed on the artwork. For some jobs, however, it was cheaper and more convenient to put correctly sized halftones called **veloxes** into place along with the type and line, and shoot the whole page in one operation.

Sometimes it may be necessary to produce a halftone from copy that has already been screened. It may not be possible to locate the original of an old illustration from a book, for example. To put a screened picture directly under the camera or on the scanner will more often than not result in unwanted moiré patterns, but there are ways of avoiding this.

Use your **loupe** (eyeglass) to see if the dots on the original are sharp

3.9 Publicity shot of Tina Turner. It does not have to be dots! But use special effect screens with discretion!

3.10 A halftone is not always "squared-up." It can also be cut out around a profile, have the highlights dropped out, or it can be made into a vignette with the usually elliptical edges fading away to white. (Bartholdi's Statue of Liberty at the entrance to New York harbor.)

and black. If the screen does not exceed 120 lines, it can be shot as line copy. This is called **dot-for-dot** reproduction, and will often result in an increase of contrast. In Photoshop, you can use a despeckle filter, or blur the image to remove the screen followed by "unsharp mask" to put it back into focus — minus the screen.

Where lines and tones appear on the same piece of artwork, for example in a pencil drawing or an ink and wash illustration, a compromise has to be made. Either the whole illustration is treated as tone, in which case the white of the paper will appear light gray and the black lines will lose their crispness. Or the artwork is shot twice, as line and as tone, and combined at the film or platemaking stage as a **line and tone combination**.

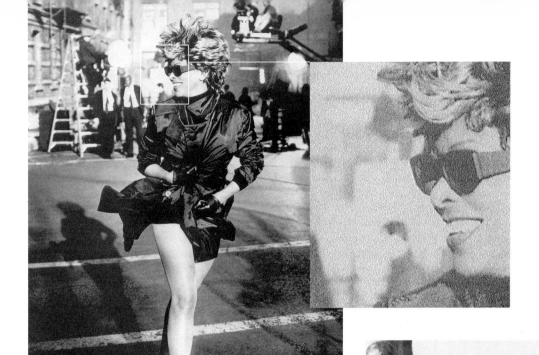

◀ **3.11** Publicity shot of Tina Turner. FM or stochastic screening uses a random scattering of spots to reproduce tone, rather than the regular pattern of dots used in AM screening.

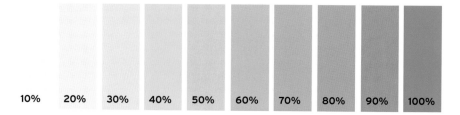

▶ **3.12** Color tints are effective when used under typesetting to draw attention to a particular passage, quotation, or checklist.

| 10% | 20% | 30% | 40% | 50% | 60% | 70% | 80% | 90% | 100% |

■ COLOR

The use of color in printing is almost as old as printing itself, but the process has always been labor-intensive and has required painstaking amounts of skill. The chromolithographs of the mid-19th century sometimes used as many as 12 separate hand-drawn plates. This created correspondingly enormous problems of positioning the successive printings into correct alignment, one on top of the other — what printers call **registration**.

Flat color

Printers can mix up any color of ink you like — you will just be charged for the cost of special ink and for cleaning up the machine afterward.

An additional color used as a design element in a layout is called **flat color**, or sometimes **match** or **spot color**. In theory, you could use any number of different colors in a design. In practice, most printing presses are designed to handle two, four, or six colors in one printing, and the more printings you ask for, the higher the cost of the job. Printers can match almost any color — from a color chart, a piece of printed work, or even the color of your eyes. But if it is consistency you're after, between jobs and other related printed items, you're going to have to be a little more scientific.

The **Pantone Matching System** (PMS) is an industry-standard collection of over 1000 colors that printers recognize and are comfortable using. (PMS 2718 — blue — is the flat color used throughout this book.) It is worth purchasing a color guide, in the form of a fan chart or **swatch book**. It will show you all the shades, along with the formulas for mixing the ink, and the effect of colors printed on both coated and uncoated paper (Fig. **3.13**). The easiest way of specifying flat color is to give the printer the Pantone

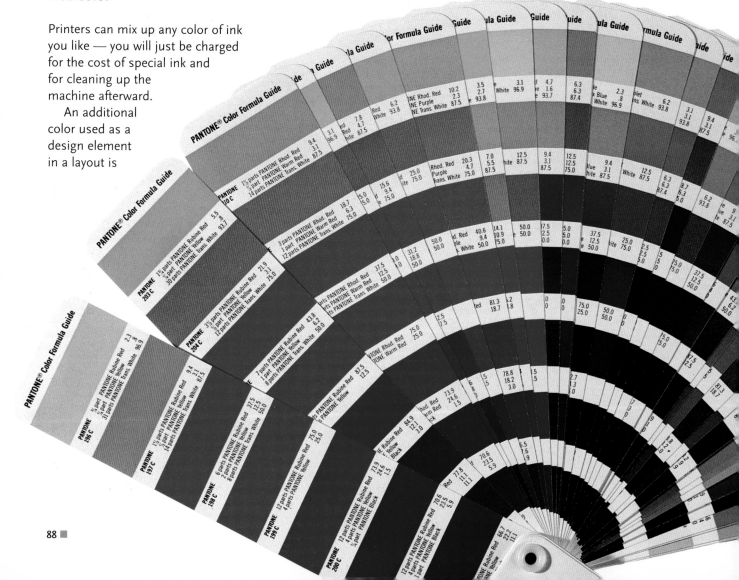

SURPRINT

REVERSE OUT

OVERPRINT

number and perhaps one of the tear-off samples that come with the swatch book.

Any color chosen from the Pantone range is made from a mixture of two or more from a set of nine basic colors: yellow, warm red, rubine red, rhodamine red, purple, violet, reflex blue, process blue, and green, supplemented by transparent white and black. There are also complementary sets of colors incorporating metallic inks, and specialist selections, such as pastel colors for packaging designers.

Flat color can be printed solid or as a percentage **tint** (Fig. **3.12**). Charts are also available that show Pantone colors in a range of percentage tints. Type can be combined with a tint of flat color in

three ways: **surprinted**, with the tint and in the same color; **reversed out** of a tint block; or **overprinted** in another color (Fig. **3.14**). Legibility is an issue, so check with printed samples to see what will work with different percentages of tint.

Printers do not like to have flat colors overlapping, because it slows down the rate of drying of the inks and introduces the possibility of smudging. A color will change shade, too, when printed over another one. But adjacent areas of flat color will need to overlap to a small extent to allow for misregistration (misalignment of successive printings). This allowance is called **trapping** (Fig. **3.15**) and is particularly important where, say, lettering is reversed out of a block of one color and printed in another. Without trapping, the slightest amount the printing slips **out of register** will cause a thin white

3.14 Text surprinted, dropped out of a tint of the same color, and overprinted in a different color.

line to appear around part of the boundary, resulting in an unwanted bas-relief effect. Generally, it is the lighter color that is extended into the area of the darker color.

Duotones

A halftone cannot always reproduce the full tonal range of a photograph. A **duotone** is a superimposition of a contrasty black halftone over a one-color halftone, which is shot for highlights and middle tones (Fig.

3.15 If a graphic or type in one flat color has to fit with a background of another color, there is always the possibility that misregistration might cause a sliver of white where they should abut — this is called bad trapping. The prevention and cure is to add a "stroke" width all round the lighter component, which will be hidden when the darker ink is overprinted.

3.13 The Pantone Matching System for specifying flat color.

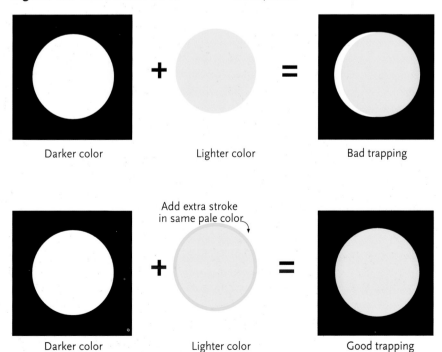

Darker color   +   Lighter color   =   Bad trapping

Darker color   +   Add extra stroke in same pale color   Lighter color   =   Good trapping

3.16), using the same image. The most commonly used colors are yellows, browns, and reds. The intention is to create a rich range of tones, and at the same time add a colored tint to the result. For high-quality work, where cost is not a constraint, a duotone may even comprise two printings in black, or in black with a shade of gray. A basic shot with the screen at 45 degrees is used for the black plate, and a second shot at 15 degrees is used for the second color.

For very high-quality publications, three passes of black or gray ink may be used to reproduce the full tonal range of a halftone. A less impressive duotone effect can be achieved by printing a black halftone over a color tint of the same size. This is called a **flat-tint halftone**. The tint must be kept quite light, as the highlights in the halftone can only ever be as light as the underlying tint.

Full-color reproduction

It is neither economic nor practical to mix up ink and print every individual color to be found in a piece of artwork or color photograph, so

another method has to be used. It should be possible to create any color from a mixture of the three primary pigments: red, yellow, and blue. Mix any two primary colors and you have the secondaries. Thus blue and yellow produce green, red and yellow produce orange, and blue and red produce purple. Theoretically, if you mix all three, you get black. Experience tells us, however, that what we really end up with is an unpleasant muddy brown. A similar result occurs with combinations of **reflected light**.

▲ **3.16** A duotone is a halftone reproduction comprising two (or sometimes more) printings — one for contrast and the other for the highlights and middle tones. More often than not, the underprinting is in a color other than black. The use of cyan here enhances the sparkle in these Art Deco glass panels, now housed in the Metropolitan Museum of Art, New York, from the ocean liner *Normandie*.

With **transmitted light** (Fig. **3.17**), things are a little better. Here, the three primaries are red, green, and blue-violet; the secondaries are yellow, **magenta** (reddish purple), and **cyan** (turquoise). Mix three such primary beams of light, and the result is pure white. Grass is green because it absorbs the red and blue-violet components of white light and retransmits the green.

The secondary colors of transmitted light — yellow, magenta (process red), and cyan (process blue) — are the ones used by printers to reproduce full-color work. In 1860, Clerk Maxwell demonstrated how colored filters could be used to record the blue-violet, green, and red constituents of any full-color subject. Filters of red, green, and blue-violet — the primaries of transmitted light, also known as **additive colors** — are used to produce **separation** negatives (Fig. **3.18**). The red filter allows only the blue and green components through, creating cyan. The green filter allows through only red and blue, creating magenta, and the blue filter lets through only the red and green, creating the yellow. The negatives taken through these filters, known as **color separations**, are screened and the positives are then used to make plates to be printed in sequence and in register (correct alignment) in the **process colors** of yellow, magenta, and cyan.

In theory, all the colors added together should produce black, but in practice printing ink, like school paint, never does produce a pure enough black. So a fourth color — black — is added to deepen the dark areas and increase contrast. This makes the scheme a **four-color**

process. In print jargon, black is referred to as **key**, so the system is known as **CMYK**. Other systems of defining color include **RGB** (red, green, blue), used for computer displays, and the more theoretical **HLS (hue, luminance, saturation)**. Hue is the part of the rainbow the color occupies — whether it is red or blue. Luminance, lightness, or **value**, is the amount of black or white that has been added, to make yellow into brown, or red into pink. Saturation, or intensity, is a measure of the color's position in the range from neutral gray to fully saturated, or bright, color.

L*a*b color is a device-independent model proposed by the CIE (Commission Internationale de l'Eclairage) in 1931 and refined in 1976. L is for luminance; a and b are chromatic components — a for green to red and b for blue to yellow. Photoshop uses the L*a*b model internally when converting from RGB to CMYK.

Pantone's **Hexachrome** system uses six colors: brighter (fluorescent) versions of CMYK plus vivid orange and green. This expands the color **gamut** (the limited spectrum of colors that a particular device can reproduce; see Fig. **3.19**) and is also referred to as HiFi color. When the image is separated, green and magenta are prevented from appearing in the same area, as are orange and cyan, so can share the same screen angles

3.17 Pure white light contains all the colors of the rainbow. Add together the three primaries — red, green, and blue-violet — and you get white. Where the primaries overlap, the secondaries appear: yellow, magenta, and cyan.

Red filter
Negative film

Green filter
Negative film

Blue filter
Negative film

3.18 All the colors in full-color copy can be reproduced from a mixture of the secondaries — yellow, magenta, and cyan — and these components of any color can be extracted using filters of the primaries red, green, and blue-violet.

3.19 The gamut of colors that an RGB monitor can display differs from the gamut of colors capable of being reproduced by CMYK four-color printing. Hexachrome adds orange and green to increase the gamut. Here, the various gamuts are plotted in a CIE (Commission Internationale de l'Eclairage) standard color space diagram. RGB can only display approximately 70 percent of the colors that can be perceived by the human eye. The CMYK color gamut is much smaller, reproducing about 20 percent of perceivable colors.

3.21 In theory, any color can be reproduced from a combination of yellow, cyan, and magenta. In practice, though, black is added for extra punch. Gray component replacement trades off some of the neutral gray created by combinations of the process colors for tints of black — it saves ink and quickens drying (see bottom row). Detail of *Scene in Harlem (Simply Heavenly)* by Edward Burra (1905–76).

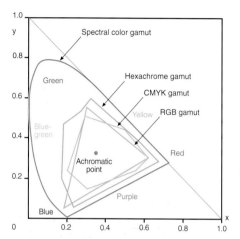

(see Fig. 3.20) and avoid any moiré patterns. When printing, black goes down first, followed by green, cyan, magenta, yellow, and finally orange.

Color separations

A color tone original, once separated by the **process camera**, is now commonly separated using an electronic **scanner**. Separations by camera were made on to continuous-tone film using three-color filters, and these were then converted into halftones by exposure through screens.

Scanners work by reading the artwork as a series of horizontal lines, or rasters. The **transparency** or artwork is wrapped around the scanner's transparent drum, which revolves at around 90 miles per hour (150 km/h). A beam of light is used to pick up the three color components. These split beams are digitized, and pass into a computer where color correction and some manipulation of the image can take place. Finally, a laser is employed to "write" the dots of the screened separations directly on to film.

The screens are laid out at different angles to keep the dots separate

— the apparent "mixing" of the colors is done by the brain and the eye — and in a pattern designed to eliminate moiré effects (Fig. **3.20**). The screens of the main colors are oriented at 30 degrees to each other, with the stronger colors at 45, 75, and 105 degrees, and the less intrusive yellow at the "difficult" angle of 90 degrees.

Some combinations of the three process colors cancel each other out to produce neutral grays, and since black is being used anyway, this can be seen as overkill. **Gray component replacement** (Fig. **3.21**),

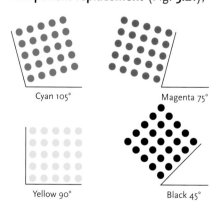

Cyan 105°   Magenta 75°

Yellow 90°   Black 45°

3.20 To prevent moiré patterns, the screens for the different color printings are set at specific angles: 45 degrees is easiest on the eye, so that is reserved for black; 90 degrees is the least satisfactory angle, so it is used for the relatively pale yellow.

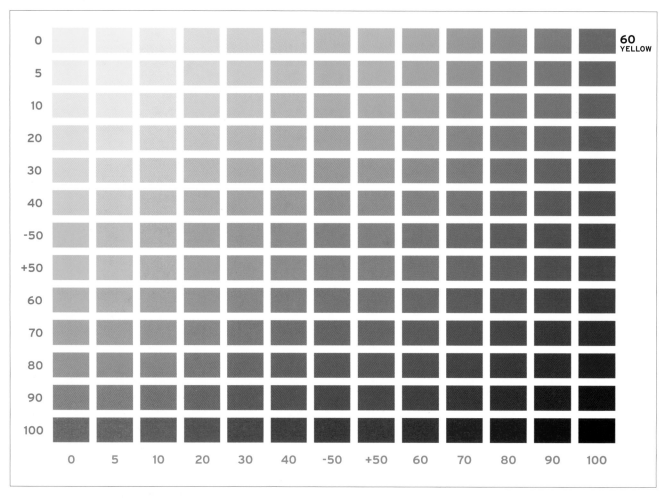

also known as **achromatic stabilization**, is a technique used at the scanning stage for cleaning up the color and reducing the amount of ink that gets to the paper. Not all the "chromatic" gray is removed and replaced by a tint of black, however. **Undercolor addition (UCA)** is a method of returning some of the process color, usually cyan, beneath the black to add depth and density to areas of deep shadow. **Undercolor removal (UCR)** reduces the amount of color in areas of shadows, to save ink and prevent problems that may occur if a new layer of ink is printed on to ink that is not quite dry.

If a solid area is to be printed in a Pantone shade along with four-color illustrations, it will be cheaper to match the color by using a combination of tints in two or more of the process colors. Pantone publishes charts illustrating various combinations of process tints printed one over the other (Fig. **3.22**). But if you plan to substitute in this way, check first with your clients. They may have strict rules about the use of specific colors for corporate-identity work — the color of a company logo, for example — and may be willing to stand the cost of an extra printing in a specially mixed Pantone shade.

To prevent potential muddiness when too many colors are mixed together, a rule of thumb has evolved that the sum of percentage components of the process colors should never exceed 240. A color comprising 30% yellow, 10% cyan, and 60% magenta (= 100%) is fine, but one containing 70% yellow, 100% cyan, and 80% magenta (= 250%) would not be allowed on the press. The color bar on a color proof has checks for this (see p. 129).

Cultural implications of color

You're wearing white for a special occasion. Where are you going? In a western country, you'd be the bride at a wedding; in Korea, you'd be at a funeral. In China, brides wear red. The bride in Jan van Eyck's Renaissance painting *Giovanni Arnolfini and His Bride* wears green — a symbol of her fertility. Color provides both visual and psychological information. But in different cultures, colors can have different meanings. Designers can control what the viewer perceives, but must always be aware that they could sometimes be sending the wrong messages.

Some colors seem to convey universal truths, and have been codified by organizations such as the Occupational Safety and Health Administration (OSHA) of the US Department of Labor. Yellow, for

3.22 Charts showing combinations of various percentage tints help you make the most effective use of process color in layouts. This chart shows the effect of changing the percentages of magenta and cyan while keeping yellow constant at 60 percent. Along the axes, 250 refers to dots that are not touching and 150 refers to ones that are.

example is a very visible color; that's why it is used on school buses. OSHA regulations designate yellow for caution and for marking (usually with a yellow and black chevron) physical hazards you might trip over. Red, for danger, is the color used for identifying fire-protection equipment and emergency stop buttons on dangerous machinery.

In many Middle Eastern countries, blue is viewed as a protective color. Front doors are painted blue to ward off evil spirits. In some communities of the southeast United States, too, front porch ceilings are painted blue to keep ghosts at bay; in the southwest United States, many Native Americans also paint their doors blue, again to keep the bad spirits away.

Colors can change their meanings over time with fashion and changing social awareness. Green used to be an unpopular color for automobiles — it was an unlucky color. This probably dates back to the 19th century when "Paris green" became a fashionable emerald shade — until it was discovered that this arsenic-based pigment had caused several deaths and was aptly renamed "poison green." Now green is back in fashion, along with greater environmental awareness. The names of colors, too, can have an influence on the perception of the color. In 1962, Binney & Smith renamed the Crayola color "flesh" to a less culturally charged "peach," and in 1992 introduced so-called "multicultural" crayons in many subtle shades of brown.

We often use colors to describe our emotions and feelings: "I was so angry, I saw red," we say, or "I'm feeling blue," or "I was green with envy."

"Paint it black" sang an unhappy Rolling Stones. But do these descriptions translate easily into other languages? Probably not that successfully, because the color may lose its associated symbolic meaning.

One link between color and emotion is the perception that red, orange, yellow, and brown hues are "warm" — inducing excitement, cheerfulness, stimulation, and aggression — while the blues, greens, and grays are "cold" — implying security, calm, and peace, or sadness, depression, and melancholy. A cross-cultural study has shown, however, that in Japan blue and green hues are perceived to be "good" and the red–purple range as "bad." In the United States, the red–yellow–green range is considered "good," with oranges and red–purples "bad."

Colors are not the same for everyone. Some languages do not contain separate words for green and blue, or for yellow and orange, and the Inuit, for example, are supposed to have 17 different words for white, as modified by different snow conditions. All languages have words for black and white. If a third hue is distinguished, it is red. Next comes yellow or green, and then both yellow and green. Blue is the sixth color named, and brown is the seventh. Finally, in no particular sequence, the colours gray, orange, pink, and purple are given names.

Architects and designers use color psychology to modify our behavior. Fast-food restaurants and coffee shops are painted orange and pink in conjunction to induce excitement. They excite you to come in, eat quickly, then vacate the table for the next set of excited

customers. Better restaurants do this more subtly using colors like burgundy. Blue is rarely used in restaurants, because it is a relaxing color. Once in the restaurant, the customers will be so relaxed that they won't want to leave. Hospitals used to be painted green to soothe patients. Pink can be energizing or calming. Prisons are painted pink to cheer up those who work there and subdue the prisoners.

Color has a significant effect on both our minds and bodies. Young children are attracted more by color than shape. As we mature, we will often become more form-dominant; however, creative people often remain color-dominant all of their lives. Eye-tracking studies of infants indicate that, regardless of sex, red and blue are the most preferred colors. Color has been shown to affect human moods, physiological responses, and perceptions of temperature, size, and ambiance. Colored light is used to treat some illnesses, and to soothe patients in hospitals and institutions. Warm colors (particularly red) increase human attraction to external stimuli, induce states of excitement, produce higher arousal levels, quicken muscular responses, and increase grip strength. In contrast, cool colors (particularly green) reduce anxiety states, and are associated with calm and tranquilizing moods.

Designing for disability access

Color-blindness is the inability to distinguish one or more of the three colors red, green, and blue. Blindness to red is called protanopia; to green, deuteranopia; and to blue, tritanopia. Red-blind people are unable to distinguish between red and green, while blue-blind people cannot distinguish between blue and yellow. Green-blind people are unable to see the green part of the spectrum. Color blindness, which affects about twenty times as many males as females, is a sex-linked recessive characteristic. A woman must inherit the trait from both parents to be color-blind.

In the United States alone, approximately 19 million people possess some form of color-blindness. While they are not technically blind, there may be some colors which are inaccessible to them, appearing as a confusing blend of grays. Designers must be ever aware of the problems of those who are color-blind, have age- or illness-related degenerative vision, or who have limited sight.

Elderly people see colors differently, but are not color-blind in the usual sense of the term. Vision declines with age, with yellowing and darkening of the lens and cornea, and a shrinking pupil size. Yellowing selectively blocks short wavelength light, so blues look darker. Moreover, the elderly have difficulty discriminating colors which differ in their blue content: blue-whites, blue-grays, green-blue greens, and red-purples. Ageing also reduces the amount of light reaching the photoreceptors. All colors will be dimmer and visual resolution lower — a moderately bright yellow may appear brownish, and dimmer blues will appear black. When designing for elderly people, use bright colors and make sure that brightness contrast is especially high.

■ CHOOSING AND PREPARING ILLUSTRATIONS

Briefing an illustrator or photographer

Graphic designers and illustrators have much in common. The most famous illustrator-turned-graphic designer, Milton Glaser, has always encouraged illustrators to do as he has done. Not only will you earn more money as a graphic designer, but you can then commission yourself to do the illustrations! Be that as it may, not every graphic designer can draw as well as he, nor is every illustrator as passionately interested in type.

A graphic designer may commission artwork and photography, or may be presented with a package of words and pictures to put together according to a design brief. If the graphic designer is involved at an early stage with the commissioning of illustration and photography, a careful eye can be kept on the quality and content of the finished job.

Perhaps the two most important pieces of information an illustrator needs to know are the deadline date, and the size of the artwork required. The content and style will be different for each job, and the choice of a particular illustrator or photographer will be made on their ability to deliver what you want, on time, and to a professional standard. There are, however, some further general principles that can be outlined.

There are two kinds of original copy. Flat artwork from the hand of the illustrator and photographic prints are termed **reflection copy**: they are viewed by reflected light. Color transparencies and film positives are known as **transmission copy**.

Almost all copy is scanned in and separated on a drum scanner nowadays, so try to encourage illustrators to produce their artwork on flexible media that will wrap around the drum. Check with the repro house the maximum size of artwork that the scanner can take. Black-and-white line artwork is often scanned as grayscale, so if you want black line, make a point of telling the repro house that black line is what you want! An illustrator may use different densities of black ink for the outline and solid color. Under the process camera, all would come out as solid black; but scanned as grayscale, you might end up with an illustration in two distinct unintended shades of gray.

Many illustrators like to work on rigid board. There is a kind of board available with a surface that can be peeled off from a rigid base and then wrapped around the drum of a scanner, but this is not to be recommended. Originals sometimes get damaged and some kinds of paint crack, so it is wise to have a transparency made first, and for this to be used in the scanning process. Bear in mind, however, that there will be a loss of quality whenever an original is copied.

Where you do have commissioning power, and when selecting images that already exist — from picture libraries, for example — insist on the following:
• Line reflection copy, such as cartoons, should be in black Indian

ink on good quality artboard, with any corrections made in process white paint. The original should be drawn no larger than twice-up, unless the lines are simple and thick enough to withstand reduction below 50 percent. Scratchboard illustrations, with their sharp lines, generally reduce well. If a line-and-tone effect is required, for example in comic book illustration, the line work and lettering should be drawn on an acetate overlay, in register, over the tonal element.

• Halftone reflection copy, such as photographic prints or airbrush drawings, should have a wide tonal range with not too much contrast. Check for the correct exposure, the graininess, and whether the part of the image you require is correctly in focus. The original should ideally be same size and, at any rate, not more than half-up. Photographs should be printed on glossy paper.

If you have access to a slide scanner, or attachment to a flatbed scanner, it is possible to scan a negative directly into the computer, where it can then be turned positive using a program such as Photoshop.

Never risk scratch marks by attaching anything to a photograph with a paperclip or staple. If color copy is to be reproduced in black and white, be prepared for a loss in clarity and contrast.

Artwork intended for flat color should be supplied in black on a baseboard, with each color drawn, in register, on a separate overlay. Artwork in which the separate flat colors do not touch or overlap can be drawn on the same board, provided that the portions to be printed in different colors are clearly indicated on an overlay. Photoshop is not very flat-color friendly — you have to save the flat-color element in black line or grayscale and color it within the page-layout program. Some designers have been known to use the duotone function to produce flat-color separations. You can also allocate a process color to a flat color and tell the printer to substitute a Pantone color on the press, but it will be impossible then to produce meaningful color proofs. FreeHand and Illustrator are much better at handling two- and three-color work.

Artwork in full color should not contain any fluorescent paints or inks as they do not reproduce well when separated into process colors. Nor do very pure secondary colors, such as purples and lime greens.

• Halftone transmission copy, such as photographic transparencies, should be chosen on a lightbox equipped with standard lighting conditions. Transparencies come in various formats: 35 mm, 5 in x 4 in, and 10 in x 8 in, for example. Because they will undergo considerable enlargement when reproduced, choose as large a format as you can afford. Check for graininess — it will increase as the transparency is enlarged. And because a transparency's tonal range will be compressed by the printing process, look for detail in both shadow areas and highlights. Check for correct exposure (ask the photographer to "bracket" the exposures, by shooting at apertures above and below the optimum f-stop, and choose the best result). Look, too, for the **color cast** found on a subject photographed against a strongly colored background. Also, scrutinize the transparencies for fingerprints, scratches, and other blemishes. Colors can be corrected to some degree at the repro house, and some retouching can be done using Photoshop, but beware — you will be charged for the service.

Ensure that each transparency is right reading — the repro house will assume that the image is correct when the transparency is viewed with the **emulsion side** facing away from you. This is not always the case, especially if the "original" is a duplicate. Double check by supplying them with a sketch of the subject on a traced overlay.

Scaling and cropping

Copy to be reproduced at exactly the same size as the original is called same size and marked **S/S**. More often than not, artwork will have to be reduced in size to fit your layout, and transparencies enlarged. This is called **scaling**, or **reproportioning**.

The simplest and clearest way to indicate the required size of artwork or photographs is to mark the limits of the image with a double-headed arrow and write "Reduce to 4 inches" or whatever you want the width (or height) to be. To avoid damaging the artwork, this is best done on an overlay, or flap, of layout paper or tissue. If you are using only a portion of the photograph or artwork, the area you need can also be outlined on the overlay. This is called **cropping**, or recomposing.

It must be said, however, that few photographers and probably no

3.23 A reproduction calculator — a device for working out the size an illustration will appear on the page once it has been reduced or enlarged.

illustrators like to have their work cropped by a graphic designer. Some sensitivity and diplomacy is required if it just has to be done. It is much better to have the size and shape of the illustration or photograph worked out in advance so that the illustrator or photographer can be briefed thoroughly. Obviously, photographs come in standard formats, and some cropping is inevitable. But give the photographers a chance to crop their images and you will be rewarded with better results.

If you are ever tempted, for the sake of a composition, to invert a photograph laterally, i.e. turn it into a mirror image of itself (and it can be done quite simply at the stripping-in stage), get out your loupe and watch out for the give-aways. These include obvious ones such as lettering and signs, but also more subtle telltales such as clocks and maps in the background, or the position of a man's suit breast pocket, or specialized equipment with controls and buttons that the reader will recognize as inverted. Some of these can be retouched, but it is often better to prevent potential embarrassment by leaving well alone, or paying out to have the photograph reshot.

It is difficult to draw **crop marks** accurately on such a small area as a portion of a 35 mm transparency, and it is better to make an enlarged photocopy, and to mark that with your instructions. These copies can be placed in position and at the correct size on the artwork (more on this in Chapter 4, p. 117).

It is often useful to know the size an image will appear once it has been reduced or enlarged, so that you can plan your layout with confidence that the scanned image or dropped-in color separations will fit. There are two methods for making this calculation. The first is to use a **reproduction calculator** or **proportional scale** (Fig. **3.23**). This is a kind of circular slide rule, comprising two discs that rotate relative to each other. Find the width of the original on the inner wheel, line up the width of the space into which is has to fit on the outer wheel, and you will be able to read off the corresponding reduction or enlargement in height. It will also give you another useful figure — the percentage reduction or enlargement.

An ordinary pocket calculator can also be used to determine the size of an illustration after reduction or enlargement — just substitute your figures into the following formula:

$$\frac{\text{height after reduction (or enlargement)}}{\text{height of original}} = \frac{\text{width after reduction}}{\text{width of original}}$$

Suppose you have a photograph 10 inches high by 8 inches wide that you have to reduce so that it will fit a column 3 inches wide. What will be the resulting height after reduction? How much room should you allocate in the layout?

Using the above formula:

$$\frac{x}{10} = \frac{3}{8}$$

Now, cross-multiply and divide to find x, thus:

$8x = 30$
$x = 30 \div 8 = 3.75$ in

The main thing to remember when using a regular pocket

calculator is to ensure that your units of measurement are consistent. *All* units must be in either inches, millimeters, or picas — but never a mixture!

To calculate the percentage reduction or enlargement, divide the intended width (or height) by the width (or height) of the original and multiply the result by 100. In this example:

$$\text{percentage reduction} = \frac{3}{8} \times 100$$

$$= 37.5\%$$

Percentages can seem confusing at first: 100 percent, for example, is same size; 50 percent is half the width or height, but a quarter the area; 200 percent is twice the width or height, but four times the area. If you increase or reduce the width, do not forget that the height will also be increased or reduced, in direct proportion. When in doubt, always mark the copy with the width (or height) at which you want the image to appear. Writing exact measurements on the copy will also make it easier to check that the correct reduction or enlargement has been made when you receive your picture proofs.

The diagonal method (Fig. **3.24**) uses geometry to help you to work out the final size of your scaled artwork. Draw a rectangle around the cropped area on the overlay, using a setsquare (triangle) or transparent grid to make sure that the corners are square. Protect the original, and draw a diagonal from the bottom left corner to the top right. If the artwork is to be reduced, measure the width you want it to appear along the bottom edge of the

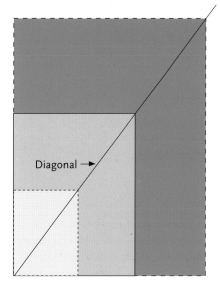

Diagonal →

rectangle using the bottom left corner as your starting point, and draw a vertical from the other end, up to meet the diagonal. Where these two lines intersect, draw a horizontal line to meet the left vertical edge of your original box. This is the height that your scaled artwork will appear when reproduced.

If the artwork or transparency is to be enlarged, trace the crop outline to the bottom left corner of a piece of paper, draw the diagonal as before, but extending it beyond the crop rectangle. Also extend the bottom edge of the box and the left

vertical. Now measure off the intended width of the enlargement, draw a line vertically to meet the extended diagonal, and read off the enlarged height. A lightbox will make the process a lot easier.

Most pictures have to fit a specified width — a column width, for example. This method can, however, be used to calculate the width of an image that has to fit a specific height.

Always label illustrations, and do so in soft pencil, preferably a non-reproducing light-blue one, or in fibertip pen (checking first that it will not bleed through the overlay). Do not stack photographs while the marks on the back are still wet without first protecting the front, and never write on the back of a photograph with a ballpoint pen. A greasy pencil, such as a Chinagraph, is best for writing on glossy surfaces. If you will be handling a lot of transparencies, invest in some lint-free cotton gloves to avoid introducing fingerprints on to the images. And always remove transparencies from glass mounts before sending them to the printers — they will break, damaging the transparency, and showering the recipient with thin shards of glass.

3.25 The main difference between "paint" and "draw" software lies in how the image seen on the screen is stored in the memory. A paint document is a bitmap — just a representation of the screen — whereas a draw document is stored in terms of the points, lines, and formulas used to create it. Thus a draw document is not restricted to the resolution of the screen, and the image can be "deconstructed" for editing and amendment.

Desktop scanning

Artwork can be scanned in the studio using a desktop scanner. The quality of the scanned images produced will be much lower than that of illustrations originated on the scanners found in repro houses, but they are improving, and coming down in price all the time.

Desktop color scanners and special slide scanners are not always up to repro quality, but they do have a place in giving the graphic designer an idea of how the layout is going to work. And they are being used as a creative tool by a new breed of computer graphics illustrators. With digital cameras, it is possible to bypass even the scanning process, and input digitized images direct to the computer (see Fig. 5.15).

Drawing and painting by computer

On a computer such as the Macintosh, there are two different ways of producing illustrations, referred to as "draw" and "paint" (Fig. **3.25**). A "paint" document is stored in the computer's memory as a bitmap, a one-to-one array corresponding to the pixels (dots) appearing on the screen — although the image can be much larger than the size of the screen. In a **paint program**, a circle intersected by a line, say, is just a pattern of dots and can only be moved en bloc. It is not possible to edit "globally" — modify every circle in a picture, for example — using just one command.

A "draw" document has more in-built "intelligence." It is stored in the computer's memory as a display list of the points and lines that make up the illustration, plus the formulas for any circles, ellipses, and curves. This is also known as object-oriented graphics, because every object — a circle, line, or curve — can be accounted for separately. In draw programs, it is possible to move the line without affecting the circle. And because the lines are not stored in terms of bitmaps, the output resolution to, say, a PostScript plotter is independent of the image's resolution.

MacPaint was the first program for the Macintosh to use bitmapped graphics, and was good for producing freehand, irregularly shaped objects and airbrush effects.

MacDraw was the original object-oriented draw program.

The original **paint system** was the Quantel Paintbox (Fig. **3.27**), best known for producing special effects for broadcast television. With ever more powerful computers and cheaper memory, much of the functionality of the Paintbox can be reproduced by programs such as Adobe Photoshop. There are also paint systems around that do their best to emulate real paint. Corel's Painter, or example, can simulate so-called "natural media" — the wet appearance of oil paint and watercolor — and produce convincing chalk and pastel effects through the use of a pressure-sensitive stylus.

It is as a medium of photomontage, however, that paint systems such as Adobe Photoshop are being

3.26 This "paint" illustration by Gary Thompson was created using Photoshop to combine multiple paint layers with typographic, EPS, and 3D elements

put to work in most design studios (Fig. **3.26**). Originally developed for **retouching** photographic images, Photoshop is now the de facto image-manipulation program. Here, so-called source or "reference material" (beware of copyright infringement!) can be scanned into the system, or "framegrabbed" by a video card, to be combined, manipulated, and recolored. This is analogous to sampling and remixing musical quotations to produce today's electronic dance music.

Some graphic designers also use paint systems as a concept design tool. If you are designing packaging for a new range of TV dinners, for example, a convincing illustration can be montaged from illustrations "grabbed" from cookery books or other sources. When the concept has been approved for go-ahead by the client, these roughs can be used as a brief for the commissioning of original illustration or photography.

The power of the computer as a conceptual tool is grossly under-

estimated. Some designers use it for nothing else, preferring to produce finished artwork traditionally, by hand. The computer allows you to play around with ideas — trying out different type, alternative positioning of elements, another color, and so on — for as long as your schedule will allow. As West Coast designer April Greiman says: "The paint never dries." And so long as you have the different versions, there is no chance of ever spoiling the original.

Retouching covers a multitude of sins: it can be as innocent as adding a few crocuses to a countryside scene, or it can be used to subvert reality completely, placing well-known characters in compromising positions, for example. Thankfully, it is mainly used to clean up images or as a purely creative medium — in fact, just as graphic designers use any other form of

3.27 The Quantel Paintbox was originally designed for television graphics. The Graphic Paintbox has a much higher resolution, more suitable for print applications.

illustration (Fig. **3.28**). What is certain, however, is that photographs are retouched routinely because it is so easy to do. And the adage that "the camera never lies" has little credibility.

Draw programs such as Adobe Illustrator and Macromedia's FreeHand are now closely linked to page-layout packages. They can be used not only for color or black-and-white illustration, but to manipulate type too (Figs. **3.29** and **3.30**).

Both use controllable freeform curves (called Bézier curves) which can be manipulated to produce complex drawings. Scanned images or bitmapped drawings from a paint program can be "imported" and traced over. However, better results can be obtained by using a specialized tracing program, such as Adobe Streamline.

Other tools are used to create boxes, lines, ellipses, and corners at any angle. Layers (overlays) are available, so that the drawing can be split up into separate elements which can be displayed and edited individually. Line attributes, pattern fills, and colors can be saved on a computer style sheet and applied to other elements later to maintain a consistency throughout a series of illustrations. There are commands for rotating, scaling, mirroring, skewing, and stretching elements. Text can be wrapped around a line or shape. Drawings thus created can be exported directly, as **EPS** (Encapsulated PostScript) files to page-layout packages such as QuarkXPress or Adobe InDesign. There they can be combined with text originated on a word-processing system.

Clip art (Fig. **3.31**) is royalty-free artwork that can be bought ready-made and en masse on a CD-rom or from the internet and incorporated into your layouts. It has always been around in book form, to be copied at will, but lately has proliferated. Some is good, most is awful, and none of it is either original or unique. It should be used with discretion, and never in work where clients are under the impression that they are paying for original artwork. Clip art maps can usually be copied with confidence, especially when they are to be customized in a program such as FreeHand or Illustrator.

Three-dimensional design programs are also increasingly

3.29 Illustrator Peter Greenwood created "Scooter girl" using Illustrator 9 on a Mac G4: note the exhaust smoke — it *is* possible to render almost airbrush effects in a vector program.

SIMPLIFY YOUR ILLUSTRATIONS

A lean and efficient illustration from FreeHand or Illustrator will output faster at the repro service bureau and save you time and money (they'll put complex jobs to the back of the queue so it doesn't hold up other jobs). Use straight lines in preference to curves whenever you can. Or use paths with as few points as possible. The number of segments the output device uses to simulate curves depends on the "flatness" value. The flatness is a number between 0 and 100 and is the difference between the polygon the output device draws and the mathematical curve. The higher the number, the rougher the curve but the faster it will print. A value of 3 should be your default, but you can probably get away with a much bigger number before detecting a loss of quality. And delete any object you can't see in preview mode — it might be hidden behind another object, but it will still have to be processed!

being used by illustrators, especially in comic books, where cartoon characters are viewed from different angles and against different backgrounds (Fig. **3.32**). Programs such as Corel's Bryce can be used to create fantastic fractal landscapes for use as backgrounds.

More and more, illustrators will be creating work on computer — images that can be shipped directly to page make-up programs with no intermediate artwork needed. There will always be a place, however, for original illustration and photography produced using traditional materials, and today's graphic designer will need to know how to make the best use of both, for a long time to come.

Copyright

What is copyright? Put simply, it is the right to prevent copying of your work. It protects the form your work takes, but not the underlying idea. Copyright for designers cuts both ways — it protects your intellectual property, but also protects the creator of the piece of work you may be tempted to copy.

Copyright is a property right — that of intellectual property — in that it can be bought, sold, inherited, willed, and leased. You can assign it, license it, or you can sell it. In some countries, such as

Germany, however, copyright is an inalienable right, which cannot be bought or sold.

How do you acquire and protect your copyright? Well, you don't really have to, as the only criterion to qualify in the case of an artistic work is that it must be original. Work that you copy (your own, of course) has a new copyright in each version you do. The main exception is in "work made for hire," when you are in full-time employment and in which case the employer, and not the employee, is considered to be the creator. It is advisable, however, to append a copyright notice to your work thus: © 2001 John Doe.

In the United States, copyright protection is provided under Title 17 of the US Code and the 1976 Copyright Act. In addition, certain authors of works of visual art have the rights of attribution and integrity. While federal copyright law is fairly specific, state variations make nationwide advice difficult to provide. The law was written before computers became commonplace, but computer-generated work is covered.

Failure to protect copyrights can lead to fines of up to $10,000 per infringement. Some state laws provide even greater fines. However, copyright law does provide some protection to intermediaries such as

3.30 A completely different use of a "draw" program is shown in this image by Henry Lyndsey — a dodo containing the names of 2000 endangered animals (right). It is a virtuoso demonstration of FreeHand's ability to set text along freeform lines.

3.31 Samples of digital clip art from the Clipper Creative Art Service.

designers and printers. But the burden falls on you to prove that you were misled, a sometimes difficult and expensive proposition.

Measures such as requiring clients to affirm that the materials you are about to incorporate into a design are in the public domain, that the copyright is owned by the customer, or that the customer has received the copyright owner's permission to print the work can all help establish proof of innocence. Include a release in your contracts (the US Copyright Office website: lcweb.loc.gov/copyright/ provides an example), and be certain that the customer understands the significance and the consequences for you and them if a copyright violation charge is brought.

In the United Kingdom, the 1988 Copyright, Designs and Patents Act gave works of art new moral rights, aimed at protecting their paternity (the right of the creator of the work to be credited as such) and integrity (the right not to have the work subjected to derogatory treatment or to be falsely attributed). The right to be identified as the author of the work can be asserted but cannot be assigned to anyone else. It can however be waived in writing.

How long does copyright last? Until 70 years after your death in most cases. Your children and grandchildren will probably be able to earn a fortune out of your work even if you don't!

3.32 Pepe Moreno used three-dimensional graphics combined with paint software to produce the artwork for the DC Comics graphic novel *Batman: Digital Justice*.

■ SUMMARY

Illustrations can be line or tone. If tone, they must be screened to convert the image into a pattern of dots for reproduction. Artwork can be drawn or painted conventionally, or created on a computer. Photographs can come in one of two forms: as reflection copy prints, or as transmission copy transparencies. Before origination, they will need to be scaled, and maybe cropped, so as to fit the size and shape of their position on the page layout. And they can be manipulated by computer, either on the level of merely correcting or changing colors, or in terms of undergoing more drastic treatment, using the image as a basis for a photomontage.

Whether you choose the mechanical or the digital method for the production of your illustrations will depend quite a lot on the processes being employed, and on the type of project. Conventionally drawn line work, such as cartoon illustrations, will have a sparkle and a fluidity that a computer program is unable to replicate. On the other hand, the consistent line weights and perfect

geometry of a computer "draw" program are ideal for technical diagrams. But as desktop scanners come down in price, a hybrid approach may rule: scanning-in line art drawn conventionally, to be manipulated further on the computer and output as a file ready to be placed in a page-layout program.

The constraints on black-and-white and color illustrations are different. If you are using a computer, it is easy enough to scan in black-and-white artwork and place it straight on to your page layout. Where photographs are concerned, the desired quality will be the decisive factor as you choose between scanning-in a coarsely screened picture or leaving its origination to the repro house. With a computer-generated or stored illustration, there is the distinct advantage that the all-important artwork cannot get lost or damaged in the mail. It can even be sent to its destination down the telephone lines. And once the image is inside the system, it can be used over and over in different shapes and forms.

For color work, illustrations usually arrive in the form of transparencies, though original artwork can produce much better results. Whichever form they take, they must be flexible enough to be wrapped around the drum of the scanner at the repro house or printer. Desktop scanners can be used to input images intended for photomontage and other forms of creative retouching. Alternatively, the scanner can produce low-resolution scans to indicate positions and crops for illustrations that will later be processed at the repro house, on better-quality equipment, as we shall discover in the next chapter.

You must be aware that colors can mean different things to different cultures, and the psychology and symbolism of color can affect our behavior. We must also take into account the needs of disabled people, especially the elderly and people with color blindness.

Computers have made it easy for anyone with the right skills and software to copy and modify text, artwork, and photographic images. As a result, knowing all there is to know about copyright has never been more important.

LUCILLE TENAZAS

LIFE STORY ■ Lucille Tenazas was born in 1953 and raised in the Philippines. She learned at an early age to accommodate both Eastern and Western ways of looking at the world: the strong US military presence familiarized her with Western culture, and she learned English alongside her native Tagalog.

Tenazas's studies in the Philippines focused on fine and liberal arts. This, coupled with design work experience at the pharmaceutical companies Bristol–Myers and Smith Kline Corporation, led her to postgraduate study in design in the United States.

Tenazas applied to Cranbrook Academy of Art in 1979, but after an initial rejection, went to California, where she studied for two semesters at the California College of Arts and Crafts (CCAC). After replenishing her portfolio and developing her skills in drawing and painting, she entered Cranbrook at the second attempt. She brought with her the visual language of California's New Wave — bright colors, geometric shapes, and a rich textural surface.

> **"My expression lies in the meaning, form, and content of the language."**

Tenazas took from Cranbook its way of thinking about design rather than an established visual style. She moved away from her colleagues' "type 'n' stripe aesthetic" to one that displayed an elegance and formal resolution.

Lucille Tenazas is principal of her own design firm based in San Francisco. Tenazas Design was responsible for the identity for the Center for the Arts at Yerba Buena Gardens, San Francisco, and was also involved in the typographic design of the New England Holocaust Memorial in Boston. Clients include the National Endowment for the Arts, the San Francisco Museum of Modern Art, California College of Arts and Crafts, Esprit, Rizzoli International, Metropolitan Furniture, Champion Paper, the Pacific Film Archive, architectural organization 2AES, and IDEO Product Development.

She is currently chair of the newly established MFA program in Design at CCAC. In 1995, she was honored as one of the "*I.D.* Forty", in *I.D.* magazine's third annual selection of leading design innovators. From 1996 to 1998 she served as national president of the American Institute of Graphic Arts (AIGA). Retrospectives of her work have been exhibited at the San Francisco Museum of Modern Art (1996) and at the Ayala Museum in her native Philippines (1998). In 1998, Lucille Tenazas became a member of the Alliance Graphique Internationale (AGI), joining a select few designers invited to represent the United States.

WORKSTATION

- Teal Triggs, "Layers of Language," *Eye*, 17/95, pp. 62–71
- Interview by Noreen Rei Fukumori, *Communication Arts*, March/April 1996, pp. 80–89
- Interview by Brad Rhodes: casa17.pac.utexas.edu/pointblank.tenazas.html
- Luanne Brown, "Designers Who Don't Do the Web": msdn.microsoft.com/ workshop/design/experts/holdouts.asp

MANIFESTO ■ **A Language of Clarity**

"My early work did not investigate language as a vehicle to explore another dimension," says Tenazas. "I started to see words as objects with a physicality that can be held and touched, and I seek to empower their meaning. My expression lies in the meaning, form, and content of the language. I'm interested in addressing the client's needs, but in ways that provoke the viewer to complete an unfinished idea that has been presented to them. This is one reason why my work has many layers.

"When I first came to the United States, my interest in English was as a form of verbal communication. My interest in the layers of language has evolved over the past six years. Since I came to this understanding later in my career, it has affected my way of teaching. The whole idea of authorship is important. I try to instil in my students that you have to make your voice heard. I feel that if you are aware of who you are, then you can ultimately take on the identities and problems a client may pose yet not lose your own voice."

Tenazas's design work spans 25 years, two continents, and two coasts and reflects an interest in the complexity of language and the overlapping relationship of meaning, form, and content. By merging the poetic and the pragmatic, she achieves a fluid and flexible approach to design, one that is human as well as critical.

Some designers fear that any subjectivity detracts from the effective communication of the client's message. But a designer's subjective voice gives the work distinction, and design that suppresses that voice becomes a dry exercise in problem-solving. Tenazas acknowledges the conflict: "Whether working for myself or for others, I've always seen opportunities to do something new. The secret is to answer the client's needs as well as satisfy my desire to further my own creative exploration."

Tenazas has also been quoted as having a dislike of computers and the internet (www.tenazasdesign.com was still under construction at the time of writing). Instead of working in front of a computer, Tenazas draws by hand, then has one of her staff members enter the image into a Mac.

"I'm not anti-technology. It's more a question of what I have an affinity for. I do what I feel most comfortable doing," Tenazas says.

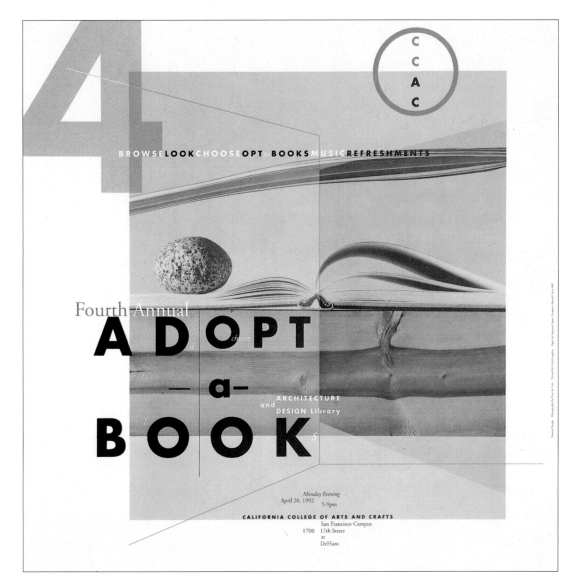

▲ **Adopt a Book**, poster for California College of Arts and Crafts, 1992. 18 in x 18 in. The printing is offset lithography and the paper is Simpson Evergreen Almond Cover 80#. As in her other posters, Tenazas uses a minimum of compositional elements to convey meanings and associations. She plays word games, both through the typography and the selection of evocative words, coaxing the reader through a subtle mental layering of interpretations.

Says Tenazas: "The Adopt a Book poster was designed just after we started working with computers. This was before any of us were adept at using the computer to produce the final mechanical art. I would say approximately 50 percent of it was designed on the computer and the other 50 percent, using more traditional methods. The mechanical production for this piece was done on an actual-size board, with acetate overlays and other color indications. The color breaks were done with color pencils.

"The typefaces used in the poster are Futura and Adobe Garamond, with PageMaker used for layout. The photograph was not commissioned for this project, but was appropriated from a previous project: a paper promotion brochure. The photographer is Peter De Lory, from Seattle, Washington.

"The Adopt a Book poster announces the fourth annual fundraising event for the library of the School of Architecture and Design at California College of Arts and Crafts. In an effort to expand the library's collection, the College sponsored a social event for architects and designers. Two Bay-area bookstores provided a display of books for potential donors to browse through and hand-pick their donations. The wide range of books on display included classical and contemporary work, as well as theoretical and technical texts. Aesthetically, the poster reveals its elements through repeated "readings," unraveling over time. The sparse photographic image is suggestive, open to interpretation. The grain in the wood below the open book and the leaves above it refer to the origins of paper. The typography adds a subtle playful tone, pulling apart words and magnifying parts, in keeping with the spirit of the event."

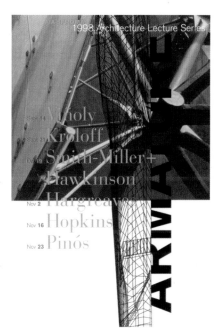

FOUR **PREPRESS**

PREPRESS

Prepress is the part of the print process in which all the design elements — the words and the pictures — are assembled into a unified whole. It is the stage in print production that ends with the making of lithographic plates, silkscreens, or gravure cylinders. This marks the point of no return, after which the presses begin to roll.

But in recent years that decisive moment has shifted. The involvement of the graphic designer has been extended, and is now much more closely tied to the outcome. A publication used to be "put to bed" with the dispatch of the mechanicals to the printer or repro house. Now, as all the data that makes up a page is digitized and stored electronically, it is feasible (though not always desirable) to make essential changes much later in the process — right up until press time, in some cases.

This chapter begins by covering the principles and terminology of layout, with tips for avoiding common design pitfalls. We take a look at grids and their usefulness in providing structure to a page; they save time too. Then imposition schemes are explained — a good grounding in how and where pages are arranged on printing plates or cylinders is important for effective prepress planning. We move on to repro and discuss the various methods of checking picture proofs, and outline what you can discover from a detailed examination of a proof's color bar.

Until only a few years ago, graphic designers could send corrected galleys, a rough layout, and marked-up illustrations along to the repro shop and expect the rest of the job to be completed by others. Now it is difficult to believe that books and magazines could possibly be produced *without* the use of computers!

Digital prepress can roughly be divided into what you the designer can do in your studio with a computer, desktop scanner, and color printer, and what still has to be done at the repro service bureau or printers with their high-end drum scanners, RIPs, imagesetters, and digital proofers. But this divide is blurring all the time, and many large design practices are effectively bringing repro in-house.

¶ Type *Tymes*

An occasional Newsletter for graphic designers, printers and typographers that is published once a millennium, if ever at all

Alphabet soup

by IMA WORDSMITH

Writing text that is meant to represent body type in layouts and type specimen books is probably the most difficult task a writer can ever be asked to undertake. Ideally, the text should contain examples of all the letters and sorts: in Roman, *italic* and **bold** and include a range of words of average length so that it looks right. Above all, it shouldn't draw attention to itself. The text is not meant to be read, merely looked at – but invariably someone somewhere will grab a magnifying glass, read it and then criticize any attempted jokes therein.

Some designers take the easy route and use real or bogus Latin text, most often a famous piece of text that begins: Lorem ipsum dolor sit amet, consectetur adipscing elit, diam nonnumy eiusmod tempor incidunt ut labore et dolo... These are, according to the FAQ (frequently asked questions) of the newsgroup comp.fonts, the slightly jumbled remnants of a passage from Cicero's *de Finibus Bonorum et Malorum*, written in 45BC, a treatise on the theory of ethics, which begins: 'Neque porro quisquam est qui dolorem ipsum quia dolor sit amet, consectetur, adipisci velit...' There is no one who loves pain itself, who seeks after it and wants to have it, simply because it is pain.]

This text has been the industry's standard dummy text ever since some printer in the 1500s took a galley of type and scrambled it to make a type specimen book; it has survived letter-by-letter essentially unchanged except for an occasional 'ing' or 'y' thrown in. The nonsense Latin was as incomprehensible as Greek: so the phrase 'it's all Greek to me' and the term 'greeking' have common roots!

But this does contain some strange, to English eyes, letter combinations. Few, if any English words contain the sequence 'eiu', for example. When short pieces of text are called for, try to make a sentence containing all the letters of the alphabet with as few duplications as possible. These are called *pangrams*.

The classic pangram used by typographers is: 'The quick brown fox jumps over a lazy dog'. Good score: all 24 letters of the alphabet in a 33-word sentence that makes sense. 'Pack my box with five dozen liquor jugs' is better, with one letter less. Another common albeit longer one is: 'How razorback-jumping frogs can level six piqued gymnasts!'

This one is not so good: 'In the vocation of typesetting, dexterity can be gained by means of quiet, judicious and zealous work'. It is more appropriate to the printing trade, but comprises 83 letters! And what about this: 'Wherever civilization extends, the services of expert and judicious typographers and printers must always be quickly called upon'. Is that grammatically correct? I don't think so. Or this: 'The bank recognizes this claim as quite valid and just, so we expect full payment'. Hmm.

Probably the shortest French pangram, at 29 letters, is: 'Whisky vert: jugez cinq fox d'aplomb'. Some pangrams of exactly 26 letters do exist, but rely heavily on odd Welsh and Hebrew words, such as cwm (a Welsh valley) and qoph (the nineteenth letter of the Hebrew alphabet) and, of course, proper nouns (which could in fact be made up from the left-over letters): 'Vext cwm fly zing jabs Kurd qoph' is a good

Page 1

¶ Type *Tymes*

An occasional Newsletter for graphic designers, printers and typographers that is published once a millennium, if ever at all

Alphabet soup

The classic pangram used by typographers is: 'The quick brown fox jumps over a lazy dog'. Good score: all 24 letters of the alphabet in a 33-word sentence that makes sense.

by IMA WORDSMITH

Writing text that is meant to represent body type in layouts and type specimen books is probably the most difficult task a writer can ever be asked to undertake. Ideally, the text should contain examples of all the letters and sorts: in Roman, *italic* and **bold** and include a range of words of average length so that it looks right. Above all, it shouldn't draw attention to itself. The text is not meant to be read, merely looked at – but invariably someone somewhere will grab a magnifying glass, read it and then criticize any attempted jokes therein.

Some designers take the easy route and use real or bogus Latin text, most often a famous piece of text that begins: Lorem ipsum dolor sit amet, consectetur adipscing elit, diam nonnumy eiusmod tempor incidunt ut labore et dolo... These are, according to the FAQ (frequently asked questions) of the newsgroup comp.fonts, the slightly jumbled remnants of a passage from Cicero's *de Finibus Bonorum et Malorum*, written in 45BC, a treatise on the theory of ethics, which begins: 'Neque porro quisquam est qui dolorem ipsum quia dolor sit amet, consectetur, adipisci velit...' There is no one who loves pain itself, who seeks after it and wants to have it, simply because it is pain.]

This text has been the industry's standard dummy text ever since some printer in the 1500s took a galley of type and scrambled it to make a type specimen book; it has survived letter-by-letter essentially unchanged except for an occasional 'ing' or 'y' thrown in. The nonsense Latin was as incomprehensible as Greek: so the phrase 'it's all Greek to me' and the term 'greeking' have common roots!

Page 1

4.1 Layouts can be symmetrical — with almost everything centered — or asymmetrical, or can combine elements of both approaches. The look you decide upon is very much dependent on the sort of job in hand, the message you wish to get across, and the fashion at the time.

◼ LAYOUT

In design, all rules are there to be broken. But first you have to know what they are. Most graphic designers are, so to speak, in the fashion business, and if asymmetrical or off-center designs are in vogue this year, then maybe a symmetrical or centered design will get noticed (Fig. **4.1**). Whenever someone writes down the rules, you can bet that someone else will come along before the ink is dry to rewrite them.

Having said that, however, there are some rules that endure and, for the majority of jobs, the desire will not be to shock, but to communicate ideas clearly, in a visual language accessible and understandable to all.

Very few designers are given a completely free hand — an open brief — to design what they will. There are always constraints, and therein lies the challenge: how to be different and eye-catching, while getting the message across, to time and to a budget. The client will expect the design to relate to the job it has to do — an annual report for a prestigious company will look very different, for example, from a newspaper advertisement for a cut-price corner store.

Designers must develop skills in communicating their concepts to the client clearly and unambiguously, through presentations, which may include rough sketches and more polished visualizations. Designers are also sometimes asked to help "sell" an idea to a client's clients by producing highly finished mock-ups or dummies that will convey a flavor of how the printed product will look.

What equipment do you need to get started?

- ✔ a sturdy tabletop or drawing board
- ✔ a pad of layout paper
- ✔ a supply of fibertip pens and soft black pencils
- ✔ a clean plastic eraser
- ✔ a pad of tissue or acetate for overlays
- ✔ a non-reproducing light-blue pencil
- ✔ a blue greasy pencil (Chinagraph) for writing on glossy surfaces
- ✔ a surgical scalpel or craft knife (such as an X-acto)
- ✔ a "self-healing" cutting mat
- ✔ a straight metal edge
- ✔ rubber cement and spatula or spray mount aerosol adhesive
- ✔ low-tack masking tape or matte frosted "magic" tape
- ✔ a large, soft brush
- ✔ talcum powder for degreasing and "lubricating" surfaces
- ✔ paper towels to mop up spillages
- ✔ process white for correcting mistakes
- ✔ sable or synthetic sable brushes, sizes 00, 1, and 3
- ✔ a loupe
- ✔ a lightbox conforming to standard lighting conditions
- ✔ a proportional scale, or calculator
- ✔ a stainless-steel pica rule or plastic typescale
- ✔ a geometry set with compasses, setsquare (triangle), and protractor for measuring angles
- ✔ a selection of type specimens
- ✔ a selection of paper samples
- ✔ a Pantone color fan and swatches
- ✔ a computer: an Apple Macintosh, IBM PC, or PC compatible such as a Compaq
- ✔ a high-definition monitor, preferably of large format (17 in/432 mm or more)
- ✔ a mouse (and mouse pad) or other pointing device, such as a rolling ball or digitizer
- ✔ a desktop scanner
- ✔ a desktop printer
- ✔ applications software, such as QuarkXPress or Adobe InDesign; also useful are FreeHand, Illustrator, and Photoshop

4.2 The page has a vocabulary of its own to describe the various parts of its anatomy. The blank spaces — the margins — are as important as the image and type areas: at the top is the head; at the bottom, the foot; nearest the inside, the back edge; and nearest the extremities, the fore edge.

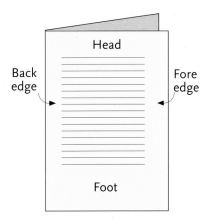

4.3 The standard proportions of medieval book pages, as discovered by the German designer Jan Tschichold. The text area and page size are in the ratio 2 : 3, the depth of text is equal to the width of the page, and the margins are in the proportions 2 (back edge) : 3 (head) : 4 (fore edge): 6 (foot).

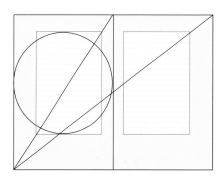

There are technical constraints in planning your layout. Paper comes in stock sizes, and so do printing plates. Insisting on so-called **bastard sizes** and non-standard shapes is wasteful of resources. Folding machines have their limitations, too. Packaging designers, in particular, may be restricted by the print technology — for example, only two non-overlapping colors may be allowable when printing a plastic container by flexography (see p. 189).

Thankfully, the offset litho process has given designers almost complete freedom over where the design elements — the type, line illustrations, and photographs — can be positioned on the page. And computer layout systems offer the chance to try out many more potential design solutions. So where do we start?

For magazine and book work, there are certain conventions to be observed. Here we are dealing with pages. Most pages are the shape of an upright rectangle, and this orientation is sometimes called **portrait**. A page with a width greater than its height is denoted **landscape**.

Page sizes are written thus: US Letter is 8$^1/_2$ inches wide and 11 inches tall, and is written 8$^1/_2$ x

11 in. The European equivalent is called A4 (see below), and its dimensions are written 210 x 297 mm. In inches, that is 8$^1/_4$ x 11$^3/_4$ in. In the United States and most of Europe, it is sometimes usual to write the width before the height; in the United Kingdom and the Far East the opposite is the case — the height precedes the width.

The white areas that frame the printed portion of the page are called the **margins** (Fig. **4.2**). The one at the top is the **head**; the one at the bottom is the **foot**. On the outer edge of the page is the **fore edge**; and the space between the printed material and the spine or fold is the **back edge**. The combined back edges of a double-page spread are called the **gutter**. This is also a term used for any vertical space — between two columns, for example. Traditionally, the foot is greater in depth than the head, and the fore edge approximately twice the width of the back edge. This means that

two facing pages will be united visually as a spread.

Much has been written about what constitutes "good" and "elegant" design. Our response to a layout is embedded in our cultural background. The German designer Jan Tschichold discovered that the margins of medieval manuscripts followed certain rules of proportion, which are still thought pleasing (Fig. **4.3**). The ratio of text area to page size was 2 : 3; the depth of the printed area was the same as the width of the page; and the back edge : head : fore edge : foot margins were of the ratio 2 : 3 : 4 : 6.

The famous **golden section** format of the Renaissance has proportions of 34 : 21 or 8.1 : 5. Superimposed on to a sheet of US Letter stock, the golden section is just over 1$^3/_4$ inches narrower (Fig. **4.4**).

4.4 The golden section is a proportion (34 : 21) that people through the ages and in different cultures have found pleasing. It has many parallels in nature — the way a snail's shell grows, for instance. Here, a sheet of paper to golden-section proportions is compared with US Letter and A4 sizes.

158   *Little Women*

'Here's a sweet prospect!' muttered Jo, slamming the stove door open, and poking vigorously among the cinders.

Having rekindled the fire, she thought she would go to market while the water heated. The walk revived her spirits; and, flattering herself that she had made good bargains, she trudged home again, after buying a very young lobster, some very old asparagus, and two boxes of acid strawberries. By the time she got cleared up, the dinner arrived, and the stove was red-hot. Hannah had left a pan of bread to rise, Meg had worked it up early, set it on the hearth for a second rising, and forgotten it. Meg was entertaining Sallie Gardiner in the parlour, when the door flew open, and a floury, crocky, flushed, and dishevelled figure appeared, demanding tartly:

'I say, isn't bread "riz" enough when it runs over the pans?'

Sallie began to laugh; but Meg nodded, and lifted her eyebrows as high as they would go, which caused the apparition to vanish, and put the sour bread into the oven without further delay. Mrs March went out, after peeping here and there to see how matters went, also saying a word of comfort to Beth, who sat making a winding sheet, while the dear departed lay in state in the domino-box. A strange sense of helplessness fell upon the girls as the grey bonnet vanished round the corner; and despair seized them, when, a few minutes later, Miss Crocker appeared, and said she'd come to dinner. Now, this lady was a thin, yellow spinster, with a sharp nose and inquisitive eyes, who saw everything, and gossiped about all she saw. They disliked her, but had been taught to be kind to her, simply because she was old and poor, and had few friends. So Meg gave her the easy-chair,

Experiments   159

and tried to entertain her, while she asked questions, criticized everything, and told stories of the people whom she knew.

Language cannot describe the anxieties, experiences, and exertions which Jo underwent that morning; and the dinner she served up became a standing joke. Fearing to ask any more advice, she did her best alone, and discovered that something more than energy and goodwill is necessary to make a cook. She boiled the asparagus for an hour, and was grieved to find the heads cooked off and the stalks harder than ever. The bread burnt black; for the salad-dressing so aggravated her, that she let everything else go till she had convinced herself that she could not make it fit to eat. The lobster was a scarlet mystery to her, but she hammered and poked, till it was unshelled, and its meagre proportions concealed in a grove of lettuce-leaves. The potatoes had to be hurried, not to keep the asparagus waiting, and were not done at last. The blancmange was lumpy, and the strawberries not as ripe as they looked, having been skilfully 'deaconed.'

'Well, they can eat beef, and bread and butter, if they are hungry; only it's mortifying to have to spend your whole morning for nothing,' thought Jo, as she rang the bell half an hour later than usual, and stood, hot, tired, and dispirited, surveying the feast spread for Laurie, accustomed to all sorts of elegance, and Miss Crocker, whose curious eyes would mark all failures, and whose tattling tongue would report them far and wide.

Poor Jo would gladly have gone under the table, as one thing after another was tasted and left; while Amy giggled, Meg looked distressed, Miss Crocker

4.7 While magazines and newspapers are meant to be browsed, books are generally intended for reading calmly and sequentially, hence the simple and comforting one-column format found in most fiction.

Grids

The layout of columns, margins, and area for text and images is usually marked out as a grid (Fig. **4.5**). It also shows the positions of any repeating headlines, or **running heads**, plus the page numbers, or folios. Before computers, a grid was drawn out on to a board or sheet of heavy paper in non-reproducing blue pencil for a one-off publication. On regular publications or books, the grid would be preprinted on layout sheets. A page-layout system will have an invisible (or visible — you choose) grid set to whatever increments of whatever units you

specify. Items can be made to snap to these grids. In addition, it is possible to set up non-printing guidelines on master pages (more of which later).

Type is set in columns. As discussed on p. 61, too wide a measure (column width) affects the readability of text. Try not to specify more than 12 words per line for books, or seven words for

newspapers and magazines. Novels and most small-format books are usually set in one column (Fig. **4.7**). If the single column goes right across the page, you are severely restricted as to where you can place any illustrations. Two or three columns give more flexibility to illustrated books. But there again, an art book may have just one relatively wide column, situated

4.5 The grid used for this book has been underprinted on this spread. A grid is the backbone of a good layout, and a great aid to consistency. It should not be a straitjacket, however. A too detailed and tight grid will result in a cold and static design.

4.6 This spread from *Spy* magazine uses a versatile five-column grid, with text at either one- or two-column measure. In the glossy magazines the principles of visual variety and stylishness are often hard to reconcile with the limited space available.

BLEEDS

Having an image, text, or block of color go right up to the edge of the page requires a **bleed**. The object to bleed must overlap the print area of the page by at least ⅛ inch (or 5 mm — check with your printer), so that when the page is trimmed the ink will truly reach the edge. Try to avoid fiddly bleeds that demand precise trimming. Adjust the design so that any accidental cropping looks intentional.

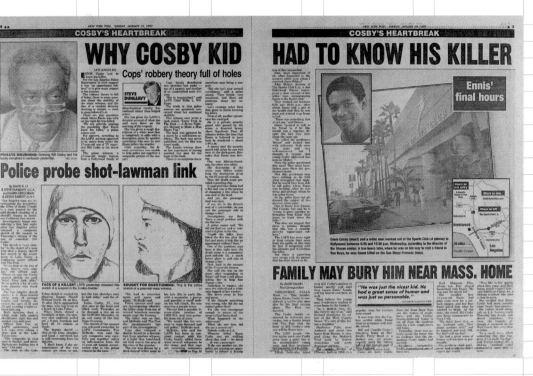

4.8 Like magazines, newspapers have relatively complex grids so as to look busy and up-to-the-minute. They tend to avoid white space altogether and use even more columns in order to cram as much text on to the page as possible. The six-column grid of this newspaper allows for flexible sizing of pictures.

asymmetrically, with lots of white space around it.

In newspapers and most popular magazines, white space means wasted space, and space is at a premium. So there will typically be many narrow columns to the page, with the possibility of photographs straddling two, three, or more of them (Figs **4.6** and **4.8**).

Horizontal lines built into the grid can be used to impose further discipline on the layout, allowing you to align the edges of photographs, say, with blocks of text. Six to eight horizontal divisions should be sufficient. Too many, and the layout will seem fussy, with no apparent thought-out design. Too few will not allow enough variety in the layout — it will appear static if the illustrations always fall in the same positions. Some grids may

show a numbered horizontal line marked out for each line of type.

A grid can seem confusing at first sight, but not all the lines and divisions have to be used on every page. Seen as an underlying structure, the grid can become an indispensable time-saving aid to producing clear and consistent layout, quickly and painlessly.

Design elements such as **crossheadings** (subheadings within a block of text), boxed copy, captions, rules, borders, and tint blocks are all devices for adding "color" to an otherwise "gray" layout. They will assist the readers' eyes, helping them follow the flow of the text, especially if it has been split to accommodate the placement of illustrations. And, if the copy does not fit exactly, they are useful and unobtrusive space fillers.

Keep your initial rough layout on paper and a complete copy of the galley proofs (see p. 46) for reference, to check that paragraphs have not been moved out of sequence or missed out altogether, and make any adjustments to the layout to avoid widows and orphans (see p. 43). The rest is up to you!

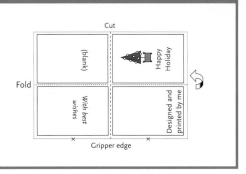

WORK AND TURN
If you are designing a greetings card, your first thought might be to put the front side of it two-up on a plate, and the reverse two-up on a second plate. You can, however, print both sides of the card using just one plate! How's it done? Using work and turn. Say you need 1000 cards: you print 500, wait until they're dry, flip the cards over and print the other side, making sure that the half of the plate with the verso is on the back of the half of the card's recto. Guillotine the result, and you have two stacks of cards, both printed both sides.

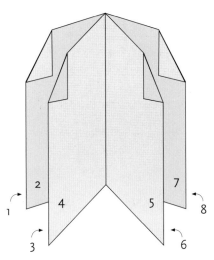

4.9 Imposition schemes can look complicated in diagram form, but all should become clear if you make a folded dummy in miniature — for your own benefit and to show the printer.

4.10 Sheetwork — the simplest form of imposition. Several pages are printed on one side of a sheet of paper, which is then turned over and printed again on the other side.

Imposition

Unless you are designing a solitary jar label, or a single-sided folder, it will help the printer considerably if you know about imposition. **Imposition** is the term used for the planning of **pagination** in folders, magazines, or books in a pattern such that when the printed sheet of paper is folded and trimmed, the resulting pages **back up** correctly and run consecutively. Page layout programs allow you to view the pages as spreads, but bear in mind that these may be broken apart when imposed. Some printers like to receive layouts and film in "printer's pairs" — like double-page spreads — if they are to do simple imposition themselves.

A sheet of paper has two sides: front and back (Fig. **4.9**). Fold it once and — to the printer, at least — it becomes a four-page folder. Fold it again, and once one of the short sides has been cut, it becomes an eight-page folder, comprising two folded sheets, one nesting inside another. Fold a third time, and the result after trimming is a 16-page folder. It is a curious fact that it is impossible to fold paper more than seven times, regardless of the size of the original sheet, or the thickness of the paper stock.

Most printers work in 16-page sections, with plates that print eight pages on each side. If your 16-page folder is numbered consecutively, with the first right-hand page as page 1, the first left as page 2, the numbers will fall as follows:

front: 1   4,5   8,9   12,13   16
back: 2,3   6,7   10,11   14,15

It is important to know which page numbers are on which side of the sheet, because you may wish to introduce flat color, or full color, into an otherwise black-and-white publication. It will save you money if you can restrict it to one side of the sheet (Fig. **4.10**).

The odd numbers are always, by convention, on the right-hand side; the even numbers on the left. In bookwork, right or front is called **recto**; left or back is called **verso**. A 16-page section of a book is called a **signature**, and each signature will usually be marked with a **backstep mark** — a letter, number, or black strip to help the binder **collate**, or assemble, the signatures in the correct order.

If the cover of a 16-page folder is to be printed in the same stock as the rest of the publication, as a **self cover**, the first page will be the outside front cover (or OFC), page 2 will be the inside front cover (or IFC), page 15 will be the inside back cover (or IBC), and page 16 will be the outside back cover (or OBC). If, however, the cover is to be printed in heavier stock, or if it alone is to be printed in color, then it will be treated as a four-page section, printed separately. This leaves you with 16 pages for the inside, making a 20-page publication.

Generally speaking, printers like to handle only 4-, 8-, or 16-page sections (though novels are often printed in 32s and 64s). A 64-page magazine with a separate 4-page cover comprises four 16-page sections, which is convenient and economical. If you increase the pagination to 68, a 4-page section would have to be added

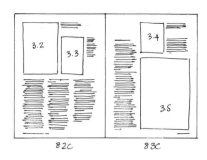

78c 79c   80c 81C   82c 83c

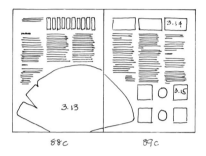

84c 86c   86c 87c   88c 89c

Leave edge

Lay edge

Gripper margin

Gripper edge

▲ **4.12** The way a sheet of paper goes into the printing press has a bearing on the layout. The gripper edge, for example, must contain an area free of all text or graphic material.

somewhere. It is possible to add a two-page section, but not recommended. If the publication is to be saddle-stitched, this would leave an unsightly strip of paper at the other side of the wire staples. It would probably be just as economic to create another two pages.

To help you find your way around an imposition scheme, it is common to draw out a **flatplan** (Fig. **4.11**). This shows diagrammatically what goes where in a publication. It also makes clear which sections or signatures can accommodate flat or full color to best effect. It is a good medium of communication on a magazine, for

example, between the editorial, advertising, and design staff.

There are many ways of drawing up a flatplan, and it is best to consult your printers first, so as to take into account the way they are used to working, and any peculiarities of their folding machines. If in any doubt about imposition, do not be afraid of making up a folded **dummy** out of scrap paper. This would be a miniature version of your publication marked with page numbers and the position of any color.

There are two distinct ways of feeding paper through printing presses. It can be done either with pre-cut single sheets (**sheetwise**) or with a roll of paper (for **web** printing). The sheetwise method uses one plate to print the front of a sheet, and another for the back. Both sides share a common **gripper edge** (Fig. **4.12**). The gripper edge is the leading end of the sheet, and is held in place on the press by finger-like grippers. An allowance of $^1/_2$ inch (15 mm) must be made on this edge when estimating the printed area of a sheet. Opposite the gripper edge is the **leave edge**, and the left side of the sheet as it passes through the press is called the **lay edge**.

An alternative, and a method used when printing booklets or

▲ **4.11** Part of the flatplan for this book. It shows at a glance not only picture sizes and text position, but gives an overview of where black-and-white and color sections fall.

sections of publications with fewer than 16 pages, is to put both sides of the sheet on the same plate. This may sound crazy, but when it is cut and folded correctly you end up with twice as many half-size sheets.

Work-and-turn (Fig. **4.13**) is a technique in which the sheet goes through the machine first one way,

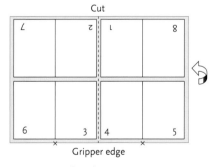

▲ **4.13** Work-and-turn is an ingenious imposition scheme that gives twice as many products as you would expect using just one plate. It is often more economical to use large plates, so one half of the sheet is put on one half of the plate, the other side on the other half. The sheet is printed, and the pile is turned over and printed again on the other side. Later the pile of sheets is cut down the middle to give you two identical half-size piles of printed sheets. Both sides share the same gripper edge.

Gripper edge

▲ **4.14** Work-and-tumble is similar to work-and-turn, except the pile is flipped head over heels and the gripper edge changes ends.

then the paper is turned over sideways and printed once more, such that page 2 prints on the back of page 1. The gripper edge remains the same. The sheet is cut in two, and the result is two piles of paper printed on both sides that can be folded and trimmed as in sheetwise imposition. **Work-and-tumble** (Fig. **4.14**) is similarly ingenious, but the paper is flipped head over heels, and the gripper edge changes ends.

Using work-and-turn or work-and-tumble is economical. This is not only because just one plate is made and there is less **spoilage**, but also because for smaller jobs the printer can **step-and-repeat** (duplicate), a set of pages and print **two-up** — twice as many again in one printing.

If you are designing a whole range of stationery, to be printed in the same Pantone colors and on the same paper stock, you can make similar savings by **ganging up** the individual items on to one plate and printing, say, three compliments slips on one sheet of A4 paper.

Web printing is usually reserved for large print runs. The possible imposition schemes are quite different from those for sheetwork. If you are

going to use this method, it is best to consult the printers at the outset.

There are other design considerations relating to the imposition scheme. A double-page spread (DPS) will be a problem if text or an image runs across two facing pages. They will only align correctly on a center spread, and even here you must take care to keep anything important — the eyes in a portrait, for example — well away from the position of a magazine's wire staples. For consistency of print density, it is best to have DPSs printed on the same side of the same section, if at all possible. **Starvation ghosting** is an unwelcome effect that results in uneven printing and is due, to some extent, to the placement of dense black elements in certain positions on the plate. If you think you may have problems, check with the printer about an alternative imposition.

There are all kinds of other imposition schemes that relate to nonstandard folders and booklets — those with fan or **accordion folds**, for example, and those having unusual shapes and sizes. Computerized imposition systems arrange page files on to large sheets of film inside an imagesetter, which are then used to produce plate-ready flats.

Factors that influence the choice of a particular imposition scheme include: the total number of pages, the print run, the untrimmed page size, and the type of folding and binding. Discuss all these with the printer before you start, and together you will be able to plan for the most economical sheet size, and the most cost-effective press, the lowest spoilage, the highest

▼ **4.15** Paper creep allowance — made to counter the effect caused by the thickness of the paper in the fold of saddle-stitched publications with lots of pages. Otherwise, after the pages have been trimmed the text area will creep nearer the fore edge as the center of the publication is approached.

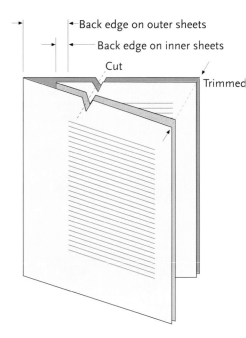

Back edge on outer sheets
Back edge on inner sheets
Cut
Trimmed

quality, and the fastest turnaround.
Paper creep allowance
A book will be bound, stitched, or glued in 16-page sections. A saddle-stitched publication, however, may have quite a number of sections nested one within the other. When these sections are collated, the thickness of the paper at the fold will add up to make pages toward the center stick out more than those near the covers. More paper will be trimmed from the fore edges of these pages, making them significantly narrower than those near the covers. To allow for this paper creep, you will need to vary the position of the margins, especially those at the outer edges.

A simple method of **paper creep allowance**, or shingling, is as follows (Fig. **4.15**). Make a folded dummy, using the same paper stock as the proposed publication. Looking down at the top edge of the dummy, measure off the inner

CROSSOVERS

A crossover is an image, text, or tint that extends from one page to a facing page. Unless you are designing a center spread or the center pages of a signature, the two halves of a crossover will be printed on separate sheets of paper. After trimming and binding, your crossover may well misalign — so avoid thin rules, small text sizes, and objects that are not placed horizontally. And consult your printer about imposing the two sides of a crossover, so that ink and color coverage are consistent.

DON'T EMBOLDEN OR ITALICIZE

Unless a font has been designed as a "type family," such as Helvetica, Times, or Zuzana Licko's Base (see p. 53), try to avoid using the "type style" options on your computer for making fonts italic or bold — use the correct font instead, for example the real Futura Oblique, not an italicized version of Futura Regular. When using the style sheets in programs like InDesign and QuarkXPress, make sure that the italic or bold boxes are left unchecked.

margin of the center pages and make a scalpel cut through the rest at the same point. Disassemble the dummy and use the position of the scalpel cuts as an inner margin reference on the layout. It will appear to move toward the fold as you approach the center pages. It is not necessary to make an allowance on every page — a cumulative allowance can be made every few pages. Trim and center marks must remain to the same measure on all the pages, and remember to mark your design "paper creep allowance made" in case a "helpful" printer decides to straighten up your seemingly wandering margins.

Page layout

The layout of the page is the graphic designer's very own domain. It is what the canvas is to the fine artist. It is the key stage in which all the copy — both text and line illustration — comes together as a unified whole ready to go to film or plate.

Once designers merely provided a rough cut and paste of photocopies to indicate their ideas to another professional, known as a **finished artist**, who did the neat job of preparing the layout for the later stages of prepress.

Before computers, designers had to prepare a **mechanical** (Fig. **4.16**), also known as **camera-ready copy** (CRC) or just plain artwork (A/W). This skill is still relevant, though almost obsolete. A mechanical is sometimes necessary for old jobs that need simple updating or when you're in a hurry and the computer is down! The difference is that the mechanical is now more likely to go on to the glass of a scanner than under the lights of a process camera.

At the printer's, a negative film is made from the mechanical. After retouching work to opaque-out scalpel marks and any other imperfections, it is **contact printed** direct to a **negative-working plate**. Alternatively, it may first be contact printed to film to produce a

positive, which is then used to produce a **positive-working plate** (see Chapter 5 for a fuller explanation of platemaking).

■ DIGITAL MAKE-UP

With a computer system, it is possible to design "on the fly," though this methodology is not always recommended! What is certain, though, is that you will be able to try out lots of "what-if?" layouts, and always end up with clean, seamless artwork, with no changes in density where paragraphs have been corrected, no scalpel cuts to be retouched, and no chance of last-minute corrections dropping off the mechanical on to the printer's floor.

Digital make-up is an immensely powerful tool, but it brings with it a great deal of responsibility for the finished product. There is no one to blame for a less than perfect layout except yourself, or perhaps a bug in the program. And there is much to learn: about operating the system, making use of the flexibility it offers, and about computers in general.

As with the totally manual method, it will always pay to sit down with a pencil and paper to plan your layout. A layout pad has been designed for that purpose, with leaves thin enough for you to trace the best parts of a previously attempted design before it is consigned to the trash. Make a sketch layout of the page. It does not have to be completely accurate, but it should be good enough for you to see what a spread is going to look like at full size. This should include the margins, columns, and the position of page numbers and running heads.

4.16 A mechanical layout can contain all kinds of design elements: text on bromide paper, PMTs, or photocopies of line art, rules and boxes, and maybe even headlines created using rub-down lettering.

Next, select your typeface. This will depend on the type of job, and what's available — both on your system, and at the service bureau. Don't forget practical considerations, such as the number of words per line and the relative x-heights (see pp. 37–8) of the different faces. Try running off some sample lines of type in the face and at the point size and measure that you have chosen, and place it on the layout. That way you will be able to judge whether you require more or less leading and tracking. Try out different sub-headings, and decide now whether the text is to be set justified or ranged left. Remember: type on the screen only approximates the output from the laser printer or imagesetter, so it is important to have a reasonable idea of what to expect.

Next, calculate how much space the type will occupy. If the text has been input using a word processor with a word counter, then that figure will be a good guide. Otherwise use one of the methods outlined in Chapter 2 (see p. 47). If it is going to be too long, or fall short, adjust the layout.

Now draw up a grid. Although the digital make-up system will have built-in rulers and construction lines, the page on the screen — even on a large format display — will look deceptively different from a piece of board on your desk. So double-check with a ruler and a same-size reference grid. Then you can key the specifications into the computer.

If the publication is mostly words, with few or no illustrations, then you can start to place the text on to the page. If, however, there is a large number of illustrations, it is best to draw up a rough plan showing where you expect them to fall. It is much easier to manage the layout (and make sure that nothing is left out) if you know exactly which elements have to be included, and roughly where.

Finally, make a written record of your specification and keep it nearby. Although it is in the computer somewhere, it can be time-consuming and disruptive to have to stop what you are doing to find a reminder of what measure, margin, or horizontal division you have been using.

Page layout programs

It is possible to make up complete pages and even multi-page documents in some of the so-called drawing programs, such as FreeHand and Illustrator, especially where their versatile type controls are required. Most off-the-shelf word-processing programs can now handle several columns of text integrated with graphics. And there are some packages on the market developed for specific design tasks:

▲ **4.17** In a digital make-up system such as Adobe InDesign the mechanical is replaced by an "electronic pasteboard." Text is imported from a word-processing system and placed on to a grid. Text can also be wrapped around illustrations.

producing display advertisements for newspapers and magazines, for example. At the other extreme, there are programs such as FrameMaker, aimed at the market for very large but relatively unsophisticated publications, such as technical manuals.

Most designers come across all kinds of jobs, however, and need a more general-purpose program. The best-known and most versatile are Adobe InDesign — a successor to PageMaker — (Fig. 4.17) and QuarkXPress (Fig. 4.18). Aldus released the first version of PageMaker for the Apple Macintosh in July 1985, and for the IBM PC in January 1987. QuarkXPress was not introduced until later in 1987. It was Aldus founder Paul Brainerd who coined the phrase "desktop publishing." PageMaker can thus rightly claim to be the original desktop-publishing package. Aldus was taken over by Adobe in 1994.

Both XPress and InDesign are based on the PostScript page-description language. Both boast a WYSIWYG (what you see is what you get) display, but the term is not strictly accurate. The printed result is far superior to the page you see on the screen, even at full zoom

4.18 QuarkXPress is similar to InDesign in many ways, but uses a different approach to placing text and graphics — XPress has linked text and graphic frames.

(magnification), because screen fonts are fundamentally different from printer fonts (see p. 72) and the illustrations may only be visible in "preview" quality. Nevertheless, what you see is far superior to what compositors have seen on screen at the typesetter's in the past. Both XPress and InDesign make extensive use of the **WIMP** (windows, icons, mouse, and pull-down menus) methodology, with "palettes" of tools (for drawing boxes, for example) and such things as style-sheet information that can be available on the screen all of the time (Fig. **4.19**).

Both systems are functionally similar; however, XPress has gained a reputation as "industry standard," and most practising designers are expected to be able to use Xpress. But there is no clear division, and designers will argue into the night about the relative merits of *their* program and its suitability to do a particular job. PageMaker will be remembered as being intuitive and simple to use. InDesign makes great play about being able to output directly to PDF format (more of which later) and its ability to open Xpress files. Xpress has always

claimed to be more accurate and with more "bells and whistles" appropriate to professional print production.

In PageMaker, and now in InDesign, the user is presented with a picture on the screen of a "paste-board" for electronically pasting on

text or graphics. Any elements not being used can be placed outside the page area on a virtual desktop until they are needed. When you open a new **document**, you are asked to enter the page size and margins in a "dialog box." (In

4.19 Both InDesign and XPress allow you to compile and edit a style sheet outlining highly specific instructions for components such as the font, leading, and tracking of body text, headlines, and captions. Thus you can maintain consistency between publications.

SCANNING AND OVERSCANNING

Scan at your target output resolution — if you are going to print at 600 dpi then scan at 600 dpi. The rule of thumb for scanning halftones is to use the following formula:

scanning resolution in dpi = [(target width (or height)/original width (or height)] x screen ruling in lpi x 2

   So if the image to be scanned is the same size as it will finish up in the final layout, then just double the screen ruling your printer recommends. Many photographs can be scanned at lower resolutions without affecting the print quality (down to 1.5 times the screen ruling), so long as they do not include geometric patterns, repeating textures, or straight lines. It is very rare to have to work higher than 240 dpi in Photoshop.

   Scanners use a row of CCDs (charge-coupled devices) to capture the image. If there are 600 of them per inch, then try to scan at a multiple of that. For the web, for example, instead of scanning at 72 dpi, scan at 100 dpi. This will use every sixth CCD — using regularly spaced CCDs will produce better results. You can then resample the scan in Photoshop.

computer language, any job you are working on is called a document, whether it is a drawing, a piece of text, or a page layout.) You will also be asked how many pages the publication will have. It is then possible to specify the number of columns, their width, and the spacing between them. All of these parameters can be changed later, if need be.

   In XPress, you start a layout by creating text and graphics boxes or frames for the design elements. It has sophisticated drawing tools based on Bézier curves and freeform paths. Complex shapes can be created by using Boolean operations (intersection, union, difference) to carve away or merge together simpler shapes — and a picture box can be created from the shape of a selection of text, to be filled, say, with an imported graphic. Text can be set on a path, can flow around all sides of an object, and clipping paths can be built around, say, the non-white areas of an imported TIFF image file. It can deal with text styles at the character level, rather than just at paragraph level: the styles palette shows the two current styles simultaneously.

   Text can be imported from a word-processor document, and a symbol is placed in the position you wish the text to start. In "auto-flow" mode it will flow down the columns until all the text is in position. In regular mode, text will flow down the first column, and then stop. In PageMaker, the text block took the appearance of a window-shade (roller blind). A red + in the "handle" indicated that there was

more text in there to be placed. A blank handle indicated that all the text was accounted for. Once placed, the text could be moved around en masse. InDesign retains this ability to place text (and pictures) directly on to the page without first creating boxes (as you must in XPress), but now the text frames are created automatically.

   There are several aids to consistency. Anything placed on "master pages" will appear on every page selected. This is useful for positioning construction lines, effectively creating a grid, and for inserting running heads and folios. You can compare alternative designs by creating a master for each idea and applying them in turn to a page of content.

   Style sheets allow you to specify body text, captions, headlines, and different grades of subheadings, as well as instructions about indents for paragraphs, kerning, and hyphenation. Entire "skeleton" documents can be saved as templates, which can be used over and over to produce documents that are going to look similar — future issues of a newsletter, for example.

   PageMaker incorporated a story editor which was virtually a word-processing package in itself — with a spelling checker, a search-and-replace command, and a word counter — and could be used for fast text entry and last-minute editing while you were working on the layout of a publication. Unfortunately, InDesign doesn't have this feature — you have to buy an additional program, InCopy.

InDesign can handle process and flat (spot) color, which can be specified by Pantone number (the color libraries also include Trumatch, Focoltone, Toyo Color Finder 1050, and DIC Color; further libraries can be imported from Illustrator), percentage tints and gradients, and also the 216 websafe RGB colors.

   Objects can be grouped, resized, rotated, or cropped — and text can still be edited while remaining in the group. Any part of the layout can be masked using objects created with the drawing tools: ovals, rectangles, and polygons. Kerning and tracking can be in 0.0001 em increments. There are four kerning options in InDesign: manual, optical, metrics using kern pairs (the default), and range (what we call tracking). A multiline composer looks ahead six lines to decide on hyphenation breaks.

   Output will generally be to a laser printer or desktop color printer for proofing and low-grade output (for a newsletter, for example), to an imagesetter for bromide or film, or direct to a digital printing press. InDesign has built-in automatic trapping, and non-printing objects, such as production notes, can be defined. A "print fit" preview shows where the document will fit on the output page, complete with register and trim marks. Limited imposition schemes can be set up, to produce booklets, for example.

   With each new upgrade, InDesign and XPress continue to leapfrog each other — if a feature in one of them proves popular, then the rival will adopt its own interpretation. InDesign has introduced

■ e-books

An e-book is simply a book in digital form. It can be a document scanned into PDF (portable document format), retaining all the formatting, typography, and illustrations of the original paper document; it can be output into PDF directly from a layout program such as QuarkXPress or InDesign or it can be just pure text. An e-book can be read from a computer screen, or — to counter the argument that you can't curl up with an e-book on holiday — from a dedicated reader, such as the Gemstar eBook from RCA (formerly known as NuvoMedia's Rocket), which can hold 19,000 pages (about 50 novels) of text and graphics at a time. And since the content is digital, text can be browsed, searched, annotated, or bookmarked in ways impossible with a traditional book. Usually, you pay the e-book vendor and then receive either an encrypted document or a password to a download site.

The ideas behind e-books are older than the internet itself. Back in 1945, Futurist Vannavar Bush imagined a "Memex" — a supplement to memory — in which people could store all their books, records, and communications to be consulted with speed and flexibility. In 1968, Ted Nelson coined the terms "hypertext" and "hypermedia" to include non-sequential text that could branch off in any direction. He later started Project Xanadu to create a "connected literature" of richly formatted text and images accessible cheaply, reliably, and securely from anywhere in the world. Project Gutenberg — an attempt to collect as many texts as possible in electronic format — began in 1971 at the Illinois Benedictine College. Then along came Tim Berners-Lee, who invented the World Wide Web.

The resolution of the average laptop, handheld, or desktop screen is only 72 or 96 dpi. This means type can appear jagged on-screen. Adobe has developed CoolType to improve on-screen text resolution using color anti-aliasing to individually manipulate the red, green, and blue subpixels on an LCD screen.

What's next? Xerox PARC has developed a technology called Gyricon, described as "digital paper." It has many of the properties of paper, but is electronically writeable and erasable. A Gyricon sheet is a thin layer of transparent plastic in which millions of tiny beads — black on one side, white on the other — are randomly dispersed. The beads, each contained in an oil-filled cavity, are free to rotate within those cavities and are charged so that when

voltage is applied they rotate to present one colored side to the viewer. The image will persist until new voltage patterns are applied.

A similar technology, called e-ink, has been developed at MIT's Media Lab. It is a liquid containing microcapsules, each containing white particles suspended in a dark dye. When an electric charge is applied, the particles either show on the surface or remain hidden in the dye. The first commercial applications were signs in J. C. Penney stores, all of which could be updated simultaneously from a central computer. An e-book made from e-ink could look just like a regular book, but could be rewritten many times — "radio newspapers" could be updated remotely. Unlike lcd displays, e-ink requires no back lighting and draws current only when the text is changed.

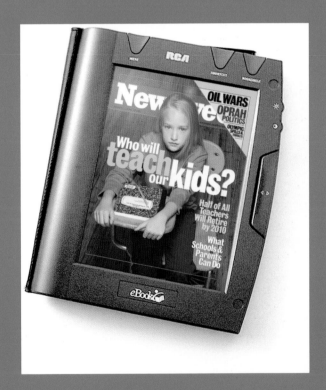

Find out more
Adobe's e-paper website has lots of tips:
www.adobe.com/epaper/ebooks/main.html
Project Gutenberg website: promo.net/pg/
Gemstar eBook: www.ebook-gemstar.com
E-ink: www.eink.com
Gyricon: www.parc.xerox.com/parc-go.html

■ Make a preflight check

Your printer isn't telepathic, so before handing over the completed job on a CD or removable hard disk along with proofs and/or thumbnails, take time to produce a list of all the settings, files, fonts, colors, bleeds etc. in a preflight check, so called because just as an airplane pilot runs through a standard checklist before take-off, so should anyone signing off electronic files. Some programs, such as Adobe InDesign and QuarkXPress can "collect for output" and produce lists automatically, but they can become unwieldy and too full of detail.

Account for every page in the publication, even blank ones. Indicate the number of color separations expected for each page, and note any details requiring special attention, such as instructions to position the saddle wires to avoid spoiling an illustration on the center spread. Keep notes brief — and include your name and telephone number just in case there are any unforeseen problems.

The "eyeball method" of evaluation is fine for simple jobs; for more complex workflows there are third-party programs such as Extensis Preflight Pro and Markzware Flightcheck which can help. Adobe's InProduction preflight-checks documents in a purely PDF workflow.

FlightCheck scans various file types including QuarkXPress, PageMaker, Multi-Ad Creator, Illustrator, Photoshop, FreeHand, CorelDraw, and PDF, and warns you of over 150 potential problems, such as incompatible graphic elements or font types. FlightCheck can investigate native document files without needing the application that created it. After verification, it reports a menu of possible problems like missing images or fonts, including fonts in EPS files.

MarkzNet, from the same supplier, is a real-time, web-based system that checks, collects, compresses, and captures job-ticket information for accounting and billing, and transmits PDF as well as native digital documents over the internet using standard FTP (file transfer protocol). It checks

digital files against a customized set of specific "ground controls" defined by the printer or service bureau. You are automatically notified of corrections required before the job is transmitted, and receive confirmation as soon as it is accepted.

PreflightPro also supports QuarkXPress, PDF, PageMaker, Photoshop, Illustrator, FreeHand, and Multi-Ad Creator. It collects all the elements of your job, including embedded fonts and images, and compresses job files into one or several archives for transfer. Like a spell-checker, the "pilot" feature takes you directly to each problem, suggesting solutions and letting you fix the problem.

InProduction scans PDF files, reports any problems, fixes some of them, and provides descriptions of the errors and any corrections performed. It can create and re-use preflight profiles for each output workflow (print, film, CTP). Descriptions of each profile provide the information you need to control the entire process. Preflight investigates document structures, page size, font status, image control, colors used, and the output for each PDF profile. When the profiles are applied to the content in a PDF document and an error is noted, the information triggers a specified response, such as ignoring or fixing the problem, and the results are saved in a report.

Trueflow, developed by Dainippon Screen and Adobe, is a web-based PDF and PostScript workflow system in which production and scheduling can be accessed and managed from any location and at any time over the internet using a standard browser. It includes preflighting, job-ticket workflow, trapping, layout, and page-independent RIPping.

Find out more
Flightcheck: www.markzware.com/elements/data/
product/flightcheck.html
PreflightPro: www.extensis.com/preflightpro
Adobe InProduction:
www.adobe.com/products/inproduction/

ROTATE IMAGES BEFORE YOU IMPORT THEM
You can save time by cropping and rotating images in Photoshop before importing them to a page-layout program such as InDesign or QuarkXPress; it will also save time at the imagesetting stage. To straighten a crooked scan in Photoshop, select the crop tool and draw a box around the image to be straightened, leaving plenty of room between the image and the edge of the scan. Now rotate the crop box. Once the edge of the box is parallel with the image, press Return for Photoshop to straighten and crop the image at the same time.

frames and a control palette like in XPress; and XPress has changed over to the pasteboard metaphor. (It is a truism in computing that you only realize what something cannot do when they bring out a new version.) InDesign has Plug-ins to add functionality to the basic program; XPress has its equivalent Xtensions. Both are also expanding from print into newer media such as CD-rom production and the internet, with features that help convert page layouts into HTML (Hyper Text Mark-up Language — see Chapter 6, p. 216) and Adobe Acrobat's PDF (Portable Document Format).

The essence of digital make-up is that you can be as rigid or as flexible as you choose. InDesign is said to be more intuitive than XPress, but some designers are convinced that XPress has more functionality, with just about every typographic control you could wish for. It is beyond the scope of this book to describe every feature of each program. The above can only give you a flavor of what both Adobe and Quark have to offer. Check with a dealer for the specification of the latest update. Both will continue to change and improve, and ultimately the choice between them is going to be a personal one.

Full-color digital prepress

In some workflows, layouts are designed on a system using only low-resolution images, in the same way that photocopies of halftones on a mechanical were once used "for position only," with transparencies sent to the repro house to be "stripped-in" later.

Printers and repro houses have been using digital scanners coupled with computers for many years. Organizations with digital prepress systems from suppliers such as Scitex and Dainippon Screen have been able to scan in and retouch color transparencies since the early 1970s. Of course, these systems have been capable of much more, but were so expensive to buy and run that printers, afraid that designers might develop the "bad habit" of asking for alterations to their images, adopted an almost conspiratorial silence.

With **OPI** (**open prepress interface**), you the designer use low-resolution images, called proxies, as for-position-only visuals to produce the "electronic mechanicals" on your desktop make-up system. High-resolution scans, straight from the original transparencies, are reunited with the layouts in the imagesetter at the repro house.

The low-resolution scans used in the computer until the proofing stage can be straight from your desktop scanner, or they can be "compressed" versions of scans from the repro house's system. As you lay out the images, the system remembers all the scaling, rotating, and cropping alterations made to the image, and conveys them to the operator at the repro house. This makes considerable savings on set-up time compared with conventional repro techniques, in which the operator has to check and measure position mark-ups on overlays.

An **EPS** (**Encapsulated Post-Script**) file can be a resolution-independent graphic from a vector program such as FreeHand, or a complete page containing bitmap images from Xpress (called **DCS — Desktop Color Separations** — in Xpress). They can also include OPI comments, which can link to other documents, such as high-resolution versions of an image.

Complex cut-outs and masks can be made and these are automatically translated into smooth high-resolution masks at the repro house, using a technique called mask-density substitution. In the same way, graduated tints (called dégradés in Scitex talk) are recreated automatically in high-resolution versions.

Most page layouts are output to an imagesetter via a **RIP** (**raster image processor**), which changes the PostScript outlines of the letters and drawings into a **bitmap** (an array of dots) that the imagesetter can print out. Once all color and mono elements are in place, the page can be proofed on a digital proofing system.

After corrections have been made, the PostScript file can be sent via CD, removable hard disk, or down an ISDN line to the repro house. This assumes, of course, that the repro house already holds the original transparencies! At the repro house, all type, tints, and images are plotted directly on to final output film, with no need for intermediate type-setting, imagesetting, or stripping-in.

The system at the repro house is built around a top-quality drum

■ Color management

One of the designer's biggest headaches is making sure that the colors you see on your computer screen and in the images you have scanned stay faithful to the originals in the finished printed publication. Of course, it is just not physically possible to reproduce on a printed page the colors we see in nature, nor is it possible to print the colors we see on a computer monitor. This is because they all inhabit different color spaces, or gamuts. RGB can only display around 70 percent of the colors that can be perceived by the human eye. The CMYK color gamut is smaller, reproducing about 20 percent of perceivable colors. These gamuts are shown diagrammatically in Fig. 3.19 against a CIE (Commission Internationale de l'Eclairage) standard color space diagram.

Scanners, computer programs like Photoshop and QuarkXPress, monitors, printers, proofers, imagesetters, and printing presses all work within their own color spaces. It is unlikely at the outset of a project that you will know the type of printing press that will ultimately be used. Nor is it likely that the printing-press operator will be able to see the photographs and artwork you have been scanning.

If all of these device-specific color spaces could be mapped into a device-independent color space, such as the CIE color space, aka L*a*b color, and if all of the computer and applications vendors could agree on the interpretation of that color space, then it would become much easier for you to mix and match equipment from different vendors into one workflow and maintain color consistency throughout the production process.

Usually, scanners have a wider gamut than printers, but optimum reproduction cannot always be attained simply by making the color space smaller. So success can either be measured subjectively, by seeing if the grays appear gray and colors such as flesh, grass, and sky look acceptable, or objectively — using a colorimeter to measure how many colors from the input device have been faithfully reproduced.

In 1993 several companies, including Apple, Microsoft, Adobe, and Kodak, formed the International Color Consortium (ICC) to tackle this problem. One of their first decisions was that color space transformations are the responsibility of the operating system. Device profiles, containing information on the color behavior of a particular peripheral, would provide the data necessary to perform these transformations.

To build a scanner profile, for example, you would scan in a reference image and compare it with what the scanned values should be. Building a profile for a printer inverts the process. Here, a set of patches evenly distributed in the output ink color space are generated and printed. These patches are then measured to provide colorimetric data. Thankfully you don't have to do all this calibration and characterization yourself, although there are instruments available to calibrate monitors (see Fig. 5.10).

Meanwhile, Apple's ColorSync has been gaining industry acceptance. It uses device profiles, usually stored as part of an image file (in the file's header or "table of contents"): these provide a description of how this image was captured, what its color space is, and more besides.

CMMs (color-matching modules) convert images from one color space to another and simultaneously apply the information in the profile to correctly render the image.

In each step of the workflow, ColorSync compensates for any deviations in the image-capturing systems of scanners, the display anomalies of monitors, and the color-imaging components of printers and output devices. The CMMs from vendors such as Heidelberg, Kodak, and Agfa are packaged in each version of ColorSync along with a CMM from Apple.

The device-independent color space used by ColorSync (and also by Photoshop to convert from RGB to CMYK, for example) is CIE L*a*b — a three-dimensional color space based on the theory that a color cannot be both green and red at the same time, nor blue and yellow at the same time. L is the lightness component, ranging from 0 to 100; a is the green–red axis; and b is the blue–yellow axis. Both can range from 1120 to 2120. The white reference point is usually based on the whitest light that can be generated by a given device.

Find out more
International Color Consortium: www.color.org/
ColorSync: www.apple.com/colorsync/

4.20 A regular desktop design system
can be used as a front-end to the
system at the repro house, mixing and matching the abilities of both to the best and most
economical advantage. Transparencies are
sent to the repro house, where both high-
and low-resolution scans are made. The low-
res scans are used in your layouts and the
high-res ones are substituted later, when the
final pages are made up.

scanner, a RIP, and a high-resolution
imagesetter (Fig. **4.20**), and one
difference between it and the
kind of system you may find in a
designer's studio is that at the repro
house all operations are carried
out in CMYK. Desktop systems
generally use RGB for image
capture and manipulation and only
convert to CMYK right at the end
of the process. Color-management
systems, such as ColorSync and
constant calibration, are critical for
the color you see on your screen to
end up on the printed page.

Late binding is a term used to
mean last-minute changes within
PostScript files while they are in the
RIP, such as adding trapping and
imposition information, particularly
for digital presses. The advantage of
supplying the repro house or printer
with the job in PDF format is that late
changes — including rearranging
pages — can be made and viewed
regardless of whether they have a
Mac, Windows, or Unix system, or
whether they have access to the
application that originally created it.

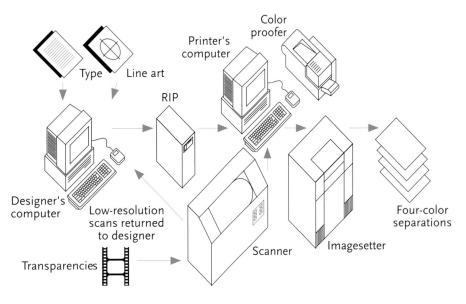

Type   Line art   RIP   Printer's computer   Color proofer   Four-color separations   Imagesetter   Scanner   Transparencies   Low-resolution scans returned to designer   Designer's computer

■ REPRO

Film make-up

For most high-quality work, and all
multicolor printing, the design
elements will still be assembled
together on **film** (Fig. **4.21**). It is
unlikely that the average graphic
designer will ever be asked to do

film make-up — the **assembly** will
be done by a professional called a
"stripper." But graphic designers
effectively have to brief the strippers
with their roughs, and check the
results, so it is important to know
what is going on.

Film used by printers has a high-
speed, high-contrast **emulsion** on a
polyester base. The emulsion side
of the film is slightly duller than the
other side, and it may be possible
to see the image on the film if it is
held up to the light and viewed at a
shallow angle. If in doubt, scratch
the film — well away from the
image area, naturally — to discover
which side the emulsion is on.

4.21 At the printer's, halftones and
tints are "stripped in" to the spaces left
in the text films. Opaque material such as
Rubylith is used to blank out black or solid
flat-color areas on positive film or white areas
on negative film.

4.23 The stripper assembles all the pages for one printing into a flat ready for platemaking, opaquing out any blemishes or marks not to be printed.

Film can be right reading, or wrong (reverse) reading. As you can view film from either side, it is important to specify "emulsion up" or "emulsion down" as well.

When the printing plates are made, the film is always put in contact with the plate for maximum sharpness. The emulsion touches the plate, i.e. the film is emulsion-side down.

The type of film most commonly used is **right-reading emulsion down (RRED)**, also known as **wrong-reading emulsion up**

4.22 For offset litho work, strippers most often use positive right-reading emulsion down film. Thus the emulsion comes into contact with the surface of the plate; the blanket is wrong-reading; and the final printed image is right-reading.

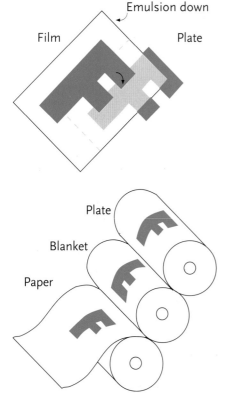

(**WREU**). The image appears the correct way round (is right-reading) when the film is viewed from the shiny side, and wrong-reading from the dull emulsion side. RRED film is used for litho printing — and for all offset processes. When the film is contacted with the plate, the image is transferred so that it is right-reading. During printing, the ink on the plate transfers as wrong-reading to the rubber blanket, and then as right-reading to the paper (Fig. **4.22**; there is more about the offset litho process on p. 179).

Wrong-reading emulsion down (WRED) film, also known as **right-reading emulsion up (RREU)**, has a wrong-reading image when viewed from the shiny side and is right-reading when viewed from the dull emulsion side. WRED film is used for direct printing processes, such as gravure. When the cylinder is made, the image is wrong-reading. It transfers ink to the paper directly, and becomes right-reading (see p. 185 for further information on gravure).

Pages can be assembled using positive or negative film. Negative film, with all the white space turned to black, is often too dense to use accurately. So most color **stripping-in** is done using positive film. The stripper uses a white board, on to which the grid (or layout) plus all the trim and center marks have been drawn or preprinted. A clear

carrier sheet of polyester or acetate is laid on to this guide, and for each page the design elements (type, line illustrations, and halftones) on film are assembled into place with the emulsion side uppermost. The film elements are cut to size with a scalpel and attached to the base sheet with pressure-sensitive tape, in order to leave a uniformly flat surface, with none of the elements overlapping.

If the layout is quite complex, with lots of design elements stuck down with tape, a copy is made on to positive-working daylight film. This is called the **final**. Every time a duplicate is made, however, there is a slight degradation in quality. The best results are obtained when film is copied emulsion to emulsion. Using normal negative-working film, the image would be reversed and another copy would have to be made to right it. Special **auto-reversing film** is used instead to keep the number of steps to a minimum.

For multicolor work, a separate clear carrier sheet is used for each of the process colors. The registration (alignment) between the separate finals has to be observed meticulously, using a **pin-register** system to line up the trim marks and multicolor elements (see below).

As discussed earlier, it is generally most economical to print several pages together, in one pass

▶ **4.24** A Cromalin color proof is a "dry" proprietary system from Du Pont which gives a good idea of how a set of color film separations are going to work together on the press.

of the printing press. Putting together the **flat** (Fig. **4.23**), or forme, to make a 16- or 32-page plate is the stripper's job, and here's how it is done.

A single-color flat with no registration problems to worry about is usually made up from film negatives, assembled together on an opaque, orange-colored paper called **Goldenrod**. Goldenrod contains a dye that prevents ultraviolet (UV) light from passing through it, and acts as a mask to protect the non-printing areas of the flat. The negative film is placed in position emulsion side up, and the whole assembly is turned over. Windows are then cut into the Goldenrod to allow UV light to pass through the image areas. The assembled flat is placed on the press plate and exposed in a **printing-down frame**.

Goldenrod can stretch, so, for work requiring close registration, the negatives are assembled first on to clear acetate or polyester sheets, emulsion side up. The assembly is

▼ **4.25** For color work, each printing must be in close register. Pin registration is a system of precisely placed holes and corresponding pins which ensure that all the films, flats, and plates are correctly aligned.

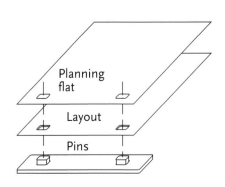

Planning flat

Layout

Pins

turned over and non-printing areas are masked using either Goldenrod or a red/amber masking film.

For multicolor printing, a positive flat is made for each of the process colors. To ensure close registration, these are pin-registered (Fig. **4.25**) with pins and a special punch used to make holes in the flats. They can be correctly located with pins on the press plate, and again the plates can be located on the press cylinder with further pins and clamps.

An alternative method is called **blue and red keys**. The first flat is assembled using either the cyan or the magenta elements. This is exposed in contact with a sheet of blue or red **dyeline** film, which produces a key image of the original image in blue or red. With blue keys, each color flat is registered in position using the blue to give accurate sightings. When complete, the flat is used for platemaking in the normal way, as the blue does not record on the plate. Red does record, however, so when red keys are used, the flat is assembled on to a clear acetate sheet with the red keys underneath, acting as a guide.

Picture proofing

Film for a single color is commonly proofed as a positive dyeline or **diazo** print (contact ammonia print), called an **ozalid**, **brownline**, **blueprint**, or **blue**. Blues (which may also be gray, brown, or other colors) often give the only opportunity to check the **alignment** of halftones and other elements. This is absolutely the last chance to make any changes before the job is "put to bed."

It may be necessary to see the printed quality of halftones, either all together in random order, as **scatter proofs**, or — probably more expensively — in their correct position on the page, as page proofs.

Color separations of illustrations and photographs can be proofed photographically or digitally, as **inkjet**, **dye-sublimation**, or **thermal-transfer prints**, or on plastic laminate systems. These are called **prepress proofs**, or **dry proofs**, and are all approximations to the finished printed result, but will give you an idea of what to expect.

Photographic systems work by exposing each process color

CHECKING PROOFS
Remember that contract color proofs will not reproduce exactly the way that ink will appear on your chosen paper stock: this is especially true for any varnishes, spot colors, and metallic inks. Check that colors are even and consistent, and check tints to make sure they are not mottled. Use printed swatches to check spot colors. Examine the color bar for lost detail. Make sure bleeds and crossovers extend beyond the trim marks. Check for weak or breaking-up type. Use a loupe to look closely at highlights and shadows. Pay attention to flesh tones and hair. Bright reflected light in the eyes should have no dot, only paper white. On fluffy clouds, magenta and yellow dots should be as small as possible, with cyan dots only slightly larger.

◄ **4.26** Epson 7500 digital proofer has 1440 dpi resolution, a six-color print-head, and can print A+ (24 in wide) proofs. The box bottom right is the 200MHz RIP Station 5100 Series III, co-developed by Epson, EFI and DuPont

separation in turn on to a three-layer photographic paper, using filters. The material is then processed to produce the color proof.

One-off transfer or integral proofs, such as Du Pont's **Cromalin** and Imation's **Matchprint**, take colored powders or pre-coated sheets representing the process colors. They are laminated in register on to white paper (Fig. **4.24**). With some systems it is possible to use the same stock as you will be using for the final printing, which is useful for checking color and inking accurately.

Plastic laminate proofs, such as Imation's **Color-Key** and Du Pont's **Cromacheck**, build up an image layer by layer on to a plastic substrate using mylar or acetate overlay film, one for each process color.

Digital proofing systems produce proofs direct from the computer's memory, using inkjet, thermal-transfer, dye-sublimation, or electro-static technologies. Adobe Press-Ready software extends color inkjet printers such as Epson's 1440 dpi Stylus Pro 7000 (Fig. **4.26**) to deliver high-quality PostScript color proofs.

Wet proofs require four plates to be made from the separations and printed on a flatbed proofing press. This should produce the most realistic representation of the finished job, and allows several sets of proofs to be made. Ensure that a complete set of color bars (see Fig. **4.27**) are run with the proof — these can later be compared with the values being recorded on the press. And ask for standard inks to be used.

A full set of **progressives** (see Fig. 3.21) can be obtained in this way. Progressives are color proofs printed in the same order in which the process colors will be applied at press time. Each color printing is shown separately and also surprinted with the other colors. A typical set comprises the individual process colors of yellow, magenta, cyan, and black, accompanied by the cumulative combinations: magenta on yellow; cyan on yellow and magenta; and finally black on yellow, magenta, and cyan. Some printers vary the sequence by running the cyan printing before the magenta. Make sure to ask for progressives in the **laydown sequence** — the order in which the finished job will be printed.

For flat color, the printer may offer a **drawdown** — a smear of ink from a smooth blade on a particular paper stock. This should not be relied upon, however, to give an accurate impression of how a particular color will print on the press.

As mentioned above, it is important, when viewing color samples, to ask for the same paper stock as will be used for the final printing. Always make allowance for the fact that **press proofs** pulled from a proofing press will be sharper and show less dot gain (see p. 196) than a high-speed production press.

Check the proofs to see that the images are the right way round — it's amazing how often they are upside-down or reversed (**flopped**) left-to-right, or both — and at the correct resolution. Low-res images sometimes slip through! Check also for the correct crop, size, position, sharpness, and mark any obvious imperfections such as spots and scratches. Black-and-white proofs need to be checked for contrast — they should have the full tonal range from shadow to highlights.

When it comes to marking proofs for color correction, tell the printer or repro house as plainly as possible what you think is wrong. Color judgment is subjective, and there may be many routes to a better end result. Just because something has a blue cast, it does not necessarily mean that there is too much cyan — the cyan may be all right but the other colors may need taking up. It is better to say "too blue" than to instruct the printer with technical certainty to "take down the cyan."

Color bars

Color bars (Fig. **4.27**) yield vital information about the performance of both the press and the inks being used. To be able to interpret them arms you with the knowledge to improve the quality of the job without being "blinded by science" at the printer's. They contain a whole range of tests: some are visual checks; others require special instruments such as a **densitometer**. And they are totally independent of the job, thus representing a consistent guide to the standard of printing you can expect.

Color bars comprise most or all of the following components:

1. Printing-down controls. There will be a series of microlines and highlight dots to assess how accurately the job has been printed down from film to plate.
2. Solid density patches for each color. These monitor ink-film thickness, and should be read using a densitometer.
3. Trapping patches. These show solid process colors printed on top of others in different combinations, and they test how ink is being accepted in **wet-on-wet** printing. There will also be a dense black made up from 100% black, 55% cyan, 42·5% yellow, and 42·5% magenta (= 240%, the maximum recommended percentage of tints; see also p. 94).
4. Screen patches. Patches for each process color at different screens are used to monitor **dot gain**. Dot

gain happens as the ink spreads around just-joined-up dots in the middle tones, tending to make these areas look darker than they should be. At one tone lighter, where the dots are not yet touching, density does not gain to the same extent. This effect can cause a visible jump in an otherwise smooth gradation of tone. Elliptical dots can help alleviate the problem.
5. Coarse and fine halftone scale. This quick visual check comprises ten steps in the form of the numerals 0 to 9 set using a screen of 200 lines, which are dropped out of a background tint screened at 65 lines. Dot gain shows as the numbers fill in and become visible — the theory is that fine tints are more sensitive to dot gain than coarser ones.
6. Slur gauge. These patches reveal any directional dot gain caused by **slurring** or **doubling**, and take the form of star targets and/or oblongs containing both horizontal and vertical lines.
7. Gray balance. If all is well, a 50% cyan, 40% magenta, and 40% yellow, printed on top of each other, should produce a neutral gray.

■ SUMMARY

Prepress is where the text set in type, the illustrations and photographs, and any other graphic elements, such as rules, boxes, and areas of flat color, all come together in a form that can be printed. The prepress process starts with the

4.27 A color bar is used by printers to assess the performance of their presses — giving information, for example, about dot gain and slurring. It appears away from the image area and is trimmed off the sheets later.

page layout on to which graphic elements — typesetting, line art, and photographs — are assembled. For simple black-and-white work, the job is completed.

For close-registration color work, however, halftones may be processed on to film, and stripped in at the printers on to flats.

For medium- and large-scale jobs, it is important to give some thought to imposition schemes. Early planning in this area can have a substantial effect on the cost-effectiveness and smooth running of a project.

The preparation of type and graphic elements at the prepress stage can also be carried out on a computer, using the electronic cut-and-paste of desktop programs such as QuarkXPress and Adobe InDesign. Layouts can then be output by laser or inkjet printers on to plain paper, or by higher-resolution imagesetters as bromide prints or film.

Whichever method or system is used, it is essential to see and to be able to understand the prepress process of proofs and color bars, so that you can be sure of quality ... and know that your design is the one that is going to be printed as you envisaged it!

DAVID CARSON

LIFE STORY ■ David Carson was born in Corpus Christi, Texas. In the late 1970s he was a professional surfer, ranking eighth in the world. In 1977, he graduated from San Diego State University "with honors and distinction" in sociology, and taught grades seven to twelve at Real Life Private School, Grants Pass, Oregon. In 1980 he took a two-week workshop in graphic design and re-enrolled at San Diego State University to study graphic design, transferring after just one month to Oregon College of Commercial Art. That same year he quit to take up an internship at Surfer Publications in Dana Point, California.

That job folded, and from 1982 until 1987 Carson was a sociology teacher at Torrey Pines High School in Del Mar, California — but after school, evenings, and weekends he was working on the fanzine *Transworld Skateboarding*. This was followed by a spell on *Musician*, then to the innovative but ultimately financially ruinous *Beach Culture* during 1989–91, to *Surfer* 1991–2, and finally international success with the music and fashion magazine *Ray Gun* from 1992 until 1995. In 1993, he was honored as one of the "I.D. Forty" in *I.D.* magazine's first annual selection of leading design innovators.

Since 1993 Carson has worked as design consultant to such clients as

> ## "Don't mistake legibility for communication

Levi's, Nike, and Pepsi and directed commercials and titling for American Express, Coca-Cola, and Sega. In 1995 he was chosen as the International Center of Photography's Designer of the Year, and won best book design of the year for *Cyclops* by Vogue photographer Albert Watson, a book making full use of FM screening for the photographs, but with a typographical cover. He has since collaborated with Watson on advertising projects, including a Superbowl spot for Budweiser.

Also in 1995 he set up David Carson Design in New York, with Mike Jurkovac, and Cyclops Productions with Jurkovac and Watson. David is the art director and designer for the Marshal McLuhan estate, and is currently designing an anthology of McLuhan. Carson directed the launch TV commercials for Lucent technologies, and designed the worldwide branding campaign for Microsoft (through Weiden + Kennedy, Portland, Oregon) and continues to design the Puerto Rican surfing magazine, *Surf in Rico*.

MANIFESTO ■ **Why Change? Why Not?**

"Don't mistake legibility for communication," asserts David Carson. "David's work communicates," says David Byrne, "but on a level beyond words — a level that bypasses the logical rational centers of the brain and goes straight to the part that understands without thinking. In this way it works just like music does — slipping in there before anyone has a chance to stop it at the border and ask for papers."

The initial reaction to Carson's magazine layouts is one of surprise, perhaps shock, and almost definitely curiosity. His work moved quickly from subculture to become the dominant style of the 1990s. Throughout a decade of magazine art direction, Carson has persistently pushed at the conventions of the medium, most controversially in his typography. This has raised cries that the work is illegible, despite the fact that for the target readers, the magazine communicates — otherwise they would not buy it.

Like Erik Spiekermann (see p. 76), Carson believes you cannot *not* communicate, as he seeks to explore the full range of expression possible within the page. The work integrates text, images, and the medium, forging a new way of reading across sequential pages. From the early *Transworld Skateboarding* spreads to *Ray Gun*, he has moved from one-off visual and verbal playfulness to, at times, pure graphic abstraction. Marks and color exist not as elements that build or frame pictures and sentences, but make emotional contact directly, as marks and color.

In these magazines Carson held the position of both art director and designer, being responsible not only for laying out pages, but also commissioning artwork and establishing the design rules for the publication. But it is the absence of rules that distinguishes Carson's spreads. The familiar structures of magazine layouts have been removed or re-engineered. Instead of a grid, pages are freeform, each one a fresh canvas onto which type and images are applied. Instead of a limited and consistent palette of typefaces, new faces were introduced with every new issue of *Ray Gun*, not as matter of novelty, but as a matter of finding new expression for new content. Rather than "why change?" the question is "why not?"

◀ Posters for Kinderlicht children's event in Mainz, Germany.

▶ Posters for the Atlantic Centre for the Arts, Florida.

▼ Typographic cover for Albert Watson's photographic book *Cyclops* — the title refers to Watson being blind in one eye.

WORKSTATION

- Website: www.davidcarsondesign.com
- Lewis Blackwell, *The End of Print: The Graphic Design of David Carson*, Laurence King, London, 1995 (2nd edition 2000)
- Lewis Blackwell, *David Carson, 2ndsight — Grafik Design after the End of Print*, Laurence King, London, and Universe, New York, 1997
- Philip B. Meggs, *David Carson, Fotografiks*, Laurence King, London, and Ginko Press, Corte Madera, CA, 1999
- David Carson, *trek*, Gingko Press, Corte Madera, CA, 2001
- *Emigre*, 27, 1993, special issue on Carson
- Rick Poynor, "David Carson Revealed," *I.D.*, November 1995, pp. 48–53, 92, 93
- *Cyclops* by Jeff Koons with James Truman and Albert Watson, designed by David Carson, Bulfinch Press, Boston, MA, 1997
- Daniel Donnelly, David Carson, Florian Brody, and Sarah ana Hahn, *Cutting Edge Web Design: The Next Generation*, Rockport Publishers, 1998

FIVE COMPUTERS

COMPUTERS & THEIR PERIPHERALS

Not so long ago, a graphic designer's studio would contain a drawing board, a Grant enlarger, and maybe a wax-coater, along with a toolkit comprising scalpels, technical pens, and sheets of Letraset rub-down lettering. Today the landscape has changed completely, with almost everything the designer needs — and more — all contained within the plastic casing of a computer.

The computer brings control and flexibility to the designer's desktop. It won't do the designing for you, of course. A computer is merely a tireless tool, to be put to work as and when necessary, alongside the pencil and layout pad. It is an extremely powerful tool, nevertheless, and it is waiting to be used.

In the past few years much of the equipment described in this chapter has become commonplace in designers' studios. It is important, therefore, to know how it works, what it is capable of, what its limitations are, and what trade-offs you will be expected to make. Thus forearmed, you will be able to take on the suppliers' salespeople, and make sound buying decisions that will ensure a successful implementation.

Simply having a computer does not make you into a better designer. If you need any evidence, take a look at the advertisements at the back of any computer magazine, especially for dealers and bureaux. Those people have offices bristling with computers, use all the software daily, and possess just about every font you could imagine. And still their ads look terrible.

But a good designer, armed with a computer, can do wondrous things. The main advantage is almost *total control* of your design, from initial concept to finished product. There is a down side to this, though. If it is control you want, you'll have to take responsibility for all your design decisions — you won't be able to blame the typesetter, for instance, if you don't get the setting you thought you'd specified. And you'll have to learn something about computers. This chapter will take you some of the way.

Finally, the health and safety aspects of a computer installation are discussed, so as to safeguard the well-being of the most valuable component of the production system — the graphic designer.

5.2 This Compaq AP550 is an IBM PC-compatible desktop computer running Windows NT 4.0. It has one or two Intel Pentium III processors with a clock speed of 733 or 866 MHz, 128 or 256 Mbyte (expandable to 1Gbyte) of 600MHz or 800MHz RAM and 9.1GB or 18.2GB SCSI hard disk drives.

What equipment do you need to get started?

✔ a computer: an Apple Macintosh, IBM PC, or PC compatible such as a Compaq
✔ a high-definition monitor, preferably of large format (17in/432 mm or more)
✔ a mouse (and mouse pad) or other pointing device, such as a rolling ball or digitizer
✔ an inkjet or laser printer
✔ a desktop scanner
✔ a back-up device, such as an external hard disk or Zip drive
✔ applications software
✔ access to the internet
and optionally:
✔ a PostScript-compatible laser printer
✔ a proof-quality thermal transfer, or dye-sublimation color printer
✔ a CD writer

■ HARDWARE AND SOFTWARE

First, some basic definitions. The stuff you can see and touch — the computer and all the ancillary equipment, the peripherals — is the **hardware**. **Software** is the unseen factor of a system which supplements the brainpower and experience of the designer and makes the hardware come alive. It arrives on a **CD-rom** in an over-large box, and is copied on to the computer's own **hard disk**. (The originals are kept in a safe place, in case anything should go wrong with your hard disk.)

The word **system** is used a lot in computer parlance. It is a catch-all term, and usually means "everything" — the hardware and software together, as in a digital prepress system. The software that looks after the internal workings of the

computer is called the operating system. And an item of software can be referred to as a program, a package, or, again, a system.

Most people recognize a computer from the name it has on the front: it may be an IBM PC, a Compaq (Fig. **5.2**), or an Apple Macintosh (Fig. **5.1**). These are all **personal computers**. A personal computer is a self-contained system

▶ **5.1** An Apple G4 with Cinema display. These come standard with dual processors: either 450 MHz or 500 MHz, delivering up to 7 billion calculations per second. When running applications like Adobe Photoshop, the dual processor 500 MHz G4 can be as fast as a 2 GHz Pentium III. The 22-inch Apple Cinema Display LCD flat panel display delivers 1600 x 1024 resolution.

that sits on the desktop, that you do not have to share, and that is powerful enough to do the job you have in mind.

The next grade up is a computer called a **workstation**, from a supplier such as Sun or Silicon Graphics (Fig. **5.3**). They are much more powerful than personal computers, but they take up more space and are more expensive. As time goes by, and PCs get more powerful, the distinction between PC and workstation begins to blur.

Although the abbreviation PC stands for personal computer, it refers to a specific class of personal computer, namely the original IBM PC and compatible computers from suppliers such as Compaq. Because IBM-compatible PCs always contain an Intel processor and mostly use the Microsoft Windows operating system, they are also sometimes referred to as "Wintel" computers.

The Apple Macintosh is a personal computer, but not a PC. It operates in a fundamentally different way to the IBM PC and compatibles. Programs designed for the PC will not work on a Macintosh, and vice versa, although *versions* of a program such as InDesign are available for both kinds of computer and will operate in similar ways. It is possible to emulate PC software on a Mac, and generally a Mac can read PC files, but not vice versa.

5.3 A Silicon Graphics Octane 2 system is a high-end workstation designed specifically for graphics applications. It is based around single or dual 400 MHz processors and runs under a Unix operating system.

5.4 This screen shot shows a WIMP (windows, icons, mouse, and pull-down menus) GUI (graphical user interface). This is a preview version of Apple's Mac OS X, which has a new GUI named Aqua, and is built around an open-source Unix-based foundation named Darwin. It includes Apple's new Quartz 2D graphics engine; OpenGL for 3D graphics and gaming, and QuickTime for streaming audio and video. The GUI includes a "dock," for organizing applications, documents, and miniaturized windows.

Software

There are many levels of software inside the computer which are mainly invisible to the user. At the lowest level, you need a program built into the machine that loads (or boots, as in "pull yourself up by the bootstraps") all the other programs.

At the next level is the **operating system**. This looks after the computer's internal workings, particularly the operation of the hard-disk memory. It is often specific to the make of computer: PCs use MS-DOS and Microsoft Windows. The Macintosh's operating system is just a number, such as OS 9. Workstations mostly use versions of AT&T's Unix (the names of the variants usually have an x in them somewhere). Linux is a public-domain operating system for PCs. The operating system comes with the computer when you buy it, and upgrades can be bought on CD-roms and installed on the hard disk. You usually see evidence of the operating system at work only when you switch the computer on. It checks that everything is in working order, then awaits your instructions. If anything is wrong, it will put an error message on the screen and you will have to refer to the manual and take remedial action.

The most visible level of software is the **application**, which you buy on CD-rom, along with an operating manual. Applications software converts the general-purpose computer, which cannot do anything, into the kind of system the user wants. It can be one of a number of things: a spreadsheet, a page-layout package, paint software, or a computer game. Software suppliers each have their own methods of numbering versions. It is important to know which version you have, to ensure compatibility, for example, between your program and the one at the **service bureau**. New versions of software packages are being released all the time — some are really significant improvements on the previous release, some are merely "fixes" that correct bugs.

A **bug** is an error in the program, hidden away in the depths of the computer code — a mistake made by the programmer. The term was coined in the late 1950s by computer pioneer Grace Hopper, who found a real insect interfering with the working of her computer.

All programs have bugs, just as all computers crash and do inexplicable things now and then. Thus there is all the more reason to save your current job to the hard disk as frequently as possible, rather than leave it in the short-term **RAM** (**random access memory**; see p. 138) memory. A few but by no means all programs do this automatically. It is a good idea also to back up (copy) anything important on to an external hard disk or a removable device like a Zip drive at the end of every session. Then put them in a safe place.

A **virus** is worse than a bug — it is a self-replicating piece of mischief, introduced surreptitiously into your computer by malicious computer addicts called "hackers."

Software is written in a programming language. The computer's own language is called **machine code**, which is expressed in hexadecimal numbers (numbers in base 16). It is gibberish to all but the most hardened hacker. Computers "think" in binary code (using the numbers in base 2: 0 or 1, on or off), but this is too cumbersome for humans to get to grips with. Binary, however, is conveniently convertible to hexadecimal. One step up from machine code is **assembler**, which substitutes short mnemonics such as MPY for multiply, one-for-one, for the hexadecimal numbers. Easiest to use are the so-called high-level languages such as **Basic** (beginners all-purpose symbolic instruction code) and **C**. These use English words, arranged using simple grammar, which is later "compiled" or "interpreted" into machine code. Even higher-level languages are sometimes available — so-called scripting languages — so that users can customize (adapt) the applications software to their own preferred ways of working.

But today it is completely unnecessary to learn a programming language. Today's operating systems contain an "intuitive" **GUI** (graphical user interface; Fig. **5.4**, p. 136) which simplifies communication between the human and the computer. Commands are chosen from lists called **menus**, and most things can be done using **tools**. A pen tool, for example, allows you to draw lines on the screen. The user selects tools by pointing at small pictures called **icons**, using a device such as a **mouse** (more of which on p. 143).

The processor

The "brain" of a computer is usually housed in a featureless box, perhaps with a CD slot in the front, and with the odd light flashing to show that the hard disk is working. The display screen rests on the box. The processor may also come in a "tower" that stands on the floor or on the desk, next to the display.

At the heart of the computer is the **cpu** (**central processing unit**), comprising a microprocessor silicon chip or set of chips (chipset). The main manufacturers are Intel (identified by the numbers 80286, 80386, 80486 . . . Pentium, Pentium II, Pentium III, Pentium 4), who supply the chips for the PC and compatibles, and Motorola (identified by the numbers 68000, 68020, 68030, 68040), who supply the chips for the Apple Macintosh. Apple PowerMacs use PowerPC RISC (reduced instruction set computer) chips, which are the result of a joint venture between IBM, Apple, and Motorola, and are numbered 601, 603, 604, and so on. The latest Mac processors are numbered G3, G4, and so on.

Raw speed in computer terms is measured by the internal **clock speed**. Clock speed is measured in MHz (megahertz, or millions of cycles per second). For example, a Macintosh Classic built around a 68000 CPU chip ran at 8 MHz, a PowerMac 9500 ran at 200 MHz, and a G4 runs at 500 MHz.

At every tick of the clock, the CPU processes an instruction, or part of one. These are not the instructions you key into the computer, though. The computer breaks down your complicated instructions into millions of simple ones, which it calculates very quickly.

Computers for graphics applications have special requirements. Compared with text, pictures take up enormous amounts of memory and to move them around, the CPUs on these systems require some help. They are therefore augmented with various speed-increasing subsystems — such as printed circuit-boards (PCBs), or cards, to control the color graphics on the screen.

All this, however, is pure speed, and, like the top figure on an automobile's speedometer, is an abstract quantity. Some computers may be able to redraw the screen after a tricky manipulation more quickly than others. But how quickly a designer actually completes a given job ultimately depends both on the efficacy of the software and on the proficiency of the operator.

Memory: ROM and RAM

Computers have two sorts of chip-based memory. **ROM** (**read-only memory**) chips have instructions manufactured into them, and they cannot be altered. These instructions remain on the chip even when the computer is switched off. ROM chips contain some of the computer's operating system, and give a computer its "personality."

Local memory, containing the immediate job in hand, is in the form of **RAM** (**random access memory**) chips which are wiped clean each time the computer is switched off (Fig. **5.5**). This, of course, includes any form of power failure, however fleeting. The amount of RAM a computer has available is measured in **bytes**, each equal to 8 **bits** (bit is short for binary digit). A kbyte, k, or kilobyte is not a thousand bytes as you may have expected, but 1024 bytes, which is equal to 2^{10} (2 to the power of 10, or 2 x 2 x 2 x 2 x 2 x 2 x 2 x 2 x 2 x 2). A megabyte, written 1 Mbyte, is more than a million bytes. A gigabyte, or Gbyte, is more than 1000 Mbytes.

The reason for the strange number 1024 is as follows. Computers count in binary numbers, 0s and 1s. (Hexadecimal, referred to earlier, is easily converted to binary and is more convenient for computer scientists to deal with.) Thus, to a computer, "round numbers" are always powers of 2 (such as 4, 8, 16, 32, 64, 128, 256, 512, and 1024), and that is why you will often see these particular numbers associated with computers.

ASCII (**American Standard Code for Information Interchange**), the worldwide format for encoding alphanumeric text, allocates a single byte per character. This chapter contains over 64.5 kbytes of information. The hard disk on my iMac computer is capable of containing 20 Gbytes, and that is quite modest by graphic design standards.

Saved data is stored in a hard-disk drive. It is advisable to back-up important data to CDs or on to DAT (digital audio tape) drives, which use cartridges that are similar to audio cassettes.

Removable hard disks, such as Iomega's Zip drive, can be added to your system. They are useful for overflow, archiving, and for

5.5 RAM comes in the form of tiny silicon chips which are encased in plastic. In a Mac, they are mounted in lines on long, thin, printed circuit-boards and are called SIMMs (single in-line memory modules) or DIMMs (dual in-line memory modules).

transporting large files to an image-setting bureau. For memory-intensive operations, you can buy optical drives that store many Gbytes of data. A device containing several optical disk drives is called a jukebox. CD-rom drives, now commonly built in to Macs and PCs, are compact-disc players for computers which can hold up to 650 Mbytes of information over several sessions. DVD-rom drives play DVDs (digital versatile disks) capable of storing over 5 Gbytes of data.

Data travels round the computer on "buses," which are like clumps of wires. There are two main buses: the memory bus and the data bus. A 32-bit computer has a data bus 32 bits wide, i.e. 32 bits of data can travel around the computer and be processed at the same time. The "width" of the bus determines how much data can be processed at each tick of the clock, and how much RAM can be managed.

A typical home PC from the early 1980s had an 8-bit processor and a 16-bit memory bus. It could thus address only 216 permutations of 0s and 1s, which equals 64 k possible memory locations in RAM. A 32-bit processor can handle several

Mbytes. Computers also commonly have "cache memory." This is a portion of RAM that holds the most recently used data from the hard disk ready for further action, thus increasing the apparent speed of access to the user.

Frame buffers

A **frame buffer** is a short-term memory store between the processor and the display screen.

The frame buffer or VRAM (video random-access memory) contains the current image in the form of a bitmap of pixels (picture elements; see p. 140). It comprises several layers or planes, with one bit (a 1 or a 0) stored for each pixel on each plane. The number of planes, and hence the number of bits allocated to each pixel, determines how many colors or "grayscale" shades the displayed pixel can be.

A mono screen, without grayscales, has 1 bit per pixel. An 8-plane system can handle 2^8 (256) different colors or grayscales. A 24-plane system can display 16·8 million, a number considered sufficient to produce realistic-looking images. A 32-bit system has 24 bits allocated to color, the rest for other

things — on a Mac, for example, the extra 8 bits are called the "alpha channel" and are available for animation and masking effects.

Displays

The computer's display is the window through which we view whatever is being designed, and through which we interact with the software. It is important to remember, however, that the image on the screen is more often than not a crude representation of the page that exists inside the computer's memory. Printed output will always be crisper, in the correct typeface, and with the letterspacing you have specified in the software. The output quality is dependent on the output device — whether it be a low-resolution laser printer or a high-resolution imagesetter — not on the quality of the screen.

The majority of computer displays are based on the **CRT (cathode ray tube)**, the tube that takes up most of the space in a television set. What make the CRT work are substances called phosphors: electrically active materials that luminesce when bombarded by electrons.

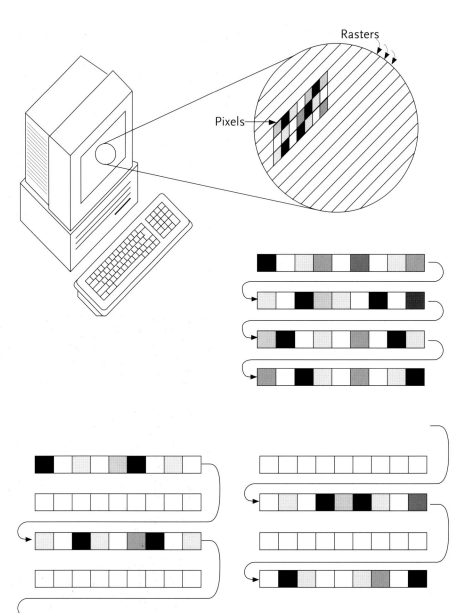

5.6 Pixels are tiny identifiable areas of the computer's display, and there is a one-to-one relationship between a pixel and a portion of computer memory. The display's electron gun scans the screen in lines called rasters. If it scans every single line in one pass, the display is non-interlaced. If it scans only every other line each pass, then the screen is interlaced.

Rasters

Pixels

Computer and television screens are called raster displays, from the Latin *rastrum*, or rake (Fig. **5.6**). The electron gun at the back of the CRT scans the whole screen in horizontal lines, top to bottom, usually 60 times a second (60 Hz). On a non-interlaced display, every line is scanned each cycle. In a television set, alternate lines are scanned each cycle, resulting in two "fields" per cycle. This is known as an interlaced display. Most computer companies make screens that are non-interlaced, because they flicker less than interlaced screens.

Each scan line is chopped into chunks called pixels (picture elements). Pixels are the screen equivalent of dots (see p. 83), and, as we discussed earlier, each pixel on the screen is described by one or more bits in the frame buffer. The resolution (fineness) of a raster display is measured by the number of pixels horizontally by the number of scan lines vertically. The resolution of a 14-inch display is 640 x 480. For higher resolutions — 1280 x 1024, for example — you may need a plug-in graphics card (printed circuit-board) and a special **high-resolution** screen (see below). A multiscan screen can display different resolutions: from 640 x 480 to 1024 x 768, for example. To display at higher resolutions, you may need to upgrade your VRAM or add a graphics card.

Other technologies, such as the flat panel LCD (**liquid crystal display**) found in laptop computers, are appearing on the market. These are more expensive than CRT screens, but take up less space on the desk, are flicker-free, and use up less power.

Meanwhile, software optical illusions such as **anti-aliasing** (Fig. **5.7**) are used to improve the perceived resolution of their screens. Anti-aliasing smooths out the staircase effect seen on diagonal lines near the horizontal. It does so by coloring the pixels around the diagonals that actually define the line or edge in subtle shades of the current foreground and background colors.

If you are doing lots of design work you will need a large-format display: either 17 inch (432 mm), or 21 inch (533 mm). Prepress operators and designers doing lots of color work will need the highest-possible quality of screen to make

5.7 Anti-aliasing is a way of fooling the eye into thinking your screen has a higher resolution than it actually has. Low-res screens produce jagged edges, especially on diagonals. Shading the pixels near the edges with a mixture of the foreground and background colors results in a fuzziness that looks smooth at a distance.

sure the transmitted RGB color of the screen faithfully predicts the CMYK color of the scan and finished printed page. The LaCie Electron monitor (Fig. **5.8**) is a professional prepress screen with an integral hood to prevent reflections and glare. Blue Eye is its matching display calibrator that adjusts each gun inside the monitor and for color management creates a Photoshop or ColorSync profile.

The color coming from a color monitor, being transmitted light, will never be the same as the color reflected from a printed page (see pp. 90–1), and the color output will change as the phosphors age. To make the colors on the screen as faithful as possible, you must **color calibrate** your screen regularly,

5.8 The LaCie Electron is a professional prepress display with a built-in hood. It comes in two versions: 19 inch (shown) and 22 inch. The 19 in version has a maximum resolution of 1600 x 1200 at 85Hz ; the 22 in version has a maximum resolution of 2048 x 1536 at 75Hz. Both use Diamondtron flat-aperture grille technology with a dot pitch of 0.24 mm.

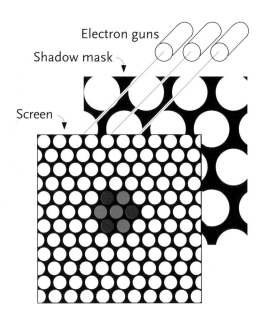

5.9 Displays are built around two distinct technologies: those based on Sony's Trinitron and Mitsubishi's Diamondtron with their vertical aperture grille (stripe-pitch) tubes, and the more conventional shadowmask (dot-pitch) screens mainly manufactured by Hitachi.

recalibrating for color "temperature" appropriate to the application and local lighting conditions (Fig. **5.10**). Color-management systems such as Apple's ColorSync and Kodak's CMS, in conjunction with application software, use device profiles supplied by the manufacturers of displays and scanners to ensure consistency between scans, what you see on the screen, and the printed product.

Color-display systems come in two parts: the color screen itself, and the graphics card that drives it. The monitor's tube comes from one of three major manufacturers: Hitachi, Sony, and Mitsubishi. The traditional tubes, which are mainly manufactured by Hitachi, have three electron guns, one each for the red, green, and blue dots on the screen (Fig. **5.9**). On their way to the screen, the beams are synchronized by a shadowmask — a metal mask with precisely placed holes through which the beams pass. A Sony Trinitron tube uses a single gun, and the shadowmask is a grid of fine vertical slots. A Trinitron tube is flatter and has a sharper, brighter picture, but it is heavier than regular screens and gives noticeable vertical lines of color. You may also be able to see two very thin dark horizontal

lines: one about a quarter from the top; the other a quarter from the bottom.

The graphics card contains the frame buffer, and is either 8-bit, for 256 displayable colors, or 24-bit, for 16·7 million colors. An 8-bit card stores information about which colors are being used (the current palette) in a color look-up table. This is like an array of pigeon holes. Each contains the "address" of four numbers: an index number, plus values for the red, green, and blue output levels that add together to

5.10 Displays must be calibrated regularly if their color reproduction is to remain faithful. A LaCie Blue Eye color calibrator makes sure that colors on the screen bear a good resemblance to printed colors. It carries out hardware calibration through a serial connection between the Mac and the display — the serial connection enables the monitor and the CPU to exchange information, allowing the monitor to be calibrated. It first adjusts each electron gun (red, green, and blue) individually until they are at an optimum setting. It then creates a ColorSync profile which can be used in applications such as Adobe Photoshop.

display your chosen color. With 24-bit color, you have direct access to all 16·7 million colors, not just a selection of 256, and there is no need for the intermediate indexing. Each color — red, green, blue — is allocated an 8-bit value, to drive the red, green, and blue electron guns in the tube.

Input devices

The input device is the means by which the designer tells the machine and the software what to do. The particular method used for human/computer interaction is called the computer's graphical user interface (GUI). Originally, you would have had to type commands using the computer's keyboard. Apple Macintosh then introduced the "point and click" approach, and almost all applications now make use of a mouse pointing device to "pull down" menus (lists of options), select icons (pictures that represent tools and documents), and open and close windows (active areas of the screen). Microsoft's Windows for PCs and X-Windows for workstations are other examples.

Computer graphics users have long abandoned exclusive use of the keyboard that always comes with the

5.11 Digitizers are essential for precision drawing and tracing. Wacom's Graphire digitizing tablets are available with both a cordless pressure-sensitive stylus and a mouse.

computer, in favor of other methods for manipulating on-screen cursors and entering shape descriptions. However, keyboard-entered shortcut commands remain popular with experienced so-called "power" users, who find mouse operations slow compared with typing "command-P" to print, for example.

There are many alternatives to the mouse, however. There are rolling balls, joysticks, thumb-wheels, and digitizing tablets — which come with a pen-like stylus or a mouse-like puck with buttons, depending on the user's preference.

Digitizing tablets like the Wacom Intuos or Graphire (Fig. **5.11**) perform a dual role: they can be used to point and pick software commands from a menu, or to make pictures. Most are electro-magnetic devices containing a grid of fine wires embedded into the work surface; others make use of sonic techniques to detect the position of the stylus or puck.

A digitizer with a cordless pressure-sensitive stylus, from a supplier such as Wacom, can be used with some draw-and-paint programs to create images more

5.13 Wacom's PL-500 digitizer has a built-in 15-inch LCD screen with a resolution of 1024 x 768 pixels and 24-bit color depth. Working with a pen with pressure and tilt sensitivity, plus the coating of the scratch-proof LCD surface, gives the user the sensation of working on paper.

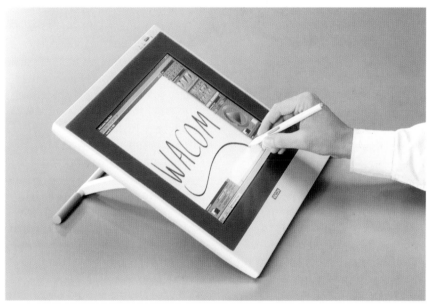

5.14 Most computers come with a standard mouse pointing device, but you don't have to stay with it. The Apple Pro Mouse has an optical tracking mechanism, so it won't stick or skip around. There is no obvious button: its body pivots up and down to activate the click mechanism.

intuitively than with a mouse and keyboard (Fig. **5.13**).

The conventional mechanical **mouse** (Fig. **5.14**) suffers from friction, or the lack of it (use a special mouse pad rather than the slippery surface of the desk, or an optical mouse). And, as it works in relative coordinates rather than absolute ones, it can get lost in space. It is fine for menu picking, but little use for drawing. Turn the mouse upside down, however, and you have the **rolling ball** (Fig. **5.12**) — a device that has been used in air-traffic control for decades. These are much more touch-sensitive than joysticks. Furthermore, they are less prone to breakage, don't trap dirt, and have a small "footprint."

5.12 Rolling balls are more touch-sensitive than mouses, have a smaller "footprint," and are more robust. The thumb-operated Logitech TrackMan Marble Wheel trackball has USB or PS/2 connection with patented Marble sensing technology. An innovative scroll wheel that's also a third mouse button provides fast scrolling in Windows or Mac applications

Digital cameras

A **digital camera** looks and feels just like a conventional analog camera, but it has one big difference. Instead of capturing an image on light-sensitive film that has to be sent away to be developed and printed, a digital camera uses an array of CCD (charge-coupled device) sensors in order to convert the image into a form that can be stored in the camera's RAM and then downloaded into your computer.

The advantages are that you don't need to buy film, you don't have to wait for the film to be developed, and there is no need to scan the photograph or transparency into your computer. The disadvantages are that digital cameras are relatively expensive, the images are generally at a lower resolution than the silver crystals of photographic film, and they can only store a limited number of images. If you are working away from the studio, and need to take more pictures, you will need a portable computer to use as a mass storage device.

5.15 Canon Digital Ixus 51 Pro camera

The Canon Digital Ixus 51 Pro, for example (Fig. **5.15**), can store 12 images at a resolution of 1600 x 1200 or 46 images at 640 x 480 pixels on an 8Mbyte CompactFlash card. Note that there are currently two different types of RAM storage cards: CompactFlash (used by Canon and Kodak cameras) or SmartMedia (Olympus and most Fujifilm cameras).

It is also possible to buy digital backs to attach to conventional 5 in x 4 in cameras. These cameras have much higher resolutions than the compact versions (up to 6000 x 7520), but must be wired directly to a computer and, as they require

long exposure times, must be used with a tripod and high-intensity lights. As RAM comes down in price, however, and the technology of the digital camera matures, there will undoubtedly come a time when a digital camera becomes an essential part of the designer's toolkit.

Scanners

A scanner converts flat artwork, photographs, or transparencies into a form that can be "seen" by your computer software. You may have a desktop scanner in your studio and you will almost certainly have to make use of the drum scanner at your repro service bureau.

Desktop scanners (Fig. **5.16**) allow the designer to input already existing images into the system — commissioned photographs, drawings, or images plagiarized from magazines. Scanned data, whether

5.16 A desktop scanner such as this Epson Expression 1640XL has an A3+ / 12.2 in x 17.2 in maximum scanning area, 42-bit color depth giving the ability to capture 440 billion colors and 16,384 shades of gray, and an optical resolution of 1600 x 3200 dpi.

5.17 A top-end flatbed scanner, such as this Dainippon Screen Cézanne, can scan reflection copy, transparencies, line art, color negatives, and printed material at high speeds.

it comes from a digital camera or a scanner, is in its raw form a bitmapped image (see p. 74). A bitmap is good enough for a paint system such as Photoshop to get to grips with. However, a drawing package will need some conversion, and the scanned image is best used as a background layer, to be traced over.

The most popular scanners for the studio are the single-pass flatbed desktops, which look similar to photocopiers. The early models worked like photocopiers, with a moving scan head containing a fluorescent tube slowly moving from end to end of the original. More recent models use CCDs (charge-coupled devices) to recognize and store images.

A rule of thumb says you should scan at a resolution that is twice the screen you plan to use for printing, if the image is to be reproduced at same size. So scanning with a resolution of 300 dpi will be able to produce a halftone at same size with a screen of 150 lines. Although this will be good enough for newspaper or newsletter reproduction, for other jobs a scanned image should be used for position only and replaced with a professionally screened image at the film stage.

Desktop color scanners (Fig. **5.17**) work by scanning the image using red, green, and blue lamps and arrays of CCD sensors. Even the cheapest scanners now can scan at true (rather than interpolated) optical resolution of 600 dpi. Scanners of 1200 dpi are within the reach of most designers. Color depth of 24 bits used to be common, but this has evolved to 36 and even 42 bits. The greater the resolution and color

depth, the greater the information at your disposal when you begin to manipulate the image. Some scanners offer a larger flatbed area; others may have a lamp in the lid and adaptors for scanning different sizes of transparencies.

Scanners used to connect to the computer via a SCSI (small computer system interface) parallel interface. More recent scanners use USB (universal serial bus), which is hot-swappable but quite a lot slower. FireWire (IEEE 1394 or I-Link) is a serial bus interface standard found mainly in digital video cameras but offering high-speed communications between computers, scanners, and hard disk drives. It can transfer data between a computer and its peripherals at 100, 200, or 400 Mbps, with a planned increase to 2 Gbps. Cable length is limited to about 15 feet (4.5 m) but up to 16 cables can be daisy-chained yielding a total length of 236 feet (72 m).

FireWire can daisy-chain together up to 63 peripherals in a tree-like structure (as opposed to SCSI's daisy-chain structure). It allows peer-to-peer device communication, such as communication between a scanner and a printer, to take place

without using system memory or the CPU. It is also designed to support plug-and-play and hot swapping. The six-wire cable is not only more convenient than SCSI cables but can supply up to 60 watts of power, allowing low-consumption devices to operate without a separate power cord.

The standard means of connecting a scanner to application software such as Photoshop is something called TWAIN, from Kipling's "The Ballad of East and West" — "... and never the twain shall meet ...," reflecting the difficulty, at the time, of connecting scanners and personal computers. The standard was first released in 1992. Because it is often seen in caps, people believed it to be an acronym, and a contest was held to come up with an expansion. None were selected, but the entry "Technology Without An Interesting Name" continues to haunt the standard!

High-end scanners — the kind found at your repro service bureau — come in two distinct types: flatbed (like studio desktop scanners) which can achieve resolutions of 5000 dpi (see Fig. 5.17) and the

5.19 Slide scanners, such as this Polaroid Sprintscan 45 Ultra, are dedicated to scanning 35 mm, 70 mm and 5 in x 4 in transparencies at up to 2500 dpi. They are also useful for scanning in color negatives from regular print film.

more traditional drum scanners which can more than double that figure (Fig. **5.18**). It is important to mount the artwork very precisely. With a flatbed scanner, you just lay the artwork on the glass plate or place transparencies into a carrier with pre-cut frames and you're ready to scan. Mounting film or flexible artwork on a drum scanner is more complicated: the drum spins very quickly, so you must secure the film well. Oil mounting (which reduces problems created by dust and scratches on the film) can be used on drum scanners: bending the film around the drum creates tension which holds it evenly against the glass. Oil mounting on flatbed scanners isn't practical, because a flat piece of film lacks the tension it needs to maintain

an even layer of oil, and air bubbles will form.

Flatbed scanners use a line of CCDs (charge-coupled devices), just like studio desktop scanners. Drum scanners use photomultiplier tubes. Separations are made by a beam splitter, which divides the light transmitted through the transparency or off the artwork into its three color components. Each beam goes through a filter corresponding to one of the additive primaries (see

p. 00) and is detected by a photocell. These signals are converted into CMYK by color-correction software.

When changing levels of magnification, both types of scanner maintain a 1 : 1 aspect ratio. To do this, drum scanners change the rate at which the optics scan across the drum. At the same time, they change the frequency with which the photomultiplier samples the image. Scanning at a lower rate captures finer lines horizontally; higher-frequency sampling keeps the vertical density the same. Flatbed scanners use lenses to map a smaller or larger area of the film on to the CCDs: when a smaller area is captured, a shorter movement by the stepper motor keeps the density of pixels the same vertically and horizontally.

Until all photographers are equipped with digital cameras, there will still be a need to scan in slides or negatives. High-end flatbed and drum scanners are happiest with large-format transparencies: 35 mm slides are small and often come in mounts that lift the emulsion away from the glass and the optimum focusing distance. Dedicated slide scanners are optimized for this kind of work and can deliver high-quality scans quickly: Polaroid's SprintScan 45 Ultra (Fig. **5.19**) has 2500 dpi resolution and can scan 35 mm or 5 in x 4 in transparencies.

5.18 This Heidelberg Primescan drum scanner has three photo-multipliers and rotates at a maximum speed of 1800 rpm. Scaling is possible up to 3000% with a maximum scanning resolution of 11,000 dpi (4330 l/cm).

▶ **5.20** This A4 Epson AcuLaser C2000 laser printer has an optical resolution of 2400 x 600 dpi and prints at five pages per minute in color or twenty pages per minute black and white.

Output devices: laser printers and imagesetters

A graphic designer will be most likely to output to a nearby laser or inkjet printer for proofing, and send a PostScript file to a repro service bureau for imagesetting on bromide paper or film. In addition, many of the output devices on the following pages can be used for undemanding short printing runs.

Laser printers work on a similar principle to laser photocopiers (Fig. **5.20**). In a photocopier, the light reflected from the white areas of an image causes a rotating drum charged with static electricity to lose its charge, so the toner doesn't stick. In a laser printer, however, there is no "original," so a laser draws a negative image on to the drum, removing charge from the white areas.

Laser printers, such as Apple's LaserWriter family and Hewlett-Packard's LaserJets, are small-format, and most print in black and white only. The resolution is never less than 600 dpi, which is great for proofing, producing artwork for publications such as newsletters, and printing short runs of simple documents. Color laser copiers are falling in price and are increasingly being used for proofing.

The original phototypesetters could only set type. With the introduction of PostScript came the imagesetter, which could output graphics and pictures as well as type (Fig. **5.21**). The ability to output all page elements in position streamlined the traditional camera and stripping operations, paving the way for totally digital prepress.

The resolution of an imagesetter is measured in dpi (dots per inch),

◀ **5.21** High-end color image-setters such as this Dainippon Screen Tanto 5120 are used to produce high-quality film separations.

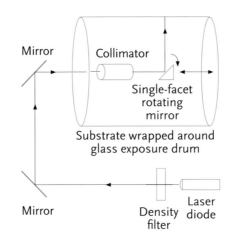

5.22 Drum imagesetter (above) and capstan (below) configurations. Each has its particular pros and cons, but the drum-based ones seem to offer the better and more consistent quality of output.

Mirror — Collimator

Single-facet rotating mirror

Substrate wrapped around glass exposure drum

Mirror — Density filter — Laser diode

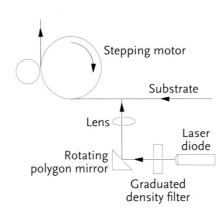

Stepping motor

Substrate

Lens

Laser diode

Rotating polygon mirror

Graduated density filter

and these should not be confused with halftone dots, which are measured in lpi (lines per inch). A halftone dot is a cluster of many imagesetter dots (which, to avoid confusion, we'll call spots). An imagesetter might deliver a resolution of up to 4876 dpi — in other words, 847 distinct spots can be laid along a line one inch long with their edges just touching. Most, however, will output at 1200 (actually 1219) or 2400 (actually 2438) dpi.

The size of a laser's spot cannot easily be altered, and so halftone dots are built up by overlapping the spots (Fig. **5.23**). The **addressability** of an imagesetter is the accuracy with which the centers of the spots can be placed in proximity with each other. Thus an addressability of 2540 dpi means that the centers of two spots can be positioned $1/2540^{th}$ of an inch apart. So, when we talk about resolution, we are more correctly talking about addressability. Other important parameters are the dot (spot) size, measured in **mils** (thousandths of an inch) or micrometers (aka µm or microns — millionths of a meter) and the repeatability, also measured in mils or microns, which is a measure of how well separations will register together.

We are told that the higher the resolution (but read: addressability), the better the print quality. But this is not always the case: there comes a point where there is so much overlapping of spots that any difference in quality is marginal. Similar results could probably be obtained using a lower setting.

There are two main types of imagesetter: capstan and drum (Fig. **5.22**). In an internal drum imagesetter, film enters and exits through a gap at the base of a large, stationary drum. Tension rollers on either side of the gap hold the film flush

against the inside of the drum. In a capstan or roll-fed imagesetter, film enters and exits the imagesetter between tension rollers, which hold the film taut and flat. Photo material — film or bromide paper — is stored in a light-tight cassette or box and then pulled across the imaging area into a receiving cassette or direct to an inline chemical processor.

Drum-based imagesetters are either internal-drum, where the film is positioned inside the drum and the imaging system moves, or external-drum systems, where the film is positioned on the outside of the drum and the drum rotates while the imaging system remains stationary. Internal drum imagesetters have an imaging laser attached to a screw which runs down the middle of the drum. As the laser spins, it slowly moves across the drum, writing the image, line by line. The film is always at the same distance from the laser. Capstan imagesetters have a stationary laser: a spinning mirror located directly above the film reflects the beam from side to side across the film.

A drum imagesetter's imaging area is limited in both width and length by the diameter and length

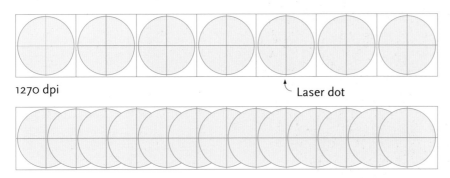

1270 dpi

Laser dot

2540 dpi

5.23 Resolution and addressability are two different, but related, parameters of an imagesetter. Resolution is the number of dots edge to edge in a line measuring an inch; addressability is a measure of how close, centre to centre, those dots can be placed next to one another.

of the drum. These imagesetters typically accept wider film sizes than do capstan devices, which are limited by the tolerance to distortion at the edges of the imaging area where the laser beam is being reflected at a steeper angle. Capstan imagesetters have to use complex optical systems to ensure that the beam reaching the film or paper is uniform in strength. Imperfections in all the extra optics can lead to slurring, and loss of brightness and contrast. This results in weaker (less sharp) dots. Typically these devices use narrower film than drum imagesetters do, but can run longer lengths of film.

Drum-based imagesetters produce more accuracy and repeatability of images for each of the four films. They use sheets of film capable of four-up standard pages. Each of the four color separations can be output on one sheet of film, or four sheets can be output on four-up pages, one for each CMYK color.

Imagesetters which, along with imposition software, produce film negatives with pages in position ready for platemaking are sometimes called **imposetters**.

There must also be some means of processing the film or bromide paper, and imagesetters will have either an inline film processor

attached, or cassettes of exposed film will have to be taken to a separate unit. Dry imagesetters output film without the need for wet chemicals and all the problems of recycling and disposal. Heidelberg (formerly Linotype-Hell) and Polaroid have collaborated on the Quicksetter (Fig. **5.24**). The film consists of a carrier layer and a top foil. Between these, under a laser-sensitive layer, is a layer of microscopic carbon particles. The laser combines the carbon with the laser-sensitive layer, and then the foil with the surplus carbon is peeled away. Finally, a laminator seals the image to the carrier film. It has two resolutions: 2540 dpi and 3387 dpi with a dot size of 7·5 μm.

In a **platesetter**, the film is replaced by plate material. Although some imagesetters have always been able to output polyester plates for black-and-white work, these days color computer-to-plate technology is a reality (see p. 182 in Chapter 6).

To print documents containing PostScript files (see p. 72) — such as type, a page layout from Quark-XPress or InDesign, or an image from a program such as FreeHand or Illustrator — an imagesetter has to operate with a device called a **RIP (raster image processor)**. These are sometimes built into the imagesetter, but are usually housed in a separate box. A RIP is a computer in its own right, and often is just that — a standard Mac or PC with lots of RAM — and all it ever does is convert PostScript into the raster bitmap an imagesetter can read and output. The RIP also takes care of the screening of halftones. A 3600 dpi imagesetter with a spot

5.25 Inkjet printers, like this Epson 870, work by shooting minute drops of ink at the paper. It has a resolution of 1440 dpi and uses a four-color cartridge.

5.26 The Tektronix Phaser 850 uses solid ink that is melted by the print head and solidifies again on the substrate. It has a resolution of 1200 x 600 dpi and a maximum speed of 14 pages per minute.

size of 7.5 μm will have a maximum screen of 500 lpi.

To do all the "ripping" on the designer's computer would be very time-consuming. A way to get round this is to send only the text, rules, and non-scanned graphics to the RIP, along with instructions describing the size, cropping, and position on the page of the scanned pictures (the high-resolution files). This is a process known as **APR (automatic picture replacement)**.

The picture commands, tagged on to the PostScript file, are part of a standard known as the **OPI (open prepress interface)**, originally proposed by Aldus. A page description can thus be transferred from a Mac or PC to a faster, more powerful workstation at the repro service bureau and then to the RIP. A designer's computer is thus

liberated to do what it does best — page design and layout.

Hardcopy: other technologies

There are many other forms of output, especially for color, and one or more of the machines described here will be found in the designer's studio. Dot-matrix printers are now virtually obsolete.

Inkjet printers (Fig. **5.25**) spray jets of microscopic electrically charged droplets of ink on to a moving roll of paper. These jets of ink are deflected by electromagnets — just like the electron beam in a television tube — to build up the image. **Bubblejet printers** have an array of thin nozzles in the print head, each of which is full of ink, held there by surface tension. A small heating element causes a bubble to form which forces the ink out of the nozzle and on to the page

5.27 In bubblejet printers, a heating element causes bubbles to form in the print head, thus forcing drops of ink to fly on to the paper.

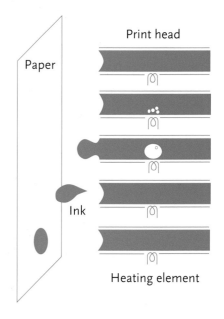

Print head

Paper

Ink

Heating element

(Fig. **5.27**). Another variation is the **thermojet plotter**, which sprays melted plastic on to the paper (Fig. **5.26**).

Top-end inkjet printers such as the Epson 7000 are used for color proofing and artists' prints. Giclée printers (from the French for "spraying" or "spreading") are medium- to large-format inkjet devices for printing on to substrates such as watercolor paper using archival ink. Output is specifically targeted to creating fine-art prints. Large-scale inkjets can be used to print posters up to A0 in size, and some can print the huge banners that hang outside buildings (Fig. **5.29**).

5.28 In the thermal-transfer process, rolls of transfer paper containing colored wax are "ironed" on to smooth paper by hundreds of individually controlled heating elements.

Roll of transfer material

Take-up reel

Heating element

Wax

Paper path

Roller

Thermal-transfer printers use an inked-roll cartridge sandwiched between the mechanism and the drawing. This acts like carbon paper, "ironing" the image on to clay-coated paper. The three process colors (and sometimes black) are applied, one at a time, by melting dots of wax on to the paper or acetate at a resolution of 300 dpi (Fig. **5.28**). The machines are cleaner and dryer than inkjets, but consumables are more expensive. **Thermal-transfer machines** produce solid, bright colors, but tend to print blues and greens darker than inkjets. **Direct thermal printers** "burn" a monochrome image into specially coated paper using thermal heads.

5.29 Large format six-color inkjet printers, like this HP DesignJet 5000, can be used to print 42" (107 cm) or 60" (152 cm) wide posters and fine art prints at a resolution of 1200 x 600 dpi.

5.30 Most output technologies can produce only one size of dot in just one intensity. This is fine for line work and flat color, but for smooth blends between colors, thermal transfer and inkjet printers have to resort to a trick called dithering, which introduces deliberate randomness into a dot pattern.

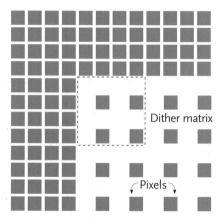

Dither matrix

Pixels

Thermal-transfer and inkjet printers produce all their colors by a process called **dithering** (Figs **5.30** and **5.31**), which is analogous to halftone screening. Pixels of cyan, magenta, and yellow (and sometimes black) are interspersed in regular patterns. Some printers use a fixed pattern of dithering, which results in a distinct step between colors. Others can make use of different patterns, leading to smoother gradations.

Laser, thermal-transfer, and inkjet printers are available with or without a PostScript driver, the PostScript versions being more expensive. It is possible to produce acceptable results without PostScript by using Adobe Type Manager or TrueType fonts. For most graphic designers committed to PostScript, and who need fast and consistent output, a PostScript-compatible printer will be essential.

5.31 Simple 1-bit dithering can be seen in this close-up — a laser plot of a chair produced by Kanwal Sharma of Lewis Sharma Design, a studio in Bristol, England, specializing in design for disabled people.

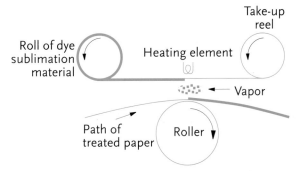

5.32 Dye-sublimation printers can produce an almost photographic quality of output, without dots or dithering, by melting and merging the inks right on the surface of the paper.

Roll of dye sublimation material

Heating element

Take-up reel

Vapor

Path of treated paper

Roller

Perhaps the best contender yet for color hardcopy is dye sublimation (Fig. **5.32**). Machines from Sony, Mitsubishi, and Hitachi mix the ink on the treated paper, without dots or dithering. So 16·7 million possible colors and 256 grayscales are smoothly blended together into a photographic-quality image almost good enough to go as artwork straight to the printer's.

Sublimation is the phenomenon whereby certain substances go directly from a solid to a gaseous form, without the usual intermediate liquid stage. The thermal head on a dye-sublimation printer varies the temperature so that the amount of dye emitted is continuously controlled.

At present, both the machines and the media for dye sublimation are expensive. With the creation of a market for digital cameras, dye sublimation will become much less expensive. Already, cheaper dye-sublimation printers such as the Sony UP-DP10 (Fig. **5.33**) can produce postcard-size prints of near-photographic quality.

Designers will sometimes want to take a 35 mm or larger-format transparency off the system. A **film recorder** (Fig. **5.34**), from companies such as Agfa and Lasergraphics,

5.33 Dye sublimation printers, such as the Sony UP-DP10, produce postcard-size images of photographic quality.

captures the image on a small, flat CRT built into the device, making three consecutive exposures through red, green, and blue filters.

A **pen plotter** will have limited use in most graphic design studios. An exception is where the graphic designer does a lot of packaging-design work. The pen plotter will be used to draw out fold-and-cut lines for the flat-pattern development of the carton or box being designed.

5.34 Film recorders are used to produce photographic transparencies direct from computer disk. They work by exposing the film three times — once for each of the primary colors — using small, flat cathode-ray tubes.

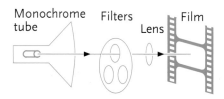

Monochrome tube

Filters

Lens

Film

5.35 Pen plotters are rarely used by graphic designers. An exception is when they are equipped with a cutting knife in place of the pen, like this Roland CAMM-1, and are used to produce masks for screenprinting or to cut vinyl letters for large signs.

A pen plotter, with a cutting knife replacing the pen or pencil, can also be used to prepare flat-color masks for silkscreen printing (see p. 189), and for cutting out vinyl letters for large-scale displays and signs (Fig. **5.35**).

There are two main types of pen plotter. Desktop plotters have the pen moving in all directions on a stationary piece of paper, held in place horizontally by a suction pump. Larger drum plotters have the pen moving in one direction and the paper in the other. These use abrasive pinch rollers to grip the edges of the paper, eliminating the necessity for sprocketed paper or film.

Roland's CAMM-1 is a desktop plotter modified for cutting vinyl

and Rubylith film. Large-format flatbed and drum production plotters/cutters are made by Zund, Wild, Aristo, and Kongsberg. Laser cutters are used for acrylics.

Plotters and cutters are vector devices, moving from point to point as on a graph, and the code that drives them conforms to a standard called HP-GL (Hewlett-Packard graphics language). PostScript is a vector format too, even though most computer devices encountered by the graphic designer work on the raster principle. PostScript to HP-GL conversion is necessary to drive a plotter directly from a PostScript package.

■ CHOOSING A SYSTEM

Turnkey systems

A **turnkey system** is a complete package of hardware and software dedicated to a particular task. You turn the (imaginary) key, and off you drive. The system may be assembled from standard pieces of equipment, bought in from well-known manufacturers and "badge engineered" (i.e. the turnkey vendor's logo is stuck on the front). Or perhaps the vendor will have modified it somewhat. The software that does the job is usually only available from the turnkey vendor. (If it is subsequently sold separately from the turnkey system, it is said to be unbundled.)

The attraction to the user is that everything needed for a working system is purchased from one source, with a single maintenance contract and one technical support person to call if things go wrong. The disadvantages are that the system cannot usually be used for other tasks — to run the studio administration, for example. And you are "locked in" to one supplier for any future updates of the hardware and software. The trend today is toward "open systems" with standardized GUIs, and the ability for programs to be able to pass information between each other. This may not be possible with a turnkey. It may have a quirky interface, and once you have learnt to use it, that knowledge will apply to that system only.

Nevertheless, there are still several turnkey systems around, aimed at highly specialized applications. There are systems targeted at packaging designers, with their need to design in three dimensions and then produce flat-pattern developments of cartons, for example. Another group of turnkeys is aimed at screenprinters and signwriters, who need to cut letters and masks out of vinyl and Rubylith.

Turnkey systems are usually much more expensive than an equivalent system assembled from component parts selected by you. The vendors have been guilty of trading on people's fear of computers by stressing that their menus, for example, make use of the terms and language peculiar to that trade. But these days, much more flexible systems can be assembled quite painlessly from standard PCs or Macs, plus any make of plotter or cutter and inexpensive, off-the-shelf software.

Selecting, upgrading, and networking the system

Selecting and cost-justifying a system is a very personal business. Read the computer magazines, visit trade shows, and talk to other users doing similar work to that of your studio. Methodologies exist that use spreadsheet programs to enable you to quantify the benefits of introducing a particular computer system into your studio. These may be understandable to an accountant or bank manager and be instrumental in securing you a loan to make the purchase. But of course they cannot predict the future. Ultimately, the success of an installation is down to you. You will have to understand what the system is capable of doing, and how it can

save you time and materials, while producing a quality product.

Once a successful installation has been established, however, expansion happens rapidly. This can take two forms: expansion of hardware — adding more systems, more memory, more output devices — and expansion into new application areas. On the Macintosh, particularly, programs have a common look and feel, which reduces the culture shock when you encounter new software.

As soon as you have more than one system, they can be networked together (Fig. **5.36**). There are three main reasons for **networking**: (1) to exchange files and messages with nearby members of your team; (2) to share expensive resources such as laser printers and disk drives; and (3) to co-operate jointly with

Mac file server with Ethernet card

PC with Ethernet card

Mac with Ethernet card

Terminating resistor

Mac with Ethernet adapter

EtherPrint device

Terminating resistor

Laser printer

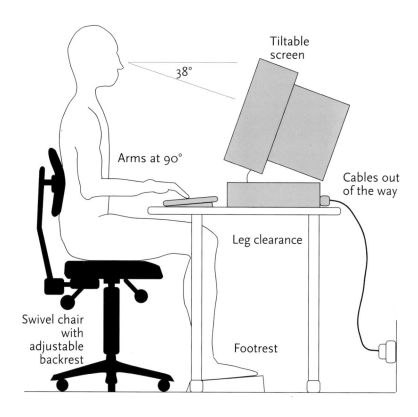

5.37 If you are to be working at the computer for long periods, it is vitally important to have the correct ergonomic conditions to reduce the possibility of computer-related health problems such as repetitive strain injury, backache, and eyestrain.

Tiltable screen

38°

Arms at 90°

Cables out of the way

Leg clearance

Swivel chair with adjustable backrest

Footrest

others in your studio on a large-scale project — in a workgroup.

Networking has a language all of its own, but all you need to know is that the most famous LAN (local-area network) is called Ethernet. It operates via a single length of coaxial cable or twisted-pair telephone cable, and was developed by Xerox, DEC, and Intel and introduced in 1980. With Ethernet it is possible to mix PCs and Macs on the same network.

Workstations were designed from the outset to be networked, so there should be no problem there. On the Macintosh, networking is fairly straightforward — Ethernet is usually built-in. Two systems can be linked using just one cable — a cross-over cable. When more than two systems are linked, one system is designated the server — the place where files are stored — and the others are called clients. Any computer in the network can act as a server. (In larger networks the file server is a dedicated computer with a large disk drive, but with no screen.) This provides shared storage for programs (though it is faster to keep your own local copy), files, or fonts that everyone on the network can access. It is the responsibility of the applications software to say who has read-only access and who has the authority to make changes to the master files.

Networking, though complicated, is not really difficult. It does, however, ultimately take you into a new league of computer management. While your studio may not want or be able to afford a systems manager, someone will have to take responsibility for the smooth operation of the system: developing filing systems, watching out for viruses, maintaining the shared resources, and so on.

Health and safety

As computers become common-place, so must health and safety issues be taken seriously. It is not yet normal, for example, to find ergonomically adjustable desks and chairs in large organizations, so what chance does the smaller design studio have? But they cost little compared with the total invest-ment in hardware and software, and can prevent lower-back damage to the most valuable component of the system — the designer. If that is not an incentive, then it should be noted that many of the recommendations are or will become legal requirements (Fig. **5.37**).

Desks should be as thin as possible and adjustable for height; chairs should be grounded sturdily and give good lumbar (lower-back) support. When you sit on your chair, upper and lower legs should be at right angles and feet comfortably on the floor. A footrest may have to be provided, subject to sufficient leg clearance, if desk height is not adjustable. The display screen should, ideally, be tiltable to an opti-mum 38 degrees below the horizon-tal. The angle between your upper and lower arm, when typing, should be 90 degrees.

There is a body of knowledge existing on such hazards as WRULD (work-related upper-limb disorders) and RSI (repetitive strain injury) —

a disorder of the hands and wrists causing numbness, swelling, tingling, and ultimately complete seizure. Keyboard operators have already suffered severe damage, and employers have already been sued for large sums, so do not wait until it is too late. Educate everyone to take frequent "thinking" breaks away from the system. To rest the eyes, a break of 15 minutes in every 75 minutes of continuous computer use is recommended.

Lighting should be diffuse and indirect. Fluorescent lights should have diffuser shades and should run parallel to the user's line of vision. Avoid glare and reflections, and excessively bright or dark color schemes. No user should have to face a window directly, and vertical blinds should be fitted, to be closed on sunny days. Regular eye tests are recommended. Because of the possibility of radiation, pregnant women should have the right to keep away from computers during pregnancy, without loss of pay or career prospects.

The health risk from static build-up and electromagnetic radiation from computers is an issue still hotly debated. Emissions from the front of a computer, i.e. through the screen, are in fact lower than from the sides or back. The computer screen should be at arm's length from your body — anyone sitting closer than 28 inches (711 mm) from the front is at some risk. Nobody should sit closer than 36 inches (914 mm) from the sides or back of a computer screen. Anti-glare screens do not help to cut down harmful radiation, unless they specifically say that they do. Radiation from mono and grayscale screens is lower than from color ones, and larger screens do not seem to emit any more radiation than smaller ones.

Photocopiers and laser printers should be placed where the air is changed at least once an hour, at least $3^{1}/4$ yards (3 m) away from the nearest person, and preferably in a separate, well-ventilated room to disperse the fumes produced by the toner. Noisy printers should also be fitted with hoods and be kept well away from the workers.

Finally, stress and anxiety can be reduced through appropriate and thorough training. This can be as simple as sitting down with the software manual for an hour or two each week to practice shortcuts, or spending time looking over the shoulder of the "resident guru" at work. Or it can involve taking time off from your paying projects regularly, to attend more formal training courses.

■ SUMMARY

Computers are here to stay. However, there is no such thing as a free lunch. There is a price to be paid for working on computers. The machinery will never be a panacea. It will never do the design work for you — in fact, it will probably make you work harder! You will have to do things that maybe before you left for the typesetter or printer to sort out. If you choose to go the computer route, the entire print-production process will become your concern ... and your responsibility. The benefits are enormous, not only in cost savings, increased creativity, and improved quality, but also in job satisfaction and personal fulfillment.

Investing in computer technology is no longer a risky venture; there is a huge body of experience within the graphics design industry for you to draw upon.

NEVILLE BRODY

LIFE STORY ■ Neville Brody was born in 1957 and grew up in Southgate, a suburb of North London. He studied fine art at Hornsey College of Art and graphic design at the London College of Printing (1977–80), where some of his tutors said he had no commercial potential. He joined the post-Punk music scene of the early 1980s, designing sleeves for Rocking Russian, Stiff, and Fetish Records, where he experimented with a graphic language that combined painting with constructivist typography. Between 1981 and 1986 he was art director for style magazine *The Face*, where his typographic experimentation influenced the look of magazines, advertising, and retail worldwide. In 1986 he set up a design studio with Fwa Richards. Jon Wozencroft's book, *The Graphic Language of Neville Brody* (see Workstation opposite) was the best-selling art book of 1988. Brody was also honored with a retrospective exhibition of the same name at London's Victoria & Albert Museum. He was just 31 years old.

For *Arena* magazine from 1987 to 1990, Brody tried to cool down the frenzy then surrounding design by developing a minimal typography, which, as the Apple Macintosh came into widespread use, he then developed into a more expressive approach. He started his own London studio The Studio in 1987 using the Mac to provide companies with templates that would enable them to carry out their own design needs in-house. He also began designing his own typefaces, such as Blur, Industria, and Insignia.

> **Digital data has a fluid form to it. As April Grieman once said, digital design is like painting where the paint never dries. It's always shiftable. It can always respond."**

Commissions from Germany and Japan, and postage stamps for the Dutch PTT, were followed by two major television graphics projects: the German cable channel Premiere and the Austrian state broadcasting company ORF.

In 1990, Brody founded FontWorks with Stuart Jensen and became a director of Erik Spiekermann's FontShop International, with whom he launched (with Jon Wozencroft) the experimental type magazine FUSE. In 1994, he changed his studio's name to Research Studios, with a subsidiary Research Arts specializing in film work. Amongst other things, he was responsible for the "electronic props" — everything that appears on computer screen — in the movie *Mission: Impossible*, displaying a version of the internet that was comprehensible to the then many non-internet users in the audience. This led him to set up Research Publishing, a web production company.

Clients include Deutsche Bank, Nike, Macromedia (if you use Macromedia products you will have seen Brody's designs on the boxes and intro screens), the *Guardian* newspaper and its website, and Channel 4. Brody now sees his role as nurturing the international team of designers at Research Studios rather than working on his own projects.

MANIFESTO ■ There is No Such Thing as Bad Design — Only Inappropriate Design

Brody on website design: he quotes with approval designer David Berlow's complaint that web design is "DTP all over again." After desktop publishing first appeared, it took a long time for designers to learn how to use it in a way that wasn't led by technological novelty. Online design has been going through the same process.

Web designers still have to get over what he calls "feature fascination": "Netscape announces a new feature and everyone immediately redesigns to take advantage, whether it works for their site or not. Start with what you want to say, not with how many ways you can say it."

The biggest problem for online design, Brody argues, is not technical. The right tools and software packages won't help if designers don't develop a new mindset. They need to stop porting print methods over to the net and start working with its distinctive features. He talks about recognizing the fluid, unfinished nature of digital design and text, about the way you can "play with time" online.

Brody suggests building websites so that no individual user ever experiences quite the same site as anyone else. "What you need is a smart site that recognizes where you've been, learns from it, and responds, so it's more of a dialogue, more user-affected. Digital data has a fluid form to it. As April Grieman once said, digital design is like painting where the paint never dries. It's always shiftable. It can always respond."

"It also means incorporating design evolution, making sure that the site feels alive to people visiting more than once. You can change information on a site all you want, but if it looks just the same after the tenth visit, those changes are no longer perceived. It feels like the same old site, like there's no more reason to visit. So design evolution becomes part of the design solution. Often people just don't get it. They think you are trying to pad your bill."

Brody is also an ethical designer: "I think intelligent, questioning design that can somehow help extend and open up people's awareness is valid. I wouldn't work for cigarette or oil companies, or even alcohol. I would find it immoral to have my persuasive skills used to encourage people to start smoking."

▼ Poster for Fuseday — lectures and an exhibition — at Manchester Metropolitan University in 1999.

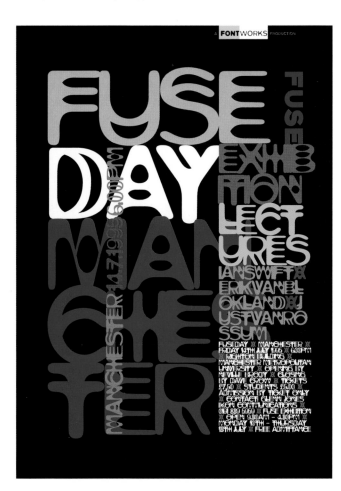

WORKSTATION

- Jon Wozencroft, *The Graphic Language of Neville Brody*, Thames and Hudson, London, 1988
- Jon Wozencroft, *The Graphic Language of Neville Brody 2*, Thames and Hudson, London, 1994
- Lewis Blackwell and Neville Brody, *G1*, Laurence King, London, 1996
- Graham Vickers, "Brody," *Creative Review*, May 2000, pp. 113–115
- Research under construction website: www.research.co.uk/index.html
- Interview by Steven Heller *Print* magazine: creativesight.com/cp/design/brody/brody_pr.htm
- *Guardian* interview: www.metagrafx.demon.co.uk/brody.html

◄ Brody designed a new identity for software company Macromedia in 1997, along with box graphics and splash screens.

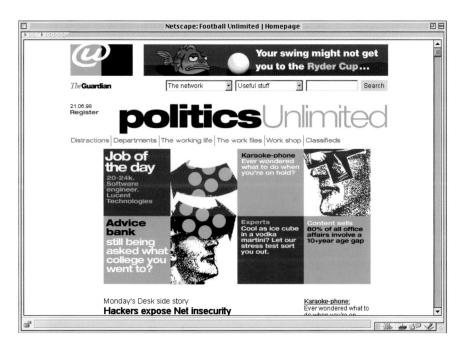

◄ Brody's *Guardian Unlimited* website (maintained by art director Ben Wuersching) beat *The Florida Times* and the *Albany Times* to win the award for Best Design of a Newspaper Online Service in the 1999 US EPpy Awards organized by *Editor and Publisher* magazine. *Guardian Unlimited* also won the Creative Achievement Award in the Pre-press and Publishing Awards 1999. Said the judges: "Aesthetically, the redesigned *Guardian* sites are streets ahead of anything on this side of the Atlantic (and much on the other side). The reader is moved effortlessly from story to story with the minimum of fuss. The color coding of the sites is a wonderful location-finder. You can't get lost in this cyberspace."

www.jour.city.ac.uk/olja99/present.html
www.guardian.co.uk

SIX ON PRESS

ON PRESS

The secret of a successful print job is a well-designed layout, some good scans for color repro, and the correct choice of paper and ink. Get all these right, and a good printing company can be relied upon to produce a pleasing result.

On press is the one part of the process that the graphic designer scarcely influences. It's now time to say goodbye to the layouts, leaving the printing work in the experienced hands of the printer.

Paper is one of the basic foundations of a good print job, but so often its choice is an afterthought. The first task in specifying paper is to think hard about what the finished item has to achieve. Then, after carefully considering the budget and availability of the stock, the designer can decide which particular characteristics of a paper are required.

Ink, too, plays a crucial role in the printing process, and the right formulation must be used for the right technology. Knowing about how inks perform will allow you to predict accurately how a job will come out. We discuss the effect of varnishing and laminating on an ink's performance, and explain the difference between die-stamping and thermography.

The printing process itself has a profound effect on print quality. The majority of designers will probably use offset litho or direct digital for most applications, but in some circumstances, gravure can become a cost-effective possibility. And when should you use flexography, or even screen printing? What are the pros and cons? This chapter gives an insight into the process of choosing the right supplier, and suggests how to go about ensuring the best-quality job.

Finally, we come to finishing — all those operations of folding, gathering, stitching, and trimming that happen to a printed sheet after it leaves the press. What are the options? Is perfect binding better than saddle-stitching? This chapter explains.

6.1 Papermaking in China, from a sequence of miniatures dating from 1811. Note that two people are required to make large sheets, a feat of coordination usually avoided by Western papermakers.

■ PAPER

Papermaking is older than any of the other printing crafts. Paper is largely a natural product — organic fibers held together by their own molecular forces. It is easy to make, but hard to make well. You can make it at home, with the help of a blender, some torn-up paper and other fibrous material (flowers, straw, cotton), and some kind of mesh to let the water drip through. Whether it will have the right degree of absorbency, strength, and surface finish required for fine printing is quite another matter.

The word "paper" comes from the Greek word "papyrus," the name of a plant that grows on the banks of the River Nile in Egypt. The writing material made from papyrus was not the kind of paper we are familiar with today. It was produced from strips peeled from the stem of the plant and pounded together into sheets.

The invention of paper made entirely from vegetable fibers — in this case tree bark, hemp, rags, and fishing nets — was announced to the Emperor of China in AD 105. However, a quasi-paper, made from pulped silk, was being made at least 200 years before that date.

Papermaking flourished in China (Fig. **6.1**), but the techniques took a thousand years to reach Europe. The first documented paper mill was established in Spain, at Xativa, around 1150. Mills were later set up in Italy, at Fabriano (a name still famous for the manufacture of beautiful paper) around 1260, and in Hertfordshire, England, around 1490. Papermaking was brought to

6.2 Papermaking is a continuous process, producing huge webs, or rolls, of paper. These are cut into sheets or made into smaller webs to feed the huge web litho, gravure, or flexo presses. Here, recycled paper is shown drying, at a mill in Minnesota.

America by a German, William Rittenhouse. The first American paper mill was established in Germantown, Pennsylvania, in 1690. Paper mills couldn't be built just anywhere. The process depends on huge amounts of pure running water — 150,000 US gallons (120,000 UK gallons or about 500,000 liters) of water, for example, are required to manufacture just one ton (or metric tonne) of handmade paper.

Until the 19th century, all paper was made by hand. The first paper-making machine was invented by Nicolas-Louis Robert in 1798 and built in France. His patents were taken up by Henry and Sealy Fourdrinier, and further developed in England. The Fourdrinier process, as it is known, allowed paper to be made in a continuous operation, producing a web (Fig. **6.2**), or roll, at the end of what are still some of the largest machines in existence.

The raw materials

Paper is made from cellulose fibers, and these come from plants or trees. Cellulose is a chemical compound of the elements carbon, hydrogen, and

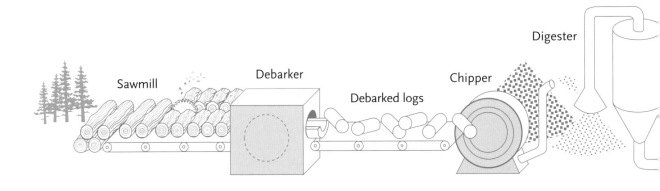

Sawmill Debarker Debarked logs Chipper Digester

6.3 Mechanical wood-pulp is made directly from logs. They are first debarked, then cut into smaller logs, and finally ground into fibers to be mixed with water and made into low-grade newsprint.

oxygen, and constitutes the cell walls of plants. Cellulose fibers are tubular, and swell when immersed in water. Allowed to dry in close contact with one another, they create their own gelatin "adhesive." Along with the bonding from the fibrillation (splitting and fraying) of the fibers, this produces an extremely strong material. The resulting paper is naturally porous and will absorb the inks and dyes used in printing. And it can be made less porous by adding a substance called **size**. It is also inert enough not to be affected by inks or photographic chemicals. The fibers are colorless and transparent, yet produce paper that is white and opaque.

Early paper mills made paper from rags. Textile production requires strong, long fibers for spinning and weaving. Papermaking is not so exacting, so papermills could recycle the shorter fibers from de-buttoned cast-off clothing and offcuts from shirt manufacturers, turning them into paper. Synthetic fibers such as nylon and rayon have put a stop to that. Artificial fibers (and animal fibers such as wool) are much more inert than cellulose. They do not bond as it does, and if they find their way into paper, they

weaken it and produce clear specks among the opaque white of the natural fibers.

One remaining source of pure cotton "rags," however, is the T-shirt industry, and its waste clippings are used to produce some of the finest papers. Another source of cotton for papermaking is from **linters**. These are the fibers left on the seed once the longer fibers for yarnmaking have been removed. The best linters come from the southern states of the United States, and from Egypt.

Clippings and linters are sorted, shredded, and placed in a large boiler. Under pressure and steam, any contaminants are removed. The fibers are washed and pulped. The dirty water is then drained off, clarified, and re-used. The pulp is bleached, and any chemicals left over are recycled into the next batch.

Chlorine bleaches, harmful to the environment, are gradually being replaced by **TCF (totally chlorine-free)** bleaches, such as hydrogen peroxide, and **ECF (elemental chlorine-free)** bleaches, such as chlorine dioxide. Although ECF bleaches do not release hazardous dioxins into the waste stream, the resulting

process water is often too corrosive to be recirculated. The pulp is then felted into board-like sheets, for ease of transport to the paper mill.

Most paper for general-purpose use is produced from wood. There are two kinds of **woodpulp**: mechanical and chemical. Mechanical, or groundwood, woodpulp is made by grinding logs under a stream of water, after first removing the bark (Fig. **6.3**). This results in the cheap but not very strong pulp used in **newsprint** and rougher grades of wrapping paper. It is the lignin left in mechanical pulp that makes the resulting paper turn brown and brittle in sunlight.

Chemical pulp relies on chemical agents such as calcium or sodium

6.4 Chemical woodpulp is also debarked, but then the chips are cooked in chemicals to remove the lignin that makes newsprint brittle and turn brown. The pulp is reduced to fibers, washed, screened to remove knots and splinters, bleached, beaten, and mixed with various additives.

6.5 More and more paper is being produced from recycled material, but it is ironical that removing and disposing of the ink can produce an ecological cost of its own.

bisulfite to separate the wood fibers (Fig. **6.4**). This way they are damaged less than in mechanical pulping, and thus paper from chemical pulp is of a higher quality. Oddly, chemical pulp is sometimes known as **woodfree**.

There are two sources of woodpulp: from softwood (coniferous) and hardwood trees. When softwood is beaten, it loses opacity. Well-beaten softwood is thus used for hard, translucent papers, such as glassine (in the windows of envelopes, and also used to wrap after-dinner mints), greaseproof, and tracing papers. Hardwoods, such as eucalyptus, produce more opaque and bulky pulp than softwoods, and can be used to produce a wide range of different papers.

Cotton products and woodpulp are the most common raw materials for papermaking. Other plants are used for producing specialized papers. Esparto grass from North Africa and Spain is used in Europe for the body of the coated papers used in color work, and for good-quality writing papers. The fibers are small and flexible, and combine to form a paper with a closeness of texture and smoothness of surface.

It also watermarks well. Straw is used for the rough board found in book jackets, and in cigarette papers. Hemp has short fibers that bond well, and is used for papers that must be thin but strong — for Bibles and air-mail paper.

Manilla fiber comes from the leaves of a plant that grows in the Philippines. It produces tough, almost untearable paper mostly used for envelopes and wrapping papers.

Other trees and plants that yield fibers for papermaking include corn (maize) stalks, bamboo, bagasse (from sugar cane), seaweed, citrus peel (a by-product of the food industry), and nettles.

Japanese papers are made from a wide range of plants, from the short-fibered *gampi*, which gives a thin, transparent paper with a fine, smooth finish, to the longer-fibered and thus stronger *mitsumata*.

Recycled paper

More than a third of the raw material fiber US papermakers use now comes from recycled paper. The US paper industry recovers for recycling 45 percent of all paper Americans use — well on the way to meeting

the American Forest and Paper Association's goal of recovering 50 percent of all paper used in the United States. The paper industry is the United Kingdom's largest recycler. During the last ten years the amount of material recovered from waste paper and board used in paper production has almost doubled from 2.5 to 4.7 million tons (2.6 to 4.8 million tonnes). Two thirds of the United Kingdom paper industry is directly involved in recycling, and 65 percent of the industry's fibrous raw material is waste/recovered paper.

All paper contains some recycled material, in the form of "broke," the waste from the papermaking process created within the paper mill. This is returned to the refiner, beaten, and turned into more paper. So-called "post-consumer" waste has always been used to manufacture board — the gray kind with specks of ink and sometimes whole letters visible.

Paper mills specializing in recycled paper prefer good clean clippings from printers — all the trimmings, with no ink or other "pernicious contraries," such as glue or metal staples, present. That apart, the next best source is office or domestic paper. There is not very much demand for newsprint, which is low-grade stock to begin with. And what mills definitely do not want are fax paper, self-adhesive envelopes, and plastic-coated papers such as milk and fruit-juice cartons. Problems are also caused by foil-stamped papers, varnishes, and anything containing ultraviolet inks.

Material for recycling is first put through vibrating sieves and centrifuges, where metal objects

6.6 Paper is still being made by hand today. Handmade paper is particularly strong and durable. Here the "vatman" is scooping the pulp from the wooden vat to form a sheet of paper in the sieve-like mold at Hayle Mill in Maidstone, England. It takes a minute's rest to change from pulp to paper, it is said, but 30 years to get it right.

such as staples and paperclips are removed. Next it is liquefied in a hydro-pulper, and washed to remove the fillers. The sludge then goes for de-inking (Fig. **6.5**). Steam and detergents are used to loosen the ink from the fibers. Air is blown through the sludge and the ink flocculates (attaches to the bubbles) and floats to the surface, where it is scraped away.

The resulting pulp is mixed with a percentage of virgin stock and printers' waste and made into paper. Virgin pulp is sometimes added for strength, for the more times that fibers go through the process, the shorter they become. Recycled paper is rarely pure white. If the ink from previous usages has not been completely removed but merely redistributed, then the paper will have a grayish tinge. This is something that has to be allowed for in color printing. Good results can be achieved by reducing the black component in four-color work, but do not expect miracles. Recycled paper tends to have greater absorbency than conventional papers. This results in dot gain (see p. 196) and reduced sharpness, and it dries more quickly after printing. It is important that you discuss the use of recycled paper with your printer. Cylinder pressure may have to be adjusted, presses run slower, and different inks used.

Off-whites and colored recycled paper can, however, have a subtlety of appearance and finish not found in conventional papers. Recycled papers are getting better all the time, and ironically, it is not always obvious to the purchaser that you are using them. Clients who want to demonstrate that they care about

the environment by using recycled paper should print a logo or statement to that effect somewhere on the publication.

Handmade paper

The tradition of handmade paper is still going strong (Fig. **6.6**). Handmade products are not only in demand from watercolor artists, but also from designers requiring exceptional strength and that slightly rough traditional finish, for limited edition books, prestigious corporate brochures, and stationery. Decorative papers incorporating plant fibers from linen, flower petals, and vine leaves are used for endpapers and book covers.

Handmade paper is always made from the finest ingredients. After all, producing it is an expensive process, and so it makes no commercial

sense to use inferior raw materials. Each sheet is slightly different, and therein lies its charm. Its extra strength comes from the process of manufacture, which requires a "vatman" to shake, or joggle, the mold to the left and to the right — an operation that the machine has been unable to imitate. This gives the paper strength in all directions, and no "grain."

Among the most obvious characteristics of handmade paper are its four **deckle** edges. The deckle — another word for the mold — is also the name given to the uneven tapering-off edge of the sheet, seen sometimes on untrimmed books of poetry.

The size of a sheet is limited to the size a person can hold, the maximum being Antiquarian at 31 x 53 inches (787 x 1346 mm). Larger sheets would need two people.

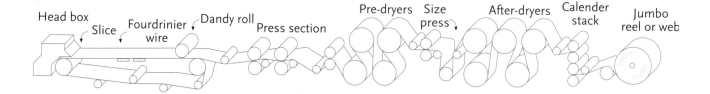

Head box | Slice | Fourdrinier wire | Dandy roll | Press section | Pre-dryers | Size press | After-dryers | Calender stack | Jumbo reel or web

Handmade paper is available in three finishes: HP (hot pressed), NOT (not hot pressed), and rough.

So-called **mold-made paper** uses a more automated procedure, producing the look and feel of handmade paper in a more consistent and reliable product.

Machine-made paper

Most printing papers are produced on Fourdrinier machines (Figs **6.7** and **6.8**). This is a continuous process: pulp goes in at one end, and rolls of paper come out at the other. Fibers, whether from cotton linters or woodpulp, are bought by the paper mill in the form of sheets. At this stage they have already undergone a kind of pre-papermaking felting process for ease of handling. These sheets are blended with lots of water for ten minutes or so to form a **slurry**. This is pumped into storage towers and then through conical refiners containing rotating bars. The amount of beating in these refiners determines the length of the fiber and the extent to which individual fibers are fibrillated. This in turn determines the kind of paper that will be manufactured: from highly beaten glassine and tracing paper to soft, bulky blotting paper that receives hardly any beating at all.

From the refiners, the pulp is moved to storage chests, and from there, via a large pump, through an

internal sizing process. Next, it is put on to a moving conveyor belt made from a mesh, where the transformation takes place from creamy pulp to solid white paper.

A process called sizing controls the absorbency of the resulting paper, and is responsible for keeping the ink on the surface and preventing **feathering**. Internal sizing does this without blocking the pores or altering the porosity of the fibers. An acidic mixture of rosin (synthetic resin) and alum was traditionally used. More recently this has been replaced by synthetic sizes such as alkyl ketene dimer, which has a neutral pH (i.e. it is neither acidic nor alkaline). The paper may later be surface-sized with starch.

Other additives such as colored dyes are also introduced at this stage. Mineral **fillers**, or loading agents, such as china clay, increase the opacity of the paper and make its surface smooth. Printing papers commonly contain up to 30 percent of fillers.

6.7 Fourdrinier machines convert pulp to paper. The first stage is the Fourdrinier wire — a conveyor belt of wire mesh that forms the paper and gives it texture. The rest of the machine is dedicated to drying and smoothing the paper.

As the pulp goes through the large pump, it comprises 99 percent water and 1 percent fibers. This is called the **furnish**. From a head box at the start proper of the papermaking machine, the furnish is released on to the wire mesh of the Fourdrinier. The rate of release and the speed the wire is traveling dictate the resulting weight of the paper. The slower the wire and greater the amount of furnish, the heavier the paper will be.

After forming on the wire, the paper is still around 70 percent water. Water drains through the mesh, and the screen is vibrated from side to side. The fibers thus tend to align in one direction, along the length of the roll, and this gives machine-made paper its characteristic **grain**. The

6.8 Papermaking machines are among the biggest production machinery in existence — some are over a mile long. This No. 4 machine at James River Fine Papers at St Andrews in Scotland has since been modernized and largely enclosed to conserve heat.

6.9 The dandy roll of a paper machine in the mill of James River Fine Papers at St Andrews, Scotland.

6.10 The watermark of William Rittenhouse, the first American paper-maker, and the fool's cap that gave foolscap writing paper its name. Some watermarks are quite complex; most are very simple.

pattern of the wire mesh gives the paper its texture. **Laid** papers have a pattern of mainly horizontal or vertical stripes; **wove** papers are created with a woven mesh.

Paper is formed as it lies horizontally on top of the wire. To create texture on the top of the sheet, a hollow dandy roll is located above the wire. This device presses a pattern on to the top surface of the paper corresponding to the pattern on the wire.

A **watermark** is created by placing a raised symbol, fashioned in wire, on the dandy roll (Fig. **6.9**). In handmade paper production, it forms part of the mold. The watermark is thinner and thus more transparent than the rest of the sheet. For large print runs, it may be

possible to have your own watermark incorporated into specially ordered paper stock. It can be an attractive design element in its own right (Fig. **6.10**), especially if it falls in the margins of a printed publication. But it can interfere with the printing, for example, by weakening a solid area of ink.

From the Fourdrinier wire onward, most of the immense length of a papermaking machine is concerned with drying the damp paper. First, it passes through a series of presses that squeeze out most of the water. These presses can also be used to impart surface texture, and the amount of smoothing affects the final bulk (though not the weight) of the stock.

The paper can then be surface coated or sized with starch, and carried on a felt belt between staggered rows of huge steam-heated cylinders. It must not get too dry, however. After leaving this section, it will still contain 2 to 8 percent of water, necessary to ensure a paper stock with good printing and folding characteristics, and the ability to **cure** in balance with the relative humidity at the printers.

Once dry, the paper is pressed in a vertical row of polished steel

calender rolls, or nips. This operation, called **calendering**, increases the smoothness and degree of gloss. The more calenders, the higher the gloss.

The distance from headbox to calenders can be a mile or more. But the elapsed time of a fiber traveling that distance could be as little as two minutes. From the calender stack, the paper is wound into large rolls called webs. These are slit and rewound into more manageable smaller rolls for shipping. If the paper mill has the capacity, they may be cut into sheets. Some papers may also require off-machine finishing such as **super-calendering** (polishing), **coating**, or embossing.

Cover paper, or board, is made in much the same way as book paper. The furnish contains more recycled material, and is beaten less, to ensure efficient drainage on the wire. Board can be single-ply, or multi-ply. Multi-ply board comprises a top liner, under liner, middle, and back liner. Generally, the liners are given conventional amounts of beating to develop strength. The middle stock, which is there as padding, is given very little. The plies may be combined on the machine or off it.

The characteristics of paper and board

By altering the furnish, and making adjustments to the papermaking machinery, mills are able to produce papers exhibiting very different characteristics. Which kind of paper you choose for a particular job will be determined mostly by the printing process. Offset litho presses require papers that are hard sized, whereas gravure presses need fast ink penetration, and hence "slack" sized paper. If you are dealing with high-quality halftones, you will need a smooth coated paper to do them justice. Economics, too, play a part. Newspapers are cheap and ephemeral, so mechanical wood-pulp is a cost-effective choice. Legal documents have to last, so a good-quality rag paper is appropriate.

Paper is specified by its characteristics, and the main ones are weight, bulk, opacity, color, and finish. In the United States, the weight (also called basis weight, poundage, or substance) is measured in pounds per ream of paper cut to its basic size. A **ream** is 500 sheets. The basic size is 25 x 38 in for book papers, 24 x 36 in for newsprint, and 20 x 26 in for cover boards. To avoid misunderstandings, a 60 lb book paper is written 25 x 38 – 60 (500). In the rest of the world, the weight is measured in grams per square meter (g/m^2, gsm, or grammage). To convert lbs to g/m^2, multiply by 1·5 (the exact factor is 1·48), and to convert g/m^2 to lbs, multiply by two-thirds (or, more exactly, by 0·6757).

Another common measurement is the **M weight**, which is the weight of 1000 sheets. To convert poundage to M weight is simple: just double the poundage figure.

The **bulk**, or **caliper**, of the paper is its thickness. Rough papers tend to be thicker than smooth papers of the same weight. Thickness is measured by a bulking number — the number of sheets to the inch, under test conditions. The ppi (pages per inch) is twice the bulking number (because there are two pages to the sheet). Another way to describe bulk is to measure four sheets of paper with an instrument called a **micrometer**. This "four-sheet caliper" is expressed in thousandths of an inch, which are commonly referred to as **mils** or points. In both continental Europe and the United Kingdom, thickness is measured in micrometers and bulk in cm^3/g.

Opacity is one characteristic not complicated by the metric system. It is the property of a paper affecting the **show-through** of printing from the other side of the sheet. Opacity is obviously influenced by both weight and bulk — the heavier and thicker a paper is, the more fibers there are blocking the passage of light. But it is also a function of the fillers added to the paper.

Visual opacity — the opacity of the unprinted sheet — is measured using an instrument called an **opacimeter**, and is expressed as a percentage. A sheet with 100 percent opacity is completely light-proof. A general idea of visual opacity can be gained by placing a printed opacity gauge under the sheet (Fig. **6.11**).

Printed opacity depends partly on how absorbent the paper is (the more absorbent, the more **strike-through** of ink), and on the paper's ink **holdout** (its capacity to keep ink on the surface). This is a difficult parameter to measure, and the subjective terms high, medium, or low strike-through are used.

The color of a paper is determined by dyes added during the papermaking process, or by coatings added afterward. Color can be affected by the raw materials used. Recycled papers are sometimes grayer than those made from virgin pulp, but this and the speckled appearance can be used as design elements in their own right. Paper also comes in several grades of whiteness, produced by adding **optical brighteners** and other chemicals. The color of paper stock always

TOP DOTS ON UNCOATED STOCK
High-quality jobs can be successfully printed on uncoated paper stock — if you compensate for dot gain and choose the correct screen ruling. Ink dries partially by absorption, so the dots will spread. As they expand and merge, detail is lost in the shadow areas and the whole image flattens. Dot gain is especially critical in the case of textured papers and on darker or warmer-toned papers, and dot-gain compensation might range from 2 to 3 percent in the highlights, to 7 to 10 percent in shadows to "open up" the dots on film. Waterless plates require less dot-gain compensation because the ink dot sits on the surface rather than being absorbed. The type of stock also dictates the screen ruling. Well-formed, ultrasmooth stock can take screens from 200 to 300 lpi; smooth vellum or wove 150–175 lpi; lightly textured stock, such as laid and antique, 120–135 lpi; while for heavily textured, open-fibered, and embossed stock, stick to 110–135 lpi.

affects the color of the ink printed on it, determining the lightest highlight in any halftone. You cannot have a highlight that is whiter than the paper, nor a shadow deeper than the color of the ink.

The finish of a paper is a description of its surface. Its texture first takes shape on the wire and under the dandy roll. As previously mentioned, wove and laid papers receive their characteristic texture here. Uncoated papers receive their smoothness in the calender stack. Coated papers are more likely to be calendered or super-calendered off the machine. Distinctive finishes such as ripple and stucco are created by embossing the paper.

For book papers, the roughest finish is called **antique**. This is an uncoated paper with high bulk. A smoother, pressed version is **eggshell**. **Machine finish** (**MF**) **paper** has been calendered and is smoother and less bulky than eggshell. **Machine glazed** (**MG**) **paper** has been dried against a highly polished cylinder and has one

6.12 All machine-made paper has grain, caused by the orientation of the drying fibers. It is important to know the direction of grain, so that it can run parallel to any folds in your publication.

glossy side with the other remaining relatively rough. It is an example of **duplex stock** — paper with a different finish or color on either side.

Coating covers the paper fibers with clay. Super-calendering coated paper gives it a highly glossy appearance. Coating produces a paper with excellent ink holdout, which is ideal for color reproduction. Thus coated papers are often called art papers.

The coating can be applied by rollers on the machine (film coating, or machine coating), or by rollers or blades off the machine (conversion coating). Conversion-coated papers generally have a thicker coating and are of a higher quality. Blade coating produces a **matte** (dull) surface. Gloss is produced by calendering and super-calendering papers after they have been coated. The highest possible gloss is called **cast coated**: the wet coated web is dried in contact with a highly polished chromium drum. **Chromo paper** is polished on one side only.

Other important characteristics include strength and wet strength, dimensional stability (the ability to stay the same size), rigidity, and **picking** resistance (a binder is used in coatings to prevent fibers from lifting on the press).

And bear in mind that all machine-made papers have grain. Paper folds more easily with than **against the grain**, and ideally books should be designed so that the printed sheets have the grain parallel to the binding (Fig. **6.12**).

Stock can be ordered grain long, with the grain running lengthwise, or grain short, with the grain

running across the width of the sheet. Grain-long paper stretches less, so gives better color registration with web offset. Grain-short paper is better for fast print runs, because it bends easily around the press rollers and speeds up the printing process.

You can determine the direction of the grain by tearing a piece of paper — it will tear straighter along the grain than against it. Here are two other methods: run one edge of the sheet between the thumb and finger, through the fingernails. If it crinkles into a wavy pattern; that's the edge across the grain (Fig. **6.13**). Or mark a swatch and dampen it: it will curl in the direction of the grain. On paper specifications, machine direction is indicated by the symbol (m). Thus 25 x 38(m) is grain long, and 25(m) x 38 is grain short.

6.13 You can test for grain either by tearing a sheet of paper — it will tear more cleanly in the direction of the grain — or by running an edge between your finger and thumb: if it crinkles, then that's the edge across the grain.

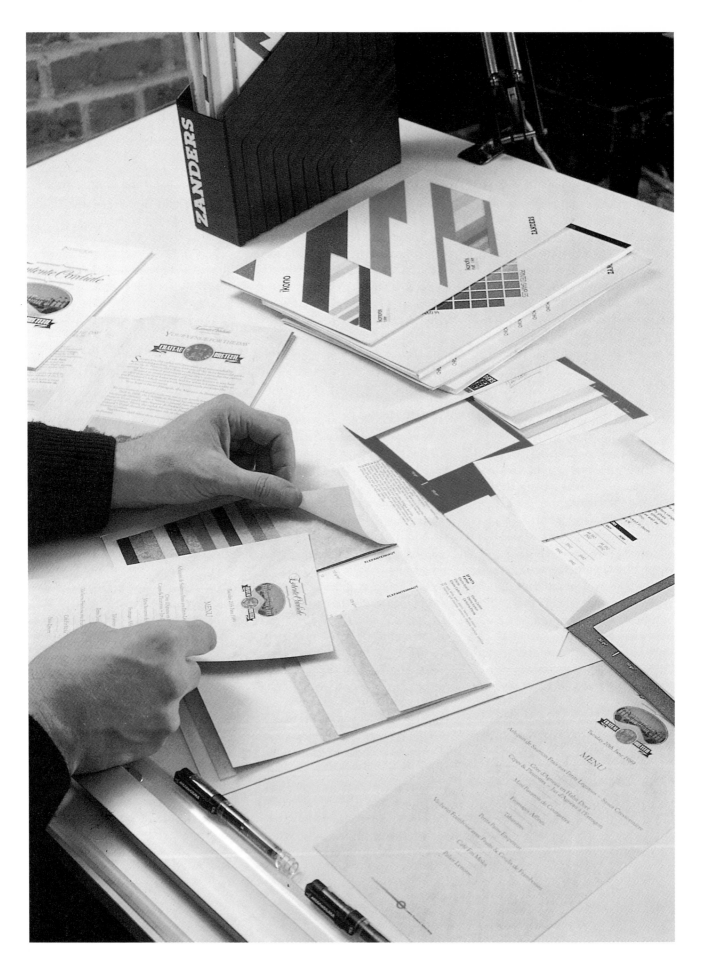

6.14 Every designer should aim to collect "designer packs" of paper samples at every opportunity. Try, too, to collect printed samples.

Choosing the right paper stock

There is a rich but bewildering range of papers available, and you should begin to collect samples, along with technical specifications on the characteristics described above. You can buy paper direct from the mill, or from a paper merchant. Paper merchants stock a wider variety of papers, obtained from many mills, both at home and abroad. Some merchants specialize in particular kinds of paper. Most mills and merchants will supply you with a designer's pack of samples (Fig. **6.14**). Collect printed samples of paper, too, and always choose a paper in consultation with the person who is going to have to print on it.

As mentioned earlier, for some jobs the printing process itself will narrow down your choice — you would never dream of putting blotting paper through a litho press, for example. Price, too, will be a limiting factor. Handmade paper must be reserved for the most prestigious jobs. And it is possible to over-specify paper. There is little point, for example, in specifying a high-gloss stock if it is to be laminated or varnished later.

Sheet-fed offset litho machines require papers with good surface strength and dimensional stability; web offset paper must also have a low moisture content. Surface finish is not such an issue, as modern offset presses can make a good impression on a wide range of surfaces. Offset ink is tacky, however, and the paper should be well sized to prevent "picking" — the pulling out of surface fibers.

The prerequisites for letterpress printing are smoothness, absorbency, opacity, and compressibility. Paper has to be smooth enough to accept a uniform transfer of ink, and strong enough to take the pressure of the sharp edges of metal type without tearing.

The most important characteristic for gravure is smoothness. However, the paper must not contain any abrasive material on its surface — as matte coated stock does. It must also be absorbent enough to draw the ink out from the cells below the smooth surface of the cylinder.

And the silkscreen process demands papers that are not too absorbent.

The trick is to find the stock that matches the brief for the job — a paper just opaque enough to prevent strike-through, but not too heavy (remember the mailing bill), and with a finish appropriate to the design content. Antique may be fine for type and line illustrations, but for good halftone reproduction you will need a coated stock. Glossy is best for color reproduction, but its shine can interfere with readability in the type sections.

Glossy art paper can sometimes feel thinner than the same weight of matte-coated stock, so you may need to increase the weight when going for glossy. Increasing the weight of the stock on some jobs — on a small print run of small-scale booklets, for example — can be a relatively inexpensive way of improving the overall quality of the print.

It is also important to think hard about what other rigors your paper will have to withstand. There may be a reply coupon on your booklet. If so, is it possible to write on the stock in ballpoint or fiber-tip pen without it skipping or smudging? And will that exquisite set of corporate stationery accept additional text from a photocopier or laser printer? A print job may leave your studio looking good, but it also has to perform well in real-life conditions.

Odd-shaped booklets and posters can seem like a good idea at the time. But they can be wasteful on paper, so find out the sizes of stock that the printer can handle, and have a sheet in front of you when you are calculating the size and shape of your layout (see Appendix A, pp. 236–7). Remember, however, that if the sheet is too large, this can affect the quality of color reproduction. And instead of requesting a paper by brand name, try asking printers what they have available — you may get a good deal. But beware — if you need reruns in the future, you may not be able to obtain that stock again.

Paper can represent a large proportion of the cost of any printed job, but, in the words of British typographer Ruari McLean, "can be a relatively inexpensive luxury, when luxuries — so often illegal, immoral, or fattening — are also harder and harder to obtain." Paper can give pleasure, and should always be chosen with a great deal of care.

■ INKS

Printing inks are completely different from the inks used for drawing and writing. They are generally thick and sticky — similar to the consistency of paint.

The various printing processes make very different demands of the characteristics of the ink: its formulation, viscosity (degree of runniness), tackiness, and rate of drying. Of course, a printer running an offset litho machine will buy ink specially formulated for offset litho (Fig. **6.15**). What a designer has to know, however, is that not all offset litho inks are the same, nor do they act in the same way. Even the standard process colors can vary subtly from manufacturer to manufacturer, and from different countries of origin. Until the discovery of phthalocyanine blue in the 1950s, process colors could be very variable indeed.

Formulation

So what are printers' inks made of? All inks are made from three basic constituents: pigments and dyes, a vehicle (or binding substance), and some additives. The **pigments and dyes** give an ink its color. Like the pigments in paint, they come from a wide range of natural and synthetic sources, some organic and some inorganic. Pigments are usually dry and powdery, and have to be ground finely. Dyes are liquid and have to be "coated" (attached to solid particles) before they can be mixed with the other ingredients. Black ink is made from carbon-black, manufactured by burning mineral oil in a restricted air supply.

6.15 Inks for offset litho are generally manufactured on three-roll mills.

Colored pigments come from so many different sources and have such individual characteristics that there has to be a great deal of adjustment to the vehicle and additives in order to make them behave with any kind of consistency. Different colored inks behave differently on the press, and dry at different rates. And because of the scarcity of certain pigments, there are variations in price between different colors. Metallic inks, in particular, are expensive. The choice

of inks has been made simpler, however, by the adoption of the four process colors for full-color work, and by Pantone's standardization of 11 basic colors, from which over 1000 flat colors can be mixed to formula (see p. 88).

The **vehicle** is the carrier that binds the dry, powdery pigment together. It can be an oil, a natural resin, or an alkyd (a synthetic resin). The type of vehicle is determined by the process. Litho and letterpress inks are oil-based. Screenprint,

6.16 The slip-resistance of many forms of printed packaging is important.

gravure, and flexographic inks are resin-based and are thinned with a highly volatile solvent, such as alcohol. Non-tainting formulations have to be specified for food packaging.

Very few printing inks are water-based, though a water-based ink would be welcomed by those caring about the environment. Litho could never use a water-based ink, because the process is based on the fact that oil and water do not mix. But water-based inks have been used, for example, for printing candy wrappers by gravure and in newspaper printing by flexography.

As well as the pigment and vehicle, printing inks contain various additives — mainly driers, but also a selection of anti-oxidants (added to stop the ink from drying in the machine), fillers, and other agents

that give the ink particular properties such as slip-resistance (Fig. **6.16**). Printers sometimes mix in further additives to meet the requirements of a specific job.

Different driers are used depending on the process, the material the job is being printed on, and the intended end use. They are metallic salts or compounds of cobalt and manganese, and speed the rate of drying chemically. Paradoxically, too much drier can slow down the rate of drying. And too much drier on the litho press will mix with the watery fountain solution and cause pigment particles to be deposited on the non-image portions of the plate.

Most inks dry by a process called oxidation. The drying oil of the vehicle absorbs oxygen from the air,

causing cross-polymerization (linking) within its molecular structure. This makes the ink gel, and then harden. Quick-drying inks and varnishes are "cured" by exposure to ultraviolet light, producing a hard and scuff-resistant film.

The quality of the paper has a marked effect on the ink's drying time. The vehicle soaks quickly into newsprint, leaving the pigment on the surface. That is why ink from most newspapers leaves your fingers (and clothes) dirty. But vegetable oils are now being used to replace the mineral oils, for improved rub resistance, as well as better brightness and sharper dots.

For the higher-quality coated stock used for magazines printed by web offset, the ink is dried in high-temperature ovens and then chilled.

6.17 Recycled papers are more absorbent and can be less white than conventional stock, and printing on them can result in colors lacking in brilliance and saturation — hence the need for different ink formulations, which may themselves be helping to destroy the environment. Calculating the ecological cost of a print job is a complex process. (Cartoon by Phil Dobson.)

The sheets are folded straight away, so the ink has to be dried quickly. Naturally, it has to be able to cope with this rough treatment, and a special solvent-based formulation called **heat-set ink** is used.

Other additives include extenders, which increase the coverage of the pigment and improve ink transfer from press to paper; distillates, which improve the flow characteristics of the ink; and waxes, which improve the slip and scuff resistance of inks employed in packaging. Inks with added wax cannot subsequently be varnished.

Viscosity and tackiness

The most important characteristic of an ink is its **viscosity** — how runny it is. This property is measured using an instrument called an **inkometer**, or tackoscope.

Litho inks have to be relatively viscous, with high **tack** (stickiness). They must also have a high concentration of pigment. The nature of the process demands the thinnest possible ink film of the strongest possible color. The amount of ink arriving at the paper during the offset litho process is half that of the more direct processes of letterpress and gravure. Litho inks are relatively transparent: yellow printed over blue will produce a recognizable green. They also have to perform well while being almost constantly "contaminated" with the water that coats the litho plate.

Letterpress inks are similar to litho inks, but contain a smaller proportion of pigments. They generally have a higher viscosity, but lower tack. Because there is no water used in the process, the chemistry of letterpress ink can be far less complex.

Inks for gravure and flexography are much more fluid than litho and letterpress inks. Gravure inks are thinned down with additional solvent before printing begins, and deposit a similar amount of pigment on to paper as letterpress. Flexographic ink is the thinnest of all, and has to be formulated so as not to attack the rubber rollers used in the process.

Silkscreen inks are semi-liquid with good flow characteristics. They have to get through the holes of the screen, but not be so fluid as to spread into the non-image areas. These inks, too, have to be thinned before printing to arrive at the correct viscosity.

Specifying inks

Some inks react unpredictably with other finishes. Colored inks for **wet-on-wet** printing on a multicolor press, for example, must be "tack graded" to arrive at an ink film of full density. Some colors will **mottle**, or change shade, when varnished; purples and reflex blue are particularly susceptible. Colors print differently on different substrates: inks on art paper may appear stronger and brighter than on recycled paper (Fig. **6.17**), and different again on plastic.

Colors appear different under different lighting conditions. Printers view colors under standard lighting conditions, an area surrounded by neutral gray and illuminated by a light source with a color temperature of 5000 Kelvin. If you are designing packaging destined for supermarkets, for example, standard conditions will give a false reading. Supermarkets use different colored lighting to seduce people into buying more things, and to make food look more succulent. The colors in the packaging must compensate for these effects — it is essential to view your designs under the lighting conditions for which they are being designed.

Lightfast inks should be specified if the job is to be exposed to sunlight. Magenta and yellow tend to fade faster than black and cyan (look at the covers of paperbacks in the windows of secondhand bookstores). Inks prone to fading are called **fugitive** inks. Silkscreen inks are more light-fast than the others.

Fluorescent and **metallic inks** often need to be underprinted to achieve a satisfactory result, just as black is often underprinted with a percentage of cyan to increase its density. Fluorescent dyes can be added to the process colors to improve the quality of reproduction

CHOOSING A PRINTER
Are you printing a rough-and-ready circular, a company's stationery or a glossy lifestyle catalog? The type of job determines which of your regular printers to use. Jobbing printers have
small-format machines able to print one or two colors in one pass. They will most likely use
plastic plates, and close registration can be a problem. They will happily print newsletters,
letterheads and disposable pamphlets, but for more demanding jobs, they will have to send
out for metal plates, and the price will rise. Better to use a mid-range printer with a press
that can handle bigger plates and more colors — you might actually save money. Stick to
standard paper and inks, the kind they always have in stock. For jobs where color matching
and premium paper stock are really important, you will need to find a printer specializing in
four-color or even hi-fi color work.

of illustrations, particularly vibrant watercolors. "Metallic integrated process printing" is a term coined by Pantone to describe a method for adding percentages of gold and silver inks to the process colors. This results in an expensive six-color process, which is printed in the sequence silver, yellow, gold, followed by the remaining process colors. Since normal photography cannot record a metallic finish, the designer or repro house has to estimate the amounts to use, based on charts supplied by Pantone. (Gold and silver can also be applied by blocking and hot-foil stamping; see p. 199.)

Other specialty inks include the magnetic inks used on bank checks and business forms, microencapsulated or "scratch and sniff" inks that add a fragrance to printed work (but be aware of an allergic reaction by some innocent end user), invisible ink for children's books and fraud-resistant lottery tickets, and moisture-resistant inks for packaging applications.

Varnishes are a kind of colorless ink used to add gloss to halftones, particularly in prestigious publications such as annual reports. They are also used to add ultraviolet protection to color work that will be exposed to sunlight. If you intend to **spot varnish** photographs or illustrations, you may need to provide artwork or keylines on the mechanical to indicate the areas to be covered. Be sure to discuss any special requirements in the design brief with your printer, and together you will be able to find the correct ink for the application.

■ SELECTING YOUR SUPPLIER

You may not be able to look over the shoulder of your printer as your design is being printed. But you can make sure that you have chosen the right supplier for the job, and that the printer is in no doubt as to your requirements. There are three main considerations: quality, cost, and the schedule. If you are running to tight deadlines, you may have to pay more. Similarly, quality means more care, and that too can cost money. This is not to say that you cannot produce beautiful printing on a small budget — there are plenty of examples of imaginative design that have used cost constraints to great advantage.

You can play your part by submitting clean, uncomplicated designs and clear, unambiguous instructions, and by avoiding any superfluous processes that are going to add labor costs to your bill — unless you decide that a special shape or finish is absolutely necessary.

How do you select the supplier appropriate to the job in hand? First, clearly you should not think of asking a small jobbing printer to undertake a complicated color job for a prestigious client. Nor should you ask a fine-art printer to bid for a short-run black-and-white newsletter. There are horses for courses. Second, do not be afraid to ask around for personal recommendations from colleagues. Look for the name of the printer on the examples of printing jobs you have collected. If their credit line is not there, ask

their client. Then obtain some competitive bids.

For small jobs, find printers somewhere nearby. If they consistently do good work, stick with them, and build up a friendly relationship. Ask them to bid for jobs, but don't make it too formal a process. They may be able to help you out of a jam one day.

For large-scale jobs, provide each prospective supplier with a clear specification of the job in writing, outlining the size, **print run**, and finish you want. Insist that their prices are to a format that you specify, so that you can compare like with like. Tell them that if they do not follow the rules, their bid will not even be considered. Listen to them, however, and give as much information as they need to make a sensible bid — you may end up working with them, after all. Listen to any suggestions they may have to reduce costs, and adapt your specification if you can. Ask what possible economies can be made, by adjusting the schedule, the imposition scheme, or the paper stock. Visit the print works if possible, to familiarize yourself with the company's equipment and its capabilities. Examine samples of work that have been done on stock similar to your job.

Indicate whether you or the prospective printer will supply color separations and film, and list the finishing operations you will require. Ask if the printer has these facilities in-house or will have to send out to sub-contractors. If the latter is the case, you may do better to negotiate finishing separately. Likewise, ascertain whose responsibility it will be to buy in the paper stock.

Show a detailed dummy to each company, and take no chances that they may misinterpret any aspect of the job. Decide also if you need a simple bottom-line figure for the whole job, or whether you need a breakdown into ink, paper, platemaking, proofing, prepress, printing, mailing, and shipping.

When you have all the bids, make a decision, and inform everyone who has quoted. You may wish to negotiate a better price, but do not try to act the bigshot by playing one supplier off against another — you may wish to use several of them at a later date. But you may want to promise bigger jobs in future, conditional on this crucial one.

You must now draw up a contract. If the deal is done on the nod or handshake, the terms of a job in the United States will automatically revert to the Printing Trade Customs, originally drawn up in 1922 by the United Typothetae of America, and amended in 1986 by the Graphic Arts Council of North America, Inc. In the United Kingdom it will be governed by the Standard Conditions of Contract for Printers, published by the British Printing Industries Federation; there are other more specialist documents such as the Customs of the Trade for the Manufacture of Books. Other countries have similar codes of conduct. It is as well to be familiar with them — ignorance is no defense.

The Printing Trade Customs formally set out the business relationship between the printer and the client. They state, for example, that quotations not accepted within 60 days are subject to review; that negatives, positives, flats, plates, and other items, when supplied by the printer, remain the printer's exclusive property unless otherwise agreed in writing; that a "reasonable variation" in color between color proofs and the completed job shall constitute acceptable delivery; and that "overruns and underruns not to exceed 10 percent on quantities ordered, or the percentage agreed on, shall constitute acceptable delivery."

Any contract made between you and your printer will have legal standing, but if any of the terms contained in the Printing Trade Customs are to be adapted, they must be spelt out precisely, in writing. An underrun of 10 percent, for example, on a print run of 10,000 is a perfectly legal shortfall of 1000 copies! You may want to prohibit a shortfall and instead risk a 20 percent **overrun**.

Make a realistic schedule that includes each stage in the process — design and mark-up of copy, typesetting, paste-up, prepress, **make-ready** (setting up the press), printing, and finishing — and let everyone concerned have a copy for comment. Anticipate any delays in ordering paper, vacations (use a calendar with weekends and holidays clearly marked), and shipping. Check proofs meticulously, bearing in mind that any error you miss will be multiplied hundreds or thousands of times. Things may go wrong, but careful planning and communication should eliminate too many surprises.

■ PRINTING PROCESSES

The various printing technologies have already been mentioned many times. Paper, ink, and printing process are all interdependent, and a choice of any one of them cannot be made in isolation. Once the decision to choose a particular printing process has been made, there is very little that a designer needs to or can do. If the mechanical is perfect, and the scans are good, then a good printer will produce a good result. There are things that can go wrong, however, and a little knowledge of how the printing processes work will go a long way in helping you to choose the right supplier and thus avoid any problems.

Printing processes can be categorized into four main types: relief, intaglio, planographic, and stencil (Fig. **6.18**). Letterpress is a form of **relief printing** invented by the ancient Chinese. Dating back to about AD 730, it is by far the oldest of the printing technologies. Flexography is another form of relief printing, which had to await recent advances in materials technology. In relief printing, the printed **impression** is made by a raised surface coated with ink and pressed against the paper, or other substrate.

Intaglio printing uses a plate with incised lines or grooves. Ink is applied, and then wiped from the surface. An impression is made when the substrate is pressed against the surface of the plate, drawing the ink out from the recesses. Gravure is a kind of

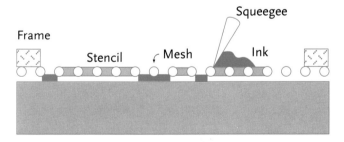

6.18 There are four main printing methods. Relief has ink sitting on the raised surface of the plate or type. Intaglio has ink in the grooves and recesses, while lithography is a planographic process with the ink on the surface, sticking only to the dry areas of the plate. And screenprinting forces the ink through a mask supported by a mesh.

intaglio process. The **planographic printing** process, of which lithography is the only example, is perhaps the most mysterious, as everything happens on the surface of the plate. It works simply because oil and water do not mix. **Stencil printing**, or screenprinting, is, like relief printing, an ancient technique; early

Oriental stencils were held together by meshes of human hair.

Offset lithography is by far the most common form of printing nowadays. There will be some designers who in the course of their careers use nothing else. It is rare these days for anyone to print by letterpress, but its historical

significance is great. Unless you work in packaging design, it is unlikely that you will ever come across flexography or screenprinting. And unless you design mail-order catalogs or glossy magazines, you may never have to work with gravure. But you never can tell!

Offset lithography

In Prague (now in the Czech Republic) in around 1798, Alois Senefelder was experimenting with Solnhofen limestone to find a cheaper alternative to engraving images on copper. His experiments with etching in relief were a failure, but he did notice that he could print just as well without the relief. That discovery, along with the invention of photography in the mid-19th century, changed the course of printing history. It rendered letterpress virtually obsolete, and made **offset lithography** the predominant print technology of the 20th century.

The word **lithography** means "writing on stone." Senefelder discovered that if a design is drawn on a limestone surface using a greasy crayon, and then the surface is "etched" with a solution of gum arabic, water, and a few drops of nitric acid, the area that has been drawn on will become permanently receptive to grease. The undrawn area desensitized by the gum solution will be permanently resistant to grease. If the stone is later dampened and greasy ink is applied from a roller, the ink will stick to the design but not to the rest of the surface. Impressions can then be taken that are exact replicas of the original design.

6.19 Plates for offset lithography are made in a printing down frame. The film or flat is put emulsion down, in direct contact with the plate, which is then developed either chemically or using a xerographic process.

Over the years, the same properties were discovered in more manageable zinc and aluminum plates. Then the **offset process** was developed to overcome the limitations of these metal plates. It involved taking an impression not directly from the plate but from an intermediate **blanket**. The offset process has several clear advantages. Metal plates are easily damaged, and offsetting the image on to rubber protects them from damage. The resilience of the rubber blanket enables impressions to be made on even quite rough papers, and other substrates such as tin plate. Furthermore, the design on the original stone had to be drawn as a mirror image of the finished design for it to print correctly; but because the image is first offset — printed to the blanket — and then on to the paper, the design for offset litho can be positive and "right reading."

Lithography would have become much more popular a lot sooner if it had not been for the fact that typesetting was a problem. It was possible to transfer type set by letterpress on to the litho plate using paper with the ink still wet. But it wasn't until the invention of photography that type could be put on to a litho plate with any kind of quality control.

Platemaking is the process by which the design is transferred on to a printing **plate** from the artwork or mechanical, either photographically or electrostatically, by a process resembling photocopying (Fig. **6.19**). Offset litho plates have to be thin and flexible enough to wrap around a cylinder. Small plates are supplied pre-sensitized with a light-sensitive diazo compound or photopolymer, and are made from metal, plastic, or paper. Paper and plastic are used for short runs, up to 1000 copies. Because they stretch and distort on the press, they are only suitable for single-color work. They are exposed under a process camera, "developed" electrostatically, and then "fixed" by heat. Alternatively, the plates are placed in direct contact with the artwork and the image is transferred using a photographic process similar to the production of PMTs (see p. 82).

Metal plates are made from aluminum with a granular surface, which gives the plate water-carrying properties, and provides anchorage to the image. Litho plates for larger machines and some smaller conventional metal plates can be exposed from either negative or positive film. As we have seen in Chapter 4, stripping and film make-up for black-and-white work is generally done using negative film. It follows that negative-working plates will be used for single-color work. Negative-working plates are less expensive than positive-working ones and are used in print runs of up to 100,000 copies. Most multi-color work, however, makes use of flats assembled from positive film, because it is easier to keep the separations in register. In this case, positive-working plates are used.

The exposure or **burn** is made by ultraviolet light in a printing-down frame which holds the plate in direct vacuum contact with the flat. On exposure, the diazo or photopolymer resin coating of a **negative-working plate** radiated by the ultraviolet light undergoes a chemical reaction to become ink-attracting. This then forms the image on the plate that will print. The rest of the coating, unexposed to the ultraviolet light, is washed off during subsequent processing. Finally, a gum arabic solution is applied to the surface to make the non-image areas water-attracting and ink-rejecting.

When **positive-working plates** are exposed in the frame, it is the sensitized photopolymer coating radiated by the ultraviolet light that is made unstable on exposure, and it is this portion that is removed during processing. The unexposed areas are the ones that will print. Again, the plate is gummed to make the non-image areas unattractive to ink. Since the image can be further de-stabilized by light, positive-working plates have a shorter life than negative-working ones. Some plates can be baked to "fix" and harden the image. Deletions can be made to a positive-working plate, by using a special eraser or brush-applied fluid. This can be useful for printing run-ons of a poster, for example, with dates or venues deleted.

All plates are subject to wear. After around 500,000 copies (or sometimes much lower numbers) have been printed, both the image and the surface grain start to break up. Multi-metal plates with surfaces of hard-wearing chromium are specially designed for long print runs of between 800,000 and a million.

Positive-working plates produce less dot gain than plates made from negatives and are popular for web offset magazine printing. Bimetal plates are even better at controlling dot gain. Here in detail are the main types of plate:

■ **Electrophotographic plates** are produced like photocopies. The photoconductor is charged using a corona discharge, and on exposure to the artwork, the charge is dissipated in those areas struck by light. The charge remaining on the unexposed areas attracts a dry or liquid toner with an opposite charge. An organic photoconductor is coated on a substrate or paper, and the toned image is either fixed or transferred to another substrate. Plates

used for laser imaging are coated on electrograined anodized aluminum. During processing, the coating is removed in the non-printing areas, and the plates are treated with etch and gum to make them water receptive. During the chemical removal process, the dots can become slightly ragged, so these plates are not recommended for fine screens and process color printing. It is also possible to make short-run polyester plates direct from a laser printer.

■ **Presensitized diazo plates** are coated with organic compounds and have a shelf life of about a year; wipe-on plates that are coated at the printers have a shelf life of one to two weeks. Most are made from negatives and, once exposed, are treated with an emulsion developer consisting of a lacquer and gum-etch in acid solution. As the unexposed diazo is dissolved by the solution, the gum deposits on the non-printing areas for water-receptivity, and lacquer deposits on the exposed images, making them ink-receptive. When developed, the plate is rinsed with water and coated with gum arabic solution. These are known as additive plates and can produce runs as long as 150,000. Some diazo plates are prelacquered and are capable of runs of up to 250,000. These plates are developed using a special solvent, and are known as subtractive plates.

■ **Photopolymer plates** are coated with inert and abrasion-resistant organic compounds and are capable of press runs up to 250,000. These

too are available as negative- and positive-working plates. Some photopolymer plates can be baked after processing to produce runs of over a million. Dye-sensitized photopolymers that can be exposed by lasers are used in digital computer-to-plate systems.

■ **Silver halide plates** are coated with photosensitive compounds similar to slow photographic film. The emulsions are very light-sensitive to blue so must be handled in yellow-filtered light. The coatings can be exposed optically using negatives, or digitally by lasers. The processing solutions contain heavy metal pollutants (silver) which must be treated with silver-recovery chemicals before being discharged into municipal sewers.

■ **Bimetal plates** use presensitized polymer coatings consisting of a metal base with one or more metals plated on to it: either copper plated on to stainless steel or aluminum, or chromium plated on to copper, which may be plated on to a third metal base. These are almost inde-structible, have good dot control and are capable of runs in the millions — they are also the most expensive. But should anything go wrong, a single acid treatment can restore the plate to its original condition.

■ **Waterless plates** consist of ink on aluminum for the image areas and a silicone rubber for the non-printing areas. Silicone rubber has very low surface tension and thus will repel ink. However, because of the pressure and heat of printing, regular

6.20 The Heidelberg Printmaster GTO 52 A3 offset printing press.

litho ink will smear over the silicone and cause scumming or toning. Waterless printing must therefore use special inks and temperature control. The technique also demands good grades of paper in order to avoid debris accumulating on the blanket.

■ **Heat-sensitive plates** are made from polymers that respond to heat rather than light, so can be handled in daylight or artificial light. They are exposed using infrared laser diodes in special imagesetters and processed in an aqueous solution. With baking, they are capable of runs of over a million.

■ **Hybrid plates** use two separate photosensitive coatings on metal plates: a silver halide coating that can be exposed either optically to film or digitally by lasers over a bottom coating of conventional photopolymer. When the top coating is processed, the bottom coating is exposed to UV light. The top coating is then removed and the photopolymer (bottom) coating used for printing.

■ **Ablation plates** are made by a laser selectively burning tiny holes into thin coatings on a polyester or metal base. These can be produced digitally, require no chemical processing, and can be printed waterless. All the plates for a job can be imaged directly on the press, simultaneously and in register.

As you can see from the above, most plate coatings can be imaged digitally by laser. High-speed dye-sensitized photopolymers, silver halide, electrophotographic, and ablation plates, coupled with PostScript-based digital systems have paved the way for **CTP** (**computer to plate**) systems. So say goodbye to the imagesetter and say hello to the platesetter. Your PostScript data comes in one end from the RIP, and out comes a plate ready for the press, with no need for film, stripping, or further processing. The main debate at the time of writing is which technology will rule: visible light-sensitive plates such as Du Pont's Silverlith, versus infrared imaging with products such as Kodak's Direct Image Thermal Plate. Visible light is a tried and trusted technology; thermal plates offer better dots (as small as 3 microns), a faster turnround, and don't need a darkroom.

The litho press
Offset litho presses range from the small-scale **sheetfed** machines found in jobbing printers all over the world (Fig. **6.20**), to the huge presses used to print magazines and newspapers on to continuous webs, or rolls, of paper. The basic principles of the process are always the same (Fig. **6.21**). A litho machine comprises: a **plate cylinder** on to which the plate is securely clamped; a resilient rubber-coated cylinder, called the **blanket cylinder**; an **impression cylinder**; a system of inking rollers called the **ink pyramid**; and a **plate-damping unit**. The litho plate is dampened, and then inked. Next, the inked image is transferred (offset) to the blanket. The paper moves between the blanket and the

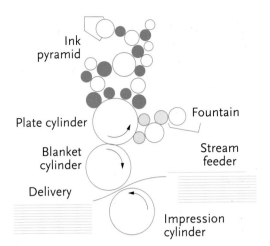

Ink pyramid

Plate cylinder

Blanket cylinder

Delivery

Fountain

Stream feeder

Impression cylinder

6.21 The layout of a small sheet-fed offset litho machine. The plate is first dampened by the fountain, then inked by the ink pyramid. The image is transferred to the rubber blanket cylinder and on to the paper, which is pressed between the blanket and the impression cylinder.

impression cylinders, which are "packed" to ensure complete contact, and the image in ink is transferred from the blanket on to the paper stock.

A single-color sheetfed machine prints single sheets in one color at a time. A mechanism called a feeder pushes each sheet in turn between the blanket and the impression cylinder. Sheets are lifted one by one by vacuum suckers, and are then sent through the machine by blasts of air and conveyor belts. High-speed presses use a **stream feeder**, which presents sheets to the rollers overlapping slightly. Detectors cut out the printing unit if a sheet is defective or if two sheets are picked up together.

The front and side lays are adjustable stops which position the sheet before it enters the machine. The grippers — sets of metal fingers on the impression cylinder — grab the sheet and pull it through. A gripper allowance of $^1/_2$ inch (15 mm) must be made when estimating the printed area of a sheet. After it has been printed it is released, and the delivery mechanism stacks it with the others, **jogging** them constantly to neaten the pile. To stop the wet image from **offsetting** on to the next sheet in the pile, anti-**setoff** spray is applied as the sheet falls on to the pile, separating it from its neighbors by a layer of fine particles.

Meanwhile, inside the machine, the damping system deposits a fine layer of moisture on to the plate's surface before it passes under the inking rollers. One or two cloth-covered rollers, supplied by a **fountain** roller, are used to regulate the amount of dampening. Alcohol can be used for up to 20 percent of the solution, to lower the surface tension and lessen the moisture uptake of the paper. Damp paper stretches, and anything that reduces this effect will improve the quality of the printing, especially in close-register color work. Because of the cost of alcohol and environmental considerations, new citrus-based fountain solutions have been developed.

Ink is introduced to the roller pyramid from a reservoir via an adjustable metal blade. Ink flow can be controlled by a computer taking densitometer readings from the printed sheets. This can also record ink settings that can be re-used if the job is to be reprinted. It is possible, though very messy and unpredictable, to print two colors from a single plate on a single-color offset press by using one color at one end of the fountain, another at the other end — the colors will blend in the middle. This is called **split fountain** printing.

A perfecting press (Fig. **6.22**) is a printing press that can print both sides of the sheet in one pass. One type of perfector is a **blanket-to-blanket press**, which has the two blanket cylinders printing at the same time, so that an impression cylinder is unnecessary.

Multicolor work can be printed in many different ways. An **in-line** machine has several single units

6.22 A perfecting press can print both sides of the sheet in one pass. Here there is no impression cylinder — the two blanket cylinders press against one another.

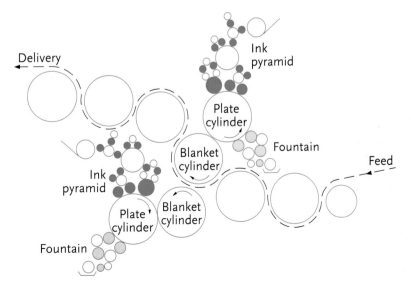

Delivery

Ink pyramid

Plate cylinder

Fountain

Blanket cylinder

Feed

Ink pyramid

Plate cylinder

Blanket cylinder

Fountain

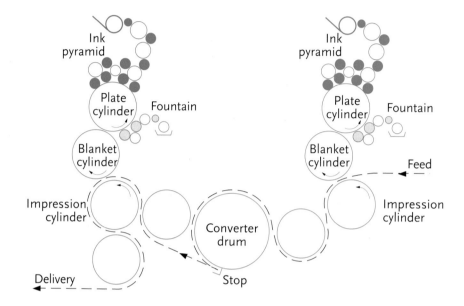

6.23 Using a converter configuration, you can either print both sides of a sheet in one pass, or one side in two colors.

arranged to print one color after another. Stock is conveyed to the next unit by grippers on transfer cylinders. A **converter** machine (Fig. **6.23**) has a drum mechanism that can reroute the paper so that it can print either two colors together on one side of a sheet or (when converted) one color on each side of the sheet. A four-unit converter can print four colors on one side, or two each on both sides.

Web-fed machines (Fig. **6.24**) print from a continuous roll of paper stock, which is printed and then folded and cut into sheets in a single pass. All web-fed machines print both sides of the sheet, and in web-offset, blanket-to-blanket designs are common. The length of the final sheet is determined by the circumference of the cutting cylinder. This cut-off length determines the press printing size you choose for a job. A single-width press with a width of 34 inches (850 mm) and a cut-off length of 24 inches (600 mm), produces eight $8^1/_4$ x $11^{11}/_{16}$ in (A4) pages to view, or 16 pages perfected (printed both sides) to a section.

A multiple-unit web-offset machine can have several web reels in operation. A five-unit web-offset machine with one reel in operation has the capacity to print four process colors plus one Pantone color, or one 16-page full-color section and one black-and-white 16-page section at the same time. A six-unit press, using only one or two printing units for each of two or three reels, can produce printings of flat color and black in many different permutations. On newspapers, for example, one cylinder might be reserved for printing late "stop press" items.

Web tension in the press is controlled by a dancer roller, which can apply a brake to the reel. When the reel runs out, the press is stopped and a new one is connected. On larger presses, this can be done automatically by a "flying paster," which attaches the end of the old reel to the beginning of the new one, then accelerates the new reel up to press speed, all while the press is running.

After printing, the web is dried in a series of gas-fired ovens, then

6.24 In this web offset configuration, the web is printed on both sides in one pass. A typical web press consists of several units like this, one after the other.

6.25 After printing and drying, the web is folded down the middle on a kite folder — as here at Headley Bros in Ashford, England.

chilled (however, newspapers often use **cold-set ink**, which does not require this treatment). To avoid smudging, it is vital that the ink is dry before the web passes over a former, or kite, which makes the first fold in the direction of motion. This is the part of the press always shown in old films, where it looks as though the web is disappearing into a slit (Fig. **6.25**). The paper is then cut into sections, and folded again down to the correct page size. Magazines are trimmed with a three-knife trimmer. Newspapers are usually left untrimmed. For books, the web is slit into ribbons, which are passed over polished turner bars on cushions of air, for better alignment during trimming.

Web machines are used for long print runs, typically over 20,000 copies, on jobs with tight deadlines. With web, all the colors can be printed, both sides, on one pass, with folding done in-line. However, registration is often not as accurate as on sheetfed presses. Trim sizes are restricted as well; non-standard sizes and finishes are better handled by sheetfed machines.

Gravure

The biggest rival to the huge web-offset presses is **gravure**. This is an intaglio process that is used to print everything from the highest quality postage stamps and banknotes, through glossy magazines and mail-order catalogs, down to rough-and-ready wallpapers and gift wrapping paper.

Although related to earlier intaglio methods of printing, such as etching and copper engraving,

gravure is a relatively recent process, invented in the middle of the 19th century by photographer Fox Talbot, as a means of reproducing **continuous tone** (see p. 19).

Present-day gravure machines are huge high-speed **rotary presses** that print from a web of paper. (Gravure is sometimes also called **rotogravure**.) The engraved cylinder is partially immersed in a bath of thin, solvent-based ink (Fig. **6.26**). Its surface is flooded with ink, and as it revolves it is wiped clean with a flexible steel blade called a doctor blade, leaving ink only in the image areas. A web of paper is pressed against the surface of the engraved cylinder by a rubber-covered impression cylinder, and the ink is transferred to the paper. The web passes to a folder and then a drier, similar

6.26 A gravure press is invariably web-fed. The engraved gravure cylinder is inked and then its surface is wiped clean by a doctor blade. The paper is printed as a result of pressure between the plate cylinder and the impression cylinder.

Impression cylinder

Reel

Doctor blade

Engraved cylinder

Ink reservoir

6.27 Conventional gravure cells have equal area but differing depth — the deeper the cell, the darker the impression (top). Other kinds of cell include those with variable area and equal depth, used mainly for packaging (center), and — for the highest quality work — those with variable area and variable depth (bottom).

Constant area, variable depth

Variable area, constant depth

Variable area, variable depth

to those found on web-offset machines.

The important point about gravure is that it prints continuous tones by means of cells — containers of ink cut into the surface of the cylinder (Fig. **6.27**). Larger-diameter or deeper cells hold more ink, and thus deposit a thicker layer of ink, hence making a darker printed image. This produces continuous-tone images that are almost screenless, as the ink from neighboring cells merges during printing. A drawback is that type is also printed this way, so it is less sharp than that produced by offset litho.

In the original process, cells were of equal size but different depths. This arrangement has been superseded either by cells of both varying depth and size, or by cells of constant depth but varying size. The latter method is used mainly for textiles and packaging design.

Preparing artwork for gravure is exactly the same as for offset litho (see Chapter 4), except that the typesetting is scanned as well as the tone. The complete artwork for the job is scanned in one pass. This is converted into signals that control a diamond engraving stylus which cuts into the surface of a blank copper cylinder, producing the pattern of cells (Fig. **6.28**). After engraving, the cylinder can be chromium-plated for extra durability. Cylinders coated with polymer resin can be cut directly by laser. These may prove to be cheaper in the long run, as the resin can be replaced and cut again.

Because of the considerable expense involved in engraving the cylinders, gravure is reserved for jobs such as glossy magazines with very high print runs — typically 250,000 copies or more — or for jobs demanding the highest quality of halftone reproduction.

Direct digital etching by laser uses an alloy that can be plated on steel like copper, but has much higher efficiency (copper reflects laser light). It is capable of etching 30,000 175 lpi cells per second.

Photopolymer plate systems for gravure consist of photopolymer coatings on stainless steel plates that can be mounted on magnetic cylinders. These plates make gravure a viable process for runs below 100,000 and can make gravure competitive with lithography and flexography for packaging runs.

Gravure was the first printing process to use digital imaging. Digital information from the prepress system is fed directly to the diamond styli in the engraving heads that produce the printing cells. This process is also called **filmless gravure**.

Letterpress

Until the 1960s, **letterpress** was the most popular form of printing. Now it is virtually obsolete, except for small limited-edition presses producing fine editions of books. The hot-metal typesetting side of the process survives, but mostly only to produce repro proofs that are then incorporated into mechanicals and printed by offset litho. Conversely, photoset mechanicals can be used to produce plates that print on letterpress machines. But increasingly, large letterpress machines are being converted to flexography (see below), in which the heritage of letterpress lingers on.

Letterpress is a relief process, invented by the Chinese. It was adapted to Western use by Gutenberg, and perfected in the late 19th century, with the introduction of iron steam-powered presses. The beautifully crafted Stanhope, Columbian, and Albion presses from the golden age of letterpress, with their ornamental cast-iron eagles and fanciful beasts, have long been relegated to science museums and the entrance halls of modern printers (Fig. **6.29**). But like steam locomotives, some have been lovingly restored by enthusiasts and put to use. They create that three-

▲ **6.28** Cylinders at the press of R. R. Donnelley in Chicago. Engraving gravure cylinders is very expensive, and thus the process is only economical for long runs.

6.29 Most old iron letterpress machines, such as this Columbian, have been relegated to the foyers of large corporations, or gardens, as mere ornamental features. Thankfully, some are being restored and put back to work.

6.31 The platen press operates like a pincer — the two halves are brought forcibly together into a vertical position by lever action.

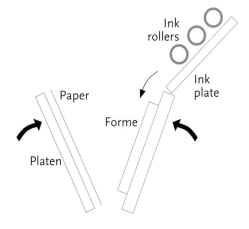

dimensional tactile quality of impression that litho and gravure cannot achieve.

There are three types of letterpress machine: flatbed, platen, and rotary. The **flatbed** is the oldest, being derived from wine and textile presses (Fig. **6.30**). The forme containing the locked-up wrong-reading type and blocks is placed horizontally on the bed of the press. Paper is placed over it, and a screw is turned or a lever pulled to apply pressure. The cylinder flatbed is a press that has the forme and paper on a bed that is inked and then moved under a heavy impression cylinder. The cylinder is lifted to allow the bed to return to its starting position.

The **platen** principle has the forme positioned vertically, with the platen — a heavy metal plate — swinging forward and upward with

the paper (Fig. **6.31**). It makes an impression as it snaps shut, like a clamshell, vertical and parallel with the forme. Platen presses can still be seen in operation, printing business cards.

A rotary press cannot print directly from the forme. A curved copy of the forme, called a stereotype, must first be cast. A *papier-mâché* mold, called a flong, is taken from the forme, and is used to make a one-piece metal, rubber, or plastic plate. It is then fixed around

the cylinder. Rotary presses can be sheetfed or web-fed. During the changeover of newspapers from letterpress to offset litho, a process called photopolymer direct relief was used to make plastic or nylon plates for letterpress from photoset mechanicals. Flexography (see the next section) uses a similar process.

Letterset is a process whereby the image is first offset on to a rubber blanket, as in offset litho. It is used for printing on metal and plastic cartons and cans.

6.30 On a traditional letterpress machine, paper is laid face down on to the inked forme and the whole flatbed assembly is moved beneath a screw- or lever-powered press.

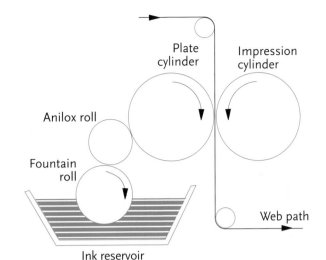

6.33 The configuration of a flexography machine is very similar to that of a gravure press. The Anilox roll even has a gravure-like cellular texture to carry the thin ink to the flexo plate.

Plate cylinder

Impression cylinder

Anilox roll

Fountain roll

Web path

Ink reservoir

Flexography

Flexography is a relief process, a form of letterpress, which prints using flexible rubber or photopolymer plates. The process was first demonstrated in 1890 by Bibby, Baron & Sons of Liverpool, United Kingdom, as a means of printing on non-absorbent packaging materials. It was further developed in the 1920s to make use of **aniline dyes**, derived from coal tar, and had various names. The term flexography was coined in 1952 as a result of a competition sponsored by the packaging industry. It was thought that any name containing the words "coal tar" had connotations that would not be acceptable by the general public in the context of packaging for foodstuffs.

Flexography presses are rotary web-fed machines, similar in layout to gravure machines (Fig. **6.33**). Like gravure, flexo generally uses thin inks, usually solvent-based. Water-based inks containing fluorescent

dyes can also be printed using flexography. It is an economical process only for very large print runs, typically measured in millions of copies.

Artwork is prepared exactly as for offset litho. The plates are produced in the same way as the stereotypes for letterpress, and are flexible enough to be attached to the printing cylinder using adhesive. Corrections can be patched into existing plates. The plates do distort in use, and some image spread should be catered for in the design. Halftones and small type should be avoided, and so should any areas of reversed-out type, which could fill in.

Because of the plates' squashiness, flexo is used for food-packaging applications that require flexibility — printing on plastic bags

and other non-absorbent stock, such as cellophane and metal foil, and corrugated surfaces (Fig. **6.32**).

The process competes with gravure for printing magazines and paperback books on cheap newsprint. The plates do have a tendency to "plug up" with fibers from rougher stocks, however.

Screenprinting

At the other end of the spectrum, the **silkscreen** process, or **screenprinting**, is used only for relatively short print runs of up to 15,000 copies. The name derives from its craft origins, when a screen of silk material was used to support the stencil bearing the image through which ink was squeezed (Fig. **6.34**). Today, the

6.32 Flexography is used for unglamorous applications, such as cardboard boxes (below), and for difficult packaging materials such as waxed paper and plastic, as the examples (right) designed by Stan Noble of designers Towers Noble show. Stan Noble often makes extensive use of a Quantel Paintbox in arriving at the concepts for his designs.

6.34 Screen-printing is mainly associated with poster and T-shirt printing, but can also be used where a non-impact process is required, for printing directly on to the surfaces of compact discs and CD-roms, for example.

screen is made from synthetic gauzes or metal meshes.

Despite its almost exclusive associations with poster design and the prints of Andy Warhol, screenprinting is an extremely versatile process. It is a simple and direct method of delivering ink, and can thus be used to print on any kind of substrate, even on curved and uneven surfaces. It can produce thick and opaque deposits of ink, in brilliant, saturated colors, and with high chemical and abrasion resistance. Applications for screenprinting range from printed circuit-boards in electronics, through bottles and cartons, to T-shirts, point-of-display

advertising, compact discs, and logos on the sides of vehicles.

The screen has two functions: to support the stencil, and to regulate the ink. The screen itself is supported in a wooden or metal frame, evenly tensioned using air-powered or mechanical devices. Most screens are made from polyester. This is a precision woven mesh for close register work, with high stability and low sensitivity to variations in temperature and humidity. Other screen materials include polyamide, which has good wear resistance and elasticity. It is used for printing three-dimensional objects. Stainless-steel screens have the

highest dimensional stability, plus chemical and physical resistance. They are used for ceramic decoration and printed circuit-boards.

The mesh has two main characteristics: the count and the grade. The **mesh count** is the number of threads per inch. The lower the count, the less support there will be for detail, and the heavier the deposit of ink. The **mesh grade** relates to thread thickness, which influences the weight of the ink film. There are four grades: S, M, T, and HD. S is the thinnest, giving a 50 to 70 percent open area; HD is the heaviest, giving a 20 to 35 percent open area. One chooses a count and grade depending on the application, ink, and halftone screen being used.

Stencils can be cut by hand from water- or solvent-soluble laminate film, and are either ironed on to the screen using heat or mounted using a solvent. A pen plotter equipped with a cutting knife can be used by the designer to cut out "line" stencils direct from a computer system. The unwanted areas are "weeded out" and discarded (don't forget enclosed areas like the bowls of letters such as b).

More complex stencils are made photomechanically. Artwork is prepared as for offset litho, and a film positive is made at the repro house. One method uses presensitized

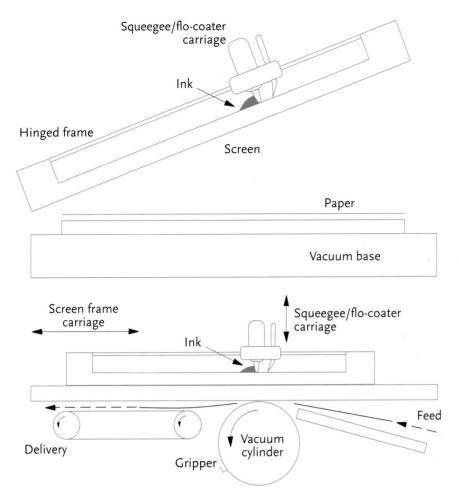

Squeegee/flo-coater
carriage

Ink

Hinged frame

Screen

Paper

Vacuum base

Screen frame
carriage

Squeegee/flo-coater
carriage

Ink

Feed

Delivery

Gripper

Vacuum
cylinder

Screenprinting is a direct non-impact process producing thick, bright colors, but it is not recommended for close registration work, nor for smaller sizes of type. Halftones pose problems because of possible moiré effects caused by the gauze of the mesh interfering with the screen. Moiré can be minimized, however, by using a stencil production system with good dot formation; by angling the mesh between four and nine degrees to the axis of the frame; or by using a "grained" or textured screen rather than a pattern of dots.

Collotype

Collotype, or photogelatin, was and still is the only process that can print continuous tone without screening (Fig. **6.36**). It is used for limited-edition art prints of

gelatin film exposed to ultraviolet light in contact with the positive. This is then hardened in hydrogen peroxide, and the sticky stencil is mounted to the underside of the frame. When it has dried, the polyester base is peeled off and discarded.

A more direct method uses a screen coated on both sides (more thickly on the underside) with a light-sensitive polymer emulsion. After exposure to ultraviolet light in contact with positive film, the image areas are washed away with water. This leaves a stencil that completely encapsulates the screen mesh.

Presses for screenprinting range from simple bench-mounted configurations operated by hand (using a rubber squeegee to force ink through the mesh) to fully automatic rotary machines (Fig. **6.35**). On bench presses, a metal blade called a flo-coater, which is mounted behind the squeegee, returns the ink to its pre-printing position. The angle,

pressure, and speed of both the squeegee and the flo-coater can be adjusted. Once set, the machine will produce consistent results throughout the print run. Fast cylinder-bed presses have the squeegee and flo-coater stationary. The stock, supported on a vacuum bed, moves in unison with the screen.

6.37 The ubiquitous photocopier — this is a Xerox 470ST laser copier.

exceptional quality, and is a slow process capable only of small print runs.

To produce a collotype, a right-reading unscreened negative is first made from the original. This is contact printed to an aluminum plate coated with light-sensitive gelatin. The gelatin hardens in proportion to the amount of light falling on it: highlights remain soft, darker areas are harder. The plate is prepared for printing by flooding it with a solution of water containing glycerine — the soft areas absorb more than the harder ones. Ink is then applied. It adheres to the hardened areas, and progressively less in the softer parts. An impression is made, producing a continuous tone image with a mottled grain.

Xerography

Xerography, or photocopying, may well replace small-scale offset litho in the near future. A photocopier can print direct from artwork or a mechanical, enlarging and reducing instantly. For small print runs, photocopying is cheaper than offset litho with all its set-up costs. The results are dense and black, and photocopiers can now print on a wide range of paper stock. Systems such as the Xerox DocuTech are used for small-scale (less than 1000) "on-demand" runs of manuals and books. Machines such as the Canon Color Laser Copier can produce full-color work direct from artwork, or from a computer system (Fig. **6.37**). The cost per sheet is

relatively expensive, but falling all the time.

Xerography was invented in 1938 by Chester Carlson, and developed by the Xerox Corporation. Artwork is placed face down on a glass plate, and is illuminated by a fluorescent light which travels the length of the image. The reflected image is directed through lenses on to an electrostatically charged drum. This charge leaks away where light from the image falls on the drum. A resin-based powder, called toner, is attracted to the image areas. This pattern of toner is transferred to a sheet of paper, where it is fixed by heat (Fig. **6.38**).

Laser copiers work like combined scanners and imagesetters by scanning the image digitally, and using a laser to write the image on to the electrostatic drum.

6.38 Inside a photocopier, a light source scans the artwork and this image is transferred via mirrors on to an electrostatically charged drum. Toner adheres to the image, and is transferred to the paper and fixed by heat. In a laser copier, all this is done digitally, just like a combination laser scanner and laser printer.

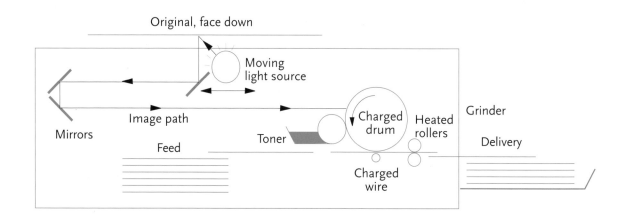

Original, face down

Moving light source

Image path

Mirrors

Feed

Toner

Charged drum

Charged wire

Heated rollers

Grinder

Delivery

Digital print

The term **digital print** covers several of the above printing processes. Broadly it can be any printed output that is imaged directly on to a blanket, plate, or substrate from an electronic file, with no intermediate film stage. The first black-and-white production devices meeting this description appeared in the 1970s. The world's first digital presses, the Indigo E-Print 1000 and Xeikon's DCP-1, were launched in 1993 (Fig. **6.39**).

The Indigo E-Print uses liquid ink to produce a result close to that of conventional offset litho. All the colors are squirted on to the plate in one go and then transferred to an offset blanket, in a similar way to conventional offset printing. Unlike conventional printing, however, the blanket of the digital printer is left clean for the next image which could well impart a different message for each printing revolution from its PostScript server. Each individual page is RIPped to the electrostatic plate in parallel with the information being held in memory before printing the next page. The printing speed of the E-Print is around 1,000 copies an hour when printing in four-color both sides on A3 or greater, at a resolution of 800 dpi.

The Indigo also has some finishing capabilities, with online collating and stapling of up to 100 pages in one go, which, with its variable page information, makes for a versatile machine. The second generation printers — the E-Print 1000+ and the Omnius, a web-fed press — are designed for the packaging market, printing on such

6.39 Indigo TurboStream sheet-fed six-color digital press can print 1000 A3 sheets an hour with electronic collation, versioning, and personalization.

materials as pressure-sensitive labels, films, foils, and other flexible packaging substrates.

The Agfa Chromapress is based around the Xeikon print engine, which uses CMYK toners and heat fusion similar to a color copier, but that is where the similarity ends. Each dot can have variable amounts of toner at 600 dpi to give a quality similar to that of offset litho and much better than a conventional color copier. Also, variable dot-density screening means that there is no dot gain, thus giving ease with consistency.

Today, there are three basic technologies being described as process color digital print:

Digital print technologies

- **Electrophotographic**, in which a dry or liquid toner is deposited on the substrate by varying its electrostatic properties and then fixed by absorption, chemical reaction, or heat. This includes xerographic photocopiers and the Indigo and Xeikon digital print engines.

- **Digital litho**, which uses a CTP (computer-to-plate) device to image a plate on press and then prints using a normal litho process. The Heidelberg Quickmaster DI (Fig.

6.40) is a four-color offset press which uses direct-imaging technology to image all plates on the press simultaneously and in register. This is achieved with four direct-imaging units with 16 infra-red laser diodes in each printing station. The laser diodes create accurate image dots on the multi-layer plates in resolutions of 1270 or 2540 dpi. No damping is required, and it is claimed that the plates should last for 20,000 impressions.

- **Inkjet**, in which a liquid ink is sprayed either directly on to the substrate, or on to an intermediate blanket.

One characteristic shared by all these devices is their ability to reduce, or almost eliminate, make-ready times. This allows short runs (roughly, up to 1000 copies) to be produced more economically than with non-digital presses. It also makes it more feasible to print "on-demand," the cut-off point to be somewhere in the area of 700 to 1000 copies. One key difference is that with digital printing every copy costs the same in material costs as the previous print. In conventional print, the more copies that are produced, the cheaper each sheet

■ Emerging print technologies

As we have seen on page 193, there are three basic technologies being described as digital print: digital litho using CTP (computer-to-plate), electrophotography (including xerography), and inkjet. Although currently used for short runs, digital print is changing the workflow pattern of print production, from "print and distribute," to "distribute (digital files such as PDF) and print" (on location).

The first digital presses were either glorified color laser copiers or, like the Indigo E-print, a converted sheet-fed offset press with a reusable organic photoconductor mounted on the plate cylinder, and the inking system replaced by a corona charger and four, six, or seven toning nozzles for applying colored liquid toner to a heated blanket. Paper either rotates one revolution for each color or (as in the web-fed Indigo Omnibus) the image is built up on the blanket before being transferred to the paper in one pass. The "ink" is comprised of microscopic particles of toner dispersed in a thermoplastic resin and diluted in a light mineral oil. The heated blanket evaporates the ink leaving a tacky polymeric film which cools and sets on contact with the substrate.

The Xeicon is web-fed and has eight LED-exposed photoconductor plates for printing four colors on both sides of the paper in one pass. Dry toners are fused by heat after imaging.

Inkjet is a non-contact technology. Printers are of two main types: continuous jets, in which charged drops of ink are deflected to form the image or fall to a gutter to be recycled; and impulse or drop on demand, such as piezo-electric, bubblejet, and solid ink/ phase change printers. Large format inkjets are used as proofers and for printing posters, displays, and fine art prints. UV curing ink can be used for light-fast and water resistant applications.

Electro-coagulation or Elcography is a novel technology developed by Canadian vendor Elcorsy. In 1971, the company's founder Adrien Castegnier was working in a rotogravure plant in Paris. He wanted to obtain photographic quality images on plain paper without the environmental problems of silver halide. His original idea was to build a gelatin gravure cell using gas bubbles generated by an electrolytic reaction. If the cavities were then filled with ink, the image could be printed on regular paper.

The Elco 400 press uses water-based polymeric ink that is sensitive to electric fields. This pigmented liquid ink is sprayed onto a metallic cylinder and coagulates into 400 dpi gel dots in 256 different thicknesses, controlled by pulses of electricity. The lightest dot is done in 100 nanoseconds, while the darkest dot is written in 4 microseconds. By comparison, the time to access data on your hard disk is a thousand times slower. The imaging cycle is repeated for each revolution of the press. It can print at 1700 pages per minute and can switch print jobs without stopping, making it ideal for short-run printing. The quick-drying water-based inks are environmentally friendly, odorless, and easy to clean with high light fastness.

Other emerging technologies include ion or electron charge deposition printing and magnetography, in which spot opaque colors are produced from a cold-fused magnetic toner and charged drum — these are used mainly for printing bar codes, tickets, and labels.

Find out more
Indigo
www.indigonet.com

Xeikon
www.xeikon.com

Elcorsy
www.elcorsy.com

6.40 Heidelberg's Quickmaster DI 46 computer-to-plate printing press reaches speeds of up to 10,000 sheets per hour in production runs, thereby ensuring that short runs of up to 500 sheets, for example, can be produced in less than 20 minutes including make-ready times.

becomes. Digital print, however, can vary text and images on a page-by-page basis creating opportunities for "tailored print" such as:

- **Personalization**, where a person's details, such as name and address, are changed between each document printed;

- **Customization**, where substantial amounts of the content of, for example, brochures or catalogues is altered to match the preferences and interests of readers;

- **Versioning**, where larger runs of a generic document are broken down into many slightly amended shorter runs (with details of a local office or staff on a sales brochure, for example).

Printing processes: the pros and cons

Offset litho
■ **Advantages** Extremely flexible and cost-effective for most jobs, wide range of presses from jobbing sheet-fed machines to large web-fed presses, relatively short set-up time, positive-working or negative-working, prints effectively on wide range of stock.

■ **Disadvantages** Needs more attention than gravure for consistency over long print runs, ink translucent and prone to more problems than in the other processes. Higher set-up costs than digital print.

Gravure
■ **Advantages** High-quality, high-speed continuous-tone reproduction and rich blacks, prints well on cheaper stock, very economical for long print runs, fast process after make-ready.

■ **Disadvantages** Type is screened, solvent-based inks, only viable for large print runs, expensive to set up, corrections require new cylinder, proofing expensive.

Flexography
■ **Advantages** Fast make-ready, prints well on non-absorbent stock, possibility of using water-based ink, prints well on cheap paper stock.

■ **Disadvantages** Image spread, poor halftones, usually have to use solvent-based ink, expensive to set up.

Screenprinting
■ **Advantages** Non-impact process, versatile, prints on any kind of substrate and on curved or uneven surfaces, can be used to produce thick and opaque deposits of ink in bril-

liant saturated colors and with high chemical and abrasion resistance.

■ **Disadvantages** Small print runs, not recommended for halftones because of the possibility of moiré effects, close registration and four-color work difficult, cannot print smaller sizes of type.

Letterpress
■ **Advantages** Quality of impression, wide range of original typeface designs (hand-set repro proofs can be taken for printing by offset litho).

■ **Disadvantages** Inflexible for design, expensive now that big presses have largely been taken out of service.

Collotype
■ **Advantages** High-quality screenless continuous-tone reproduction.

■ **Disadvantages** Slow, very expensive, short print runs only.

Xerography
■ **Advantages** Inexpensive for short print runs, no set-up costs, no film or plates, no ink, can print direct from computer disk.

■ **Disadvantages** Cannot print large sheets, color reproduction often poor and almost always variable, restricted paper stock.

Digital print
■ **Advantages** Cost-effective for short runs, print can be personalized, very fast turnaround, electronic collation, delivers a book or brochures that only need trimming and gluing to be ready for delivery.

■ **Disadvantages** Expensive machinery and consumables, requires a digital workflow.

6.41 Catch-up.

6.42 Hickies

Things that can go wrong

There are all kinds of problems associated with the paper, the ink, and the press, and how they interact with each other. Some of these have been mentioned earlier, but for the sake of completeness, they will be listed here in alphabetical order.

- **Backing** is a lightening of color that occurs if ink removed from the fountain roller is not replaced by the flow of new ink.
- **Catch-up** occurs in offset litho when insufficient water on the plate causes non-image areas to print (Fig. **6.41**).
- **Chalking**, or powdering, happens mainly with matte coated stock and is caused when the vehicle from the ink is absorbed, leaving only pigment on the surface. It becomes apparent when dry ink starts to rub off the image or smudge, and unfortunately is noticed only after the job is finished. In emergencies, the original plate can be used to overprint a layer of transparent size to try to bind the ink to the paper.

- **Color variation** during a run is caused by altering ink-to-water balance, or by stopping the press.
- **Crawling** is an imperfection in the surface of the ink, occurring when thick ink overprints wet ink.
- **Crocking** is smudging or transfer of dry ink on to printed sheets.
- **Crystallization** is a result of careless overprinting. If the ink of the first printing dries too hard before overprinting is done, it can repel the second color.
- **Damper** marks are patterns over the print caused by worn damper covers or too much pressure.
- **Dot gain** shows when halftone shadows fill in or if the print looks too dark, and is caused by bad film-to-plate contact, over-exposure of the plate, over-absorbent paper, or over-inking. However, it will always occur to some degree, so an allowance should be made at the proofing stage.
- **Doubling** — two dots where there should be only one — is caused when wet ink is picked up by the blanket on a subsequent printing. If it is slightly off register, it prints as a ghost dot nearby.

- **Emulsification** is what happens when water gets into the litho ink. Most litho inks are designed to accept some emulsification, but too much results in a wishy-washy appearance.
- **Flocculation** produces a surface like orange peel, and is an ink defect. It occurs when the pigment is not properly dispersed in the vehicle.
- **Ghosting** is the word for feint areas, usually in solid blocks of color, caused by some parts of the image taking more than their fair share of ink, leaving other areas deficient. Some ghosting problems can be foreseen, and imposition schemes can be changed to prevent them. On small-format jobs, try to distribute solid areas evenly. Ghosting is also the term used to describe the dull image on the reverse side of a sheet caused by a printed image that has affected the drying and trapping of ink applied to the other side.
- **Halation** appears in halftones as a halo-like light around a dark area, and is a prepress problem that should be picked up before plates are made.

- **Hickies** are dark spots surrounded by uninked halos, or just plain white specks, that appear at random (Fig. **6.42**). They are caused by dust, paper fibers, or foreign bodies from the ink which have found their way on to the blanket. A solution is to run uninked paper through the press, and then wash the blanket.
- **Linting** is a problem created by paper fibers that get on to the blanket, plate, or rollers of a press.
- **Low spot** is a loss of image caused by an indentation on the blanket, often because plate and blanket are insufficiently packed.
- **Moiré patterns** are unwanted "basket-weave" effects. They occur when the screen angles on multi-color work have not been set correctly, or sometimes when there is regular patterning on an image, or when a halftone has been rescreened.
- **Mottle** is an uneven, blotchy application of ink, caused by a mismatch between ink and paper stock, or too much dampening water on the blanket.
- **Offset** *see* Setoff.
- **Paper curl** can be caused by too much dampening water, or can happen because the stock has not acclimatized to the relative humidity of the press room. Wavy edges appear if the stack of paper has a lower moisture level than the surroundings. Tight edges are caused by a higher moisture level in the stack. *See also* Tail-end hook.
- **Picking** is a lifting of the paper's surface most noticeable in solid areas, caused by ink that is too tacky, a press running too fast, or a paper surface with too low a "picking resistance."

- **Piling** is caused by a build-up of ink on the press rollers, or by particles from uncoated stock which adhere to the blanket and break up the image on the following sheets.
- **Registration problems** are caused by poor stripping at the flat stage (check the proofs) or by paper stretching on the press (Fig. **6.44**).
- **Scuffing** is a problem in packaging design, where print is likely to receive rough handling. Choose a scuff-proof ink or try a coat of varnish.
- **Scumming** is when ink starts to appear on the non-image parts of the plate. It can be caused by a badly done deletion, or more likely it's time for the plate to be replaced.
- **Setoff**, or offset, occurs when the wet image on a sheet of paper prints on to the paper above or below it in the pile, or later rubs off in a bound book (Fig. **6.43**). Anti-setoff spray should separate each sheet with a fine layer of particles.

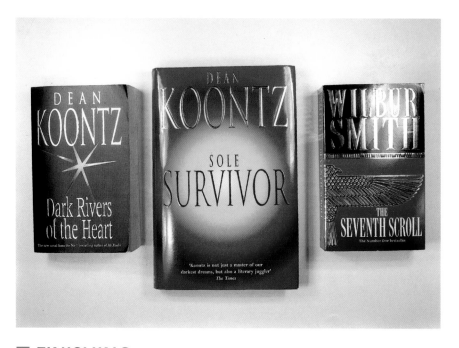

6.45 Die-stamping is used to add glamor to the kind of blockbuster paperback book you see on airport magazine booths. They can be stamped blind, giving a subtle three-dimensional effect, or inked, or foil-blocked in gold, silver, or other metallic colors.

- **Show-through** is when you can see right through a sheet of paper to the printing on the other side. Choose a more opaque stock next time.
- **Skewing** is a problem that occurs during printing if the paper, blanket, and cylinder are not in proper contact.
- **Slurring** is when halftones start to fill in, and is caused by too much ink, or slippage from smooth paper. There is a portion of the color bar on the proof specifically for indicating slurring.
- **Snowflaking** in solid areas is a problem caused by water droplets in the litho ink. In gravure it can happen because inadequate pressure prevents the paper from taking the ink from one or more cells.
- **Spreading** is an enlarging of the image caused by too much ink, or too much pressure between blanket and plate.
- **Sticking**, or blocking, occurs when there is so much setoff that the sheets stick together.
- **Strike-through** is like show-through, only worse — it is when the ink penetrates the whole thickness of the sheet. Change stock, or use a different ink formulation.
- **Tail-end hook** — when solid areas near the back edge of a sheet make it curl down — is caused by paper adhering to the blanket too tightly as it is pulled off by the delivery grippers, and it happens if the ink is too tacky.
- **Tinting** happens when pigment finds its way into the fountain, discoloring the background.
- **Tracking**, or stripping, is when several colored images are printed in a row and inking becomes uneven as a result.

■ FINISHING

All the processes that convert the printed sheets into folded and bound publications are collectively known as **finishing** operations. These can also include print-related operations such as die-stamping, thermography, varnishing, and laminating.

Die-stamping is a process for producing a three-dimensional low relief effect on paper or cover board (Fig. **6.45**). It works as a kind of heavy-handed letterpress, with the additional assistance of a hollowed out recess on the other side. The hollowed out recess is in fact the die; the stamping part, the counter-die. The die is placed face upward beneath the paper. It is made in steel from artwork, either etched photographically like a process block, or engraved by a computer-controlled machine tool.

Die-stamping can be used **blind**, to produce the subtle effect found on letterheads, or inked. Or the die can be used with metal foil, to make the bold impression that is so popular on the covers of blockbuster paperback books. **Die-cutting** uses sharp steel rules in a wooden die to cut shapes from paper.

Laser die-cutting is used to produce intricate patterns and designs on greetings cards and/or for see-through logos on business cards. Note that you must include small tabs of 0.3 to 0.5 mm to prevent the inner bowls of letters, for example, from falling out.

A cheaper way to obtain a low relief is by means of **thermography**. A freshly printed image is dusted with transparent thermography powder. This sticks to the ink and, when heated, swells into the third dimension; high-gloss and matte finishes are available. It is worth bearing in mind, however, that sheets printed using thermography can later be a problem when put through laser printers, as the thermographic printing can melt.

Embossing, similar to die-stamping, also gives the stock an area of texture. The lettering on the

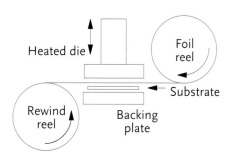

6.46 In hot-foil blocking, the foil passes from a roll and is stamped on to the substrate by the action of heat.

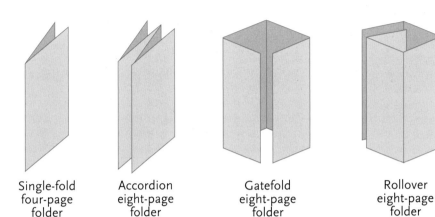

Single-fold
four-page
folder

Accordion
eight-page
folder

Gatefold
eight-page
folder

Rollover
eight-page
folder

6.47 There are many different ways to fold a folder. Here are some examples — but remember to make economical use of your printed sheet before you specify an exotic fold.

spine of a hardback book is formed by **blocking** in gold or silver leaf using a brass, or die. This time, the die is in relief and the effect is below the surface of the substrate.

Hot-foil stamping, or leaf stamping, transfers a foil coating from a carrier roll of polyester, by means of a heated die (Fig. **6.46**). The coating can be metallic, matte, pearl, or even a **hologram**.

Spot varnishing of halftones to add gloss and intensity has already been mentioned in the discussion of inks (see p. 176). Overall **varnishing**, as a finishing operation, is carried out by running printed sheets through rollers. Machine varnish (lacquer) can be applied using a

conventional litho machine, but the sheen it produces is barely noticeable. High-gloss or liquid lamination is a nitrocellulose coating requiring a special machine. Ultraviolet varnish, which dries on exposure to ultraviolet light, also produces high gloss and scuff-resistance. Two layers of varnish, printed wet-on-wet, give a very smooth glossy finish.

Lamination adds strength as well as gloss. Film lamination is glued to the stock as it goes through a heated roller under high pressure. It is applied from a roll on to overlapping sheets, leaving the gripper edge and the sides free for any other processing. But laminated sheets must be left for two days for the adhesive to dry completely, before operations such as guillotining or embossing can be performed with confidence. Ultraviolet lamination cures more quickly.

Ink that is to be varnished or laminated should be quick drying, with little residual solvent, and absolutely no wax additives. Too much anti-setoff spray can have an adverse effect on either process. Metallic inks are a problem, and should be left alone. They have their own sheen, after all.

Folding and binding

After these print-related finishes have been applied, the stock can be folded (Fig. **6.47**). There are three types of folding machine. **Buckle folders** (Fig. **6.48**) are the most commonplace. The sheet enters a pre-set distance and is stopped and buckled back at the fold line by two inward-revolving rollers. These nip the flat sheet, then fold it and carry it forward to the next "plate," where the process is repeated. **Knife folders** (Fig. **6.49**) are used in bookwork. Here a blunt knife is used to nip the sheet between two rollers. They are very precise, but slower than buckle

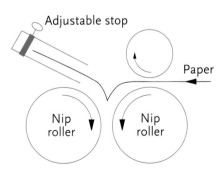

6.48 In a buckle folder, the sheet is brought to rest by an adjustable stop before being forced between a pair of nip rollers.

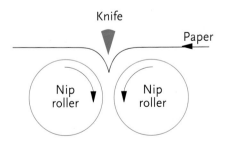

6.49 A knife folder is used for more exacting work — a knife-like device pushes the sheet between two nip rollers, producing a much sharper fold.

SCORE BEFORE FOLDING
Heavy paper or card should always be
scored before folding — enough to produce
a raised ridge. A fold should always be
made with the ridge or hinge on the inside.
Booklet covers must have a score wide
enough to accommodate all the pages to be
inserted inside.

Right

Wrong

Score

Hinges

Signature
feed

Signature
feed

Wire stitchers

To trimmer →

Guillotine

Guillotine

Delivery

Face trimmed

Head and foot
trimmed

▲ **6.50** In saddle-stitching, the folded
and collated signatures move along a
conveyor on saddles the shape of inverted
Vs. Wire staples are then inserted along the
fold of the spine.

folders. **Combination folders** give the
best of both worlds.

Single-sheet jobs then go straight
to the guillotine for trimming. Multi-
page jobs first have to be united
with the other pages, **gathered** on
conveyor belts, bundled flat, and
collated (put in order). For books,
the sections are gathered one next
to the other. Printed marks on the
spines of sections, called backstep
marks, indicate the correct
sequence visually. Letters or

numbers printed on the signatures
serve as a double check.

Loose **inserts** are single sheets of
paper or even sometimes booklets,
which are added, generally by hand,
to a magazine. They fall out when
the magazine is shaken.

Tipping-in is adding a single page
to a publication, either by pasting
down the inside edge, or by wrapping a short strip around the fold.
This is a labor-intensive process, and
thus very expensive. Illustrations that
were printed intaglio, or on art paper,
used to be tipped in to books.
Tipping-on is pasting a smaller illustration, an erratum slip, or a reply
coupon on to a page.

▲ **6.51** In side-stabbing, the wire staples
are inserted through the front of the
signature, along the back edge close to
the spine.

Perforation can be done on the printing press, by means of a perforating strip attached to the impression cylinder (eventually ruining the blanket), or on a special finishing machine.

Magazines and booklets are bound in one of two ways: by saddle-stitching or perfect binding. **Saddle-stitching** (Fig. **6.50**) is a fancy way of saying stapling, though the wire staples used in saddle-stitching are longer and rounder than office staples. Saddle-stitching gets its name from the inverted V saddle on to which the sections are placed. Sections are opened out and placed one inside another, inserting larger sections inside smaller ones, and with the cover on top. This is the least expensive form of **binding**, but can only be used with publications of up to around 128 pages, depending on the paper stock. On thicker publications, take note of paper creep — pages near the center will be narrower after trimming than those near the covers (see p. 116). Specify stainless steel wires so that they don't rust.

Side-stabbing (Fig. **6.51**) inserts the wires from front to back, near the spine, disguised by the creased **hinges** of the covers.

6.52 Spiral binding is used for calendars, manuals, and cookery books — wherever the publication has to fold perfectly flat. Wire-O gives a neater finish.

Calendars, cookbooks, and technical manuals are sometimes **spiral-bound** (Fig. **6.52**) so as to lie flat. The sheets are punched with a line of round or slotted holes near the **spine**. Wire is then coiled through the holes and crimped. **Wire comb**, or Wire-O, bindings and **plastic comb** bindings give a more finished look.

Perfect binding (Fig. **6.53**), unsewn binding, or cut-back binding, can be far from perfect unless a good glue is used. For this process, the sections are gathered and collated as before, and presented to the machine spine down. The edge is notched, or milled off and roughened, and adhesive is applied. The covers are folded, scored, and wrapped around the pages. The adhesive is then cured by heat, and the pages are trimmed. Perfect-bound magazines have a flat spine, on to which a title, date, and a résumé of the contents can be printed. But the process is slower and more expensive than saddle-stitching, and double-page spreads can be a problem with copy disappearing into the gutter. Fold the magazine back and it falls apart! Mass-market paperback books are often printed two-up, head to head, and only cut apart after perfect binding.

Hardback books are sometimes perfect bound, but the sections can instead be sewn through the spine with thread — this is called **section sewing**. They are then gathered together into a book block. **Thread-**

6.53 In perfect binding, the signatures are collated, then the spines are cut off, roughened, and spread with glue to attach the covers.

sealing combines features of perfect binding and section sewing (but no thread runs between sections).

Side-sewing is a method used for children's books, in which the thread goes front to back, as in side-stabbing. This produces a stronger binding than section sewing, with the disadvantage that the book will not lie flat when folded.

A case-bound, or hardback, book (Fig. **6.56**) has a hard case made apart from the pages. The book-block and cover are assembled, along with tipped-on endpapers, at the final stage of binding. Endpapers are usually of heavier stock than the text pages, and are sometimes decorated. **Rounding and backing (R & B)** is a combined operation that puts a rounded shape into the spine of the book-block, and a joint below the shoulder (Fig. **6.54**). Some books are rounded; others are left with flat

Roller

Threads

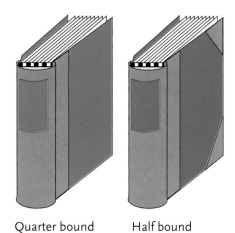

6.54 **6.54** The thread used to sew the book-block makes it thicker at the spine. Rounding keeps the book in good shape; backing produces a neat shoulder.

a hardback book look attractive is known as the covering. It can be of non-woven material, such as embossed paper, fiberfelts, or plastic-coated fiber, or a form of starch-filled cloth or **buckram**. A **quarter-bound** book (Fig. **6.55**) has the spine and an adjacent strip of the cover bound in an expensive material, maybe leather, with the rest of the sides in something cheaper. A **half binding** has, in addition, triangles at the corners in the expensive material. Leather, embellished with gold blocking and tooled decorations, is reserved for expensive limited-edition books.

After binding and counting, the job is parceled up in waterproof packaging or shrink-wrapping, is boxed, correctly labeled, put on to pallets, and shipped to its destination — and your job is done.

Quarter bound   Half bound

6.55 A quarter-bound book and a half-bound book, with its additional triangles at the corners.

spines. Linings are glued to the spine; **headbands** and **tailbands** — and perhaps a bookmark — are added; and the endpapers are glued to the insides of the cases. Book jackets can be wrapped around the cased book by hand or by machine.

Cases are made from heavy board, with the grain parallel to the spine to prevent warping. The material used to make the case of

6.56 Case-bound books consist of a book-block, a hard cover, and end-papers that are assembled at the final stage of binding.

Thread

Thread

Sewn signatures

Endpapers   Endpapers
      Book block

Strip of
crash glued on

Headband and
case added

■ SUMMARY

On press is that part of the production process over which the graphic designer has the least amount of hands-on control. What the designer does possess, however, is the power of *selection*. An appropriate choice of paper, ink, and printer should ensure a predictable outcome, given that the designer's input is as near perfect as can be, and bearing in mind the merits and limitations of the various printing processes.

Paper, ink, and printing process are all interlinked. The size of the print run and the budget for the job are also important considerations. Offset litho and letterpress demand thick and sticky inks; conversely, the inks for gravure and flexography need to be thin and runny. Consequently, gravure and flexo are able to print at high speed on to relatively poor stock — and flexo can print on to the most difficult surfaces, such as cellophane and waxy board. But there is a trade-off. Flexo and gravure cylinders are expensive to produce, and so the process is only viable for large print runs.

Most designers will spend most of their careers working with offset lithography, which is perhaps the most economical and versatile process of all. But there will perhaps come a time when you need to produce a design for a plastic carrier bag, for example, and have to evaluate the relative advantages and constraints of flexography and screenprinting, and modify the design appropriately. Or there may come a time when you wish to produce a high-quality invitation card on handmade paper using letterpress. With the information outlined in this chapter, you will be confident of making the right choice.

So, too, with finishing. The expected end use of a printed product and the budget are key factors in the choice of perfect binding, say, over wire stitching, or varnishing over lamination. Only experience will teach you to make the correct choices every time, but, forearmed with the knowledge contained in this chapter, you will at least be aware of all the options open to you.

MALCOLM GARRETT

LIFE STORY ■ Malcolm Garrett was born in Northwich, England, in 1956. He studied typography and psychology at Reading University from 1974 to 1975, and graphic design at Manchester Polytechnic from 1975 to 1978. His first professional work in 1977 made an immediate impact with his album sleeves for Manchester punk-rock band The Buzzcocks. In the late 1970s and early 1980s, Garrett was identified, along with colleagues Peter Saville, Jamie Reed, and Neville Brody, as one of the most influential designers working for youth-culture clients. In 1983, with partner Kasper de Graaf, he set up Assorted images (Ai).

> "If you don't speak to an audience in a language it can understand then communication is unlikely to take place. This either means that you educate an audience in the nuances of your own personal language, or you explore the languages that exist, which can be efficient yet conceptually restrictive."

In projects for Simple Minds, Duran Duran, and Culture Club, Garrett applied corporate identity to pop groups. Using logos, emblems, and other decorative typographical devices, and the iconography of technology, he turned bands into brands. Other work in the entertainment industry followed, including television graphics. Over the years, Garrett has designed using every possible spelling of his own name (one R, two Rs, one T, two Ts) and under various trade names, including Aesthetic Images and Assorted images. Ai could mean "love" in Japanese or stand as an acronym for artificial intelligence.

Ai was an early advocate of computer graphics — first with an Apple II-based CAD system (yes, Apple II not Mac II) called the Robocom Bitstik, used to distort and stretch logos, then more mainstream Macs. In the late 1980s, Garrett's focus shifted decisively in the direction of new technology, and in 1994 he broke with Ai and joined up with multimedia director Alasdair Scott, with whom he had collaborated since 1989. Together they set up AMXdigital in London (now AMXstudios). Since March 1998, AMXstudios has been part of the Havas Advertising Group.

AMX has developed DVD, Enhanced CD and CD-based multimedia titles and internet sites for Saatchi & Saatchi, Guinness Brewing (for Ogilvy & Mather), *Dazed&Confused* magazine, and WEA records. They have been pioneers in developing "webcasts" in Europe, for Apple Computer, Warner Music, Pulp, Oasis, the Spice Girls, and many others.

Garrett has taught multimedia design at the School of Visual Arts in New York, and Savannah College of Art & Design, Georgia, and is Visiting Professor of Interactive Communications at the Royal College of Art, London, and Visiting Professor at Central St Martins, London. In 2000, he was honored with the title of Royal Designer for Industry for his achievements in New Media Design by the Royal Society of Arts.

MANIFESTO ■ **A Pragmatic Anarchist**

The primary objective when designing digital media is to hide the technology, to make the design transparent, and make it do the right job for the user in an effortless manner. Garrett is a big believer in communication. His definition of good design is: does it do its job? Did message A get communicated to audience B? "If you don't speak to an audience in a language it can understand," says Garrett, "then communication is unlikely to take place. This either means that you educate an audience in the nuances of your own personal language, or you explore the languages that exist, which can be efficient yet conceptually restrictive." His work often seems to adopt a vernacular approach, but is not constrained by convention. He's a pragmatic anarchist.

Garrett has always loved technology. "If you're going to succeed and move forward, you do have to be pigeonholed. So despite calling myself Assorted images in an early idealistic vision of never being pigeonholed, I figured, well, if I'm to be pigeonholed anyway, it will be for computers, technology, something I'm good at, something I've got involved in early on, something I have a view about. I decided it was time perhaps to have people reappraise what they think I'm about. I would much rather be known as Malcolm Garrett, the guy who plays with computers, than Malcolm Garrett, the guy who designs record sleeves.

"I'm genuinely excited by the things that are happening now and things that haven't happened yet. I figure it is my job to be this kind of blinkered believer. You know: I am the new futurist, I will live in the technological world. That appeals to me and I will ignore the current technical problems because someone else will sort out the technology. That's the Japanese approach. You go to Japan and everybody is positive and optimistic and you look at what Japan's done in the last 50 years. If it can happen, it should. Is that irresponsible?"

Saatchi & Saatchi Award for Innovation in Communication website (1997). Creative direction: Malcolm Garrett. Designed by David Loosmore at AMX.

The Saatchi & Saatchi Award for Innovation in Communication website was launched in autumn 1997.

The crux of the navigation system for the site was the image of a brain, representing the origin of all human creative thought, each half of which was drawn differently to indicate different types of information available on the site — practical and conceptual. By "scanning" the brain using an interactive navigational controller, visitors could access the information about the award, or read about the judges, who included William Gibson, Laurie Anderson, James Burke, and the astronaut Buzz Aldrin.

The "conceptual" section aimed to excite the visitor with online demonstrations of recent inventions, which themselves could have been contenders for the award had the scheme been running the previous year. Making judicious use of technologies such as Real Video, Real Audio, and Flash, inventions such as the Micromap, Trevor Bayliss' award-winning wind-up radio, and vision-enhancing glasses were brought to life in a visually sympathetic manner.

This site was one of the very first sites in the United Kingdom to use Macromedia Flash software to bring animation to the site and was the first site in Europe to win the coveted Macromedia "Shocked site of the day."

The record sleeve for The Buzzcocks' *Orgasm Addict* (1977) was Garrett's first published work, produced at the beginning of his final year studying graphic design at Manchester Polytechnic. It features a montage by Linder, a fellow student of illustration with whom he collaborated throughout 1977 and 1978. It was first photocopied to degrade the image. The typography was a combination of stenciled lettering, modified rub-down lettering, and metal type hand-set in the college typography department.

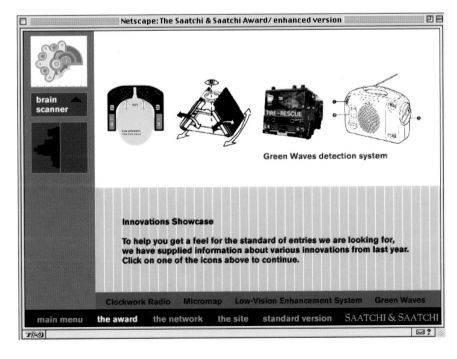

WORKSTATION

- Website: www.amxstudios.com
- Interview by Alan Pipes, *Design*, July 1985, pp. 44, 45
- *Graphis* Nov/Dec 1988, No. 258
- *Emigre* 11, 1989, Ambition/Fear issue
- *Emigre* 13, 1989, Redesigning stereotypes issue
- Malcolm Garrett, "The book is dead," *Graphics World* Feb 1991, No. 90
- Malcolm Garrett, "Multimedia — who needs it?" *Baseline* No. 18, 1994, pp. 30–33
- Interview by Rick Poynor, *Eye* 12/94, pp. 11–16
- Interview by Joe Shepter, Adobe, www.adobe.com/web/gallery/amx/main.html

SEVEN   THE INTERNET

THE INTERNET

Imagine: you are reading this book and you come across a term you don't quite understand or the name of a person or place you'd like to know some more about. The words may be highlighted by being in **bold type**, so that means you can flick to the back of the book and look them up in the glossary. But think how amazing it would be if you could just "click" on the word somehow and be transported to a place with all the answers in as much detail as you need! Well, if you were online to the internet, that's exactly what would happen.

What is the internet? It is simply a global network of computers, and a means of connecting your computer, TV, or mobile telephone to other computers. It is merely a medium. But on the internet you'll find lots of useful tools, the main three being email (electronic mail), newsgroups, and the World Wide Web.

With email, you can send messages and digital "attachments" — anything from computer-generated images, scanned photographs, and artwork to sound samples — anywhere in the world.

Newsgroups are online "bulletin boards" or discussion groups that enable you to keep in touch with other designers, exchange tips and experiences, or download "shareware" fonts and programs.

The World Wide Web (WWW) is a collection of "pages," probably running into several billions by now, containing text, images, sound, movies, and, most importantly, "hot links" to other pages. You view these pages using a program called a browser, such as Netscape Navigator or Internet Explorer. WWW pages can also have forms built in so that you can, say, order books from an online bookstore or DVDs from the Cyber Mall, or send fan mail (or a job offer) to an illustrator or photographer who's showing their virtual portfolio at an online gallery.

So what's in the internet for the designer? First, it is a cheap and fast way to send artwork to the client and printer. Second, it's an inexpensive and effective way to advertise yourself and your work worldwide. Third, it is a potentially huge source of new clients and job opportunities.

■ WHAT IS THE INTERNET?

In only a decade or so, the internet has become an essential part of most people's lives, as indispensible as a telephone or television. But what exactly is it? And how does it work? The internet is a global network of computers or, more accurately, a network of computer networks — the network of networks — after all, there is only one internet. It enables you to connect your computer to every other computer on the internet, initially via a telephone line. It is basically a medium of communication, like the telephone network, but capable of much more.

First, as always, some history. In 1962, Dr J. C. R. "Lick" Licklider was chosen to head research into improving the military's use of computer technology. The result was ARPAnet (ARPA stands for Advanced Research Projects Agency — the funding body), which was set up to connect together just four computers at sites around the United States in order to distribute resources where they were needed. Computers were extremely expensive in those days (even though they probably only had around 12 k of memory each) and had to be shared around. The first ARPAnet node was installed at the University of California at Los Angeles in September 1969. Additional nodes were soon added at Stanford Research Institute, the University of California at Santa Barbara, and the University of Utah.

This was all made possible by packet switching. The reasoning went that in a nuclear war, the communications infrastructure — the networks of wires, command centers, antennae — would become prime targets. By decentralizing the network, communications would keep flowing even if parts of the network were destroyed. The key idea was that messages were broken down into "packets" and sent off in the general direction of their destination, where they would then be reassembled. Paul Baran of the Rand Corporation published such a scheme in 1964. The National Physical Laboratory in the United Kingdom set up the first test network based on these principles in 1968.

ARPAnet was developed from the outset to be both resilient and decentralized — designed, in other words, to survive a nuclear attack. By 1971 approximately 20 nodes had been installed. In 1972, the First International Conference on Computer Communications was held in Washington DC to discuss communication protocols in order that different kinds of networks around the world would be able to "talk" to each other. The International Network Working Group (INWG) was created, and Vinton Cerf, who was involved with ARPAnet at UCLA, was chosen as the first chair. The first international connections to the ARPAnet were made in 1973: to University College, London, and the Royal Radar Establishment in Norway.

In September 1973, Bob Kahn and Vint Cerf presented their basic internet ideas at a meeting of the INWG at the University of Sussex in Brighton, United Kingdom. The

7.1 A modem converts the digital signal from your computer into an analog signal that can travel down the telephone line. Modems are being replaced by ISDN terminal adaptors that act as virtual modems, like this Hermstedt Leonardo for light or medium ISDN usage on either Macs or PCs. This external USB adaptor will allow you to send or receive data at up to 128 kbit/s.

system of protocols they came up with became known as the TCP/IP, after the two initial protocols developed: Transmission Control Protocol (TCP) and Internet Protocol (IP). These were first published in September 1981, became the standard internet protocols in January 1983, and are still used today.

The internet was opened up to commercial networks such as CompuServe and America OnLine in 1991 and continues to grow and grow. The number of computers on the internet reached a million in 1992 and by the end of 1993 this number had doubled. At the time of writing, the number of computers connected to the internet was estimated at 340 million.

Who invented the internet? Who coined that word? The definitive primary source for internet history is the collection of email memos called RFCs (Requests for Comments). RFC791, for example, is the September 1981 specification for Internet Protocol (IP). The oldest reference to the word "internet" that I could find was in the title of

RFC675: V. Cerf, Y. Dalal, and C. Sunshine, "Specification of Internet Transmission Control Program," dated 1 December, 1974.

So who runs the internet? No one actually owns the internet and no one body runs it. That is both its strength and its weakness. If a resilient network has been designed to find a route around physical damage, so it can always find a route around censorship. Some people see the internet as much more than a collection of cooperating computer networks. They see a new community called Cyberspace, with its own culture, language, and laws. But fascinating as that concept might be, it is really outside the scope of this book. Check out Further Reading, pp. 250–1, if you'd like to know more.

In summary, the internet is:

- A network of networks based on the TCP/IP protocols
- A community of people who use and develop those networks
- A collection of resources that can be reached from those networks.

■ HOW TO GET STARTED

You may already have access to the internet at home, school, or college. If not, you can rent time at a Cybercafé or invest in your own equipment. You will need a **modem** (Fig. **7.1**) and an account with an **ISP** (Internet Service Provider). The modem connects your (digital) computer to the (analog) telephone network and your ISP should be a local telephone call away. You will need **TCP/IP** (Transmission Control Protocol/Internet Protocol) software and either **SLIP** (Serial Line Internet Protocol) or **PPP** (Point to Point Protocol) software. These will generally be built into the operating system of your computer. Don't worry, your ISP will usually supply you with all the software you need to get started, plus instructions on how to configure the software. Modems are rated by their data throughput — 56 kbits per second is the state of the art at the time of writing. Modems can also be used to send faxes directly from your computer or can be used to set up a direct connection (i.e. direct from your telephone to their telephone, not via the internet) with your repro house.

You can cut out the modem altogether and gain a faster connection by leasing a dedicated digital **ISDN** (Integrated Services Digital Network) line. This requires a terminal adaptor — either a card or box that attaches to your modem port and acts as a virtual modem. ISDN operates at 64 kbits per second, or

128 kbits per second if you use two lines.

ADSL (Asymmetric Digital Subscriber Line — or loop) can be even faster. Here the bandwidth available for downstream connection is significantly larger than for upstream and is well suited to web browsing and client–server applications as well as some emerging applications such as video on demand.

The data-rate of ADSL depends greatly on the length and quality of the line connecting the end-user to the telephone company's exchange. Typically the upstream data flow is between 16 and 640 kbits per second while the downstream data flow is between 1.5 and 9 Mbits per second.

A **cable modem** allows people to access the internet via their cable television service, and can transfer data at 500 kbits per second or higher, but the actual transfer rates in practice may be lower, depending on the number of other simultaneous users on the same cable.

■ EMAIL

With **email (electronic mail)** you can send messages and "attachments" to other people connected to the internet: you type a message on your computer, connect to the internet, and send it down the telephone line to your local ISP (Fig. **7.2**). It then finds its way to the destination computer and waits in the recipient's "mailbox" until they check their mail. If they wish to reply, they hit the "reply" button on their computer, type a message (perhaps highlighting parts of your original message), and — you have new mail.

Trivial, you may think. But it's much easier and faster than faxing, it's the cost of a quick local phone call, and you have a digital record of the correspondence. What's more, you can send "attachments," which could be scanned-in drawings or photographs, digital artwork, programs, sound samples, anything that can be digitized. It's fast, cheap (the cost of a local phone call), and

energy-saving (green); another plus point is that precious artwork doesn't get delayed, lost, or bent in the mail.

In October 1963, computer-consulting company Bolt, Beranek, and Newman (BBN) published a paper demonstrating that users could communicate remotely with computers using ordinary telephones. BBN had already patented the modem earlier that year.

In 1971, Ray Tomlinson of BBN invented email. By the second year of ARPAnet's operation, the main traffic was news and personal messages. Researchers were using the network not only to collaborate on projects and trade notes on work, but to gossip. People had their own personal-user accounts on the ARPAnet computers, and their own personal addresses for electronic mail. It wasn't long before the mailing list was invented, with which a message could be broadcast to anyone "subscribing" to a particular list. One of the first mailing lists was for science-fiction fans.

7.3 Newsgroup screenshot taken from a comp.fonts discussion thread. The program is Newswatcher.

Eudora (named after Eudora Welty, the author of "Why I live at the P.O.") is a popular email program for Macs; Outlook Express is an email program for Wintel PCs and Macs. Most email programs allow you to store contact lists of recipients and to add your "signature" to the end of each and every message.

Decoding internet addresses

Everyone on the internet has an email address in the form **username@site.dom**, in which **username** is your name or a nickname you have chosen, **site** locates your ISP or server computer, and **dom** is a "domain" type, possibly including subdomains. These are generally separated by periods.

Domain types include:
.com commercial organizations
.edu educational institutions

Note that most of the sites in the .com and .edu domains are in the United States. Outside of these functional domains, sites in the States have the .us domain, and there are subdomains for the 50 states, each generally with a name identical to the state's postal abbreviation. Within the .uk domain, there is an .ac subdomain for academic sites and a .co domain for commercial ones. Note that .ca can be both California and Canada, depending on the context.

It is a good idea to register your own domain while it is still available. Not only will you have an easy-to-remember email and website address, but if you should change

your ISP, you won't have to inform all and sundry about your change of address. The domain acts like a mail-box number — your mail is redirected to your actual address. Domain names are administered by Network Solutions, Inc. in the United States and Nominet in the United Kingdom, but as you must have two servers for the domain to "live on," it is usual to buy a domain through a third party. Prices have come down, but beware of companies that charge you exorbitant amounts if you choose to move your domain at any time in the future.

■ NEWSGROUPS

Usenet (Unix User Network) was established in 1979 between Duke University and the University of North Carolina to exchange news and views. The original programs were written by graduate student

Steve Bellovin. These were rewritten and extended by Steve Daniel and Tom Truscott.

Usenet is an example of a **client–server** architecture. A user (the client) connects to a machine (the server) where the Usenet postings for the past few days, weeks, or hours are stored. You can look at the headings of postings in the newsgroups of interest, and then request the full text of a particular posting (message or article) to be forwarded to your machine (Fig. **7.3**). You may then read or store the article, reply directly to the poster via email, or post a follow-up article (starting or joining a "thread"). You can also initiate a new subject heading with a new posting. The newsgroup program on your computer keeps track of which articles you have already read.

Newsgroups are supposed to be limited to a single topic, and the name of the group should give you some idea of the content to be expected. In 1986 to 1987, seven main hierarchies were created: **comp**, **misc**, **news**, **rec**, **sci**, **soc**, and **talk**. The **alt** hierarchy was proposed at a barbecue in Mountain View, California, on 7 May, 1987, and implemented by subterfuge.

At the time of writing, there were over 60,000 different newsgroups, covering everything from keeping fish (rec.aquaria.freshwater.goldfish) to font design (comp.fonts). Not all ISPs carry all newsgroups, however. Some refuse to carry some sexually explicit groups, especially those used for posting "binaries" (image or sound files), which also take up a lot of "bandwidth" (here meaning throughput of traffic).

Newswatcher is a popular newsgroup program for Macs; Free Agent is a newsgroup program for Wintel PCs.

Chatting on the net

There may be times when you'd like to communicate with other netizens live in almost real time. With **IRC** (Internet Relay Chat) you can. It is a text-based system, so you'll need to know lots of acronyms in order to keep up with the conversations. First you join a channel, #Brighton for example, and then you can either broadcast your comments to everyone else on that channel or choose a person to talk to in private. If you have prearranged a conference with someone, you can create your own channel in which to speak privately. Homer is a popular IRC program for Macs; IRC2 is an IRC program for Wintel PCs.

With a microphone attached to your computer, you can speak to other net users anywhere in the world for the price of a local call. Video conferencing is possible on the net, using a program such as CU-SeeMe, so long as you also have a video camera attached to your computer.

Netiquette

Network etiquette, or **netiquette**, is something that a **newbie** (new user) will come across sooner or later. In the absence of any governing body, certain netizens take it upon themselves to police the newsgroups and will **flame** any transgressors (post a harshly critical message in public on Usenet or send very long messages to you via email). Newbies are encouraged to **lurk** for a while (a lurker is someone who reads but never posts) and consult the newsgroup's FAQ (Frequently Asked Questions) list before posting for the first time.

Postings that are "off topic" often elicit a flaming. **Crossposting** (posting the same message to several groups) is particularly frowned upon, but real venom is reserved for **spamming** (from the Monty Python song "Spam"), which is crossposting a carelessly inappropriate message or advertisement to many different groups or individuals. Messages set all in capitals (interpreted as "shouting") or with overlong signatures (especially ones containing so-called ASCII art) are discouraged, but it is considered very bad form to criticize a poster's poor grammar or spelling. The latest versions of newsreading

programs, such as Newswatcher, have useful "kill files" which enable you to filter out unwanted messages from particular people or on particular topics.

Acronyms and smileys

Because of the need to conserve bandwidth, and for speed of typing, many acronyms are in common use. Here are a few you may encounter:

AFAIK	as far as I know
BTW	by the way
FYI	for your information
IMHO	in my humble opinion
LOL	laughs out loud
ROFL	rolls on the floor laughing
RT*M	read the * manual (clean version!)
YMMV	your mileage may vary

And because gestures or inflections of speech are impossible on the net, symbols made from ASCII characters, called smileys or "emoticons" have evolved. These are particularly useful to avoid causing offense — your harmless joke may be taken literally, but a smiley makes everything OK! Here are a few (turn your head 90 degrees to the left):

:-) or :) basic smiley
;-) or ;) winking smiley (for irony)
:-(or :(sad smiley

You may also see these non-smileys:

<g>	grins
<s>	sighs

MAKE YOURSELF KNOWN

Search engines such as AltaVista and Lycos send out robots to rove the web, reading the first few words of websites and then trying to classify them so that someone initiating a search with a few key words will not be inundated with thousands of likely matches to plow through. Help them out by using the <META> tag in your HTML document so that search engines will know all about you. Place something like this in your document and you will stand a good chance of coming top of the list in an Alta Vista search for Palo Alto poodle parlors:

```
<HEAD>
<TITLE>Acme Pet Parlor</TITLE>
<META NAME="description"
CONTENT="We specialize in grooming pink poodles.">
<META NAME="keywords"
CONTENT="pet grooming, Palo Alto, dog">
</HEAD>
```

7.4 You can download software or upload your ISP's server using an ftp program such as Fetch.

Ftp: uploading and downloading

Ftp (File Transfer Protocol) lets users transfer files between computers. There are many sites around the internet where users can **download** programs, documents, and images (Fig. **7.4**). **Mirror sites** keep copies of the files from the main sites, but may be geographically closer to you. If you have a **WWW** site (see next section), you will use ftp to **upload** your files to the server. Fetch is a popular ftp program for Macs; Ws_ftp is an ftp program for Wintel PCs.

Telnet lets you log on to another computer, anywhere on the internet, as if you were using a terminal attached to that computer. You may

use Telnet, for example, to check your email while round at a friend's house or to run programs remotely. Gopher and Archie are other terms you may come across: they are ways of locating files via ftp. However, they are becoming much less important as the World Wide Web and all-in-one browsers such as Netscape Navigator take over their original role.

■ WORLD WIDE WEB (WWW)

While consulting for CERN (the European Laboratory for Particle Physics) between June and December 1980, Tim Berners-Lee wrote a

hypertext-based program called "Enquire-Within-Upon-Everything." In October 1990, the name **World Wide Web** (**WWW**) was decided, and in November, with Robert Cailliau as co-author, the first WWW program was developed. On 30 April, 1993, CERN placed the software for the WWW in the public domain.

In September 1993 a group of graduate students from the University of Illinois at Champaign-Urbana developed Mosaic, a software package that used the WWW protocol. Mosaic was a major factor in the explosion of business interest in the internet, because it made the internet accessible to inexperienced users. Many other browsers have evolved since Mosaic's development,

including its direct descendant
Netscape Navigator and Microsoft's
more recent Internet Explorer.

The World Wide Web is a huge
collection of interconnected "pages,"
probably running into several billions
by now. These pages are viewed by a
browser (which, like most internet
software, can be downloaded for
free) and can contain text, images,
sound, movies, and hypertext "hot
links" to other pages, which may
reside on servers anywhere around
the world (Fig. **7.5**). These pages can
be about anything: football, recipes,
bands, illustration. The biggest
growth area is in commercial sites
(see Malcolm Garrett, pp. 204–5),
where corporations entice users to
visit their online "advertisements"
with the promise of free screen-
savers and other entertaining
programs to download. Pages may
also have built-in forms, so that you
can, say, order books from an online
bookshop or CDs from the Cyber
Mall pages, or send fan mail (or a
job) to an artist showing at an online
gallery. Many sites encourage you
to register (giving them valuable
marketing information), and you
are issued with a password for
subsequent visits.

Most people on the net have a
home page. Your ISP or college may
provide you with disk space on their
server, and there are many sites
around the world that offer free
space for home pages. These can
also be used as test areas to
develop your web design skills.

The WWW is based on a
client–server model where the client
(your browser) communicates with
the servers (the sites storing the
web pages you want to view) using

HTTP (Hyper Text Transport
Protocol). **HTML** (Hyper Text
Markup Language) is used to create
and communicate the page. The
address of a page or its **URL**
(Uniform Resource Locator) is thus
in the form: http://www.yourISP.
com/username/index.html

Designing for the World Wide Web

The World Wide Web is a wonderful
opportunity for the graphic
designer, but it does have some
curious challenges. For a start, until
recently you didn't have a lot of
control over how your designs and
layouts would be seen! You can only
specify fonts that the user already
has, but have little control over what
size they will be viewed at or the
measure used. You have very little
influence over the use of white
space, and there are many trade-offs

to be made to keep downloading
time to a minimum (if your page
doesn't download quickly then it
won't be seen — the user will just
carry on surfing!)

You have to accept that your
design is going to appear differently
on different browsers and on different machines. On some browsers,
for example, the user can increase
the viewable text size — this is
great news for the partially sighted,
but it can play havoc with your carefully crafted layouts. But on the
upside, some designers find these
constraints liberating: you don't
have to worry about the resolution
of images (everything is 72 dpi),
CMYK concerns, or anything at all
to do with print production! The

7.5 Netscape screenshot showing
the use of frames to create a separate
scrollable contents list to a site on steam
locomotives.

web is an ideal publishing medium: it is cheap (almost free), global, instantaneous, and, despite what was said earlier in this paragraph, extremely versatile.

So what is there left for the designer to do? Basically what all graphic designers do all the time in any case: communicate the client's message in the most effective way; make it easy for the user to "navigate" around the site; and make the pages distinctive, attractive, eye-catching, and entertaining. You may have to use ingenious work-arounds to achieve all the results you envisaged at concept stage, but the web is also a great leveler — college graduates in their back bedrooms have exactly the same tools available to them as the most prestigious design groups working for the largest multinational corporations.

Perhaps the biggest difference between designing for print and for the WWW — and this applies equally to CD-rom design — is that the layouts for a book or magazine are designed in linear fashion: readers are expected to start at the beginning and work their way through to the end. In interactive media like the WWW, the reader is encouraged to leap from one hot link to another, so page organization is important. Designing a WWW site is more akin to making a movie, but one with multiple narratives, to boot. Remember, the reader may be entering any page in your site from an outside link, so every page must be self-contained, with all the navigational aids necessary to help them carry on surfing. A concept plan with flowcharts and maybe a storyboard is essential (Fig. **7.6**). WWW designers need directorial skills too — with sound and animation available, you may well be asked to coordinate the efforts of a whole team of other professionals.

Do designers really have to learn HTML?

Well, yes and no. The internet at present is rather like the early days of automobiles, when you had to carry a toolkit around with you and know enough about the engine to make running repairs. There are plug-ins to QuarkXPress and InDesign that can convert existing page layouts into HTML, but the results generally need fine-tuning later, particularly in relation to making links work.

There are several very good standalone WYSIWYG web-design programs, such as Adobe GoLive and Macromedia Dreamweaver (Fig. **7.7**) which claim that you can design web pages without ever having to come into contact with HTML code — after all, you don't need to be able to program in PostScript to lay out pages in QuarkXPress, do you? In practice, however, you will need a working knowledge of HTML to delve into the code if something peculiar happens to your design. GoLive can toggle between the layout and code, which is very useful for troubleshooting. There are excellent programs that never allow you to look at the code. Freeway, for the

GETTING YOURSELF ORGANIZED
Append notes to yourself in your HTML code by using the tag
<!—a note to myself—> to make future debugging easier,
especially if someone else has to maintain your pages. It can be
harder than you think to update complex HTML pages, even if you
created them yourself. And use lots of white space between paragraphs — unless you use <P> or <BR> any formatting in the code
will be ignored by the browser. And remember to turn off curly
quotes if you're writing HTML on a word processor: browsers
only understand feet (') and inches (").

7.6 Concept design of a website for the 1997 British General Election, designed by New Media Labs for the *Guardian* newspaper.

7.7 Programs such as Adobe GoLive enable you to create web pages quickly.

Mac, has a QuarkXpress feel to it, with a pasteboard, master pages and text boxes. It can import Photoshop images and convert them to GIFs or JPEGs (more later). And when you have finished, the program "compiles" and exports (and ftps) the entire website.

Most websites are now so complex that it would not be economic to write the code by hand, and programs like GoLive and Dreamweaver are essential if you are working with freeform layouts using tables (more later) and frames, with mouse rollovers and other Javascript effects, or developing database-driven e-commerce sites.

A complete description of HTML is beyond the scope of this chapter, but there are many excellent books on the subject (see Further Reading, pp. 250–1), and the joy of the inter-net is that there are many online teaching resources available. To start with, your browser will have built-in links to "How to ..." pages, and your ISP's home page is always a good place to start surfing for advice. If you do find a page that you like the look of, all you have to do is hit the "View document source" button on your browser for it to display the HTML code for the page you are viewing (so long as it is not a frames-based page!). It's then a relatively easy step to figure how that designer achieved that effect.

Writing your own home page
A good way to get a taste of HTML is to design a simple **home page**. A first encounter with the internet is often quite a culture shock. It's like going back 20 years in time to

the days of ASCII-only typewriter terminals. Email and newsgroups are ASCII based — thus many charac-ters are unavailable, and you have to remember to insert carriage returns at the ends of lines. HTML is no exception; the simple reason is that the web is accessed by every possible kind of computer — the files that travel around the internet must be of the lowest common denominator, and that means ASCII text. Likewise, images have to be in a format under-standable by all types of computer, and that means they are most commonly in **GIF** (Graphics Inter-change Format) or **JPEG** (Joint Photographic Experts Group) format.

A simple web page will thus comprise a text document plus GIF and/or JPEG files all in the same directory (equivalent to a Mac folder), or with the images in a sub-folder. To create a home page, you

will need either a simple-text editor, such as Simpletext for a Mac or Notepad on a Wintel PC, a word processor that can output text files (but remember to turn "smart quotes" off), or a simple shareware web page design program such as PageSpinner which will also provide menus of useful commands and options. You will also need a graph-ics program, such as Photoshop, that can export GIF and JPEG files. And finally, you will need ftp access to a server — you can create the pages on your computer, but for anyone else to be able to see them they must first be "published" by uploading them to a server.

HTML works its magic by the use of **tags** that the browser inter-prets as the web page arrives from the server to the client. Tags nearly always have a start and an end, "containing" the item in question.

Production for graphic designers 3rd edition Chapter 7 1/23/01 18

7.8 PageSpinner screenshot showing the HTML code of your home-page document.

The first part of the tag turns an attribute on and the second turns the attribute off. Tags themselves are surrounded by angled brackets (the < "less than" and > "greater than" symbols), and the closing tag is usually preceded by a forward slash symbol (/). For example, the tag for the title of your page is written in HTML like this:

<TITLE> My home page</TITLE>

All HTML documents contain the following code:

```
<HTML>
<HEAD>
<TITLE>My home page</TITLE>
</HEAD>
<BODY>
Text and images to be placed here.
</BODY>
</HTML>
```

A program such as PageSpinner will present this sequence whenever you open a new document — it also colors the tags to distinguish them from the text (Fig. **7.8**). The <HTML> tag tells the browser that an HTML document is on the way. The name of the text document should end with the suffix ".html"

(although PC users, restricted to file names of eight characters plus a three-letter suffix, can use just ".htm" for their extension). By default, the first page of a website is always called index.html.

The text within the <TITLE> tags will appear at the head of your browser window and as the description of a URL in the bookmark file of your browser. Everything within the <BODY> tags will appear in the main window of the browser.

Note that HTML is not case sensitive: <title> will be interpreted exactly the same way as <TITLE> or even <TiTlE>, but for legibility, we will use upper case. File names should always be in lower case.

```
<HTML>
<!—This file was created on
1/1/01 by me—>
<HEAD>
<TITLE> My home
page</TITLE>
</HEAD>
<BODY>
<H1>Welcome to my
world!</H1>
<P>This is my as yet still
under, construction home
page.</P>
It was last updated on 1
January 2001.
</BODY>
</HTML>
```

7.9 This is how the HTML code in the text will look when interpreted by the browser.

Production for graphic designers 3rd edition Chapter 7 1/23/01 18

7.10 This is how the HTML code in the text will look when interpreted by your browser. Note that the hot links are underlined and are usually in a different color to the regular text.

Now you can import or type in a heading and some text (Fig. **7.9**):

Headings. Unlike in print, in web design you cannot specify the font and sizes of headings; all you can say about a heading in HTML is that it will (probably) be bigger and bolder than the regular text. There are six headings in HTML: H1 through H6. The default for an H1 heading is 24 pt Times. It is best always to start with an H1 heading and not to skip levels. If you miss off the </H1> end tag, the whole document will be one big heading! H6, strangely, will be smaller than the body text, at around 9 pt.

Anchors. One of the best things about the web is that you can create hypertext "hot links" to other parts of your page, to other pages on your site, or to other unrelated pages on any other computer anywhere in the world. To do this, you insert anchors: either local relative ones pointing to another text file in the same directory, or absolute ones containing the full URL of the page you want to link to. An anchor is the form

<A HREF="URL">the hot text</A>

where the URL is either relative, i.e. music.html — another page on your site — or absolute, i.e. http://www.elvisnet.com, the URL of the ElvisNet site. If you are experimenting with HTML in a word processor, remember to turn off the "curly quotes" option. HTML only understands the inches (") symbol. An example of anchors in use follows (Fig. **7.10**):

```
<HTML>
<!—This file was created on
1/1/01 by me—>
<HEAD>
<TITLE>My home
page</TITLE>
</HEAD>
<BODY>
<H1>Welcome to my
world!</H1>
<P>This is my getting-there-
slowly home page.</P>
<P>My favorite artiste of all
time is<A HREF="http://
www.elvisnet.com">Elvis
</A></P>
<P>You can find more musical
links on my <A HREF="
music.html"> Music</A>
page. </P>
<P>This page was last
updated on 1 January 2001.
<BR>
Why not email me with your
comments on
<A HREF="MAILTO:pipes@
brighton.co.uk">pipes@
brighton.co.uk</A>
</BODY>
</HTML>
```

Note that other type of anchor at the end: the MAILTO: attribute automatically creates an email form within the browser.

Character formatting. You can influence the choice of font to some extent, but must give the end user a lot of leeway: if you specify <FONT FACE= "Verdana,Arial,Helvetica, Swiss,Geneva,Sans-serif">, for example, then if the user has Verdana, the browser will use it, if not it will use Arial or Helvetica, or at least any old sans serif face instead of the default Times. You can at least make words **bold** or *italic*. HTML, however, has two classes of styles: logical and physical. Logical styles, such as <STRONG> tag the text according to its meaning, while physical styles, such as <BOLD> indicate the specific typographical appearance of the text.

Logical tags are supposed to help enforce consistency in your documents. Remember, the WWW was developed by scientists used to the conventions of academic papers, not graphic designers with their own set of needs. Most

SIZE YOUR IMAGES
Use the size attributes WIDTH = 200 HEIGHT = 150 within the <IMG> tag for all your GIFs and JPEGs. You can find out the size of your image in pixels in Photoshop or one of many shareware programs. The browser will then leave space for them and load the text that follows the images. The viewer will then have something to read as the images are downloading. And add text descriptions to images for readers who can't read the graphics by putting an ALT 5 "text description of image" into the <IMG> tag. Reuse the same image over and over whenever possible to speed up page loading.

browsers render the <STRONG> tag in **bold** text. However, it is possible that a browser might display the word in bright red instead. If you want something to be displayed in **bold** (for example) and do not want a browser's setting to display it differently, use physical styles. *Italic* is best avoided, however — the browser's version of italic is usually an oblique version of the roman font and nearly always illegible.

Try to be consistent about which type of style you use. If you tag with physical styles, do so within the whole document. If you use logical styles, stick with them throughout a document.

Here are some of the logical styles:

<EM>   for emphasis, typically displayed in italics
<CITE>   for titles of books, films, etc., typically displayed in italics
<STRONG>   for strong emphasis, typically displayed in **bold**.

And here are some examples of physical styles:

<B>   **bold** text
<I>   *italic* text
<TT>   typewriter text, i.e. fixed-width font, usually Courier.

Escape sequences. Three ASCII characters — the left angle bracket (<), the right angle bracket (>), and the ampersand (&) — have special meanings in HTML and therefore cannot be used "as is" in text. (The angle brackets are used to indicate the beginning and end of HTML tags, and the ampersand is used to indicate the beginning of an escape sequence.) Double quote marks may be used as is, but a character entity may also be used (").

To use any of these in an HTML document, you must enter their escape sequence instead:

< is the escape sequence for <
> is the escape sequence for >
& is the escape sequence for &

Color. By default, the background color in Netscape is gray and the text is black. Hot links are blue and these change to purple when that link has been visited (browsers have a cache, a portion of your hard disk, in which they store recently visited sites). These can be changed, however, by adding attributes to the <BODY> tag. The bad news is that the RGB colors you specify must be converted to hexadecimal! Programs such as Photoshop allow you to do this quite painlessly. For example,

<BODY TEXT="#000055"
BGCOLOR="#CCFFFF"
LINK="#CC0000"
VLINK="#005522">

results in dark blue text, a light blue background, and red hypertext links which, when visited, change to green.

Website designers get to work in RGB all the time, and at screen resolution of 72 dpi (dots per inch), so what they see on the screen will be the same as in the finished product. There are slight differences, however, in the way Macs and PCs display colors, and how browsers, such as Netscape and Explorer, interpret the color information. Most people are assumed to have at least a 256-color monitor, and, taking into account the above constraints, we arrive at 216 "web-safe" colors, which will be displayed without resorting to dithering (optically mixing two or more colors). Thus white is FFFFFF and black is 000000.

Web colors are described using three sets of hexadecimal numbers, one each for red, green, and blue. Some web creators prefer to specify colors by name rather than by hexadecimal value. There are 136 standard colors with names that are recognized by most browsers. Many of these colors are not among the 216 browser-safe colors, and may be dithered. These include such exotic names as Blanched Almond (FFEBCD), Chocolate (D2691E), Dodger Blue (1E90FF), Fuchsia (FF00FF), Old Lace (FDF5E6), Thistle (D8BFDB), and Tomato (FF6347). Charts of websafe colors can be found on the internet: try www.lynda.com/hex.html and the-light.com/colclick.html

Images. To add an image, use the tag <IMG SRC="picture.gif">, where picture.gif is the file name of the image, in this case a GIF file. IMG says place image here and SRC tells the browser that the source is an image in the same directory as the text file called picture.gif. By default, images are ranged left, but you can center them using the <CENTER> tag. It is also useful to specify the dimensions of the image, in pixels, using WIDTH and HEIGHT attributes. If you do this, the browser will leave a space for the image and display any text that follows without waiting for the image to load. Images always take longer to download than text and this gives the user something to read while waiting for the pictures. The ALT attribute describes the image in text and is a courtesy to users with a browser, such as Lynx, that doesn't support graphics, and to visually disabled people who rely on their computer to speak the websites out loud.

Other attributes define the space between the image and text, and whether the image has a border or not. You can use an image as a link, and the default is a blue rectangular border, which looks odd on an image with an irregular outline. For example,

```
<CENTER><IMG SRC="fido.gif"
ALT="my poodle Fido"
WIDTH=200 HEIGHT=50
BORDER=0></CENTER>
```

displays a centered image without a border. If you were using a browser such as Lynx or had your images switched off, all you would see was the text "my poodle Fido."

Optional extras

You can also use GIFs to tile a background, you can create tables of data, and forms for feedback using CGI (Common Gateway Interface) scripts. You can make a graphic into an "imagemap" — when users click on specified portions of the graphic they are linked to other pages. A feature called "frames" will divide the main window into lots of smaller scrollable ones (see Fig. 7.5) — so that you can have a permanent table of contents in a sidebar, say, with the current content in the main window (and a clock in the corner).

There are advantages and disadvantages to using frames. The benefits include faster performance, easier navigation, easier branding of a website by having a logo, say, in a frame of its own, and easier maintenance — if you have to change an item on the menu, you only have to do it once. Frames can also solve a lot of layout problems, such as true centering of page elements within the browser window, and the use of different background colors or gifs in different areas of the window. The drawbacks include uneven browser support, difficulty in bookmarking specific pages within the website, and being listed by search engines, and problems printing out the pages. Frames also cause confusion to the speech programs that help visually impaired people.

With programs such as Macromedia Flash and Director, Real Audio, and Apple's QuickTime, you can add audio, animations, movies and virtual-reality panoramas to your website. But until the plug-ins become a standard part of the browser software, your end user will have to download up-to-date plug-ins from the vendor's website. Programs such as Macromedia Fireworks and Adobe LiveMotion help you create animated buttons and other graphic elements.

Sun's **Java** programming language (named after the amount of Mount Java coffee drunk during its development) allows you to incorporate "applets" (no relation to Apple computers) into your HTML code. These are tiny programs embedded into the HTML which, when downloaded, will run on any computer to produce animations, for example. Sun describes Java as a "simple, robust, object-oriented, platform-independent, multi-threaded, dynamic general-purpose programming environment." With Java you don't need to download plug-ins — the ability to run Java is built into browsers such as Netscape's Navigator.

Javascript allows you to have features such as mouse rollovers on your website, where the graphic changes as your mouse moves over it. Web-design programs such as GoLive, Dreamweaver, and Freeway help you create these without having to learn Javascript.

Remember the automobile simile earlier? Web design is also like the early days of "desktop publishing" when anyone purchasing a copy of PageMaker or QuarkXPress and a handful of fonts was led to believe that they too could be a graphic designer. And the result? A lot of publications looking like Victorian handbills. Just because you can do something, you don't have to incorporate every feature into every document. Everything can be used appropriately somewhere, but in general try to exercise some restraint!

There are sound reasons for this: the more features you add to your pages, the longer they will take to download and the more chance there is that the user will get bored and move on. It may be convenient

7.11 This is the same page as in Figure 7.5 but viewed in another browser — in this case Microsoft's Internet Explorer.

for you to write the page in Director, say, but it can be a bore to have to download the latest version of a Shockwave plug-in first, and then to have to wait ages for the Shocked "movie" to download before you can even decide whether to surf on to another page. Some of the better pages, in my opinion, have few frills, just plain white backgrounds, the minimum amount of graphics, a logical structure, and legible text.

Standard and non-standard HTML

HTML 4.0 sets out the specifications for "standard" HTML, as agreed by international committees. However, vendors such as Netscape and Microsoft (Fig. **7.11**), driven by the demands of graphic designers, add so-called extensions or enhancements to their browsers

plus the corresponding HTML code to make them work. As they have a large market share of the browser-installed base, this is not seen as a problem, but it makes internet purists mad! If a browser sees a tag it doesn't understand, it should ignore it — but unpredictable results can sometimes occur.

CSS (cascading style sheets) is an extension to HTML to allow styles — color, font, font sizes, and other attributes — to be specified for certain elements of a hypertext document. Style information can be included within the HTML file or in a separate CSS file (which can then easily be shared by multiple HTML files). Multiple levels of CSS can be used to allow selective overriding of styles.

DHTML (Dynamic HTML) is a term used by some vendors to describe the combination of HTML, style sheets, and scripts that allows

documents to be animated. It is a non-standard extension of HTML, giving greater control over the layout of page elements and the ability to have web pages that change and interact with the user without having to communicate with the server.

DHTML was created by Microsoft and can be viewed in Internet Explorer 4.0 (and later) and Netscape Communicator 4.0 (and later) but, as usual, Microsoft and Netscape disagree on how it should be implemented. The Document Object Model Group of the World Wide Web Consortium is developing standards for DHTML.

More acronyms and standards: SGML (Standard Generalized Mark-up Language) is a generic mark-up language for representing documents — an International Standard that describes the relationship between a document's content and its structure. Since 1998, almost all development in SGML has been focussed on XML — a simple (and therefore easier to understand and implement) subset of SGML suitable for use on the World Wide Web. XHTML is a reformulation of HTML 4.01 in XML. (For more information, check out www.w3.org/XML.)

Tables were originally introduced to display tabular matter. But they are also a useful workaround for laying out text. A table with a single row and a single column, for example, can be used to display a single column of text with some degree of control over the measure (set the border to zero: BORDER="0".) A table of two columns can be used to place a graphic, say, flush left with the text running alongside it. Behind the scenes, Freeway uses elaborate arrays of tables with some cells containing differently sized "invisible" GIFs to implement your layouts.

So our nearly finished home page might now look like this (Fig. **7.12**):

```
<HTML>
<!—This file was created on
1/1/01 by me—>
<HEAD>
<TITLE>My home page</TITLE>
</HEAD>
<BODY
TEXT="#000055"#BGCOLOR=
"#CCFFFF"#LINK="#CC0000"
VLINK="#005522">
<CENTER><H1> Welcome to my
world!</H1>

<P><IMG SRC="fido.jpg"
ALT="my poodle Fido"
WIDTH=200 HEIGHT=319
BORDER="0 ">
</P>

<P><FONT SIZE="+3"
COLOR="RED">T</FONT>his is
my getting there slowly

<B>home page</B>. </P>
<P>My favorite artiste of all time
is<AHREF="http://www.
elvisnet.com"> Elvis</A>. </P>
<P>You can find more musical
links on my <A
HREF="music.html"> Music</A>
page.</P> </CENTER>

<HR SIZE=4 WIDTH=90%
ALIGN=CENTER>

<FONT SIZE="-1">This page was
last updated on 1 January 2001.
<BR>
Why not email me with your
comments on
<AHREF="MAILTO:pipes@
brighton.co.uk">
pipes@brighton.co.uk</A>
</FONT>
</BODY>
</HTML>
```

The only way at present to have total control over the appearance of your layout is to use an Adobe Acrobat file in PDF (Portable Document Format), but once again this is yet another file to download and read

later — you will need the proprietary software to create the files, and the user will need a plug-in or viewing software to read them.

Graphics formats: GIFs and JPEGs

Another way to be in control of the look of your pages is to put all the typography into graphic images — and some web designers do. On a lot of web pages, you will find that headings are often GIFs, and so are other graphic devices such as bullets and buttons. The GIF (Graphics Interchange Format) was originally developed for CompuServe (it's still called CompuServe GIF on the Photoshop menu) and it is very good at compressing 8-bit (256-color) files that have areas containing flat color, such as logos and typographic headings. A later version, called GIF89a, also supports transparency (so that images with irregular outlines can appear to blend into the background) and interlacing, so that the image first appears as a highly pixelated picture that sharpens up as it downloads (Fig. **7.13**). GIF89a also allows

7.12 This is how the code below looks in Netscape.

7.13 An interlaced GIF looks rough at first, but sharpens up as the image downloads.

animated GIFs to be assembled from a series of still frames in programs such as Adobe Image-Ready (bundled with Photoshop).

All browsers (except completely non-graphical ones like Lynx) support GIFs. Most also support JPEG (Joint Photographic Experts Group) files. JPEGs (files with the suffix .JPEG, or .JPG for PC users) can display 24-bit color and are much better than GIFs for displaying continuous-tone photographic images. Photoshop 6 has a "Save for web" feature that does wonders to compress JPEG and GIF images.

There are other formats in use, but these are the most common. PNG (Portable Network Graphics) is a lossless, portable format coming into use which provides a patent-free replacement for GIF and can also replace many common uses of TIFF.

Whichever you use (remember GIFs are good for graphics with areas of flat color; JPEGs are best for photographs) you must keep the file sizes to a minimum. And that means 30 k maximum for any one image. For designers dealing with print images of several megabytes, this may seem an impossible task, but remember you are only dealing with resolutions of 72 dpi and using as few colors as you can get away with.

GIFs have less obvious uses too. Graphic designer David Siegel (www.dsiegel.com/tips) has lots of tips for web designers, but his neatest trick is the single-pixel GIF. He has a clear (transparent) GIF for creating "white" space in a layout. Replacing x and y in the tag

```
<IMG HSPACE=x VSPACE=y
SRC="dot_clear.gif">
```

where x is the number of pixels horizontally and y is the number of pixels vertically, will create rectangles of space of any size, and because these tiny GIFs are cached in your hard disk, they can be used over and over with no drop in performance. You can also use various colored ones to create solid blocks and bullets. The most ingenious single-pixel GIF trick is to use a black dot to construct an em rule, thus:

```
<IMG ALIGN=ABSMIDDLE
WIDTH=11 HEIGHT=1
SRC="dot_black.gif">
```

What's more, you can download these GIFs from David Siegel's ftp site.

Testing your pages

Web pages are cheap and fast to produce, and the temptation is to "publish" as soon as you possibly can. After all, if there are mistakes, then they can soon be rectified and the original files at the server overwritten. True, but it is still good practice to test, test, and then test again.

You can view your emerging pages on a browser such as Netscape without going online, and this should be the first step. Then try viewing your pages on another browser, such as Internet Explorer (they can all be downloaded free, or can be installed from CD-roms that come with computer magazines). Try uploading your pages to a home page site and go online to check that they still look OK and that everything works.

If you designed the pages on a Mac, find a friend with a PC and see how they look on that platform. PCs have different color tables, and your subtle background color could turn into a dithered mess, or even render the text illegible. A PC might have a 96 dpi monitor, so your text will appear larger and your 72 dpi graphic will appear smaller! The default font on most browsers is Times, and the Times New Roman on PCs is different from the version of Times on Macs!

Remember: some users may still have black-and-white screens, so increase the contrast in your graphics. And finally, pity those (few?) users out there whose only access to the internet is via text-only browsers such as Lynx — at least give them something to read!

You may not need or want to start writing Java applets or CGI scripts, so make friends with your local HTML geek: the local newsgroups are a good place to start. And talk to the people at your ISP about what you can and can't do at the server end. You will at least now know what is possible.

Publicizing your pages

How do you tell the world that you have a website? You can send out postcards, by snailmail. Add your URL to your letterheads and to the signature on your email and newsgroup postings. And you can make it easy for people searching for your site to find it!

7.14 Alta Vista is a popular search engine that presents you with possible sites based on keywords. Sometimes a good deal of lateral thinking is needed to find a particular site.

Some people still seem to think that the internet is one huge encyclopedia — you type in a word somehow and it comes up with an answer. Well, not yet. But there are search engines that can help. The best known is Yahoo, which is more a directory of websites that have been nominated, reviewed, and indexed by its staff. You can speed up the process by sending them details of your site. AltaVista sends out "robots" to search out pages and then tries to classify them. Users can search for words and phrases using logical operators; for example, to find a bedtime story, type "fairy tale" + frog – dragon (Fig. **7.14**). Sometimes you have to use quite a lot of lateral thinking to find a site you know is there — and that's where the surfing comes in. It's like detective work: one page leads to another, nearer and nearer, until you find what you're looking

for. Some search engines just look at the first few words of a page, and you can have some influence by using the <META> tag at the head of your page:

<META NAME="description" CONTENT="We specialize in grooming pink poodles.">
<META NAME="keywords" CONTENT="pet grooming, Palo Alto, dog">

will result in a "hit" if you type in either poodle or dog.

Human factors in website design

Surfing the web and trying to take in information are hard on the eyes. It is estimated that reading speed and comprehension of websites is a quarter of that of print. People don't want to read a lot of text from

computer screens, so avoid long pages and use plenty of subheads; to avoid the reader having to scroll, break long pages into screen-size pages. Use radio skills to boost readability: one idea per sentence; one breath per idea. Try to use italics sparingly as they are hard to read online. Instead use bold or colored text for emphasis. Text on navigation bars and buttons should be concise but not cryptic — reading a heading should tell the user quickly what the page or section is all about.

Impatient users tend not to read streams of text fully. Instead, they scan text and pick out keywords, sentences, and paragraphs of interest while skipping over those parts of the text they care less about. Jacob Neilson (www.useit.com) is a web-usability guru. In his research, he found that 79 percent of test users always scanned any new page; but only 16 percent read word-by-word. As a result, he recommends that web pages employ scannable text.

Because the reader can determine the order of access and choose which ideas to pursue, make each page a self-contained entity, with navigation back to the home page and perhaps your email address. Online readers arrive through many portals and can go anywhere they like — they will not necessarily read the pages in sequential order.

Links can be useful to take readers to extra information, but they can also disrupt flow – be careful when peppering a site with external links. Place them in a "Find out more" section. Grouping links to

TV DESIGN DANGERS
Computer monitors have non-interlaced screens; television sets are interlaced (see p. 140) — so avoid very thin horizontal lines (one pixel thick or a small, odd number of pixels) and tight patterns (like herringbone), or they will flicker. The same applies to fonts with fine serifs, like Bodoni — use sturdy, bold faces like Verdana and Century Schoolbook instead. Avoid excessive kerning and type below 14 pt. TV tubes aren't as sharp as computer monitors and have a narrower color gamut, and bright, saturated colors, particularly yellows and reds, can cause problems of "blooming," so use the NTSC/PAL filter in Photoshop to make sure your colors are broadcast-legal. And keep important elements away from the edge of the screen — they may be lost!

other sites at the website's end means readers are retained and rewarded. You also have space to describe the link before the users choose to go there.

What can you do online for your target audience that you can't do on paper? Would the site content be brought alive by including multimedia and interactive elements? Pop-up windows that bring a page up in a smaller window over the top of the page you were looking at can be used to display bigger versions of maps, photos, and illustrations. You can also use them for glossaries or box stories. Consider how repeat visitors will know what has been changed or added. "Sticky content" is the stuff that keeps users coming back day after day, week after week for their fix. Unlike print, websites can be updated fairly easily, but they can also easily be neglected. So think hard about what "sticky content" will bring lasting enjoyment to your audience.

■ DESIGNING FOR THE SMALL SCREEN

Until recently, graphic design for print, and graphic design for screen-based applications such as television and multimedia were seen as two distinct disciplines, employing very different kinds of designer. Print designers have long been used to working with high-resolution but static visual information; screen designers have to think more like movie makers. The popularity of the internet has been responsible for breaking down some of these divides and many designers are now

expected to "repurpose" their layouts for use in many diverse and different kinds of media.

As we have seen earlier in this chapter, designing a website is more than just feeding a QuarkXPress document into an HTML plug-in and uploading the result to an ISP. A job destined to be published both in print and on the internet will ideally have to be planned very carefully to take advantage of the strengths of both media while avoiding their relative weaknesses. And even if you can turn your hand to designing wonderful web pages, creating designs for television and multimedia means taking on an entirely new set of challenges. For television and film work, designers used to produce lettering on boards, which were then placed in front of the camera. Nowadays, everything is created on a computer system and output direct to video, or, in the case of sports and current-affairs programs, broadcast live (Fig. **7.15**).

Programs like Flash have introduced designers to animation and the possibilities of sound. You can add the time dimension to graphic design — the words and letters can move! Cheaper digital video cameras and programs like Apple's iMovie may have tempted you into film making. Designing for television is not an unreachable aspiration. Everyone is now familiar with the clichés of flying chrome-plated logos and drop shadows, but you don't need to use sophisticated solid modeling with photorealistic rendering techniques such as ray tracing to achieve a memorable effect, as the award-winning idents

for British TV's BBC2 by Martin Lambie-Nairn prove.

Other areas opening up to graphic designers include interaction design — designing the icons and interfaces of software applications — and interactive database design, for use in art galleries and museums, or for distribution on CD-rom. These may also take the form of freestanding "kiosks" with touch-screen interaction.

Collectively known as hypermedia, and created using computer programs such as Macromedia Director, these "stacks" mimic conventional books. The difference is that the "reader" can flip around at will, usually by pointing to a highlighted word in the text, or by choosing a new topic from a menu. The problem for the designer — apart from organizing the stack so as not to frustrate the reader with too many dead ends — is one of legibility. The amount of text on any one page must be kept to a minimum (although it is possible to scroll a large amount of text within a window) because low-resolution text on a screen is tiring to read. The graphics must also be carefully laid out to avoid unwanted effects such as "pixel beards," where a letter or graphic interacts unfavorably with a background tint.

■ SUMMARY

What's in the internet for the designer? Many things. First, it is a cheap and fast way to transport artwork to the client. Second, it's a cheap and effective way to advertise yourself and your work worldwide, using online galleries of work. You

▲ ▶
7.15 The Building the Biggest title sequence for UK TV station Channel 4 was designed by Emmy-winning designer Bernard Heyes using Quantel's Hal video editing system with added effects by Discreet Logic's Flame. It incorporates computer-aided design imager provided by architects Norman Foster and Partners, which was rendered using Alias Wavefront's 3D animation package Maya.

don't have to wait for a source book or CD-rom to come out, and you can change round your portfolio daily, if need be. OK, putting lots of graphics on to WWW pages makes them slow at present, but technology is improving all the time.

Third, it is a source of new work and clients. The fastest growing area of graphic design is in making the WWW pages themselves, as many of our Trailblazers can testify. Everyone has to have one — you only have to watch TV commercials to see how often "something dot com" addresses appear these days. As with CD-rom design and production, huge opportunities exist for designers who understand and appreciate the possibilities (and limitations) of the medium.

You may not wish to learn all the ins and outs of HTML, but with the working knowledge you have gained here you will be able to assemble sample WWW pages quickly and clearly using a wysiwyg page designer, and then be able to fine-tune the source code. You will at least be able to produce a working prototype of the look and feel for a site, which can then be completed by a team of other professionals. You may even be inspired to do it all yourself. At long last, in WWW design, the entire concept-to-production cycle is back in the hands of the designer. Gutenberg must be smiling.

TOMATO

LIFE STORY ■ Tomato is a collective of designers, film makers, writers, and musicians based in Soho, London. It was founded in 1991, and, unlike many design groups, its structure has no hierarchy — all the members are free-lancers and describe themselves as "a group of friends who meet each day to share experiences." Tomato is, in fact, a company and all members are shareholders. It acts like a not-for-profit agency, retaining just enough percentage for overheads and a fund for personal work before paying the rest to the members. When a project comes in, they decide amongst them-selves who should contribute.

The founding members were John Warwicker, Steve Baker, Dirk Van Dooren, Karl Hyde, Richard Smith, Simon Taylor, and Graham Wood. Jason Kedgley joined in 1994 and Michael Horsham in 1996.

Taylor started with Maru Takeshi, the Tokyo- and London-based fashion label Urban Action. Smith and Hyde also comprise the music group Underworld. Tomato Films was begun in 1998, and produces commercials, short films, music videos, and film titles. In April 1999, Tom Roope, Anthony Rogers, and Joel Baumann, along with Tomato formed Tomato Interactive — to explore mixed media, digital, and interactive design.

> Tomato's works are expressive: "an attempt to snatch and log the fleeting multiple details and momentary atmospheric sensations of daily experience."

Clients have included Nike, Adidas, Coca-Cola, Levi's, Microsoft, Kodak, Sony, Intel, Volvo, and Volkswagen. Along with these more specifically commercial projects, Tomato have collaborated on creating the visuals used in Underworld's live shows, whilst their two books, *Process* and *Bareback*, are also examples of more personal experimentation.

Other areas of interest include architecture and installations — such as the three-acre Federation Square cultural and civic centre in Melbourne, Australia — and exhibitions in Manchester, Tokyo, and Munich. In 2000, Tomato began a series of workshops and schools, designed around commu-nicating and sharing in the process of conversation and exploration. Tomato have also begun the development of "amato" — a product range due for launch in May, 2001.

MANIFESTO ■ The Final Outcome is Less Important Than the Process Itself

Tomato's works are expressive: "an attempt to snatch and log the fleeting multiple details and momentary atmospheric sensations of daily experience."

Tomato is, and always has been, about conversation.

Ideas come from this conversation, and these ideas are formed in any media as an appropriate response.

There are no rules — only when rules are required.

This part-intuitive, part-intellectual response gives Tomato the freedom to discover and experiment with many different media. Sometimes the conversation is purely within Tomato, and at other times it is with those outside.

Sometimes Tomato forms the space where this expression exists (in published works and in the Tomato Gallery), sometimes others offer a space for their work to inhabit.

WORKSTATION
• Website: www.tomato.co.uk
• *Process: A Tomato Project*, Thames and Hudson, London, 1996
• *Bareback: A Tomato Project*, Laurence King Publishing, London, 1999
• Noreen O'Leary, "tomato," *Communication Arts*, May/June 1999, pp. 94–102
• Patrick Burgoyne, "Fresh Tomato?" *Creative Review*, September 1999, pp. 29–32

Dirk Van Dooren and Michael Horsham designed a series of posters and magazine ads for the launch of the Sony PlayStation 2 in 2000

Early day my DNA was boss; real one hundred percent cop.
Now, I man balancer, a sleeping bullet

CD cover of Underworld's Beaucoup Fish (1999) for label Junior Boys Own

US Standard Paper Sizes

Grade classification	Basis size*		Weights, lb/ream	Design applications
	in	mm		
Bond	17 x 22	432 x 559	13, 16, 20, 24, 28, 32, 36, 40	Letterheads, newsletters
Book	25 x 38	635 x 965	30, 40, 45, 50, 55, 60, 65, 70, 75, 80, 90, 100, 120	Books, catalogues, calendars, annual reports, brochures, magazines
Text	25 x 30	635 x 965	90, 100, 120, 140, 160, 180	Posters, self-mailers, announcements
Cover	20 x 26	508 x 660	25, 35, 40, 50, 55, 60, 65, 80, 90, 100	Business cards, annual report covers greeting cards

*Basis size: the standard size in a particular grade that determines basis weight

US BOOK SIZES

Grade classification	in	mm	Name	in	mm
Medium 32mo	3 x 4³/₄	76 x 121	Medium 12mo	5¹/₈ x 7²/₃	130 x 195
Medium 24mo	3⁵/₈ x 5¹/₂	92 x 140	Demy 8vo	5¹/₂ x 8	140 x 203
Medium 18mo	4 x 6²/₃	102 x 169	Small 4to	7 x 8¹/₂	178 x 216
Cap 8vo	7 x 7¹/₄	178 x 184	Broad 4to	7 x 8¹/₂	178 x 216
12mo	4¹/₂ x 7¹/₂	114 x 191	(up to 13 x 10) (330 x 254)		
Medium 16mo	4¹/₂ x 6³/₄	114 x 171	Medium 8vo	6 x 9¹/₂	165 x 254
Crown 8vo	5 x 7¹/₂	127 x 191	Royal 8vo	6¹/₂ x 10	165 x 267
Pos 8vo	5¹/₂ x 7¹/₂	140 x 191	Super Royal 8vo	7 x 10¹/₂	178 x 267
			Imperial 8vo	8¹/₄ x 11¹/₂	210 x 292

Note that American and European usage is to express the width dimension of the book first. In the UK and Far East, depth is shown first. Sizes quoted are not absolute and may vary slightly.

TRIMMED PAGE SIZES FROM STANDARD US SHEETS

Trimmed page size in (mm)	Number of pages	Number from sheet	Standard paper size in	mm
3¹/₂ x 6¹/₄ (89 x 159)	4	24	28 x 44	711 x 1118
	8	12	28 x 44	711 x 1118
	12	8	28 x 44	711 x 1118
	16	6	28 x 44	711 x 1118
	24	4	28 x 44	711 x 1118
4 x 9 (102 x 229)	4	12	25 x 38	635 x 965
	8	12	38 x 50	965 x 1270
	12	4	25 x 38	635 x 965
	16	6	38 x 50	965 x 1270
	24	2	25 x 38	635 x 695
4¹/₂ x 6 (114 x 152)	4	16	25 x 38	635 x 965
	8	8	25 x 38	635 x 965
	16	4	25 x 38	635 x 965
	32	2	25 x 38	635 x 965
5¹/₄ x 7⁵/₈ (133 x 194)	4	16	32 x 44	813 x 1118
	8	8	32 x 44	813 x 1118
	16	4	32 x 44	813 x 1118
	32	2	32 x 44	813 x 1118
6 x 9 (152 x 229)	4	8	25 x 38	635 x 965
	8	4	25 x 38	635 x 965
	16	2	25 x 38	635 x 965
	32	2	38 x 50	965 x 1270
Oblong 7 x 5¹/₂ (178 x 140)	4	8	23 x 29	584 x 737
	8	4	23 x 29	584 x 737
	16	2	23 x 29	584 x 737
8¹/₂ x 11 (216 x 279)	4	4	23 x 35	584 x 889
	8	2	23 x 35	584 x 889
	16	2	35 x 45	889 x 1143
9 x 12 (229 x 305)	4	4	23 x 38	665 x 965
	8	2	23 x 38	665 x 965
	16	2	38 x 50	965 x 1270

US STANDARD ENVELOPE SIZES

Commercial/official Window

Number	Size, in
6	3³/₈ x 6
6¹/₄	3¹/₂ x 6
6³/₄	3⁵/₈ x 6¹/₂
7	3³/₄ x 6³/₄
7³/₄	3⁷/₈ x 7¹/₂
Data Card	3¹/₂ x 7⁵/₈
8⁵/₈	3⁵/₈ x 8⁵/₈
9	3⁷/₈ x 8⁷/₈
10	4¹/₈ x 9¹/₂
10¹/₂	4¹/₂ x 9¹/₂
11	4¹/₂ x 10³/₈
12	4³/₄ x 11
14	5 x 11¹/₂

Booklet

Number	Size, in
2¹/₂	4¹/₂ x 5⁷/₈
3	4³/₄ x 6¹/₂
4¹/₄	5 x 7¹/₂
4¹/₂	5¹/₂ x 7¹/₂
5	5¹/₂ x 8¹/₂
6	5³/₄ x 8⁷/₈
6¹/₂	6 x 9
6³/₄	6¹/₂ x 9¹/₂
7	6¹/₄ x 9⁵/₈
7¹/₄	7 x 10
7¹/₂	7¹/₂ x 10¹/₂
8	8 x 11¹/₂
9	8³/₄ x 11¹/₂
9¹/₂	9 x 12
10	9¹/₂ x 12⁵/₈
13	10 x 13

Catalogue

Number	Size, in
1	6 x 9
1³/₄	6¹/₂ x 9¹/₂
2	6¹/₂ x 10
3	7 x 10
6	7¹/₂ x 10¹/₂
7	8 x 11
8	8¹/₄ x 11¹/₄
9¹/₂	8¹/₂ x 10¹/₂
9³/₄	8³/₄ x 11¹/₄
10¹/₂	9 x 12
12¹/₂	9¹/₂ x 12¹/₂
13¹/₂	10 x 13
14¹/₂	11¹/₂ x 14¹/₄
14¹/₂	11¹/₂ x 14¹/₂

Announcement

Number	Size, in
A-2	4³/₈ x 5⁵/₈
A-6	4³/₄ x 6¹/₂
A-7	5¹/₄ x 7¹/₄
A-8	5¹/₂ x 8¹/₂
A-10	6¹/₄ x 9⁵/₈
Slim	3³/₈ x 8⁷/₈

INTERNATIONAL "A" SIZES OF PAPER

Size	mm	approx. in
4AO	1682 x 2378	$66^1/_4$ x $93^3/_8$
2AO	1189 x 1682	$46^3/_4$ x $66^1/_4$
AO*	841 x 1189	$33^1/_8$ x $46^3/_4$
A1	594 x 841	$23^3/_8$ x $33^1/_8$
A2	420 x 594	$16^1/_2$ x $23^3/_8$
A3	297 x 420	$11^3/_4$ x $16^1/_2$
A4	210 x 297	$8^1/_4$ x $11^3/_4$
A5	148 x 210	$5^7/_8$ x $8^1/_4$
A6	105 x 148	$4^1/_8$ x $5^7/_8$
A7	74 x 105	$2^7/_8$ x $4^1/_8$
A8	52 x 74	2 x $2^7/_8$
A9	37 x 52	$1^1/_2$ x 2
A10	26 x 37	1 x $1^1/_2$

•*Nominal size: in the A series, this equals one square meter

All A series sizes mentioned here are trimmed. "A" sizes can be cut from two stock sizes – R, for trims, and SR, for extra trims or bleeds. A listing of R and SR metric sizes and inch equivalents is below.

Size	mm	approx. in
RAO	860 x 1220	$33^7/_8$ x $48^1/_8$
RA1	610 x 860	$24^1/_8$ x $33^7/_8$
RA2	430 x 610	17 x $24^1/_8$
SRAO	900 x 1280	$35^1/_2$ x $50^3/_8$
SRA1	640 x 900	$25^1/_4$ x $35^1/_2$
SRA2	450 x 640	$17^7/_8$ x $25^1/_4$

▼ Paper sizes

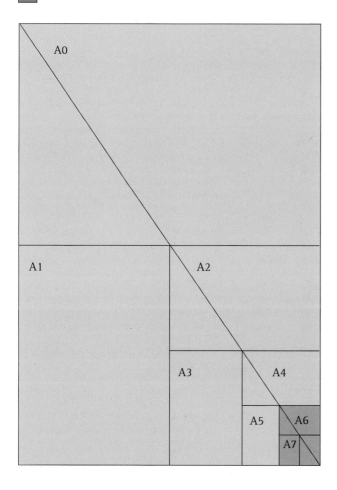

ISO "B" AND "C" SIZES OF PAPER

Size	mm	approx. in
BO	1000 x 1414	$39^3/_8$ x $55^5/_8$
B1	707 x 1000	$27^7/_8$ x $39^3/_8$
B2	500 x 707	$19^5/_8$ x $27^7/_8$
B3	353 x 500	$12^7/_8$ x $19^5/_8$
B4	250 x 353	$9^7/_8$ x $12^7/_8$
B5	176 x 250	7 x $9^7/_8$
B6	125 x 176	5 x 7
B7	88 x 125	$3^1/_2$ x 5
B8	62 x 88	$2^1/_2$ x $3^1/_2$
B9	44 x 62	$1^3/_4$ x $2^1/_2$
B10	31 x 44	$1^1/_4$ x $1^3/_4$
CO	917 x 1297	$36^1/_8$ x 51
C1	648 x 917	$25^1/_2$ x $36^1/_8$
C2	458 x 648	18 x $25^1/_2$
C3	324 x 458	$12^3/_4$ x 18
C4	229 x 324	9 x $12^3/_4$
C5	162 x 229	$6^3/_8$ x 9
C6	114 x 162	$4^1/_2$ x $6^3/_8$
C7	81 x 114	$3^1/_4$ x $4^1/_2$
C8	57 x 81	$2^1/_4$ x $3^1/_4$

ISO ENVELOPE STANDARDS

Sheets from the A series can be inserted in the C series envelope, flat or folded. For example, a C5 envelope will accommodate an A5 sheet flat, or an A4 folded once. ISO envelope sizes are all taken from B or C size sheets.

Envelope	mm	approx. in
C3	324 x 458	$12^3/_4$ x 18
B4	250 x 353	$9^7/_8$ x $12^7/_8$
C4	229 x 324	9 x $12^3/_4$
B5	176 x 250	7 x $9^7/_8$
C5	162 x 229	$6^3/_8$ x 9
B6/C4	125 x 324	5 x $12^3/_4$
B6	125 x 176	5 x 7
C6	114 x 162	$4^1/_2$ x $6^3/_8$
DL	110 x 220	$4^1/_4$ x $8^3/_4$
C7/6	81 x 162	$3^1/_4$ x $6^3/_8$
C7	81 x 114	$3^1/_4$ x $4^1/_2$

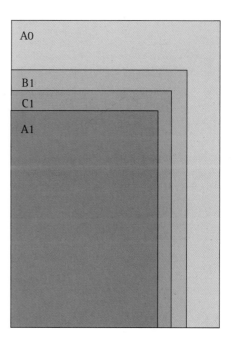

ABLATION PLATES In OFFSET LITHO printing, a laser is used to burn tiny holes into thin coatings on a polyester or metal base. These can be produced digitally, require no chemical processing; and can be printed waterless. All the PLATES for a job can be imaged directly on the press, simultaneously and in register.

ACCORDION FOLD or **CONCERTINA FOLD** A folding method in which two or more parallel folds are made in opposite directions

ACETATE A clear film used as an overlay on a MECHANICAL, for the production of SEPARATIONS for FLAT COLOR, for example, or KEYLINES

ACHROMATIC STABILIZATION See GRAY COMPONENT REPLACEMENT

ADDITIVE COLORS The primaries of TRANSMITTED LIGHT: red, green, and blue-violet

ADDRESSABILITY A measure of how close the centers of the dots that make up type or images can be placed next to each other on an output device such as a LASER PRINTER; see also RESOLUTION

ADSL (ASYMMETRIC DIGITAL SUBSCRIBER LINE — OR LOOP) Telephone line for connecting to the INTERNET in which the bandwidth available for downstream connection is significantly broader than for upstream

AGAINST THE GRAIN Folding or feeding paper stock at right angles to the orientation of the fibers

AGFAPROOF A proprietary PREPRESS color-proofing system

ALIGNMENT Placing type or images so that they line up either horizontally or vertically

ALPHANUMERIC CHARACTER SET A complete set of letters, numbers, and associated punctuation marks; see also FONT

AM SCREENING (AMPLITUDE MODULATED) Conventional screening which uses an array of differently sized dots; see also FM SCREENING

ANCHOR In HTML code, a means of pointing your BROWSER to another web page. The TAG is of the form <A HREF= "URL"> the text to be linked </A> where the URL is either relative, i.e. music.html — another page on your site — or absolute, i.e. http://www.elvisnet.com, a site elsewhere on the INTERNET

ANILINE DYE Synthetic dye used in flexographic ink

ANTI-ALIASING An optical trick to make hard, jagged edges on low-RESOLUTION computer screens and color output look smoother

ANTIQUE PAPER A book paper with a rough finish

APPLICATION Computer software that does a particular task, such as page layout

APR (AUTOMATIC PICTURE REPLACEMENT) This uses a low-RESOLUTION HALFTONE in a digital page layout, which will be relaced later at the repro house by a high-resolution scanned image

ASCENDER The part of a lower-case letter such as k or d that extends above the body of the type

ASCII (AMERICAN STANDARD CODE FOR INFORMATION INTERCHANGE) A text-only format of 256 codes used to represent ALPHANUMERIC CHARACTERS with no additional information about size, font, or spacing

ASSEMBLER A low-level computer-programming language which uses mnemonics, such as MPY for multiply

ASSEMBLY Collecting and arranging design elements on film to create the FLAT used for platemaking

AUTHOR'S CORRECTIONS Corrections that are made to a GALLEY PROOF by the author or editor, which may contain new material or changes of mind that will have to be paid for

AUTO-REVERSING FILM Film that can be used to copy negative-working film to negative-working film without the need for an intermediate positive

AVATAR On the INTERNET, in IRC, your visual human-like representative in a virtual scene speaking your words. In mythology, an avatar is an incarnation of a Hindu deity

BACK EDGE The MARGIN closest to the SPINE

BACKING A problem of lightening of color in printing which occurs when ink removed from the FOUNTAIN roller is not being replaced by the flow of fresh ink

BACKSTEP MARK Black mark printed on a SIGNATURE which shows where the final fold will be. After collation, the marks should fall in a stepped sequence

BACK UP Printing on the other side of the sheet; in computer terminology, to copy important work onto floppy disks, removable hard drives, or other storage media

BAD BREAK In JUSTIFIED setting, hyphenation of a word which looks wrong

BARYTA Smooth paper used for LETTERPRESS repro proofs

BASELINE The imaginary — or, where a computerised layout GRID is used, the actual — horizontal line on which letters sit

BASTARD SIZE Any non-standard size, especially of paper

BINDING Fixing together folded SIGNATURES into multipage publications, using glue, thread, or metal wires. Also the cover and backing of a book

BIT The primary unit in computing — a binary digit (a 1 or a 0)

BITMAP An image or letter made from a pattern of dots or PIXELS on a RASTER device such as a computer screen or LASER PRINTER

BLANKET The intermediate rubber roller on an OFFSET LITHO press which transfers the image from the PLATE to the paper

BLANKET CYLINDER The cylinder on an OFFSET LITHO press to which the BLANKET is attached

BLANKET-TO-BLANKET PRESS An OFFSET LITHO press that can print both sides of a sheet in one pass — the sheet passes between two BLANKET CYLINDERS and there is no need for an IMPRESSION CYLINDER

BLEED Part of the image that extends beyond the TRIM MARKS of a page

BLIND A method of DIE STAMPING or EMBOSSING in three-dimensional low relief without foil or ink

BLOCKING Producing the lettering on the SPINE of a hardback book, usually in gold or silver leaf, by means of a die; see also STICKING

BLUE AND RED KEYS A method for ensuring the close REGISTRATION of COLOR SEPARATIONS using a key image in blue or red as a guide

BLUEPRINT or **BLUE** A DYELINE PROOF for checking the position of design elements and STRIPPED-IN HALFTONES before the PLATE is made, also called OZALID

BODY TYPE Type below 14 POINT, used for the main body of text, as opposed to DISPLAY type

BOND A durable grade of paper, used mostly for stationery

BRIGHTNESS The brilliance or light reflectivity of paper

BROMIDE Smooth, high-contrast photographic paper used for PMTs and as output from IMAGESETTERS

BROWNLINE or **BROWNPRINT** A PROOF made from a LITHOGRAPHIC negative similar to a BLUEPRINT but producing a brown image

BROWSER A computer program that allows you to view and interact with WWW pages on the Internet. An example is Netscape Navigator

BUBBLEJET PRINTER A form of INKJET PRINTER in which a heating element causes bubbles to eject the ink

BUCKLE FOLDER A folding machine that uses an adjustable stop to buckle the sheet, which is then forced between two nip rollers

BUCKRAM A heavy, coarse-thread BINDING cloth

BUG A mistake in a computer program which makes unexpected things happen

BULK See CALIPER

BURN Exposure of a LITHO PLATE

BURNISHING Rubbing down pressure-sensitive lettering such as Letraset

BYTE Eight bits, corresponding to one ASCII character

C++ A structured computer-programming language, the basis of JAVA

CALENDERING Smoothing and compressing paper as it travels through the paper machine

CALIPER The thickness of paper, also called BULK

CAMERA-READY COPY or **MECHANICAL** A complete and finished layout of type and images ready to be scanned or photographed by a PROCESS CAMERA

CAST COATED Paper with a high-gloss finish

CASTING OFF Calculating how much space the text in a manuscript will occupy when set into type

CATCH-UP Printing on non-image areas, caused by insufficient water

CD-ROM (COMPACT DISC — READ-ONLY MEMORY) A plastic disc, like an audio CD, on to which tiny holes are "written" by a laser beam to store up to 650 Mbytes of digital data or programs; see also DVD-ROM

CEPS (COLOR ELECTRONIC PUBLISHING SYSTEM) Low-RESOLUTION images are used as for-position-only visuals. High-resolution scans, straight from the original TRANSPARENCIES, are reunited with the layouts in the IMAGESETTER at the repro house

CHALKING PIGMENTS smudging or rubbing off, caused by improper CURING of paper which results in too rapid an absorption of the binding vehicle in ink

CHASE In LETTERPRESS, the rectangular metal frame holding type and blocks; when locked-up, it is called a FORME

CHROMO PAPER A type of paper polished on one side only

CLIENT–SERVER ARCHITECTURE A user or a user's program is the client and connects to a remote machine (the server) where, for example, USENET postings or WWW pages are stored

CLIP ART Copyright-free illustrations

CLOCK SPEED The length of the processing cycle in a computer, measured in MHz

CMM (COLOR-MATCHING MODULE) Converts images from one COLOR SPACE to another and simultaneously applies the information in the profile to correctly render the image

CMS (COLOR-MANAGEMENT SYSTEM) A library of scanner, monitor, and output device profiles to ensure consistency of color reproduction by mapping color from the GAMUT of one device, such as a display, into a device-independent model, and then to the gamut of another device, such as a color printer; see also COLORSYNC

CMYK Cyan, magenta, yellow, and key (black). This is the system used to describe and separate colors for printing. Other color systems include RGB (red, green, blue) for transmitted color, such as for computer screens, and HLS (hue, luminance, saturation), a more theoretical description. The PANTONE MATCHING SYSTEM matches colors by mixing 11 basic colors

COATING Adding a layer of china clay to paper to increase its smoothness

COLD-METAL SETTING or **STRIKE-ON** Typesetting produced directly on to paper using a typewriter or rub-down lettering

COLD-SET INK Solid ink that is melted and used with a hot press, solidifying when it contacts the paper

COLLATING or **GATHERING** Bringing pages and SIGNATURES together for BINDING

COLLOTYPE Printing process using plate coated with gelatin, the only process to reproduce CONTINUOUS-TONE images without screening

COLOR BAR A printer's check appearing on color PROOFS to show up any faults in color REGISTRATION, print density, DOT GAIN, and SLURRING

COLOR BLINDNESS The inability to distinguish one or more of the three colors red, green, and blue. Blindness to red is called protanopia; to green, deuteranopia; and to blue, tritanopia

COLOR CALIBRATE To adjust the output values of a computer screen to correspond more faithfully to printed colors

COLOR CAST An unfaithful color on a color image, often found on a subject photographed against a srongly colored background

COLOR-DISPLAY SYSTEM The color computer display screen or monitor itself, and the graphics card that drives it

COLOR-KEY A 3M proprietary dry-proofing system using plastic laminates

COLOR-MANAGEMENT SYSTEM See CMS

COLOR SEPARATIONS A set of films for the cyan, magenta, yellow, and black components of a full-color image

COLOR SPACE See GAMUT

COLORSYNC Apple's proprietary COLOR-MANAGEMENT SYSTEM

COMBINATION FOLDER A folding machine that uses both the KNIFE and BUCKLE methods in combination

COMPACTFLASH RAM storage cards for Canon and Kodak digital cameras; see also SMARTMEDIA

COMPOSING STICK A device used in hand setting for assembling a line of type

COMPOSITOR The person who sets type

COMPUTER-TO-PLATE (CTP) or **DIRECT TO PLATE** Making OFFSET LITHO PLATES in a PLATESETTER direct from a PostScript file without the need for film

CONCERTINA FOLD A type of fold in which two or more parallel folds are made in opposite directions, also called an ACCORDION FOLD

CONTINUOUS-TONE COPY Artwork or photography containing shades of gray, as opposed to LINE copy, also called contone

CONTRACT PROOF A color PROOF representing an agreement between printer and client on how the finished job should look

CONVERTER An OFFSET LITHO press that can be converted to print either two colors on one side of a sheet or one color on both sides in one pass

COPY The raw material of the graphic designer: the text, type, artwork, and mechanicals

COPYFITTING Marking up type so that it fits a given space in a layout

COPY PREPARATION Adding the instructions to text that define how it is to be set; MARK UP is the manual method of copy preparation

COPYRIGHT The right in law to prevent copying of your work

CPU (CENTRAL PROCESSING UNIT) The "brain" of a computer, a microprocessor, chip, or chipset

CRAWLING An imperfection in the surface of the ink, occurring when thick ink overprints wet ink

CROCKING Smudging or transfer of dry ink on to printed sheets

CROMACHECK Proprietary off-press proofing system from Du Pont which uses plastic laminates

CROMALIN Proprietary off-press PROOFING system from Du Pont which uses dry toners and light-sensitive sheets

CROP MARKS Lines to indicate which portions of a photograph or illustration are surplus to requirements

CROPPING Choosing not to use portions of a photograph and marking an OVERLAY on the original to indicate which portions of the image are to be printed

CROSS-HEADINGS DISPLAY TYPE used to interest the reader and break up gray areas of body type

CROSSOVER When an image, text, or tint extends from one page of a publication to a facing page, which may or may not be from the same printed sheet

CROSSPOSTING Posting the same message to several newsgroups on the INTERNET — not a good idea, especially if it is off-topic

CRYSTALLIZATION When the ink of the first printing dries too hard before OVERPRINTING, it can repel the second ink and produce poor TRAPPING

CSS (CASCADING STYLE SHEETS) An extension to HTML to allow styles — color, FONT, font sizes, and other attributes — to be specified for certain elements of a hypertext document

CURE Acclimatize paper to the temperature and humidity of the press room

CUSTOMIZATION In digital print, where substantial amounts of the content of, for example, brochures or catalogs is altered to match the preferences and interests of particular groups of readers

CUT-OUT Photograph in which certain portions are removed to make a subject stand out

CYAN PROCESS blue — really more a turquoise

DAMPER MARKS Patterns over the print caused by worn damper covers, or too much pressure

DECKLE The natural wavy edge to paper; also the frame used to make handmade paper

DENSITOMETER An instrument used to measure the density of printed color

DESCENDER The part of a lower-case letter such as p or g that extends below the BASELINE

DHTML (DYNAMIC HTML) A term used by some suppliers to describe the combination of HTML, style sheets, and scripts that allows documents to be animated

DIAZO PROOF made by direct contact with film positives; see also BLUEPRINT and BROWNLINE

DIDOT POINT A unit of measurement used in continental Europe equivalent to 0.0148 inch (0.376 mm), 7 percent larger than the American POINT

DIE-CUTTING Using sharp steel rules in a wooden die or laser to cut shapes from paper

DIE-STAMPING Producing a three-dimensional low relief effect on paper or cover board using a metal die and counter-die

DIFFUSION TRANSFER A semi-automatic process for making enlargements or reductions of LINE or HALFTONE copy. A negative is produced in the PROCESS CAMERA and transferred to a receiver sheet to create the BROMIDE positive; see also PMT and VELOX

DIGITAL CAMERA Instead of capturing an image on light-sensitive film that has to be sent away to be developed and printed, a digital camera uses an array of CCD (charge-coupled device) sensors to convert the image into a form that can be stored in the camera's RAM and then downloaded into your computer

DIGITAL LITHO A press which uses a CTP (COMPUTER-TO-PLATE) device to image a PLATE on press and then prints using a normal litho process

DIGITAL PRINTING Any printed output that is imaged directly on to a BLANKET, PLATE, or SUBSTRATE from an electronic file, with no intermediate film stage

DINGBAT A symbol or ornament such as h or + treated as characters in a FONT

DIRECT DIGITAL PRINTING POSTSCRIPT files are sent directly to special OFFSET PLATES (direct to press) on the press or to ELECTROPHOTOGRAPHIC cylinders in XEROGRAPHY machines, without the need for artwork or film

DIRECT THERMAL PRINTER An output device that burns an image into special paper

DIRECT-TO-PLATE See COMPUTER-TO-PLATE (CTP)

DISPLAY TYPE Type above 14 POINT SET for headlines or other display purposes; some fancy display faces are available in capitals only

DITHERING A crude computer method of screening. THERMAL TRANSFER and INKJET printers produce their colors by interspersing PIXELS of CYAN, MAGENTA, and yellow (and sometimes black) in regular patterns, grouped together in either two-by-two or four-by-four MATRICES

DOCUMENT In computer language, any job you are working on is called a document, whether it is a drawing, a piece of text, or a page layout

DOT-FOR-DOT A method of screening already screened HALFTONE to prevent MOIRÉ patterns

DOT GAIN or **DOT SPREAD** As individual dots begin to join in darker areas of a HALFTONE there can be an apparent jump in what should be a continuous tone

DOT-MATRIX PRINTER An output device that uses pins striking a ribbon to transfer ink on to the paper

DOUBLING Two dots where there should only be one. It is caused when wet ink is picked up by the BLANKET on a subsequent printing. If it is off REGISTER, it prints as a ghost dot nearby

DOWNLOAD Use FTP to transfer files from a remote server to your computer

DPI Dots per inch, a measure of the RESOLUTION or ADDRESSABILITY of a RASTER device such as a LASER PRINTER

DPS Double-page spread, two facing pages treated as one design layout, also called a spread or double truck

DRAWDOWN A smear of ink from a smooth blade used to check the quality of an ink on a particular paper stock

DRAW PROGRAM or **OBJECT-ORIENTED PROGRAM** A computer program that stores and manipulates images in terms of the lines and curves used to create them, usually in POSTSCRIPT; see also PAINT PROGRAM

DROP CAP A large initial letter dropping into the lines below and signaling the beginning of the text

DROP-OUT Complete removal of the dots in highlight areas of a HALFTONE

DRY PROOF A color PROOF made without ink, such as a Cromalin

DTP desktop publishing — digital page make-up

DUMMY A "concept model" of a publication, usually a miniature folded version, showing the position of pages; also a book without printing made up to the correct number of pages in a particular paper stock for the purpose of weighing, designing the dust jacket, and generally seeing how the finished product will look

DUOTONE A high-quality HALFTONE with a full tonal range made from two printings, either black and one other color, or black twice

DUPLEX STOCK Paper that has different finishes or colors either side

DUSTING Accumulation of paper particles on the BLANKET of a LITHO press, also spraying powder on to sheets coming off the press to stop wet ink touching the other sheets above and below

DVD-ROM (DIGITAL VERSATILE DISK READ-ONLY MEMORY) A storage medium similar to a CD-ROM but which can hold more than 5 Gbytes of information

DYELINE See DIAZO

DYE SUBLIMATION PRINTS Color PROOFS of near photographic quality produced by mixing vaporized dyes on the surface of the paper

EARMARKS Distinguishing features of a TYPEFACE used for identification, named after the ear of a lower-case g

E-BOOK A book in digital form. It can be a document scanned into PDF (portable document format), retaining all the formatting, typography, and illustrations of the original paper document it can be output into PDF directly from a layout program such as QuarkXPress or InDesign or it can just be pure text

ECF (ELEMENTAL CHLORINE FREE) In papermaking, chlorine-free bleaches, such as chlorine dioxide; see also TCF

EGGSHELL PAPER A smooth, pressed type of book paper

ELECTRO-COAGULATION (ELCOGRAPHY) DIGITAL PRINT using water-based polymeric ink sprayed on to a metallic cylinder which coagulates into 400 dpi gel dots in 256 different thicknesses, controlled by pulses of electricity

ELECTROPHOTOGRAPHIC PRINTERS DIGITAL PRINT technology in which a dry or liquid TONER is deposited on the SUBSTRATE by varying its electrostatic properties and then fixed by absorption, chemical reaction, or heat. This includes XEROGRAPHIC photocopiers and the Indigo and Xeikon digital-print engines

EM The width of a letter M, or a square em-QUAD space, which will be different for each typeface, unlike a PICA EM, which is $1/6$th of an inch

EMAIL (ELECTRONIC MAIL) A means of sending messages and "attachments" to other people, mainly connected to the INTERNET, but also within organisations on a local-area network or INTRANET. You type a message on your computer, connect to the Internet using a MODEM, and send it down the telephone line to your local ISP

EMBOSSING A FINISHING process producing an image in low relief

EMULSIFICATION What happens when water gets into the litho ink. Most litho inks are designed to accept some emulsification, but too much results in a wishy-washy appearance

EMULSION SIDE The duller side of film, which can be scratched

EN The width of a letter N, half an EM

EPS (ENCAPULATED POSTSCRIPT) A format for transferring drawings created in Illustrator and Freehand, for example, into digital layout programs

ESCAPE SEQUENCES The left angle bracket (<), the right angle bracket (>), and the ampersand (&) have special meanings in HTML and cannot be used "as is"; you must enter their escape sequence instead — &amp, for example, is the escape sequence for &

ETHERNET A local-area network developed by Xerox, Intel, and DEC for connecting PCs, Macs, and printers together so they can share data

EZINE A magazine that exists only on the INTERNET or on CD-ROM

FACE See TYPEFACE

FAMILY A set of FONTS related to a basic ROMAN TYPEFACE, which may include italic and bold plus a whole spectrum of different "weights"

FAQ (FREQUENTLY ASKED QUESTIONS) A list of questions and answers, usually relating to a particular NEWSGROUP. NEWBIES are encouraged to consult the FAQ before posting, so as not to annoy the old hands

FEATHERING Ink spreading from the edges of type, caused by poor-quality ink or paper

FILLERS Additives in papermaking that improve the properties of the stock, for example increasing BULK and preventing FEATHERING

FILLING IN When HALFTONE dots or the bowls of letters such as a or b fill solid with ink

FILM High-contrast photographic film used to transfer the image to the PLATE; can be positive (when the image is the same as the MECHANICAL) or negative (the white areas show black and vice versa)

FILMLESS GRAVURE In GRAVURE printing, digital information from the prepress system is fed directly to the diamond styli in the engraving heads that produce the printing cells

FILM RECORDER Output device for making TRANSPARENCIES from an image created in the computer

FINAL Film containing all the pages and design elements assembled ready to make the plate

FINISHED ARTIST Person who makes a neat camera-ready MECHANICAL from a designer's rough layout

FINISHING All the processes that convert printed sheets into folded and bound publications

FIREWIRE (IEEE 1394 or I-Link) A serial bus interface standard found mainly in digital video cameras but offering high-speed communications between computers, SCANNERS, and HARD-DISK drives; see also SCSI and USB

FLAME To post a harshly critical message in public on USENET or send very long abusive messages via EMAIL

FLAPPING An overlay of tissue or ACETATE protecting artwork and mechanicals

FLAT All the film assembled by the STRIPPER to make a 16- or 32-page plate

FLAT COLOR, MATCH COLOR or **SPOT COLOR** A single printing of a PANTONE color, printed solid or as TINTS, in REGISTER with the black

FLATPLAN A diagram showing the position of pages in a publication along with a brief description of their content, used mainly to identify full-color and FLAT-COLOR sections

FLAT-TINT HALFTONE A black HALFTONE printed over a TINT of color, faking a DUOTONE

FLEXOGRAPHY (FLEXO) A form of relief printing, using fast-drying inks and rubber or plastic PLATES on a rotary LETTERPRESS

FLOCCULATION An ink defect that produces a surface like orange peel, caused by the PIGMENT not being properly dispersed in the VEHICLE

FLOPPED Laterally inverted — normally applied to HALFTONES that have been STRIPPED into film wrongly

FLONG See MAT

FM SCREENING (FREQUENCY MODULATED) or **STOCHASTIC SCREENING** Using dots arranged randomly to reproduce CONTINUOUS-TONE artwork; see also AM (amplitude modulated) or conventional screening, which uses an array of differently sized dots

FOLD LINES Marks usually in the TRIM areas showing where sheets are to be folded

FOLIO Page number, or a single sheet of a manuscript

FONT A complete set *in one size* of all the letters of the alphabet, complete with associated LIGATURES (joined letters), numerals, punctuation marks, and any other signs and symbols

FONT MASTERS A set of type designs in one or more sizes that are scaled (enlarged or reduced) to create all the intermediate sizes

FONT METRICS The information about horizontal spacing built into a TYPEFACE by its designer

FOOT The bottom MARGIN of a page

FORE EDGE The MARGIN of a page furthest from the SPINE

FORME A locked-up CHASE in LETTERPRESS; also another name for a FLAT

FOUNTAIN The ink reservoir in LETTERPRESS, or the container for the solution that dampens the rollers of an OFFSET LITHO press

FOUR-COLOR PROCESS Full-color printing in which colors are approximated by various percentages of the PROCESS COLORS CYAN, MAGENTA, yellow, and black. A full-color image is separated by filters into four different films — one for each of the four process colors — and four PLATES are used for the printing

FRAME BUFFER Computer memory that holds the current image on the screen; see also VRAM

FRAME GRABBER An input device that uses a television camera to capture a picture or three-dimensional object, or a video frame; it converts it into digital form readable by a computer program

FTP (FILE TRANSFER PROTOCOL) A protocol to let users transfer files between computers

FUGITIVE Inks that fade when exposed to light

FURNISH The liquid pulp that is converted into paper

GALLEY A typesetting PROOF for checking the setting before the type is made up into pages; they are generally long and thin

GAMUT or **COLOR SPACE** The range of colors that can be reproduced on a color display, output device, or by a particular color-printing method — some colors available on a computer screen may not be printable using the CMYK process

GANGING UP Grouping together several TRANSPARENCIES to be scanned together; also printing a group of different jobs on the same sheet of paper using a single PLATE

GATHERING See COLLATING

GHOSTING Printing fault of a repeated image appearing next to the correct image, caused by faulty IMPOSITION; also a dull image on the other side of the sheet — this happens when the printed image affects the drying and TRAPPING of wet ink on the reverse

GICLÉE (from the French for "spraying" or "spreading") Medium-to-large format INKJET devices printing onto SUBSTRATES such as watercolor paper using archival ink

GIF (GRAPHICS INTERCHANGE FORMAT) A common format for graphics containing flat areas of color, see also JPEG

GOLDENROD Orange or yellow opaque masking paper used to make up a final

GOLDEN SECTION An aesthetically pleasing proportion with many examples in nature; the ratio is 34:21 or 8.1:5

GRAIN The orientation of fibers in paper, which lie in the direction of flow in a papermaking machine. "Grain long" means the grain is in the direction of the sheet's length. "Grain short" means the grain is in the direction of the sheet's width

GRAVURE or **PHOTOGRAVURE** An INTAGLIO PRINTING process in which the image is etched below the surface of a cylinder. The deeper the ink, the darker the tone.

GRAY COMPONENT REPLACEMENT or **ACHROMATIC STABILIZATION** Removing percentages of CYAN, MAGENTA, and yellow that cancel each other out to produce neutral grays, and replacing them with a tint of black

GREEKING Gray lines that indicate the presence of type on a computer screen; also the nonsense setting (usually Latin!) used by designers to show the position of type on a rough layout or DUMMY

GRID The underlying structure for a page layout as prescribed by the designer, usually preprinted onto layout sheets or boards, or programmed into master pages in a digital page-layout program

GRIPPER EDGE The edge of a sheet held by metal fingers in the press — a term used in IMPOSITION. The gripper margin is the allowance that avoids any damage caused by the grippers to the printed image

GUI (GRAPHICAL USER INTERFACE) What you see on the screen when you want to communicate with the program, the most famous being the WIMP (windows, icons, mouse, pull-down menus) interface of the Apple Macintosh, derived mostly from the Smalltalk project at Xerox's PARC. Other "standards" include Windows for the PC and X-Windows for workstations.

GUTTER The combined MARGIN of a book or folder on each side of the SPINE; the margin on one side of the spine is called the BACK EDGE. The term gutter is also used for any vertical space, such as that between two columns

GYRICON "Digital paper" having many of the properties of paper, but electronically writeable and erasable

HAIRLINE RULE A rule thinner than 0.5 POINT

HALATION or **HALO EFFECT** When ink builds up around letters or dots, leaving the center lighter

HALF BINDING The SPINE, adjacent strips of the cover, and triangles at the corners are bound in one material, maybe leather, and the rest of the book in a less expensive material

HALFTONE A CONTINUOUS-TONE image converted to line by turning it into a pattern of dots, either digitally, by laser, or by photographing it through a screen

HARDCOPY Output from a computer system that you can hold in your hand — usually a paper PROOF

HARD DISK Permanent magnetic memory, usually within the computer

HARD DOT A clean, regular, and sharp HALFTONE dot

HARDWARE The parts of a computer system that you can see and touch

HEAD The MARGIN at the top of a page

HEADBAND A decorative feature added to a case-bound book at the top of the SPINE

HEAT-SET INK Web ink that is dried quickly by heat and then chilled

HEXACHROME A proprietary six-color system from PANTONE using brighter (fluorescent) versions of CMYK plus vivid orange and green; also referred to as HiFi color. See also FOUR-COLOR PROCESS

HICKIES Imperfections in LITHO printing caused by any dry, hard particles on the cylinder or BLANKET, also called fisheyes, bull's eyes, donuts, and Newton's rings

HIGH-FIDELITY PRINTING or **HIFI PRINTING** Uses additional process inks to increase the GAMUT. PANTONE's Hexachrome, for example, adds green and orange inks to the regular CMYK

HINGE The crease in a book cover near the SPINE

HINTING In computer FONTS, a method for changing the shapes of characters — especially those of small sizes — so that they look better on low-RESOLUTION printers

HLS (HUE, LUMINANCE, SATURATION) A method for specifying color; see CMYK and RGB

HOLDOUT The property of paper that makes it resist the absorption of ink

HOLOGRAM A three-dimensional image created by laser photography, reproduced by hot-foil stamping or embossing on to reflective-backed mylar

HOME PAGE Your own WWW site, in which you can indulge your hobbies, try out your INTERNET skills, or publish an EZINE

HOT-FOIL STAMPING Transferring a foil coating from a carrier roll of polyester to paper or cover board by means of a heated die

HOT METAL SETTING Casting molten metal into molds to produce type for LETTERPRESS printing

HOUSE STYLE Standards of consistency concerning spelling and use of English (or any other language) as laid down by a particular publisher, or to be used within a particular publication

HTML (HYPER TEXT MARK-UP LANGUAGE) Text-based language used to create and communicate WWW pages

HTTP (HYPER TEXT TRANSPORT PROTOCOL) The protocol of the World Wide Web

HUE The rainbow parameter of a color that distinguishes, for example, red from blue

HYPHENATION The division of words, usually between syllables, pairs of consonants, or pairs of vowels

ICON A small picture on a computer screen representing an application, tool, or document

IMAGESETTER A high-RESOLUTION output device that produces film or BROMIDE prints from a POSTSCRIPT file, so called because it can output LINE art and HALFTONE images as well as type; see also PLATESETTER

IMPOSETTER IMAGESETTER which, with imposition software, produces film negatives with pages in position ready for platemaking

IMPOSING TABLE In LETTERPRESS, the place where GALLEYS are assembled

IMPOSITION The layout of pages such that after printing, folding, collating, and trimming they will all end up in the correct order and the right way up

IMPRESSION The process of transferring ink from PLATE to paper during printing

IMPRESSION CYLINDER In an OFFSET LITHO press, the cylinder that presses the paper against the BLANKET CYLINDER

INDESIGN A page-layout program from Adobe, and successor to PAGEMAKER

INKJET PRINTER An output device that creates an image by spraying tiny drops of ink on to paper; see also BUBBLEJET PRINTER

INKOMETER or **TACKOSCOPE** An instrument for measuring the tackiness of ink

INK PYRAMID In an OFFSET LITHO press, the system of rollers that conveys ink to the PLATE

IN-LINE An in-line press has several single units arranged to print one color after another; also a process, such as folding or gluing, that happens straight after the printing, in the same pass

INSERT Any printed material that is included during BINDING. Material wrapped around a SIGNATURE is called a wrap. A loose insert is not attached to the "parent" publication and will fall out when it is shaken

INTAGLIO PRINTING A method in which the ink is contained in grooves below the surface of the PLATE and transferred to dampened paper by pressure

INTERNET A network of networks based on the TCP/IP protocols, a community of people who use and develop those networks, and a collection of resources that can be reached from those networks

INTRANET A local network, such as within a corporation, using the same tools as the INTERNET EMAIL and WWW pages, for example

IRC (INTERNET RELAY CHAT) A means of communicating in text in real time with other INTERNET users employing a program such as Homer

ISDN (INTEGRATED SERVICES DIGITAL NETWORK) A dedicated digital telephone line — you don't need a MODEM

ISP (INTERNET SERVICE PROVIDER) The company you dial up to get on to the INTERNET

JAVA A C11 based programming language from Sun that is object-oriented and platform-independent — tiny programs called applets are downloaded and embedded in the HTML code

JOGGING Vibrating paper stock before trimming to bring all the edges into alignment

JPEG (JOINT PHOTOGRAPHIC EXPERTS GROUP) A common format for graphics containing CONTINUOUS TONES of color, such as photographs; see also GIF

JUSTIFIED Type set with edges that are aligned both left and right. Justified setting requires hyphenation and variable spacing between words

KERNING Adjusting the spacing between pairs of letters, such as T and A, to improve the aesthetic appearance; see also TRACKING

KEY Black in four-color printing; see CMYK

KEYLINE The marks on a MECHANICAL's OVERLAY that indicate the position of TINTS, HALFTONES, and BLEEDS. A keyline artist is a person who assembles the finished mechanical

KNIFE FOLDER A folding machine that uses a knife to force the sheet between two nip rollers

k–p DISTANCE The distance from the top of a letter k to the bottom of a letter p

L*a*b A device-independent color model

proposed by the Commission Internationale de l'Eclairage: L is for luminance; a and b are chromatic components — a for green to red, and b for blue to yellow

LACQUER See VARNISHING

LAID A paper texture created on the Fourdrinier wire; it has a characteristic lined appearance

LAMINATION Coating paper or cover board with a clear film to add strength and gloss

LANDSCAPE The orientation of a page when the width is greater than the height

LASER PRINTER An output device in which TONER is attracted to an image on a drum that has had electrostatic charge removed by the action of a laser; the image is transferred to paper and fixed by heat

LATE BINDING The term used to mean last-minute changes within POSTSCRIPT files while they are in the RIP, such as adding TRAPPING and IMPOSITION information, particularly for digital presses

LAYDOWN SEQUENCE The sequence in which colors are printed — usually yellow, MAGENTA, CYAN, and finally black

LAY EDGE The left side of the sheet as it passes through the press; the lay edge will change to the right side if the sheet is to be printed on the reverse

LCD (LIQUID CRYSTAL DISPLAY) Thin, flicker-free computer-display technology

LEADING or **INTERLINE SPACING** The space between lines of type; in LETTERPRESS these were strips of lead

LEAVE EDGE The edge of a sheet opposite the GRIPPER EDGE

LETTERPRESS A RELIEF PRINTING process, in which ink is transferred from the raised surface of metal or wooden type directly on to paper

LETTERSET An indirect LETTERPRESS printing process, in which the image is first transferred to a BLANKET, and then on to the paper

LIGATURE Two or more letters, such as fi and ffl, joined together into one character

LINE Artwork in black (or any other single color) and white only, with no intermediate tones of gray, which will print without first being screened

LINEN TESTER See LOUPE

LINOTYPE A typesetting machine for LETTERPRESS in which a whole line of type (line o' type), or SLUG, is cast in one operation

LINTERS In papermaking, the fibers left on the cotton seed once the longer fibers have been removed for yarn-making

LINTING A printing problem caused by paper fibers that get on to the BLANKET, PLATE, or rollers of a press

LITERALS In proofreading, the spelling mistakes and transposition of letters caused by typing errors

LITHOGRAPHY A PLANOGRAPHIC PRINTING process in which greasy ink is transferred from the surface of a dampened plate or stone directly on to paper. OFFSET LITHOGRAPHY, usually shortened to offset

litho, prints first on to a rubber or plastic BLANKET, and then on to the paper

LOUPE Designer's magnifying glass, also called a linen tester or eyeglass; used for checking color TRANSPARENCIES and HALFTONE dots

LOW SPOT Loss of image caused by an indentation in the BLANKET of an OFFSET press

LUMINANCE See VALUE

MACHINE CODE The lowest level of computer language — lists of hexadecimal numbers

MACHINE FINISH (MF) Paper that has been CALENDERED and is smoother and less bulky than EGGSHELL PAPER

MACHINE GLAZED (MG) Paper that has been dried against a highly polished cylinder and has one glossy side while the other remains relatively rough

MACHINE PROOF See PRESS PROOF

MAGENTA The PROCESS COLOR red, really more a purple

MAILING LIST An EMAIL discussion group, in which a message sent to the list server is broadcast to anyone "subscribing" to that particular list

MAKE-READY Setting up the press ready to print

MAKEUP To assemble, position, and paste type and graphic elements to produce a MECHANICAL or FLAT

MANUSCRIPT The original COPY for typesetting, shortened to Ms

MARGINS The areas of white between the text and the edges of the page

MARK UP To write instructions on text to define how it is to be set in type

MASK Shape cut out of opaque material such as RUBYLITH or GOLDENROD to shield film from exposure to light; also used in image manipulation programs such as Photoshop

MASTER PROOF A clean and neat PROOF on to which the corrections and comments of all interested parties are collated

MAT or **FLONG** In LETTERPRESS, a papier-mâché mold taken from the FORME and used to make a STEREOTYPE; an abbreviation for MATRIX

MATCH COLOR See FLAT COLOR

MATCHPRINT A proprietary prepress proofing system from Imation

MATRIX A metal mold used to cast metal type; also any array or pattern of PIXELS, as in DITHERING; see also MAT

MATTE Dull finish, the opposite of glossy

MEASURE The width of a line of type — usually the column width, specified in PICA EMS

MECHANICAL Camera-ready artwork on boards, or all the LINE artwork for a page layout with the HALFTONES marked "for position only", also called camera-ready copy. Mechanical SEPARATIONS are sets of OVERLAYS in REGISTER containing the artwork for FLAT COLOR

MECHANICAL TINTS Patterns of dots simulating shades of gray or FLAT COLOR

added by the process blockmaker (Ben Day tints) or printer according to the designer's instructions

MENU In computing, a list of options or commands from which you are invited to choose

MESH COUNT A measure of the fineness of the mesh in the screens used in SCREEN-PRINTING — the number of threads per inch

MESH GRADE Thread thickness in the screens used in SCREENPRINTING

METALLIC INKS Inks that contain metal dust, producing a sheen when printed

MICROMETER An instrument for measuring very small distances, such as the thicknesss of paper; also one millionth of a meter

MIL One thousandth of an inch

MIRROR SITE Stores copies of files from main sites, but may be geographically closer to you

MODEM (MOdulator DEModulator) A device to convert digital data from your computer into analog data that can travel down the telephone line

MOIRÉ PATTERNS Unwanted "basket-weave" effects caused by superimposed regular patterns, such as HALFTONE dots. Screens must be set at angles that minimize the moiré effect

MOLD-MADE PAPER Paper made by a semi-automatic process to resemble handmade paper

MONO, MONOCHROME Black and white, or the various tones of one color

MONOTYPE A LETTERPRESS typesetting machine that casts individual metal letters in a two-stage process

MOTTLE An uneven impression caused by too much dampening water or the wrong choice of paper and ink

MOUSE In computing, a small pointing device used to control a cursor on the screen

M WEIGHT The weight of paper as measured per thousand sheets

NEGATIVE-WORKING PLATE OFFSET LITHO PLATE prepared by exposure to negative film

NETIQUETTE A code of conduct or good manners for the INTERNET

NETWORKING Linking computers together so that they can communicate with each other and share output devices such as LASER PRINTERS and file servers

NEWBIE A new user to the INTERNET, particularly to NEWSGROUPS

NEWSGROUP A "bulletin board" of articles on a specific topic, arranged in threads; see also USENET (UNIX USER NETWORK)

NEWSPRINT Inexpensive, rough, absorbent paper used for printing newspapers and some magazines

NTSC (NATIONAL TELEVISION SYSTEMS COMMITTEE) The US standard of the FCC (Federal Communications Commission) for broadcast television

OFFSET Abbreviation for offset lithography; also the same as setoff — when ink transfers from one printed sheet to the back of another

OFFSET LITHOGRAPHY or **OFFSET LITHO** A PLANOGRAPHIC PRINTING process in which greasy ink is transferred from the surface of a dampened PLATE first on to a rubber or plastic BLANKET, and then on to the paper

OFFSET PROCESS See OFFSET LITHOGRAPHY

ONE-UP Printing a single job on one PLATE. Quality is better controlled, but it is usually more economical to print two-up, i.e. two different jobs, or the same job in tandem, on one plate

OPACIMETER An instrument for measuring the opacity of paper

OPACITY The property of a paper affecting the SHOW-THROUGH of printing from the other side of the sheet

OPERATING SYSTEM Behind-the-scenes computer software that takes care of the internal workings of the computer

OPI (OPEN PREPRESS INTERFACE) A protocol, originally proposed by Aldus, which enables files from different digital prepress programs to be used together

OPTICAL BRIGHTENERS Additives to paper that increase its brightness by glowing under the influence of ultraviolet light

ORIENTED POLYPROPYLENE (OPP) LAMINATION The standard bookjacket lamination film

ORPHAN(S) A single word or a few words, usually less than a third the MEASURE of the setting, forming a line of its own at the end of a paragraph; see also WIDOW

ORTHOCHROMATIC Film sensitive to the blue end of the spectrum used for LINE work — red records as black, and marks in light-blue pencil are invisible; see also PANCHROMATIC

OUT OF REGISTER The blurred effect that occurs when film SEPARATIONS or PLATES are misaligned

OVERLAY A sheet of ACETATE or tissue over a photograph or in REGISTRATION with a MECHANICAL, containing artwork for FLAT COLOR, KEYLINES, or instructions to the printer

OVERMATTER Setting or images that are excess to requirements, to be used in the next issue of a magazine, for example

OVERPRINT Color, usually black, printed over FLAT COLOR

OVER RUNS or **RUN-ONS** Sheets printed beyond the quantity specified, to compensate for spoilage or for the client's own use

OZALID See BLUEPRINT and BROWNLINE

PAGEMAKER A page-layout program from Adobe, originally developed by Aldus, and superseded by InDesign

PAGE PROOF A PROOF showing type arranged on a page, along with FOLIOS, RUNNING HEADLINES, captions, and sometimes the position of illustrations

PAGINATION The sequence of pages in a book or folder

PAINT PROGRAM or **PAINT SYSTEM** A computer program that stores the image

on the screen as a bitmap; see also DRAW PROGRAM

PAL (PHASE ALTERNATION LINE) The standard in the UK and most of Europe for broadcast television

PANCHROMATIC Film that records all colors equally, as opposed to ORTHOCHROMATIC which does not "see" the blue end of the spectrum

PANTONE MATCHING SYSTEM (PMS) A widely used proprietary system for specifying FLAT COLOR in percentages of eleven standard colors; papers and markers corresponding to Pantone colors can also be purchased

PAPER-CREEP ALLOWANCE Allowing for the thickness of paper at the SPINE of a thick, SADDLE-STITCHED publication by shifting the MARGINS on the MECHANICAL so that the margins remain consistent after the sheets are trimmed

PAPER CURL Wavy edges caused by the stack of paper having a lower moisture level than the surroundings, or tight edges caused by the stack having a higher moisture level

PASTE UP To cut and assemble typesetting, LINE art, and HALFTONES on to board using gum or wax, so as to produce a MECHANICAL

PDF (PORTABLE DOCUMENT FORMAT) A DOCUMENT format that uses a reader such as Adobe Acrobat to recreate the appearance of FONTS and spacing in your page layout

PEN PLOTTER A point-to-point output device used mainly for engineering drawings; if equipped with a knife in place of the pen it can be used to cut stencils for SCREEN-PRINTING or vinyl letters for signs

PERFECT BINDING Trimmed single sheets of paper bound with glue to produce a book or magazine with a flat SPINE

PERFECTING PRESS A press that prints both sides of the sheet at the same time

PERFORATION Producing the tear-along lines on coupons or stamps, for example, by piercing with sharp metal strips

PERSONAL COMPUTER A stand-alone desktop computer; a PC is an IBM Personal Computer or a software-compatible system from a supplier such as Compaq

PERSONALIZATION In digital print where a person's details, such as name and address, are changed between each DOCUMENT printed

PHOTOGRAVURE See GRAVURE

PHOTOTYPESETTING or **PHOTOSETTING** A process in which type is set on to BROMIDE paper or film by exposure of light through a MATRIX containing tiny negatives of the letters, or directly by the action of a laser beam

PICA or **PICA EM** A unit for measuring type equal to 1/6th of an inch, or 12 POINTS; on a typewriter, the normal PITCH of 10 characters per inch

PI CHARACTERS Greek and mathematical signs, used with but not typically part of a FONT

PICKING Removal of some of the surface of paper during printing

PIGMENTS AND DYES Components of printing inks that give it color

PILING Sticking or caking of ink PIGMENT on the BLANKET or PLATE

PIN REGISTER Accurate positioning system for COLOR SEPARATIONS — both films and plates — with punched holes and corresponding pins

PITCH On typewriters, the number of characters per inch

PIXEL Pixel is short for picture element and is the dot on a computer display. The RESOLUTION (sharpness) of a RASTER display is measured by the number of pixels horizontally by the number of scan lines vertically, e.g. 1280 x 1024

PLANOGRAPHIC PRINTING Any process using a PLATE on which both the printing and non-printing areas are on the same surface, e.g. LITHOGRAPHY

PLASTIC COMB A type of ring BINDING found on reports and manuals

PLATE A metal or plastic sheet with photosensitive face on to which an image is chemically etched, either changing the characteristics of the surface as in LITHOGRAPHY, or cutting below the surface as in RELIEF or INTAGLIO PRINTING

PLATE CYLINDER In an OFFSET LITHO press, the cylinder to which the PLATE is attached

PLATE-DAMPENING UNIT In OFFSET LITHO, the system of rollers that dampens the plate before inking; see also FOUNTAIN

PLATEN A small LETTERPRESS that acts like a clamshell, bringing a flat PLATE and the paper together in an opening and closing motion, as opposed to a ROTARY PRESS

PLATESETTER A device that processes PLATES direct from a POSTSCRIPT file; see also IMAGESETTER

PMT Photomechanical transfer, a DIFFUSION TRANSFER process for enlarging or reducing LINE art; also called a BROMIDE

PNG (PORTABLE NETWORK GRAPHICS) A lossless, portable format coming into use that provides a patent-free replacement for GIF and can also replace many common uses of TIFF

POINT A unit for measuring type equal to approximately $1/72$nd of an inch (exactly $1/72$nd of an inch in computer systems), abbreviated pt; also a measure of paper BULK equivalent to one thousandth of an inch (a MIL)

PORTRAIT The orientation of a page when the height is greater than the width

POSITIVE-WORKING PLATE An OFFSET LITHO PLATE prepared by exposure to positive film

POSTSCRIPT An outline description language for type developed by Adobe and licensed to suppliers such as Linotype, Monotype, Agfa, and AM Varityper. Type 1 PostScript FONTS contain HINTING and encryption; see also EPS and TRUETYPE

PPP (POINT-TO-POINT PROTOCOL) The gateway from your client SOFTWARE, e.g. Eudora for EMAIL, to the INTERNET, see also SLIP

PREFLIGHTING Checking output from page-layout programs such as InDesign and QuarkXPress to see if all images and FONTS are present and that there will be no problems with files at the printers

PREPRESS PROOF A PROOF taken directly from the film SEPARATIONS, to check that the color will print correctly

PRESS PROOF A PROOF taken from the PLATES that will be used to print the finished job, and on the specified paper stock, usually on a special proofing press, also called MACHINE PROOF or WET PROOF

PRINTING-DOWN FRAME In OFFSET LITHO, a device for holding the film and PLATE in contact during exposure to ultra-violet light

PRINT RUN The number of copies to be produced in one printing, also called the press run

PROCESS CAMERA A camera designed to enlarge or reduce artwork and MECHANICALS, and produce film positives and negatives

PROCESS COLORS the four colors — CYAN (process blue), MAGENTA (process red), yellow, and key (black) — used to approximate full-color artwork

PROGRESSIVES A set of PROOFS showing the four color SEPARATIONS printed in various combinations; also called Hollywoods or progs

PROOF Hardcopy that allows you to check the accuracy of setting, the position of design elements on a page, or the fidelity of color after separation

PROOFING PRESS A small press used to produce PROOFS

PROPORTIONAL SCALE See REPRODUCTION CALCULATOR

QUAD A square space in typesetting used as a unit of measurement, such as an EM quad or EN quad

QUARTER BINDING The SPINE and adjacent strips of the cover are bound in one material, maybe leather, and the rest of the sides in a less expensive material

RAM (RANDOM ACCESS MEMORY) Quick-access temporary memory in a computer, containing the job in hand, in the form of chips

RANGED LEFT/RIGHT Ranged left is a method of setting type in which the type is aligned on the left-hand side and ragged on the right. Ranged right is ragged on the left and aligned on the right

RASTER A horizontal scan line on a computer screen or output device

REAM 500 sheets of paper

RECTO The front of a sheet of paper, or the right-hand page of a publication; opposite of VERSO

REFLECTED LIGHT Colors from an object or flat artwork, as opposed to TRANSMITTED LIGHT from a light source or TRANSPARENCY

REFLECTION COPY Any original art viewed by light reflecting from its surface, as opposed

to TRANSMISSION COPY such as a 35 mm slide

REGISTER or **REGISTRATION** Correct positioning of one COLOR SEPARATION in relation to the others during printing. A register mark is a symbol used on COPY and film to ensure accurate registration

RELIEF PRINTING A printing process, such as LETTERPRESS and FLEXOGRAPHY, in which ink lies on the raised surface of the PLATE but not in the grooves and is transferred to the paper by pressure

REPRODUCTION CALCULATOR or **PROPORTIONAL SCALE** A slide-rule type instrument for estimating the size of an illustration after reduction or enlargement

REPRODUCTION PROOF or **REPRO PROOF** A crisp PROOF on art paper of LETTERPRESS setting to be used on a MECHANICAL

REPURPOSING Adapting an existing page layout to become a different format or medium, such as a WWW page

RESIST A substance used on PLATES for preventing the non-printing areas from etching

RESOLUTION A measure of the fineness and quality of an output device, usually measured in dots per inch (DPI) — the number of dots that can be placed end to end in a line an inch long; see also ADDRESSABILITY

RETOUCHING Modifying or correcting photographic images either manually with dye and airbrush, or electronically to a scanned image using a program such as Photoshop or Quantel Paintbox

REVERSED OUT When type is set in white against a black or flat-color background

RGB (RED, GREEN, BLUE) A system for specifying color on a computer screen; see also CMYK

RICH BLACK A black object or area that prints even darker with the use of undercolors, usually CYAN

RIGHT-READING EMULSION DOWN (RRED) Film used for OFFSET LITHO platemaking in which the image appears the correct way round when the film is viewed from the shiny (non-EMULSION) side, also called wrong-reading emulsion up (WREU)

RIGHT-READING EMULSION UP (RREU) Film used for direct forms of platemaking, such as LETTERPRESS and FLEXOGRAPHY, in which the image appears the correct way round when the film is viewed from the dull EMULSION SIDE, also called wrong-reading emulsion down (WRED)

RIP RASTER image processor — a device that converts a POSTSCRIPT file into a BITMAP that can be output from an IMAGESETTER or PLATESETTER

RIVERS Unwanted space running vertically and diagonally in chunks of (mainly JUSTIFIED) type — to be avoided

ROLLING BALL A pointing device that controls the position of a cursor on the computer screen

ROM (READ-ONLY MEMORY) Permanent unalterable computer memory in the form of chips; also abbreviation for ROMAN

ROMAN Normal type, as opposed to italic or bold; also a kind of type with SERIFS such as Times New Roman

ROTARY PRESS A press that uses a cylinder as its printing surface, as opposed to a FLATBED or PLATEN press

ROTOGRAVURE See GRAVURE

ROUNDING AND BACKING (R&B) Putting a rounded shape into the SPINE of a book-block, and a joint below the shoulder

RUBYLITH A red, transparent MASKING material

RUNAROUND Type set around a photograph or other design element, deviating away from the normal MEASURE

RUNNING HEADS Headlines that appear in the same (or a symmetrical) position on every page of a publication, except where chapter titles occur or if illustrations outside the GRID area displace them

SADDLE STITCHING A BINDING method using wire staples along the fold of the publication

SANS SERIF A typeface without SERIFS

SATURATION or **INTENSITY** A measure of the color's position in the range from neutral gray to fully saturated, or bright, color

SCALING Enlarging or reducing — usually applied to an image — and calculating the percentage of enlargement or reduction so as to anticipate the space it will occupy in a layout

SCANNER An electronic device used to convert artwork or TRANSPARENCIES into digital form

SCATTER PROOFS PROOFS with several illustrations printed randomly together on one sheet, not in their correct positions on the page

SCORE Creasing a sheet of paper or board so that it will fold easily

SCREEN A piece of glass or plastic used to convert CONTINUOUS-TONE COPY into a HALFTONE; also the frequency of dots, expressed in lines per inch or lpi

SCREENPRINTING A printing process using a stencil supported on a mesh or screen; ink is forced through the open mesh but is prevented from reaching the non-image areas of the paper by the stencil

SCSI (SMALL COMPUTER SYSTEM INTERFACE) A parallel interface used to connect computers with SCANNERS and other peripherals; see also USB and FIREWIRE

SCUFFING A problem in packaging design, where print is more likely to receive rough handling; scuffproof ink, LAMINATION, or a coat of varnish is the solution

SCUMMING A printing problem caused when the plate accepts ink where it shouldn't

SECTION SEWING A BINDING method in which SIGNATURES are sewn through the SPINE with thread before being casebound

SELF COVER A cover printed on the same paper stock as the rest of the publication, using the same PLATE as pages from the inside

SEPARATION Film in REGISTER relating to one of the four PROCESS COLORS; also artwork or film in register relating to FLAT COLOR

SERIES A complete range of sizes in the same TYPEFACE

SERIF The mark that terminates the ends of the letters in some TYPEFACES

SERVICE BUREAU A place where you can rent expensive equipment by the hour, or have laser prints, BROMIDES, and film output from an IMAGESETTER from your disk at a price per sheet

SET The width of a letter

SETOFF or **OFFSET** This occurs when the wet image on a sheet of paper prints on to the paper above or below it in the pile. Anti-setoff spray should separate each sheet with a fine layer of particles

SET SOLID Type set without LEADING, for example 10/10pt

SET-UP TIME The time it takes to MAKE-READY and set up the press to run your job

SGML (STANDARD GENERALIZED MARKUP LANGUAGE) A generic MARK-UP language for representing DOCUMENTS — an international standard that describes the relationship between a document's content and its structure

SHEETFED A press taking single sheets of paper

SHEETWISE A form of IMPOSITION using one PLATE to print the front of a sheet, and another to print the back

SHINGLING See PAPER-CREEP ALLOWANCE

SHOW-THROUGH or **STRIKE-THROUGH** Being able to see through a sheet of paper to the printed IMPRESSION on the other side

SIDE BEARINGS The space allocated on either side of a letter by its designer to stop adjacent letters from touching and to achieve an aesthetically pleasing appearance when words are set

SIDE SEWING A form of BINDING used mainly for children's books in which the thread is sewn near the SPINE, front to back, as in SIDE STABBING

SIDE STABBING A form of BINDING in which wire staples are inserted near the SPINE from front to back

SIGNATURE Several pages for a book, printed from the same PLATE and arranged so that they can be folded and trimmed to make a section, usually of 16 pages. A BACKSTEP MARK on the SPINE shows how several signatures are to be arranged so they bind in the correct sequence

SILKSCREEN See SCREENPRINTING

SIZE In papermaking, substances added to the FURNISH to make the paper less absorbent, which can also be coated or sprayed on to the WEB at a later stage of the process at the size press; sizing can also be used to mean SCALING

SKEWING A printing problem that occurs when paper, BLANKET, and cylinder are not in proper contact

SLIP (SERIAL LINE INTERNET PROTOCOL) The gateway from your client SOFTWARE,

i.e. Eudora for EMAIL, to the INTERNET; see also PPP

SLUG A line of LETTERPRESS type from a LINOTYPE machine, or a piece of metal used for word spacing

SLURRING Distortion of the image, with dots appearing elongated or smeared, caused by too much ink or slippage of stock

SLURRY In papermaking, fibers with lots of water

SMARTMEDIA RAM storage cards for Olympus and Fujifilm DIGITAL CAMERAS, see also COMPACTFLASH

SMILEY Symbol made from ASCII characters meant to convey emotions, e.g. :-)

SNOWFLAKING In OFFSET LITHO, a problem of water droplets in the litho ink that spoil solid areas; in GRAVURE the effect is caused by inadequate pressure which prevents the paper from taking the ink from one or more cells

SOFT DOT HALFTONE dot slightly out of focus

SOFTWARE The list of instructions that turn a general-purpose computer into a machine for a particular purpose, such as digital-page layout or image manipulation

SORTS In LETTERPRESS, individual pieces of metal type

SPAMMING (from the Monty Python song "Spam") CROSSPOSTING a carelessly inappropriate message or advertisement to many different groups or individuals

SPINE The bound edge of a book or magazine, where the fold is

SPIRAL-BOUND A method of BINDING used for calendars, cookery books, and manuals, using a wire spiral inserted through holes in the pages

SPLIT FOUNTAIN Printing two colors on an OFFSET press by using one color at one end of the FOUNTAIN and another at the other end — the colors blend in the middle

SPOILAGE Wasted printed sheets that are discarded

SPOT COLOR See FLAT COLOR

SPOT VARNISH Applying patches of varnish, often to make HALFTONES glossy

SPREADING An enlarging of the image caused by too much ink, or too much pressure between BLANKET and PLATE

STANDARD LIGHTING CONDITIONS A light source with a color temperature of 5000 Kelvin

STANDARD VIEWING CONDITIONS An area to view color PROOFS, surrounded by neutral gray and illuminated by STANDARD LIGHTING CONDITIONS

STARVATION GHOSTING An unwelcome effect that results in uneven printing and is due to some extent to the placement of dense black elements in certain positions on the PLATE

STENCIL PRINTING A printing process, such as SCREENPRINTING, using a stencil supported on a mesh or screen; ink is forced through the open mesh but is prevented from reaching the non-image areas of the paper by the stencil

STEP-AND-REPEAT A method for copying film, so that two or more parts of the same job can be printed from one PLATE

STEREOTYPE or **STEREO** A LETTERPRESS PLATE made by casting lead in a *papier-mâché* mold (a MAT or flong) taken from the FORME. It can be flat for flatbed presses or curved for ROTARY machines

STET A proofreading mark meaning reinstate, or "let it stand," i.e. print what was there originally

STICKING or **BLOCKING** So much SETOFF that the sheets stick together

STOCHASTIC SCREENING or **FM SCREENING** Using dots arranged randomly to reproduce CONTINUOUS-TONE artwork; see also AM (amplitude modulated) or conventional screening which uses a regular array of differently sized dots

STREAM FEEDER A mechanism on high-speed sheetfed presses that presents sheets to the rollers overlapping slightly

STRIKE-ON SETTING See COLD-METAL SETTING

STRIKE-THROUGH See SHOW-THROUGH

STRIPPING IN Inserting HALFTONES on film into the film made from a MECHANICAL. A stripper is a person who assembles film into the final

STYLE SHEET A paper DOCUMENT or feature of a page-layout program that sets out the specifications for a publication or series of publications, listing such things as the TYPEFACE, size, LEADING of body text headlines, and captions

SUBSTRATE Any sheet material to be printed — paper, board, plastic, or another substance. Also the carrier material in film, for example, on to which a layer of emulsion is deposited

SUPER-CALENDERING Smoothing paper by pressing it between highly polished cylinders, done off the machine

SURPRINT Superimposing type on to a TINT of the same color — they share the same film and are printed together

SWATCH BOOK A book of tear-off color samples; the most commonly used come from PANTONE

SWOP (SPECIFICATIONS FOR WEB OFFSET PUBLICATIONS) Standard ink colors and DOT-GAIN tolerances established by the Magazine Publishers Association

SYSTEM A catch-all term meaning all the computer equipment you need to make things work (as in "the system's down"); also the operating system (as in System 7); or a set of SOFTWARE tools (as in a digital prepress system)

TACK The adhesive property of an ink

TAG HTML code that the BROWSER interprets "on the fly" as the web page arrives from the server to the client. Tags usually have a start and an end, "containing" the item in question. The first part of the tag turns an attribute on and the second turns the attribute off. Tags are surrounded by angled brackets (the "less than" and "greater than" symbols) and the closing tag is usually preceded by a slash symbol (/)

TAILBAND A decorative feature added to a casebound book at the bottom of the SPINE

TAIL-END HOOK When solid areas near the back edge of a sheet make it curl down, caused by paper that adheres to the BLANKET too tightly as it is pulled off by the delivery grippers because the ink is too tacky

TCF (TOTALLY CHLORINE FREE) In papermaking, chlorine-free bleaches, such as hydrogen peroxide

TCP/IP (TRANSMISSION CONTROL PROTOCOL/INTERNET PROTOCOL) The standards that enable computers to pass information between each other on the INTERNET

TELNET A program that lets you log on to another computer, anywhere on the INTERNET, as if you were using a terminal attached to that computer

THERMAL-TRANSFER PLOTTER An output device that prints by "ironing" colored wax on to paper by the action of heat

THERMAL-TRANSFER PRINTS Color PROOFS produced by melting colored waxes on to paper

THERMOGRAPHY Creating a raised IMPRESSION by using a heat-treated resinous powder

THERMOJET PLOTTER A form of INKJET printer which sprays melted plastic onto the paper, also known as a phase-change inkjet

THREAD-SEALING A combination of some of the features of PERFECT BINDING and SECTION SEWING, but no thread runs between sections

TIFF Tagged Image File Format, a protocol for dealing with scanned photographs in digital prepress programs

TINT Shades of a FLAT COLOR created by patterns of dots similar to HALFTONES, specified as a percentage of the solid color

TINTING A printing problem of PIGMENT finding its way into the FOUNTAIN, discoloring the background

TIP IN A page-size INSERT glued to the edge of a SIGNATURE

TIP ON A small insert glued to the surface of a page, such as a coupon

TONER Digital "ink," used in photocopiers and digital presses

TOOL A facility in a computer program that makes something happen — a circle tool, for example allows you to draw circles in different ways; tools are usually represented by ICONS

TRACKING Adjusting the spacing between all letters, as opposed to KERNING, which only adjusts the space between pairs of letters; also, when several colored images are printed in a row and inking becomes uneven as a result

TRANSMISSION COPY COPY, such as TRANSPARENCIES and film positives, viewed by TRANSMITTED LIGHT

TRANSMITTED LIGHT Colors from a light source or a TRANSPARENCY, as opposed to REFLECTED LIGHT from a print or flat artwork

TRANSPARENCY A color slide, usually either 35 mm, 5 in by 4 in, or 10 in by 8 in, so-called TRANSMISSION COPY

TRAP A small nick in the design of letters to allow for ink spread, especially around junctions

TRAPPING Creating an overlap between areas of FLAT COLOR to compensate for any misregistration — usually the lighter color overlaps the darker; also any area of color overlapping another. A spread traps a light foreground object to a dark background; a choke traps a light background to a dark foreground object. Rich blacks require keepaway: the undercolor is made smaller than the black, so that should the inks misregister the undercolor is covered by the black

TRIM AND CENTER MARKS Indications of where paper sheets are to be trimmed and folded; they mark out the finished page area

TRUETYPE An outline description format from Apple and Microsoft which rivals POST-SCRIPT

TURNKEY SYSTEM A packaged and integrated assembly of HARDWARE, SOFTWARE, and support. Turnkey suppliers buy in equipment from third parties and repackage or "badge engineer" the components, perhaps adding some proprietary go-faster boards as well as their own software, before passing on the "value-added" system to the end user

TWAIN Standard for connecting SCANNERS and PERSONAL COMPUTERS, from Kipling's "The Ballad of East and West" — "... and never the twain shall meet..." aka "Technology Without An Interesting Name"

TWO-UP See ONE-UP

TYPEFACE The design of a FONT

TYPE SPECIFICATION A list of all the TYPEFACES, sizes, and LEADING to be used for body type, headlines, captions, and so on, in a publication or series of publications; see also STYLE SHEET

UNDERCOLOR ADDITION (UCA) Adding a TINT of PROCESS COLOR to add density to a black; see also RICH BLACK

UNDERCOLOR REMOVAL (UCR) Reducing the amount of color in areas of shadows, to save ink and improve TRAPPING

UNITS Letters of different widths in a TYPEFACE are allocated different numbers of units in accordance with a scheme that is devised by the typographer and the type foundry and dependent on the output process being used

UPLOAD Using FTP to send a file from your computer, such as your WWW home page, to a remote server

URL (UNIFORM RESOURCE LOCATOR) The unique address of a WWW page, of the form:
http://www.your_ISP.com/user_name/index.html

USB (UNIVERSAL SERIAL BUS) A hot-swoppable interface used to connect computers with SCANNERS and other peripherals, see also SCSI and FIREWIRE

USENET (UNIX USER NETWORK) A collection of NEWSGROUPS, each containing articles on a specific topic, arranged in threads

VALUE or **LUMINANCE** The parameter of color describing lightness or darkness, changed by adding black or white to a particular HUE

VARNISHING Coating areas of a page with a colorless varnish or lacquer to improve gloss on HALFTONES, for example

VEHICLE The component of a printing ink that carries and binds the PIGMENT

VELOX A HALFTONE on BROMIDE paper that can be pasted on to a MECHANICAL and used for undemanding printing

VERSIONING In digital print where larger runs of a generic DOCUMENT are broken down into many slightly amended shorter runs (with details of a local office or staff on a sales brochure, for example)

VERSO The back of a sheet of paper, or the left-hand page of a publication, opposite of RECTO

VGA (VIDEO GRAPHICS ARRAY) Developed by IBM for the PS/2 computer. Its standard resolution is 640 x 480 PIXELS, extendable to 1024 x 768, and it can display 256 colors from a palette of 256k

VIGNETTE A HALFTONE that fades to nothing around the edges

VIRUS A pernicious and self-replicating piece of mischief that can cause havoc in a computer or via the INTERNET

VISCOSITY The amount of flow and tack in an ink

VRAM Video random-access memory; also known as FRAME BUFFER

VRML (VIRTUAL REALITY MODELING LANGUAGE) A platform-independent language for describing 3D virtual-reality scenes

WATERLESS PLATES In OFFSET LITHO printing, waterless plates consist of ink on aluminum for the image areas and a silicone rubber for the non-printing areas. Silicone rubber has very low surface tension and thus will repel ink.

WATERMARK A symbol or mark manufactured into paper which can be seen when the sheet is held to the light

WEB A continuous roll of paper used on web-fed presses, cut into sheets after printing; also short for World Wide Web

WEBSAFE COLORS 216 colors that will be displayed by a BROWSER without resorting to DITHERING (optically mixing two or more colors)

WET PROOF See PRESS PROOF

WET-ON-WET One color is still wet as another is printed

WIDOW A single word or part of a word from the end of a paragraph left at the top of a new column or page; see also ORPHANS

WIMP Windows, icons, mouse, and pull-down menus (or windows, icons, menus, and pointing device), the original Mac GUI with which the user tells the computer what to do by pointing and clicking at ICONS (little pictures) and MENU items (lists of available options) on the screen using a MOUSE or other pointing device

WINDOW A transparent hole in a negative awaiting a HALFTONE to be STRIPPED IN; also an active and independent area of a computer screen

WINDOWS A Mac-like operating system for PCs developed by Microsoft

WINTEL A name for PCs that use WINDOWS and Intel microprocessor chips

WIRE COMB A form of spiral BINDING used for reports, cookery books, and manuals

WOODFREE Chemical woodpulp for paper-making

WOODPULP Wood that has been debarked and separated into fibers for papermaking, either by grinding (mechanical woodpulp) or by cooking in chemicals (chemical or woodfree woodpulp)

WORK-AND-TUMBLE An IMPOSITION scheme in which both sides of a job can be printed, in two passes, by a single PLATE: one side is printed, then the sheet is turned head-over-heels so that the GRIPPER EDGE changes ends

WORK-AND-TURN An IMPOSITION scheme in which both sides of a job can be printed, in two passes, by a single PLATE: one side is printed, then the sheet is turned sideways so that the lay edge changes sides but the GRIPPER EDGE remains the same

WORKSTATION A type of networkable computer, more powerful than a personal computer, made by companies such as Sun and Silicon Graphics

WOVE A paper texture introduced on the Fourdrinier wire; it has a characteristic woven appearance (or sometimes no detectable texture); see also LAID

WRONG-READING EMULSION DOWN (WRED) See RIGHT-READING EMULSION UP (RREU)

WRONG-READING EMULSION UP (WREU) See RIGHT-READING EMULSION DOWN (RRED)

WWW (WORLD WIDE WEB) Interconnected INTERNET "pages" viewed by a BROWSER, such as Netscape Navigator, containing text, images, sound, movies, and hypertext "hot links" to other pages

WYSIWYG (WHAT YOU SEE IS WHAT YOU GET) In computer SOFTWARE, a screen-based representation of a printed or WWW page that approximates what you will see in the finished product, as opposed to a list of computer code

X-HEIGHT The height of a letter x in a particular TYPEFACE — a typographic measurement which ignores the height of the ASCENDERS and DESCENDERS

XEROGRAPHY A copying process using black TONER attracted to an image on an electrostatically charged drum; the toner is transferred to paper and fixed by heat

XHTML A reformulation of HTML 4.01 in XML

XML (EXTENSIBLE MARKUP LANGUAGE) A simple subset of SGML suitable for use on the World Wide Web

XPRESS A digital page-layout program from Quark

AFAIK as far as I know
AM amplitude modulated
APR automatic picture replacement
ASCII American Standard Code for Information Interchange
ADSL asymmetric digital subscriber line — or loop
A/UX a workstation operating system, a version of Unix
A/W artwork
BTW by the way
C11 a high-level computer language
CCD charge-coupled device
CD-ROM compact disk read-only memory
CEPS Color Electronic Publishing System
CIE Commission Internationale de l'Eclairage
CMM color-matching module
CMS color-management system
cm³/g cubic centimeters per gram
CMYK cyan, magenta, yellow, key (black)
cpu central processing unit
CRC camera-ready copy
CRT cathode ray tube
CSS cascading style sheets
CTF computer-to-film
CTP computer-to-plate
DHTML Dynamic HTML
DMA direct memory access
dpi dots per inch
DPS double-page spread
dtp desktop publishing
DVD digital versatile disk
ECF elemental chlorine free
EPS Encapsulated PostScript
FAQ Frequently Asked Questions
FM frequency modulated
Ftp File Transfer Protocol
FYI for your information
Gbyte gigabyte
GIF Graphics Interchange Format
g/m² grams per meter squared
gsm grams per square meter
GUI graphical user interface
HD grade of mesh for screenprinting with 20–35% open area
HLS hue, luminance, saturation
HP hot-pressed, a handmade-paper finish
HP-GL Hewlett Packard graphics language
HTML Hyper Text Markup Language
HTTP Hyper Text Transport Protocol
Hz Hertz, or cycles per second

IBC inside back cover
IBM PC a make of personal computer
ICC International Color Consortium
IFC inside front cover
IMHO in my humble opinion
IRC Internet Relay Chat
ISDN Integrated Services Digital Network
ISP Internet Service Provider
JPEG Joint Photographic Experts Group
k kilobyte, 1024 bytes (kbyte is more accurate usage)
kbyte kilobyte, 1024 bytes
L*a*b L is for luminance; a and b are chromatic components — a for green to red and b for blue to yellow
LAN local-area network
l.c. lower case
lcd liquid-crystal display
lpi lines per inch
M grade of mesh for screenprinting
(m) machine direction in paper
Mbyte megabyte
MF machine-finish paper
MG machine-glazed paper
MHz megahertz, or millions of cycles per second
MIPS millions of instructions per second
Ms manuscript
MS DOS Microsoft — Disk Operating System (PCs operating system)
NOT not hot-pressed, a handmade-paper finish
NTSC National Television Systems Committee
OBC outside back cover
OFC outside front cover
OPI open prepress interface
OPL oriented polypropylene lamination
OS operating system
OSHA Occupational Safety and Health Administration of the US Department of Labor
PAL Phase Alternation Line — broadcast television standard in the UK
PC personal computer
pcb printed circuit board
PDF Portable Document Format
PMS Pantone Matching System
PMT photomechanical transfer
PNG portable network graphics
ppi pages per inch
PPP Point to Point Protocol
pt point, a measurement of type size

ram random-access memory — short-term computer memory
R&B rounding and backing
RC resin-coated
RGB red, green, blue
RIP raster image processor
RISC reduced-instruction-set computer
ROFL rolls on the floor laughing
rom read-only memory — permanent computer memory
RRED right-reading emulsion down
RREU right-reading emulsion up
RSI repetitive-strain injury
RT*M read the * manual (clean version!)
S grade of mesh for screenprinting with 50–70% open area
SCSI small computer system interface
SGML Standard Generalized Mark-up Language
SIMM single in-line memory module
SLIP Serial Line Internet Protocol
SPARC scaleable-processor architecture
S/S same size
stet reinstate deleted material
SWOP Specifications for web offset publications
T grade of mesh for screenprinting
TCF totally chlorine free
TCP/IP Transmission Control Protocol/Internet Protocol
TIFF tagged image file format
TDP two-page display
TWAIN Technology Without An Interesting Name
u.c. upper case
UCA undercolor addition
UCR undercolor removal
URL Uniform Resource Locator
USB universal serial bus
UV ultraviolet
VGA video graphics array
VRML Virtual Reality Modeling Language
WIMP windows, icons, mouse, and pull-down menus
WOB white on black
WORM write once read many — computer optical drives
WRED wrong-reading emulsion down
WREU wrong-reading emulsion up
WRULD work-related upper-limb disorders
WWW World Wide Web
WYSIWYG what you see is what you get
XML Extensible Markup Language
YMMV your mileage may vary

FURTHER READING

David Bann, *The Print Production Handbook*, Suntree, 1998

Michael Barnard, *The Print and Production Manual* (8th edn), Pira International, Leatherhead, 1998. Authorative manual on all aspects of print production, now available in PDF format on CD-rom.

Fernand Baudin, *How Typography Works (and Why it is Important)*, Lund Humphries, London 1989. An idiosyncratic handwritten text based on a series of blackboard lectures by the Belgian graphic designer.

Michael Bierut (ed.), Jessica Helfand (ed.), Steven Heller and Rick Poynor, *Looking Closer 3: Classic Writings on Graphic Design*, Allworth Press, 1999. A comprehensive look at the people, ideas, and social and economic forces that have shaped graphic design in the 20th century.

Lewis Blackwell, *The End of Print* (revised edn), Chronicle, San Francisco, and Laurence King, London, 2000. A book about and designed by innovative graphic designer David Carson.

Lewis Blackwell, *David Carson: 2nd Sight: Grafik Design After the End of Print*, St Martin's Press, New York, and Laurence King, London, 1997. The sequel to *The End of Print* examines David Carson's intuitive approach to graphic design.

Lewis Blackwell, *Twentieth-Century Type Remix*, Gingko Press, Corte Madera, CA, and Laurence King, London, 1999. A decade-by-decade look at typography and graphic design.

Lewis Blackwell and Neville Brody, *G1*. Rizzoli, New York, and Laurence King, London, 1997. A collection of work by contemporary graphic designers, including Zuzana Licko and P. Scott Makela, along with the found images that have inspired them.

Michael H. Bruno (ed.), *Pocket Pal: A Graphic Arts Production Handbook*. A handy, concise pocket-sized guide to graphic design. International Paper, Memphis, TN 2000 (18th edn). A handy concise pocket-sized guide to graphic-arts production.

David Carson and Philip B. Meggs *Fotografiks*. Gingko Press, Corte Madera, CA, and Laurence King, London, 1999. Explores the synergy between photography and graphic design.

Rob Carter, *American Typography Today*, John Wiley & Sons, New York, 1997. A guide to the work of 24 contemporary American typographers from Frank Armstrong to Dietmar Winkler, with a chronology of other important typographers.

Rob Carter, Philip B. Meggs, and Ben Day, *Typographic Design: Form and Communication*, (2nd edn), John Wiley & Sons, New York, 1993. An overview of the fundamentals of typographic design, incorporating desktop publishing, digital type, and bitmapped design.

Sebastian Carter, *Twentieth-Century Type Designers* (2nd edn), W.W. Norton & Company, New York, and Lund Humphries, London, 1995. A standard reference work on the lives of 24 designers worldwide, from Frederic W. Goudy to Carol Twombly.

David Collier *Collier's Rules for Desktop Design and Typography*, Addison-Wesley, Wokingham, England, 1991. A lively and graphic look at digital design by a former partner of DeCode design.

James Craig, *Production for the Graphic Designer* (2nd edn 1990), Watson-Guptill, New York, 1976. An updated version of Craig's definitive work.

James Craig and William Bevington, *Designing with Type: A Basic Course in Typography* (4th edn), Watson-Guptill, New York, 1999. Discusses type fundamentals and examines five classic typefaces in detail.

Design, Print and Production Handbook, Hartford Publications, 1989.

Adam C. Engst, *Internet Starter Kit* (4th edn), Hayden Books, Indianapolis, IN 1994 1996. Definitive guide to the internet.

Bruce Fraser, *Print Production Essentials*, Adobe Press, 2001. How to use Adobe graphics and prepress programs.

April Greiman and Liz Farrelly, *Floating Ideas into Time and Space (Cutting Edge)*, Watson-Guptill, New York, 1998. The ideas and creative process behind Greiman's influential work.

Kenneth J. Hiebert and Armin Hofmann, *Graphic Design Sources*, Yale University Press, Yale, CT, 1998. Practical advice for those seeking to understand the principles and process of good design.

Steven Heller and Karen Pomeroy, *Design Literacy: Understanding Graphic Design*, Watson-Guptill and Allworth Press, New York, 1997. An analysis of the key works of 20th-century graphic design, exploring 100 classic and contemporary works, explaining why they are aesthetically significant and how they function as good design.

Steven Heller, *Design Literacy (Continued)*, Allworth Press, 1999. The sequel to *Design Literacy: Understanding Graphic Design* a collection of essays examining the significance and histories of objects from vintage

fair and concert posters of the 1930s to a Rolling Stones CD cover from the 1990s.

Steven Heller and Teresa Fernandes, *Becoming a Graphic Designer: A Guide to Careers in Design*, John Wiley & Sons, New York, 1999. A clear and comprehensive overview of the many types of careers available to today's graphic designer: advertising, corporate work, editorial, and other key design disciplines, with case studies from Pentagram, Margo Chase design, and Landor Associates.

Seven Heller (ed.), *The Education of a Graphic Designer*. Allworth Press, 1998. Twenty-five designers and educators, including Milton Glaser and David Carson, examine how graphic design is taught, learned, and practiced.

Steven Heller and Anne Fink, *Less Is More: The New Simplicity in Graphic Design*, North Light Books, Cincinnati, OH, 1999. Explores the emerging "less is more" attitude in graphic design through work and insight from 96 of today's hottest (and coolest) designers.

Steven Heller and Louise Fili, *Typology: Type Design from the Victorian Era to the Digital Age*, Chronicle Books, San Francisco, 1999. Introduces the culture and aesthetics of the period, discusses how individual styles developed, and offers insights into the artistry of key typographers and foundries.

Jost Hochuli and Robin Kinross, *Designing Books: Practice and Theory*. Chronicle Books, San Francisco, and Hyphen Press, London, 1997. The basic principles of "macrotypography" by the Swiss designer with a detailed commentary of 27 of his designs by a design historian.

Dard Hunter, *Papermaking: The History and Technique of an Ancient Craft*, Dover, New York, 1978. An authoritative history of papermaking.

Dean Kuipers (ed.) and Marvin Scott Jarrett (introduction), *Ray Gun: Out of Control*, Simon & Schuster, London, 1997. Since 1992, Ray Gun has set the parameters of the cutting edge in publishing. David Carson served his apprenticeship as Art Director at *Ray Gun*.

Jeremy Leslie and Lewis Blackwell (introduction), *Issues: New Magazine Design*, Gingko Press, Corte Madera, CA, and Laurence King, London, 2000. An examination of the whole culture of magazines from the point of view of their design.

Ellen Lupton, *Mixing messages: Contemporary Graphic Design in America*, Princeton

Architectural Press, New York, and Thames & Hudson, London, 1996. Catalog of an exhibition held at the Cooper Hewitt National Design Museum, Smithsonian Institution, New York.

Ellen Lupton and J. Abbott Miller, *Design Writing Research: Writing on Graphic Design*, Phaidon Press, London, 1999. A critical study of graphic design and typography, from the history of punctuation and the origins of international pictograms to the structure of modern typography.

Patrick J. Lynch and Sarah Horton, *Web Style Guide: Basic Design Principles for Creating Web Sites*, Yale University Press, Yale, CT, 1999. The essence of the Yale University Center for Advanced Instructional Media's wonderful online website-design guide translated in traditional print format.

Ruari McLean, *How Typography Happens*, Oak Knoll Books, CA, and the British Library, London, 2000. Based on the Sandars lectures at Cambridge University in 1983.

Ruari McLean, *The Thames and Hudson Manual of Typography*, Thames and Hudson, London, 1992. An authoritative history of typography from an eminent typographer and designer.

Ruari McLean (ed.), *Typographers on Type: An Illustrated Anthology from William Morris to the Present Day*, W.W. Norton, New York, and Lund Humphries, London, 1995. An illustrated anthology of essays from type designers as diverse as William Morris and Matthew Carter.

Philip B. Meggs, *History of Graphic Design*, John Wiley & Sons, New York, 1998. A definitive and well-illustrated history of graphic design through the ages.

Jennifer Niederst, *Web Design in a Nutshell: A Desktop Quick Reference*, O'Reilly & Associates, Sebastopol, CA, 1998. Slim but full of understandable, readable segments.

Jakob Nielsen, *Designing Web Usability: The Practice of Simplicity*, New Riders Publishing, Indianapolis, IN, 2000. Web usability guru sets out many of the design precepts all web developers should follow.

Rick Poynor, *Typography Now Two: Implosion*, Booth-Clibborn Editions, London, 2000. This follow-up to *Typography Now: The Next Wave* updates the story of typography in the late 1990s, focusing on the most innovative designers and projects in print, advertising, and the moving image.

Rick Poynor, *The Graphic Edge*, Booth-Clibborn Editions, London, 1995. Consists of an exploration of contemporary trends in typography and design, and contains over 200 examples from combinations of raw typography and organic fonts.

David Siegel, *Creating Killer Web Sites*, Hayden Books, Indianapolis, IN, 1997. Web-design theory plus the nuts and bolts of successful page production.

David Siegel, *Secrets of Successful Web Sites: Project Management on the World Wide Web*, Hayden Books, Indianapolis, IN, 1997. Practical nitty-gritty on the less glamorous side of building a site.

Erik Spiekermann, *Rhyme & Reason: A Typographic Novel*, H. Berthold AG, Berlin, 1987. A beautifully made treatise on typography, in the style of *Tristram Shandy*.

Erik Spiekermann and E.M. Ginger, *Stop Stealing Sheep & Find Out How Type Works*, Adobe Press, Mountain View, CA, 2000. The title refers to a quotation by Frederic

Goudy: "Anyone who would letterspace lower case would steal sheep."

Fay Sweet, *Metadesigns: Design from the Word Up*, Watson-Guptill, New York, and Thames and Hudson, London, 1999. Erik Spiekermann's multidisciplinary design firm is one of the world's largest consultancies applying its fresh ideas to everything from websites to corporate identities.

Tomato, *Process: A Tomato Project*, Gingko Press, and Thames and Hudson, London 1996. Tomato's output in its first five years — an eclectic mix of artistic concepts and working ideas which offers a glimpse into the creative processes that inform their projects.

Tomato *Bareback: A Tomato Project* Gingko Press, Corte Madera, CA, and Laurence King, London, 1999. Stunning collection of personal work by the members of Tomato, from poetry to photography.

Jan Tschichold (Ruari McLean, translator), *The New Typography: A Handbook for Modern Designers*, University of California Press, Berkeley, CA. Since its initial publication in Berlin in 1928, this has been recognized as a definitive treatise on book and graphic design.

Rudy Vanderlans, Mary E. Gray and Zuzana Licko, *Emigre: Graphic Design into the Digital Realm*, John Wiley & Sons, New York, 1997. Brimming with ground-breaking Mac-generated typography, illustration, and graphic design, and oversized to do justice to its pictorial content.

Jon Wozencraft, *The Graphic Language of Neville Brody 2*, Universe Publishing, New York, and Thames and Hudson, London, 1996. The fruits of five years' experimentation, alongside Brody's new typefaces: Blur, Pop, and FF Gothic.

WEB SITE RESOURCES

The internet is full of wonderful resources for web-design tips and tutorials. It is not possible here to list every vendor's website, but here follows a by-no-means exhaustive selection. To find a particular vendor's website, try a search engine such as AltaVista or Yahoo.

Adobe — home of Acrobat, Illustrator, InDesign, Photoshop, and GoLive
www.adobe.com

ArtConnex — an information site for finding the technical and legal advice, employment, resources, publications, supplies, and organizations affiliated with the graphic-arts industry
www.artconnex.com

Core77 — resources for designers
www.core77.com

David Siegel's Tips for Writers and Designers
www.dsiegel.com/tips

Digital Type Review
www.typereview.com

FontFont Finder Typographic Resource
www.fontfont.de

Goudy Center Typeface Database
www.rit.edu/~goudyctr

Jakob Nielsen's useability website
www.useit.com

Macromedia — home of Dreamweaver, Flash, Fontographer, and FreeHand
www.macromedia.com

Microsoft's typography website
www.microsoft.com/typography/default.asp

QuarkXPress
www.quark.com

Vincent Flanders' "Web pages that suck" — learn good design by looking at bad web design
www.webpagesthatsuck.com

Web-builder tutorials
home.cnet.com/webbuilding/0–3880.html

Webmaster Reference Library
www.webreference.com

Web-safe color charts
www.lynda.com/hex.html
the-light.com/colclick.html

Yale web-style guide
info.med.yale.edu/caim/manual

■ **USA**

American Printer
29 North Wacker Drive
Chicago, IL 60606
www.americanprinter.com

Communication Arts
110 Constitution Drive
Menlo Park, CA 94025
ca@commarts.com
www.commarts.com

Design Quarterly
Walker Art Center
Vineland Place
Minneapolis, MN 55403
www.walkerart.org

Emigre
4475 D Street
Sacramento, CA 95819
www.emigre.com

Graphic Arts Monthly
Cahners Publishing Co.
345 Hudson Street
4th Floor
New York, NY 10014
www.gammag.com

Graphic Design USA
79 Madison Avenue
Suite 1202
New York, NY 10016
www.gdusa.com/

Graphis
307 Fifth Avenue
10th Floor
New York, NY 10016
www.graphis.com

HOW
F&W Publications, Inc.
1507 Dana Avenue
Cincinnati, OH 45207
editorial@howdesign.com
www.howdesign.com

I.D.
116 East 27th Street
Floor 6
New York, NY 10016
edit@ID-Mag.com
www.idonline.com

DT&G Magazine
15 Southgate
Harrisonburg, VA 22801
www.graphic-design.com

MacWorld
IDG Publications
501 Second Avenue
San Francisco, CA 94107
macworld.zdnet.com/

Print
104 Fifth Avenue,
New York, NY 10011
info@printmag.com
www.printmag.com

Publishers Weekly
245 West 17th Street
New York, NY 10011
www.publishersweekly.com

Serif
PMB 377
2038 North Clark St
Chicago, IL 60614
www.quixote.com/serif

Seybold Reports
428 East Baltimore Avenue
PO Box 644
Media, PA 19063
www.seyboldreports.com

Step-by-Step Graphics
Dynamic Graphics, Inc.
6000 North Forest Park Drive
Peoria, IL 61614–3592
www.dgusa.com/dgstore/a/
sbshome.htm

u&lc
International Typeface
Corporation (ITC)
200 Ballardvale Street
Wilmington, MA 01887–1069
www.itcfonts.com/itc/ulc
/index.html

x-height
DsgnHaus, Inc
1375 Kings Highway East
Fairfield, CT 06430
www.fordesigners.com/xheight
/index.cfm

■ **UK**

Baseline
Bradbourne Publishing Ltd
East Malling
Kent ME19 6DZ
www.baselinemagazine.com

British Printer
Sovereign Way
Tonbridge
Kent TN9 1RW
www.dotprint.com

CGI (Computer Generated Imaging)
3 St Peter's Street
London N1 8JD
www.cgimag.com

Computer Arts
30 Monmouth Street
Bath BA1 2BW
www.computerarts.co.uk

Creative Review
Centaur Communications Ltd
50 Poland Street
London W1V 4AX
www.mad.co.uk/cr/

Digit
99 Gray's Inn Road
London WC1X 8UT
www.digitmag.co.uk

Design Week
Centaur Communications
50 Poland Street
London W1V 4AX
www.mad.co.uk/dw/

Graphics International
The Mill
Bearwalden Business Park
Wendens Ambo
Saffron Walden
Essex CB11 4JX

Eye
Quantum House
19 Scarbrook Road
Croydon CR9 1LX
US subscriptions: PO Box 10812
Birmingham, AL 35202

MacWorld (UK edition)
IDG Publications
99 Gray's Inn Road
London WC1X 8UT
www.macworld.co.uk

Printing World
Sovereign Way, Tonbridge,
Kent TN9 1RW
www.dotprint.com

ORGANIZATIONS

US

American Forest and Paper Association
1111 19th Street, NW, Suite 800
Washington, DC 20036
info@afandpa.org
www.afandpa.org

American Institute of Graphic Arts
1059 Third Avenue
New York, NY 10021
www.aiga.org

American Printing History Association
PO Box 4922
Grand Central Station
New York, NY 10163–4922
scrook@printinghistory.org
www.printinghistory.org

Digital Printing & Imaging Association
10015 Main Street,
Fairfax, VA 22031
www.dpia.org

Flexographic Technical Association
900 Marconi Avenue
Ronkonkoma, NY 11779–7212
membership@flexography.org
www.flexography.org

Graphic Arts Technical Foundation
200 Deer Run Road
Sewickley, PA 15143–2600
www.gatf.org

The Gravure Association of America, Inc.
1200–A Scottsville Road
Rochester, NY 14624
www.gaa.org

IAPHC The International Association of Printing House Craftsmen
7042 Brooklyn Boulevard
Minneapolis, MN 55429
headquarters@iaphc.org
www.iaphc.org

Institute of Paper Science and Technology
500 10th Street, NW
Atlanta, GA 30318
www.ipst.edu

National Association of Printing Ink Manufacturers, Inc.
581 Main Street
Woodbridge, New Jersey
07095–1104
napim@napim.org
www.napim.org

National Association for Printing Leadership (formerly National Association of Printers and Lithographers)
75 West Century Road
Paramus, New Jersey 07652
www.napl.org

National Soy Ink Information Center
4554 NW 114th Street
Urbandale, IA 50322–5410
soyink@soyink.com
www.soyink.com

NPES The Association for Suppliers of Printing, Publishing, and Converting Technologies
1899 Preston White Drive
Reston, Virginia 20191–4367
npes@npes.org
www.npes.org

Printers' National Environmental Assistance Center
www.pneac.org

Printing Industries of America Inc.
100 Daingerfield Road
Alexandria, VA 22314
www.gain.org

Screenprinting & Graphic Imaging Association International
10015 Main Street
Fairfax, VA 22031–3489
sgia@sgia.org
www.sgia.org

TAPPI Technical Association of the Pulp and Paper Industry
PO Box 105113
Atlanta, GA 30348–5113
www.tappi.org

US Screen Printing Institute
605 South Rockford Drive,
Tempe, AZ 85281
sales@usscreen.com
www.usscreen.com

Waterless Printing Association
PO Box 59800
Chicago, IL 60659
wpaone@waterless.org
www.waterless.org

UK

British Printing Industries Federation
11 Bedford Row
London WC1R 4DX
www.bpif.org.uk

The Paper Federation of Great Britain
Papermakers House
Rivenhall Road, Westlea
Swindon SN5 7BE
www.paper.org.uk

Periodical Publishers Association
Queens House
28 Kingsway, London WC2B 6JR
www.ppa.co.uk

Pira International
Randalls Road
Leatherhead, Surrey KT22 7RU
www.pira.co.uk

Printing Historical Society
St Bride Printing Library
Bride Lane, Fleet Street
London EC4Y 8EE
www.rdg.ac.uk/~ltssmimm

The Publishers Association
1 Kingsway, London WC2B 6XF
www.publishers.org.uk

St Bride Printing Library
Bride Lane, Fleet Street
London EC4Y 8EE
www.stbride.org

Screen Printing Association (UK) Ltd
Association House
7a West Street
Reigate, Surrey RH2 9BL
www.martex.co.uk/spa/index.htm

International

Icograda
The International Council of Graphic Design Associations
PO Box 5, Forest 2
B–1190 Brussels, Belgium
secretariat@icograda.org
www.icograda.org

International Society of Typographic Designers
c/o David Jury
Colchester Institute
Sheepen Road, Colchester
Essex CO3 3LL
david.jury@colch-inst.ac.uk

International Women Designers' Network
www.ds.fh-koeln.de/iwd/eindex.html

Organization of Black Designers
300 M Street, SW
Suite N110
Washington, DC 20024–4019
OBDesign@aol.com.
www.core77.com/OBD/welcome.html

PICTURE CREDITS

The author and publishers would like to thank all individuals, agencies, museums, and companies that supplied pictures for use in this book. Special thanks to those designers — Neville Brody, David Carson, Malcolm Garrett, Zuzanna Licko, Erik Spiekermann, Lucille Tenazas, and Tomato — who provided material for the Design Trailblazers spreads.

Chapter 1
1.1 Mansell Collection, London; 1.3–5 Ann Ronan Picture Library, Taunton, Somerset; 1.6 Mansell Collection, London; 1.7 Nick Day, Brighton; 1.8–9 Ann Ronan Picture Library, Taunton, Somerset; 1.11 Mary Evans Picture Library, London; Photoshop manipulation by Dave Kemp; 1.12 David Foenander, Milton Keynes; 1.13 Henry Hyde of H@://wired, Brighton; p. 24 top: The Kobal Collection, bottom: the Bell Symbol was reproduced with the kind permission of BellSouth Intellectual Property Marketing Corporation; the AT&T Symbol was reproduced with the kind permission of AT&T Public Relations; p. 25 top: The Kobal Collection, bottom: British Heart Foundation, Brighton (Neil Gower)

Chapter 2
2.2–3 Mansell Collection, London; 2.4 British Library, London; 2.5–6 Crazy Diamond Design, Manchester; 2.7 Ann Ronan Picture Library, Taunton, Somerset; 2.9 Alan Pipes; 2.10 Mary Evans Picture Library, London; 2.16 Alan Pipes; 2.20 Alan Pipes; 2.25 Alan Pipes; 2.32 Alan Pipes; 2.37 Mary Evans Picture Library, London; 2.41 Carol Kemp; 2.42 Fontworks UK, London; 2.43 Zefa Picture Library, London (J. Pfaff); 2.45 Art Directors Photo Library, London; 2.46 Zefa Picture Library, London;

2.47 Zefa Picture Library, London (J. Pfaff); 2.51–53 Alan Pipes

Chapter 3
3.1 Mansell Collection, London; 3.3 Art Directors Photo Library, London; 3.4–5 Rex Features, London (Ron Sachs); 3.8 Roger-Viollet, Paris; 3.9 LD Publicity; 3.10 Hulton Getty Picture Collection Ltd, London; 3.11 LD Publicity; 3.16 Metropolitan Museum of Art, New York; 3.17 Paul Brierley, Harlow, Essex; 3.19–3.20 Alan Pipes; 3.21 Lefevre Gallery, London; 3.23 David Foenander, Milton Keynes; 3.24 Zefa Picture Library, London (J. Pfaff); 3.26 Gary Thompson, Brighton; 3.28 John Avon, Brighton; 3.29 Peter Greenwood, Brighton; 3.32 DC Comics Inc., New York

Chapter 4
4.1–4 Alan Pipes; 4.9–10 Alan Pipes; 4.12–16 Alan Pipes; p. 121 RCA/Thomson Multimedia; 4.20 Alan Pipes; 4.21 Art Directors Photo Library, London; 4.22–23 Alan Pipes; 4.24 Du Pont UK Ltd; 4.25 Alan Pipes; 4.26 Espson (UK) Ltd, Hemel Hempstead

Chapter 5
5.1 Apple Computer; 5.2 Compaq Computer Ltd; 5.3 SGI, Mountain View, CA; 5.4 Apple Computer; 5.5 Performance Direct, Egham, Surrey; 5.6 Alan Pipes; 5.8 LaCie UK, London; 5.9 Alan Pipes; 5.10 LaCie UK, London; 5.11 Wacom Europe GmbH; 5.12 Logitech Europe SA; 5.13 Wacom Europe GmbH; 5.14 Apple Computer; 5.15 Canon UK; 5.16 Epson (UK) Ltd, Hemel Hempstead; 5.17 Dainippon Screen BV, Netherlands; 5.18 Heidelberger Druckmaschinen AG; 5.19 Polaroid (UK) Ltd; 5.20 Epson (UK) Ltd, Hemel Hempstead; 5.21 Dainippon Screen BV, Netherlands; 5.22 Alan Pipes; 5.23 Alan Pipes; 5.24 Heidelberger Druckmaschinen AG; 5.25 Epson (UK) Ltd, Hemel Hempstead; 5.26 Xerox Corporation (Tektronix); 5.27 Alan Pipes; 5.28 Alan Pipes; 5.29 Hewlett-Packard Company; 5.30 Alan Pipes; 5.32 Alan Pipes; 5.33 Sony Computer Peripherals and Components Europe, Weybridge; 5.34 Alan Pipes; 5.36–37 Alan Pipes

Chapter 6
6.1 Sonia Halliday, Weston Turville, Bucks; 6.2 Science Photo Library, London; 6.3–4 Alan Pipes; 6.5 Art Directors Photo Library, London; 6.6 Art Directors Photo Library (John Frye); 6.7 Alan Pipes; 6.8–9 James River Fine Papers, St Andrews, Scotland; 6.10–13 Alan Pipes; 6.14 Zefa Picture Library, London; 6.17 Phil Dobson, Brighton; 6.18 Alan Pipes; 6.19 Art Directors Photo Library, London; 6.20 Heidelberger Druckmaschinen AG, Heidelber, Germany; 6.21–4 Alan Pipes; 6.25 Art Directors Photo Library, London; 6.26–7 Alan Pipes; 6.29 Art Directors Photo Library, London (Archie Miles); 6.30–1 Alan Pipes; 6.32 Zefa Picture Library, London; 6.33 Alan Pipes; 6.35 Alan Pipes; 6.37 Xerox Corporation; 6.38 Alan Pipes; 6.39 Indigo; 6.40 Heidelberger Druckmaschina AG, Heidelber, Germany; 6.45 (left to right) Hodder Headline, Hodder Headline, Pan Books; 6.46–56 Alan Pipes

Chapter 7
7.1 Hermstedt Ltd, London; 7.6 Simon Waldman, New Media Labs, *Guardian* newspapers, London; 7.15 Bernard Heyes Design, London